Dynamics of Indian Rural Economy

Growth Perspective

Dynamics of Indian Rural Economy

Growth Perspective

Uma Narula

ATLANTIC
PUBLISHERS & DISTRIBUTORS (P) LTD

Published by
ATLANTIC
PUBLISHERS & DISTRIBUTORS (P) LTD
7/22, Ansari Road, Darya Ganj,
New Delhi-110002
Phones : +91-11-40775252, 23273880, 23275880, 23280451
Fax : +91-11-23285873
Web : www.atlanticbooks.com
E-mail : orders@atlanticbooks.com

Branch Office
5, Nallathambi Street, Wallajah Road,
Chennai-600002
Phones : +91-44-64611085, 32413319
E-mail : chennai@atlanticbooks.com

ISBN 978-81-269-1444-9

Printed in India at Nice Printing Press, A-33/3A, Site-IV, Industrial Area, Sahibabad, Ghaziabad, U.P.

Dedicated to millions of villagers in India who have awakened to achieve quality of life by participation, and to other stakeholders who support their efforts

For my family
Atul and Tara
Ameeta and Vivek

Acknowledgements

This book is the outgrowth of my years of rural development work in India from communication perspective for socio-economic issues, research and reflections on the current status of rural economy in the last two decades or so of the twentieth century.

For up-to-date assessment of the countrywide situation, I have relied on data and reports from the Rural Development Division of the Planning Commission, and NGO's websites. My sincere thanks to them.

Uma Narula
New Delhi

Preface

The development story of India's rural population since more than 60 years is quite unique. Interestingly, 90 per cent of the Indian population has been living in villages. The present rural population is 75 per cent since over time, the 15 per cent have moved to urban areas in search of jobs and better life. These 15 per cent are on the periphery of urban areas and mostly live in urban slums.

Probably from historical perspective, villages must have been the hub of productivity and prosperity. During British colonial period, they suffered from gradual neglect, and surfacing of exploitative linkages, and the people suffered. They were ignorant, superstitious and fatalistic, and grew as traditional society, less amenable to social change in the subsequent periods. Agriculture remained the main occupation but it was becoming less productive. For inexplicable reasons, the beautiful traditions of arts and crafts dwindled, got neglected and were lost. They were not promoted to develop as art or for living.

The British for their own reasons focused on urban development of places which were going to be their seat of ruling and living. They exported much of the produce such as cotton and spices to England to develop their home markets and earn trade profits. In the process, villagers never had full utilization and consumption of their own produce to prosper. Even the rural physical infrastructure of roads, etc. suffered neglect though the British had constructed railway to connect urban towns and cities. At later stages, most of the villages got connected after Independence. They also built canals on rivers mostly in Punjab area for irrigation and that did help to develop the arid land of Doaba in Punjab. They also built small dams to facilitate irrigation. They opened schools and then colleges for boys and girls in urban areas to promote education for an educated support staff for their administration in India. May be the British too had the limitations of funds and technology and also they were driven by profit motives in ruling India. But in the process, 90 per cent of rural population became underdeveloped and poor over time.

The Indian government and its national political leaders focused on developing the villages and their inhabitants after India's Independence in 1947 from British colonial rule through an ambitious plan of 'villageism'. It has been a tremendous task and was beset with limitations of physical and financial resources all these years. The visions of development of villagers through social change and modernization were very commendable but sadly, during the six decades or so after Independence, village people have not developed rural economy and its social institutions. Their performance and achievement did not match with the envisaged goals. Whatever development took place was not commensurate with the efforts expended by the Indian government and its national leaders. In fact, 15 per cent of its people migrated to urban areas to be on the peripheral growth.

It is not difficult to see why all this happened. The ruralites in India in the early 60s were fatalistic, contented with the stagnant state of affairs in their life and work, and at one point they were getting discontented with the way government was not able to improve their situations. They were dependent on government, and they also believed in ethics of proportional efforts suggesting why they should put more efforts which will benefit the majority. These attitudes continued till late 80s.

In the 90s the impact of globalization, exposure to media explosion, and many corporations and NGOs taking interest in rural development made people demanding, asking for transparency and accountability for their low economic growth. And it was through hard way that they learnt that the key is their own participation and motivation as well as demanding transparency and accountability of actions of all contact agents.

Villagers' passive compliance of 50s and 60s turned to complaining and angry distrust of the government in 80s and 90s.

In the 1990s the realization dawned on the villagers that their aspirations for quality of life will only come through their own participation along with other participants in P4 model for development efforts and aggressively demanding such efforts from others. This was the turning point. The episodes of the different decades goaded me to explore the dynamics of India's rural economy and envision what will be the drivers of its growth.

India's participation in globalization impacted urban growth through economic reforms of 90s and technological breakthroughs. The book studies various aspects of growth of rural economy after India's Independence and reflects Indian government's concern and focus to develop these villagers and villages through their commendable visions, reviving villageism, adding from the experiences they gained from their earlier failures. There is will and the vision that a Rural Economic Model can drive rural economic growth just as economic reforms of 90s have brought urban growth. The benefits of technology and globalization will also support these visions.

Organization of the Book

Introduction recounts the failures and the successes, demands and discontents of people and the government which become the impediments for growth of a vigorous rural economy.

Chapter 2 puts forth the thesis that rural economy could be the driver of future economic mainstream growth through dynamics for economic growth. The rural economy is at periphery growth because of dysfunctional factors in rural economic development. A Rural Economic Model is imperative for future growth of both rural economy as well the mainstream economic growth. Perhaps, changing the way we think about the future of our nation requires a departure from talking about an urban-rural-suburban divide.

Chapter 3 focuses on income generating rural occupations of agriculture and village enterprises which could be the drivers of future economic growth. Chapter 4 discusses the challenges of rural life in India for providing quality of life for ruralites such as healthy physical environment, education, rural employment, rural health care efforts and policies. Chapter 5 focuses on rural infrastructure development of water, sanitation, environment, housing, energy, rural electrification and rural roads and transport.

Chapter 6 advocates that technology breakthroughs have brought rural growth, and these communication technologies bridges of television, telephone, computerization and Internet access in rural India have given connectivity to ruralites. Chapter 7 highlights the necessity of building business markets for village economy by development of rural markets segments of low-end markets and rural markets for the bottom of the pyramid. Rural business models put forth are rural markets and consumerism. Chapter 8 discusses rural policy frames, rural policies development with particular focus on rural economic policies for social spending on development schemes and programs. Current rural policies in operation are also discussed.

Rural Integrated Transformation highlights my observations and focuses on challenges and opportunities for ruralites and development community in gearing rural economy, and attempts to visualise what could be the future scenario.

The models given in the book are based on the research done in the 60s, 70s and 80s. Indian Development Decades Model, Rural Communication Model, and Panchayat System are given in Appendix 1. Process of Establishing Rural Business Hubs is provided in Appendix 2, while Social Security and Related Programs and Health Technology are given in Appendix 3A and 3B respectively. Appendix 4 focuses on Telecommunications in India, and Appendix 5 on the 'Loop Model' and Interconnected Interactions.

The book has targeted academic and practioners audience. It will interest government departments; academic and research institutions; civil society organizations and advocacy groups; relevant private enterprises in the context of multi-stakeholder partnership; professional associations and other development participants.

Uma Narula

Contents

Acknowledgements *vii*

Preface *ix*

1. **Introduction** 1

Historical Perspective of Indian Village Development 1

Rural Research Experiences 3

Panchayat System—Reconstruction 15

Panchayat System Structure in 1950s 15

Panchayat System Restructure in 1980s 16

Rural Scenario in 2000 Decades 20

2. **Rural Economy: Future Economic Growth** 22

Drivers of Future Rural Economy 22

Dynamics for Economic Growth 23

Rural Economy: Periphery Growth 24

Dysfunctional Factors in Rural Economic Development Then and Now 26

Rural Economic Model 27

Rural Economy: Future Growth 28

Challenges Ahead 33

3. **Rural Occupations** 35

Rural Income: Income Generating Occupations 35

Agriculture 35

Agriculture Development Models in India 37

Agriculture Development Model P3 37

Agriculture Development Model 2 38

Agriculture Development Model 3 40

Other Agriculture Development Efforts 41

Farmers' Loans 41

Agriculture Loans 2009 42

Rural GDP Growth 42

Boosting the Farm Sector 45

Seeds 46

Seeds Development 47

Direct Seeding Venture 49

Fertilizers 49

Irrigation 51

Sustainable Agricultural Production 52

Impact of Economic Reforms Process on Indian Agricultural Sector 52

Salient Agriculture Programs to Boost the Agro Production 53

Safe Drinking Water and Sustainable Agriculture 53

The Field Fresh Agri Excellence Center 54

The Low-cost Agro-animal Technologies by the Defense Institute of High Altitude Research (DIHAR) 55

ITC e-Chaupal 55

Expanding the Food Product Supply 55

National Food Security Mission

Information Availability 56

Research and Extension Agriculture Model 56

Agricultural Knowledge Initiative 58

Agricultural Resources Information System 59

Application of Geomatics Technology 60

Salient Projects 61

Effective Networking of Research and Extension: Information Technology 64

Knowledge & Information Focus 64

Multi-agency Research and Extension Providers 65

NARS & NAES 65

Some Major Sectors in Rural Economy of India 66
Village Enterprises 68
Rural Art and Crafts Industries 70
Khadi and Village Industries Commission 70
Rural Outsourced Production Enterprises 75
ICT Applications and Rural Cyber Café 76
Rural Business Hubs 76
Challenges Ahead 77

4. Human Development: Ruralites 79
Challenges of Rural Life in India 83
Quality of Life for Villagers 85
Healthy Physical Environment 85
Education Model in India 86
Education Bill 88
Public-Private Partnership Model in School Education 90
Rural Model of Education 97
Initiatives for Village School Education 97
Government Initiatives for Village School Education 100
Private Initiatives for Rural School Education 101
International NGOs 102
Domestic NGOs 103
Community Initiatives 104
Rural Tele-centers Educational Initiatives 105
Corporate Social Responsibility Initiatives 107
The Dilemmas of Rural Education 108
Rural Employment 111
Rural Employment Programs 113
Rural Health Care Efforts and Policies 118
Primary Health Care System in Rural Areas 119
National Rural Health Mission 127
Strengthening of Rural Health Care Infrastructure 129

Revamping Primary Health Care Infrastructure 132
A Convergence Approach 143
Salient Rural Health Programs 145
Population Control in Villages 145
Rural Dental Health Programs 146
Rural Eye Health Care 148
Eye Care Efforts 149
PPP in Health Care 150
Private Initiatives: Eye Health Care 150
LV Prasad Eye Institute Focus 150
Approaches and Strategies for Eye Care 152
Pediatric Ophthalmology 153
Nimmagadda Foundation—LVPEI 154
Pyramid Eye Care Model 154
Aravind Eye Care Hospital 159
Sankara Eye Care Institutions 161
ICT: Rural Eye Health Care 162
Mobile Phone Health Monitoring System 162
Sehat Saathi 163
Mobile-based PHC Management System 164
George Foundation Technology Use: Rural Health Care 165
Aravind Eye Health Care: Technology Use 166
Enabling Eye Care in Rural India—Research at Intel 166
Challenges Ahead 172
5. Rural Infrastructure Development 174
Rural Infrastructure Development 174
The Rural Infrastructure Development Fund (RIDF) 175
Water, Sanitation, Environment 175
Rural Water Supply Program 176

- Accelerated Rural Water Supply Program 177
- Rajiv Gandhi National Drinking Water Mission 179

Safe Water and More 180

Gujarat Environmental Health Improvement Program 183

Sustainability of Water System 185

SM Sehgal Foundation 185

Water for Irrigation 187

Rural Sanitation in India 189

- Community-led Total Sanitation Program 191
- Total Sanitation Campaign 191

Salient Projects in Sanitation 194

- Ecosystem and Ecotechnologies for Sanitation 194
- National Workshop on Sustainable Sanitation 195
- Eco Sanitation 199
- Grey Water Use 199
- IFS/SIDA Sustainable Sanitation Initiative 200

Environment 201

Rural Housing 203

The Action Plan for Rural Housing in 2009 206

- Credit-cum-Subsidy Scheme for Rural Housing 206
- Innovative Stream for Rural Housing and Habitat Development 207
- Rural Building Centers 207
- Samagra Awaas Yojana 208
- Equity Support to HUDCO 208
- National Mission for Rural Housing and Habitat 209

Focus on Improving Rural Housing 209

Rural Housing Survey (2008-09) 210

Salient Private Partnership Efforts for Rural Housing 212

- Holcim Initiative for Rural Housing 212

SDC Initiatives and Rural Housing 213
An Assessment of Future Scenario 215
Observations 215
Rural Electrification 215
Rural Electrification Programs 218
Accelerated Rural Electrification Program 218
Rajiv Gandhi Grameen Vidyutikaran Yojana 219
New Initiatives for Creating Renewable Energy 221
Solar Electrification in Rural Areas 222
Copper Wiring Helps Rural Electrification 222
Micro-utility Initiative for Rural Electrification 223
Nimbkar Agricultural Research Institute 223
Rural Electricity Supply Technology Mission 224
DRUM Project 225
USAID and GE Project 226
Rural Roads 227
Two Approaches 228
Prime Minister Rural Roads Program 228
Improvement of Rural Roads, Bridges and Drainage Structures 230
Rural Road Planning and Construction 230
Self-help Group Initiative 230
GIS for Planning and Management of Rural Roads 232
GIS Potential Use for Rural Roads 232
GIS Application in Planning 233
Construction and Execution 233
Maintenance Planning and Management 234
Infrastructure Finance 235
Infrastructure Policy 236
Challenges Ahead 239

6. Technology for Rural Growth **241**

Connectivity: Communication Technologies Bridges 243

Rural Telecommunication Policies 243

Current Broadcasting Scenario 244

Television in India 244

Rural Television: Historical Perspective 245

Television and Public Policy 248

Rural Telephony 251

Rural Telephony: Current Perspective 2008-09 252

Cellular Technology: Rural 256

USO Fund Activities 258

Rural Telephony in India: Historical Perspective 258

Investments in Rural Telephony 260

Technology Issues for Rural Telephony 263

Infrastructure to Accelerate Rural Telephony 265

Salient Current Rural Telephony Programs 266

Computer 270

Computerization in Rural India 270

Computer Literacy Initiatives 270

Discover the PC Initiative 271

Computerization for Village Functionalities 273

Computerization: Post Offices 276

IT and Rural Economy 277

Rural BPOs 277

Internet 281

Internet Access 281

Internet Promotion 281

Internet Content 282

Internet Cost 282

Rural Broadband 283

Broadband Policy 284

Investment in Rural Broadband 286

ICTs Initiatives in Rural India 287

Microsoft Saksham Project 289
National Alliance Mission 2007 292
Pratham 292
Bridge Digital Divide: 2000 Decades 295

7. Business Markets for Village Economy 298
Development of Rural Markets 298
Rural Market Segments 300
Low-end Markets 300
Business Models for Rural Markets 300
Basic Rural Business Model 301
Co-Creation Business Model 302
Needs Assessment Business Model 303
Government Rural Business Models 304
Rural Markets and Consumerism 306
Building Consumer Base 306
Rural Markets and Rural Consumption in India: Emerging Practices 308
Rural Retailing 311
Rural Business Hubs 312
Special Segments Markets 325
Commodity Exchanges 325
Consumer Markets 325
Rural Financials 326
Emerging Microfinance Practices 328
Emerging Microfinance Practices in India 328
Unique Rural Banking Services 335
Disaster Loan Funds for Ruralites 339
Industrial Initiatives 339
Government Efforts 340
Mobile Wallet: m-payments 343
Observations 345

8. **Rural Policies** 347
Rural Policy Frames 347
Rural Policy Development 348
Rural Economic Policy 351
Current Rural Policies in Operation 353
Panchayat Raj Policies 354
Rural Housing Policies 355
Overview of Housing Policies and Outlook 356
Farm Economy—Farm Practices and Management Policies 358
Rural Tourism Policy 358
Rural Tourism Infrastructure Development 364
Infrastructure Investment 365
Rural Tourism Constraints 365
Rural Entrepreneurship Policies 366
Social Security Rural Policies 367
Integrating Rural Economy with National Economy 372
Rural-urban Integrated Policies 373
Monitoring Rural Policies & Programs 379
Rural Policy Research 379
Eleventh Five Year Plan: Mid-term Appraisal 379
Economic Survey 2009 381
Economic Survey 2010 382
Observations 393

9. **Rural Integrated Transformation** 395
Observations 396
First Paradigm Shift 397
Second Paradigm Shift 399
Third Paradigm Shift 403
Challenges and Opportunities 404
Ongoing Challenging Issues 405
Salient Challenges: Ongoing Rural Programs 406

Monitoring, Evaluating, and Reporting on Outcomes 414
Outcome Approach 416
Unique Identity Scheme 419
Rural People Empowerment 420
Future Scenario Envisioned 423
Appendices 427
Bibliography 447
Subject Index 454

1
Introduction

Historical Perspective of Indian Village Development

India experimented with the Gandhian Plan of rural reconstruction during the three years between independence in 1947 and the first formal developmental plan. Concept of 'villageism' was the base of Gandhian Plan. In Practice, this was an attempt to produce powerful village communities by initiating participatory communication, developing self-reliant village Panchayat—the local governing councils, enforcing reform of land ownership, and encouraging the development of rural industries. The village was seen as the unit of social planning. It should be self-reliant and provide the basic necessities of food, shelter, clothing, education and justice. Village industries would provide employment. The natural and necessary cooperation among villagers would produce popular participation. This is Gandhian Meta Model.

In plans for rural reconstruction, the quality of life for human being was the focus; by providing the basic minimum needs. Next, the programs attempted to re-order structural changes such as removing exploitative linkages of feudal land lords—Zamindars who created more poor people and bonded laborers by instigating economic dependency, moneylenders, caste impediments, and social and economic inequalities. Rigid caste system institutionalized 'marginals' who were completely isolated from the economy. The traditional attitude towards large family and male children resulted in population explosion swallowing any increase in material resources. Gandhian Meta

Model suggested vigorous attempts to mend, if need be replace outlived social, economic and political institutions.

At that point of time, infrastructure of roads, water, sanitation, fuel, schools, medical facilities, were non-existent in many villages. Media exposure was negligible in most of the villages. Low literacy was accountable for the absence of print media, government community radio in 50s and community TV in 70s was being provided to few electrified villages, and only transistors could be bought by few. Their aspirations were far and few and women were suppressed, and they would not have thought about empowerment at all.

Gandhian Meta Model was never implemented as such but its various parts were the basis of much of the subsequent development experience in India. It remained a conceptual model. Community development programs for social and physical reconstruction were focused in 1st plan to give power to the people and Block Development program and Panchayat Raj for decentralized rural administration. The emphasis was on rural participation and democratic decentralization.

Communication Models, programs and experiments on which government was focusing rural development is highlighted in Figure 1.1. 'Indian Developmental Decades' given in Appendix 1.

A re-reading of history of village development since 50s shows an inherent tension between the objectives of socialism and democracy in the context of economic stress but noted that Indian government pursued both.

During those years, the interaction of planners, change agents and masses in context of development is non-summative combination of the interactions, interpretations, and actions of each participant and shows how the pattern of interaction is dissimilar to social realities of each of the actor involved in it.

Why these programs could not be implemented effectively? Administration of development programs was major problem. Country did set up planning commission to plan development plans for the country through 5-year National plan; the 1st plan was for 1951-1956 and then, subsequent plans till date. Second, the development of programs did not commensurate with the efforts that government had expended and did not match the performance expected.

Through 'villageism', government wanted to develop the villagers, these were the practical social realties for 90% of India's rural population at that time; and village economy would have prospered but it did not even after 62 plus years of conceptualization of the plan, as at that time, people were not ready to accept development among many other reasons (see Appendix 1 Indian Development Decades Summary Villageism Efforts, 'villageism' re-Gandhian Meta Model). Since last decade, there have been intensive and extensive efforts to develop the village and villagers on the lines of 'villageism' re-Gandhian Meta Model.

Rural Research Experiences

I narrate rural development scenarios in four time periods—1956, 1958, 1972-75, 1982-83 to highlight the slow progress and the developmental issues. These were villages in North India close to Delhi—the capital of India, seat of Indian government and having quick access to many national and international development programs. Even then, socio-economic growth of these villages was low. Three sampled villages were selected from Alipore Block—the progressive block at different time periods (1956, 1958, 1982-83) to assess the overtime developmental growth. Study in 1972-75 in sampled villages focused why there was satiation in certain development programs.

In 1956, rural research for planning commission projects was about 'Impact of urbanization and social change in villages'. Nayabans in Alipore block was one of the sampled villages. We have to walk from main road to the village. There were only patches of dirt road to the village, all dirt roads within the village and for connecting with surrounding villages. Mostly, thatched huts for living, a brick layered (pucca) yard for Panchayat and village meetings was there. Farming was the main occupation. Women were the main contributors for farm work. No electricity, water was drawn from traditional wells segregated by higher and lower caste wells and no sanitation;

people were using open fields for toilets, no cleanliness around the villages or systemic garbage disposal could be seen.

As far as impact of urbanization was concerned, the four indices of urbanization: Education, Economic and Political participation, Mass-media exposure were totally missing from sampled village and villages around. There were no village schools, no radio or TV, newspapers or any other print material or mobile cinema van visiting the village. The only contact with urbanization was back home visits of a few persons working in the nearby towns or Delhi. They will tell the urban experiences and sometimes bring newspapers in Hindi. They were also not the educated set.

People's aspirations were limited. Their biggest aspiration was to migrate to cities where they would have better life, though they could not describe exactly what that better life would be. On the social side, there were no schools in the village or around but they aspired for education for children, medicine availability in the villages, and low domestic violence for women and empowerment of women (aspired by women only). On the occupation side, training and facilities to improve agriculture productivity and other village enterprises were given, since the land was limited per family. Women also wanted agriculture training since they were the main persons working in the fields whereas they were always given sewing training; there were lots of gender differentiations. On the material side, they only aspired for cycles so they could commute to villages around and interact with people.

Lerner (1958, Lerner's Model of Modernization 1.4 in appendix 1) argued that villages in underdeveloped world could not exploit their resources because of attitudes and practices that constituted 'traditional' society. One of the first objectives of development was, therefore to change individuals and bring social change for modernization. The role of communication was to show traditional individuals that there was a world outside their experience, to enable them to relate to persons from diverse backgrounds and to persuade them to adopt a particular set of beliefs and values that would facilitate their participation in the industrialized society being developed.

By increasing mass-media exposure, the 'passing of traditional society' can be speeded. At that time, India had very low mass-media exposure even in urban areas and they were not in a position to develop mass-media exposure speedily in villages with very low literacy rate; *so they focused on Interpersonal channels of communication to bring social change.*

Rogers (1971, 76, 83—diffusion of innovations Model 1.5 in appendix 1) advocated that development is modernization of the social system through a process by which individuals change from a traditional way of life to a more complex traditionally advanced, rapidly changing style of life by diffusion of social and material innovations to create overtime awareness, knowledge, attitude change through persuasion, and behavioral change through adoption or rejection of the innovations. Both, Mass-media and Interpersonal communication channels can facilitate social change.

Inkles and Smith (1976) talked about social change in the villages and villagers as "an informed participant citizen, has marked sense of personal efficacy, is highly independent and autonomous, and is ready for new experiences and ideas". These were antithetical to traditional Indian village culture at that time.

Through project research feedback, government in 50s and 60s focused on strategies for creating awareness, knowledge and motivation for change of attitudes and behavior of the village masses towards issues such as education, personal hygiene and cleanliness to major issues of women empowerment, mother and child reproductive health and family planning issues for controlling population explosion.

In 1958, I was associated with rural anthropological research project. An American couple and I lived in the village to experience the day-to-day life, their customs, aspirations, etc. This sample village Holombi in Alipore Block was also close to Delhi, around the village sampled for 1956 research. In the intervening 2 years, the dirt road coming from main road and all other dirt roads within the village and with surrounding villages were paved now though not with concrete or tar but still easier to walk on the paved road. There was daily bus service from the main road connecting the village with Delhi and other towns. There were 2-3 brick houses. The one in which we were staying was brick house and two storied and had dry indoor toilet—the only one in the village. Water was drawn from wells, but no electricity, people used petromax lamps, wood fuel was mainly used for cooking but sometimes kerosene stove by well-off villagers was also used. The caste impediments were there, violence against women was still prevalent. There was very little change in exploitative linkages of feudal landlords—Zamindars and bonded labors, moneylenders, caste impediments, and social and economic inequalities, and the traditional attitudes for large family and male children which resulted in population explosion.

People were getting aware of family planning programs through government programs, through radio broadcasts and other interpersonal channels. Men expressed hostility to such campaigns; women liked the idea but were helpless and had no say even in their own health matters.

Government had installed one community radio in every village, which was usually kept in Panchayat yard. Mainly, males would watch the programs as women were not allowed to sit with males. Agriculture and other development programs were being broadcast—and discussion group forum were also set up, along with few entertainment programs. Occasional government mobile vans would come over to show documentaries. More people have started going to work in Delhi and narrate urban anecdotes now and then. Though Panchayat Raj has been set up since 1950, yet its tiers like gram-sevak (VLW) for their daily visits to village were missing earlier and even now. Panchayat Raj was still dysfunctional.

Agriculture remained the main income generating occupation. Government agriculture extension workers would be coming to villages for occasional agriculture training for the males and the related radio broadcast forums created some interest. Few tractors and harvesting machines and other small mechanical tools could be seen in the fields.

On the social side, they aspired for education for male children, a small school was set up in the village but either the teacher or students would be irregular. Medicine and medical services availability in the villages were negligible, and women were subjected to domestic violence and empowerment of women (aspired by women only) was negligible. Villagers aspired for more economic gains to buy the necessities and good things of life and even a transistor since it has come in the market or even an occasional visit to the city for a movie. Women were the most suppressed and never wanted to say aloud what their aspirations or wishes were.

As witnessed in 1958, there was slow and inconsistent change, village society still remained conservative. In the meantime, government had spent tremendous resources in these eight years to bring changes in attitudes and behavior but self-sustaining social and economic progress was not resulting in commensurate with the efforts that government had expended. That was puzzling. Was communication strategies adopted by government was satiating the masses to have no effect or plateau effect or the social structures in the rural society were more overpowering?

In 1972-75, my research team did extensive research in East Uttar Pradesh State, in forward and backward villages, to study the satiation of family planning campaigns through five integrated studies from medical and sociological aspects, and focusing on IEC (information, education, communication) for these campaigns.

FP Campaigns: The results for impact and success of these campaigns were startling. The family planning campaigns through media—mostly radio reach were getting ineffective but they were alleged to be 'stale presentation, not attractive' or to tell them nothing new. The major flaw was that people had lost faith in the programs, the way they were carried coercively by rural agents of the government who were getting more and more target-oriented especially for males, rather than IEC oriented. Even women were not easily approachable by rural women government agents for traditional reasons and hostility by the husbands. Thus, Interpersonal communication channels were getting satiated and needed innovative approach to boost the FP programs. The media campaign could reach backward villages as government had provided community sets. The campaigns remained flat or low appeal as the women could not watch or listen to these programs because of gender segregations; and males would intentionally block information from women.

During the years from 50s onwards, government had focused on the health issues along with the FP campaigns and set up rural medical infrastructure of a village level worker attending to first aid, a dispensary for walkable cluster of villages, a Primary Health Center (PHC) for more villages put together with doctors, midwife and more medical facilities to diagnose and dispense medicines, and a community hospital to treat diseases and indoor patients, and to refer them to other bigger hospitals in towns for advance level diagnosis or treatment. These medical facilities tiers were also supposed to be IEC for FP and help in using the devices. But research results showed government scheme was laudable but not effective for health because of lackadaisical attitude of VLW to doctors towards treating the public, attending the clinics, etc. and imparting IEC for FP and help in using the devices.

During the 5-year experiments in these areas, government had spent lot of resources but the results were poor. The good point was that the apathy to FP itself was changing as they expressed better facilities for it. Women craved for more interpersonal contact on the sly as media was unapproachable. Earlier, FP interpersonal people were not welcome and were pelted with stones.

The Research Findings: Health care administrators were concerned about providing good health care facilities at the medical centers in the villages, i.e. providing adequate number of doctors and paramedical staff and quality medicine. The lack of personnel was the major impediment and was more than problem of funding. Not many medical doctors and paramedical staff were ready to serve outside urban centers where they would lack basic living comforts and commuting daily could not be worked out. (It was never envisaged at that time to provide daily commuting conveyance to a group of doctors and paramedical staff for number of villages around;

just as it is working for commuting BPO staff at all odd hours and in distant places now-a-days). Quality of medicine was poor in part because of widespread corruption. Many of these factors are still problematic for effective delivery of health services in villages.

The social structure of masses and their action patterns caused problems for effective delivery of medical services. For instance, high caste villagers boycotted a medical center because water to be used for medical procedure had been brought to the center by a low caste. In another case, a high caste won't give his building on rent for medical center because people from the low class would be treated there. High caste would demand exclusive facilities for themselves. Political office holders and community factions would often demand that regardless of the needs, medical centers should be set up in places they favor.

IEC programs have been successful in creating a desire for healthcare among the masses and then, in making them aware of the day-to-day solutions to environmental health hazards. They have been effective in making masses conscious of the need for safe drinking water though government was unable to provide it to them.

Sociologically, women were getting aware of health issues, UNICEF Aganwari programs were also helpful in creating such awareness but still felt disempowered to take decisions to limit their families as they have to consult their husbands or even mother-in-law if they wanted to use FP devices.

People were complaining about lack of Village Schools and roads. More people were migrating to urban areas. There was more urban contact also as more people commuted for work to nearby towns. There is increased contact with media and agriculture extension workers. Road infrastructure needed improvement, safe drinking water problem is pervasive for all and few villages have electricity. Panchayati Raj and rural opinion leadership had become dysfunctional. People had low purchasing power and did not have easy access for rural loans which was even available for agriculture machinery and implements only.

In 1981-83, extensive research was undertaken in north India villages from dynamics perspectives. The sampled village is Lampur village in Alipore Block.

Village Lampur in the study is a 'progressive' village. There is a primary, co-educational, one teacher school, a woman's charcha mandal—organized discussion group that meets once a month, but no bank or medical dispensary in the village.

The approach road and all roads to the village are metallic. Except for 20-30 mud houses, others are made of brick and cement. The village is fully electrified but no street lights outside the village. Open drains exists both in and outside the village. The use of open space outside the village for toilet is matter of discontent. Lack of privacy, fear for women of going out of village unaccompanied in dark, and the risk of health, are all cited as problems but villagers contended that it is the government who has to do something about and not the villagers themselves.

Some of the villagers are quite prosperous, possessing TV, radios, cassette recorder, refrigerators, washing machines, room coolers, ceiling fans and well-furnished houses. The prosperous persons are mostly farm owners, they have tractors and other agriculture machinery. Less prosperous are agriculture labors, marginal farmers, poorly paid government service workers who commute to nearby towns. Many of the poorer people and women are underemployed.

Most of the younger male generation has high school education, though there is only primary school in village, the boys commute to high schools in nearby villages and most of those over forty are illiterate. The headman (pradhan) of the village is elected by the villagers and also woman opinion leader heading charcha-mandal is elected by the villagers but still they feel that both leaders promote the interest of their own castes.

Participation and Adoption Rates: The rates for development programs in Lampur are comparatively quite good. The masses are aware of the benefits of the development. Those who commute to Delhi for jobs bring back ideas about higher standard of living and political and social news. They also bring newspapers. Some of the younger married women are from Delhi and bring with them urban influences such as women's education, personal rights, opportunities for gainful employment, luxury goods, privacy inside the houses especially toilet privacy and demanding tap water in homes delivered by the government. Compared to some other nearby villages, Lampur women enjoy good status, there is no inhibition about education for girls, and women are quite aggressive about demanding their rights in the village and from the government.

Communication Media Infrastructure: A government community TV set is in the village, and the male pradhan controls its daily operations. About 90% own transistors and radios, very rarely government field publicity vans come to show any documentary or feature films. Nearest cinema house is about 5 km away in a nearby town, so males visit cinema but women attend cinema much less frequently. The village is frequently visited by block development office personnel or by development program specialists to discuss innovations and to hear their complaints. There is Panchayat with its administrative tiers in the village.

Opinion Leaders: They were an important communication link in Lampur. People accused opinion leaders of being corrupt, failing to convey masses' demands effectively to the authorities, and serving vested interests in dissemination of information and redress grievances. Further, they blamed the opinion leaders for not organizing them (people) for self-reliant participation in development activities. People even do not give feedback to the contact agents, VLW, etc. since they find them unreceptive or absent.

Rural Elites or the Opinion Leaders: They block information from the masses and take advantage of the opportunities themselves. They often meet the visiting developmental officials and give them incorrect information about the village and pass on to the poor distorted reports of government offers. Since the elites control the community TV set, they can block the poor people's access to information by turning off the receiver. It is local social structure that often undermines the developmental efforts of the government. (Does that mean, government should provide TV for women, low caste, poor for their information!). Thus both, mass media diffusion and development contact is filtered to the poor and weaker sections; and thereby rural elites become filters of development efforts by the government. Weak, ineffective local leadership, sluggish motivation and communication gap accounts for low development efforts by the masses. (Fig. 1.9 in appendix 1).

Planners: They were (still) in charmed loop of perpetual responsibility for incessant development planning and programs for the masses. Planners' concept of how development works by perception of development problems by the government and planning and administrating the same through its contact agents who were working through opinion leaders—the intervening factor and they would influence the masses. Government sponsored IEC campaigns through media (TV, radio, print low, wall paper, cinema low) and interpersonal channels of Government contact agents and Panchayat Raj tiers, Agriculture extension workers, and rural opinion leaders.

Research revealed that planners have consistently blamed themselves, i.e. the centralized bureaucracy for falling considerably short of the mark and not having the desired impact on the people, for not giving adequate technical and other guidance for development programs, blamed the administrators for poorly coordinating with NGOs, and not *delegating implementation and planning to the people.*

Government Contact Agents: They worked in villages at three levels of contexts: the most encompassing context is the socio-eco programs in general including health care public facilities, public transit and agriculture development. At the second level are particular relationships and arenas for action, including interaction with Panchayat and village leaders, people's development participation, local development strategies and administrative decisions. The third and most specific levels of contexts are specific episodes in the villages itself such as cleaning and garbage disposal, village pond as a health hazard, brackish quality of water, malfunctioning of medical facilities due to political pressures and unavailability of medical and paramedical staff, etc.

Change agents feel effective in offering need based programs if they have more frequent and periodical reviews and discussions with higher level functionaries about successes and failures of the ongoing programs. They feel effective when they have executive powers for problem solving actions.

An enduring problem for all change agents is ratio between resources and need; they always have to choose among deserving projects leaving important things undone. More than the sheer size of the task, however, they feel the quality of their interaction with the masses, and with other components of the bureaucracy make them ineffective and sap their motivation. They feel powerless to plan and implement feedback programs and thus feel constrained about their development role.

Masses presume contact agents' efforts have created development awareness and discontents with the existing situations but they (contact agents') are to be blamed for development disappointments and ineffective delivery. Masses are dependent on government to deliver development, but masses are passive in participation.

Panchayats: They are no longer remaining a democratic forum for village participation. Panchayat is set up by government to provide autonomy and administrative leadership to the villages. But this innovation has not been fully effective. Although, they are elected by the community, they are not necessarily community-oriented; rather their decisions are often governed by vested interest. Because of the growing feeling among the masses that village Panchayats have become corrupt and are reflecting only their own vested interests, or narrow village factions, the people are losing faith in their own Panchayat representatives.

Government Intentions: The intentions of the government have been to improve the material quality of life of the villagers, inform them, emancipate them from exploitative linkages within the feudal social structure and elicit their active participation in this national effort. At the same time, they wanted to work through the local community structure and extolled the virtues and values of village life (Panchayat etc.). In hindsight, these objectives are not fully compatible.

The government was successful in making the masses discontented, aware of innovations, informed about their personal rights and ready to demand redresses of grievances but government only created learned dependency where the masses 'participation' was in government gifts as 'owed' and complaining that government was not doing enough and failing in specific ways to do its job well. Thus, it was negative participation. They have learned to distrust the local social structure, but instead of developing autonomous initiative, have transferred their dependency to the central government.

***Development Communication Patterns in Lampur*:** The most frequent and most important patterns of communication are horizontal among the masses. They interact with friends, family, and opinion leaders. But they are limited in effectiveness because they contain relatively little information, authority and specific solutions. Interpersonal channels of top-down communication are more important than mass media for most purposes. In the village, Interpersonal communication channels as well as oral communication play a significant role in development awareness, information and feedback and in sensitizing the government about masses' needs and demands. Rural males and females discussed development information with family, friends, radio change agents, opinion leaders and visiting program specialists. Development feedback links are change agents, opinion leaders and visiting program specialists for males but females prefer visiting female program specialists as there were no female opinion leaders or change agents.

Model 1.1 given in appendix 1 based on the researches done in 60s to 70s highlights that development communication patterns have changed over the past 20 years due to developmental efforts. This model emphasizes the central role of local leadership who expresses development demands and imposes sanctions. Secondly, masses discontent was focused on communication strategies of the government and perceived government planning as irrelevant for them. The processes of development communication have made the social environment of the villages more complex than they were. They were deeply enmeshed in traditional social patterns and were resistant to change and modernization. The masses have to be made aware of a problematic familiar condition. They have to be informed about a new practice that would solve the problem and they were urged to accept it.

Model 1.2 given in appendix 1 based on the researches done in 80s highlights the changes in the development attitudes. Researches reveal masses are aware of developmental needs and projects, and are discontented because their demands have not been met. They have moved from an earlier belief that government has no concern and interest in their economic and social conditions to a perception of the government as a failed provider of goods and services. They are more knowledgeable about development bureaucracy and have a much improved notion as which communication channels ought to be useful to them. The resistant to change is less and attitude towards modernization has improved. Now the masses are aware of the existing problematic conditions, and the new practices to solve them. Now the diffusion is needed to make masses adopt the new practices with which they are already familiar now.

Both the models highlight that masses do not display high level of active participation from 60s to 80s; and the prevailing passive participation is a major threat to the goal of self-sustaining development.

Panchayat System—Reconstruction

Panchayat System Structure in 1950s: In 50s, there was Single tier Panchayat system where block is the unit of implementation of development programs, block development officer is the head of the Panchayat Samiti and responsible for and supervision of development programs. Block extension staff consists of Panchayat inspectors for various development programs, the Panchayat secretaries and the village level workers (VLW). The VLWs are assigned 2 or 3 villages depending on the size of the villages and the Panchayat secretaries are assigned 3 or 4 villages according to the work load produced by the villages. The village Pradhan is the member of the Panchayat Samiti and is the elected leader of the villagers, heads the local Panchayat.

Although the Panchayati Raj institutions have existed for many years, owing to inherent weaknesses in the systems, they were not very effective in the implementation of rural development programs. Through constitutional amendments, a third tier of local self-government has been set up and steps have been taken to remove the inherent shortcomings of the system. It is expected that the new Panchayati system should now provide the much needed non-bureaucratic institutional support to rural development programs. With a more aware rural population, the prospects for success are perhaps brighter.

Implication of these research experiences suggested that the dysfunctional effect of development programs was produced by: absence of strong local leadership, inadequate and inefficient delivery of goods and services by the development program functionaries, towards public participation and creation of counter-productive effects. These dysfunctional effects suggested a poor communication dialogue and participation effectiveness of rural masses and governments' ineffective means to intercept the spiral of discontent and dependency.

Panchayat System Restructure in 1980s: The mid-1980s saw the emergence of an influential movement to revitalize local self-government structures in India and link them with the agricultural and rural development process. There were two basic reasons for this. The first was the belief of the then Prime Minister Rajiv Gandhi that India was too 'large' a country to be ruled from a central place. The responsibility of the centre for many functions had to be at the local level. This would lead to accountability in the long run, although in the short run, resources would have to be allocated at the local level (if accountability was to be enforced) and these resources could be misused. Rajiv Gandhi, however, believed that in the long run, democratic policies would take care of such abuse and so insisted on the political and economic enfranchisement of poorer groups (Scheduled Castes, Scheduled Tribes and women).

The second reason was the fact that India's initial agricultural planning systems were somewhat linear in nature, emphasizing, for example, canal and tube-well irrigation and high-yielding varieties and led to the favored region, favored crop strategy. The mid-1980s saw this strategy being questioned and the whole issue of widespread agricultural growth raised in terms of an agro-climatic plan. This in turn raised the question of local participation and voluntary organizations and the associated question of resource allocation and functioning of decentralized markets. The question raised was the manner in which special programs for employment and rural development could be integrated with the agricultural development.

The revised Panchayati Raj Bill (1989) was an initiative not only to decentralize power, but to politically enfranchise the poorer sections of society, such as Scheduled Castes, Scheduled Tribes and women, who form a large part of the landless laborer and artisan populations. The Jawahar Rozgar Yojana (JRY), a nationwide employment scheme, attempted to put economic power behind this change. The new Panchayat system should now provide the much-needed non-bureaucratic institutional support to the poverty alleviation programs and with a more aware rural population; the prospects for its success are perhaps brighter (Alagh 1993).

Panchayats have been empowered by the Seventy-third Amendment. Access to and effective control over resources is a critical component of this empowerment. The real issues of such access are knowledge and awareness of the needs of the people, legal rights, availability and accessibility of social and economic resources. These changes in procedures and organizations have as yet not fully taken place as envisaged in the legislation. It also requires restructuring relationships including looking at gender issues both at the micro and macro level.

Panchayat Empowerment and Accountability Scheme (PEAS) is an existing scheme under the central sector plan which has been recognized as a powerful instrument to incentivize States to empower the Panchayats and put in place accountability systems to make their functioning transparent and efficient. Acknowledging the need to build in incentives for encouraging States to devolve funds, functions and functionaries and set up an institutional framework for such devolution, the Government proposes to substantially expand the scheme by making suitable allocations.

Effectiveness of Panchayat depends on three factors: Firstly, a genuine attempt at giving flexibility to local institutions in implementing major developmental initiatives such as the Basic Minimum Services Program and the Special Employment Program (JRY). The second is the need to involve local institutions in the country's economic liberalization and restructuring programs. Without restructuring, local bodies will not be able to mobilize resources for such development. This restructuring has to be done at three levels—local, state and central. Finally, when the three tier system has been set up, its development will need continued emphasis on transparency, genuine transfer of power and administrative coordination and reform, particularly in planning and implementation.

It would be thus possible to take a holistic view of the development needs of the area. This enables the village Panchayat to meet the critical gaps in rural infrastructure and also to generate income via supplementary wage employment to those willing and able to do manual work. It is hoped that with greater people participation in decision making, formalized through the institutions of Panchayati Raj, there will be greater transparency in the functioning of these institutions eventually leading to fuller accountability.

The basic local institutions for participatory planning in India have been set up. However, these institutions ought to have adequate autonomy as units of self-government so as to decide on the local needs and priorities and design and implement the necessary action. The challenge of making this new phase of democratic decentralization successful depends on the commitment of the political leadership, bureaucracy and the people themselves. Sufficiently clear and workable regulations have to be framed to streamline the inter-tier relationships and functions of each tier.

The involvement of the people in the planning process is necessary to take into account their felt needs, to mobilize local resources, to increase the speed of implementation by securing the people's cooperation, to increase the acceptance of the plan and projects and also to bring about a change in the power structure in people's institutions in favor of the poor. Strong leadership and political will are the necessary conditions for facing the challenge of enabling the local self-government institutions to become effective instruments of social and economic development of rural areas.

The 'tragedy of commons' is that when one used a natural resource say water, it is overused because no one can control its usage and each person has incentive to use it before others do. The insight has helped us to understand much of human behavior and has led people to advocate government regulation or private ownership (Garrett Hardin). It led to the view that resources that are commonly shared must be highly regulated or privatized.

Ostram Elinor, Noble Prize winner for economics 2009 challenges the 'tragedy of commons' that when people share a common resource, they will end up by destroying it. She proposed several rules for communal ownership for managing common-pool resources. Rules define: Who gets what, good conflict resolution methods, people's duty to maintain the resources proportional to their benefits, monitoring and punishing is done by the users or someone accountable to the users, and users are allowed in setting and modifying the rules. There is absence of government top-down solutions. As development economics highlight Top-down solutions do not help poor countries. Simple formulas focusing on formal ownership particularly solely on government ownership will not solve the problem of resource use. Common resources like water, climate change should be managed through institutions, networks and other ways of interacting. Institution structures humans build to solve real-world problems. Her work highlights that voluntary associations work to manage the resources.

Rural Scenario in 2000 Decades

Introduction highlights the commendable visions of India's political leaders to develop villages and villagers. Despite these visions, the development was slow paced and initially nothing seemed to be working as visualized. There were limitations of the funds and other resources and technology. Our earlier discussions have pointed out that why 'villageism' plans did not work and what went wrong despite of those visions.

Most of us, the urbanites or the so-called "outsiders", have a nostalgic view of rural India. We think of villages as peaceful havens where people live simple lives, where the air is pure, and the land is green as far as the eye can see. Some of those images are indeed true, but the realities of day-to-day life for a majority of the rural people are nothing short of misery. It is a living story of economic deprivation, social injustice, and hopelessness that outsiders cannot comprehend.

To the rural poor, deprivation is both economic and social, which in turn is the direct result of exploitation and lack of opportunities. The condition of life for the rural poor is characterized by malnutrition, illiteracy, sufferings from diseases and long-term health problems, inadequate shelter and unhygienic conditions, high infant mortality, oppression of women, and social treatment devoid of human dignity. Much of it is concealed from view, as outsider interaction is usually limited to village heads and "authorities", unless one chooses to study the low caste colonies and interior villages that are not easily accessible. That is not to say that government programs do not target these people, or non-governmental organizations (NGOs) do not work in these areas. What is missing is adequate emphasis in dealing with the root causes of these closely interrelated problems.

The current scenario in 2000 decades is that learning experiences have forced ruralites to shed their learned dependency on government, be participatory and self-reliant.

Government role is to create awareness, knowledge, and discontentment with stagnant; and facilitate people-government partnership through dialogue strategies. Media Exposure also has tremendous role to play. Rural programs focusing on socio-economic initiatives in P4 model can be driver for growth of its economy. It is important to know the rural society and their development threshold before setting schools, banking-financial systems and village enterprises.

Rural Situations in 2000 Decades: Infrastructure has improved, villagers aspirations are rising, drivers for economic growth are focused, economic scenario is changing because of change in attitude both by villagers and government themselves. There is more connectivity through technology. We are all pushing for the next change towards progressive and enlightened villages, and development demanding villages. We highlight these changes in the book chapters.

Earlier 60+ years have been slow; we want to focus on the rural-centric economic growth and prosperity for the coming years. As we wing through the chapters and discussions, we would realize the inclusive growth—rural economic growth may be the result of ruralites aspiration for quality of life as well as their active participation and cooperation to achieve it.

The government had planned the villageism plan in 50s but failed to achieve it but today, it's the people who are likely to achieve it through their own efforts for their own benefits because they will do so.

2

Rural Economy: Future Economic Growth

Changing the way we think about the future of our nation requires a departure from talking about urban-rural-suburban divide.

Drivers of Future Rural Economy Growth

We are supporting rural-centric economy in India more in 2000 decades since the worldwide economic meltdown in 2007. The country has by and large developed a consensus around accelerated inclusion of the rural economy in the wider growth process. We develop the rural economy through investment in rural infrastructure and by creating additional employment opportunities, providing quality of life to ruralites and take initiatives to integrate the rural economy with the national economy. Even as there is ongoing global economic slump, there are stirrings of a significant change in rural India, home to about two-thirds of the country's 114.5 crore population. Associated chambers of India, a business body also urged RBI to take measures to ensure "financial inclusion" of the rural economy, which accounts for half of India's GDP. This explanation ties up with the mounting evidence of the rural economy having escaped the slowdown almost unscathed so far.

To create *rural economy growth, the focus is economic prosperity, environmental sustainability, and social equity*. The drivers of rural economy growth are fourfold: One, development of income generating occupations namely agriculture and rural enterprises; two, rural based products and services; thirdly, rural infrastructure including building roads, dams and highways and irrigation canals etc. and infrastructure for potable water and sanitation, and giving connectivity to people through media, telecommunication; and fourth is development of rural markets and financials. The major focus of these fourfold growth drivers is to improve quality of life for ruralites and bring them at par with mainstream economy.

The drivers of rural economic growth could be providing quality of life to villagers through education, employment, capital flow, connectivity and healthy physical living environment on one hand and on the other hand, focused business markets for rural segments. ***These new markets require partnerships not only with other companies but also with local communities, non-profit organizations and Corporations have to deal with them to create a much more inclusive and interesting business model.***

The focus on rural economic growth has to be at multi-pronged levels: marginals, middle class and prosperous ruralites. The focus is on expanding opportunities for all these three levels to bring them at par and at their own comfortable levels. There will remain some gaps even among these three levels but the collective efforts have to be to pull all at comfortable levels. Who pushes ahead depends on their achievement motivation, competition and initiatives. This is likely to check rural migration to nearby towns and cities and even may reverse the migration back to villages so the family earner is back at village with the family for a cohesive family life.

Dynamics for Economic Growth

Dynamics for economic growth are awareness, discontent, demand, motivation and participation for action. These are the real drivers for economic growth achievement. Awareness about opportunities, threats and limitations about various factors operating in rural milieu, discontent with the state of affairs in work and life styles environments, based on these discontent, the ruralites would look for change and demand change, discontent and demand motivate them to achieve the opportunities seeking a combination of favorable circumstances or situations; they are motivated to participate for action individually, in collaboration with community, local government and with other drivers of economic growth. Over and above, the ruralites would demand transparency and accountability for implementation by the community and other contact agents.

Rural Economy: Periphery Growth

Economic boom in India has focused on urban development and rural economy also gaining on the periphery. In the current plans, India wants to focus specifically on developing the rural economy through development of the common man. Rural economy is seen as the driver of future economic growth of India.

For the last sixty-two years after independence of the country, government has mainly focused on developing the social development of the villagers through its development schemes. It has focused on even initiating and developing village autonomy through setting up local democratic institutions. But it has not commensurate with the efforts and resources spent to make villagers self-reliant and self-governing. It is puzzling why rural areas and its population could not achieve even minimum level of well-being and economic prosperity as compared to urban population where fewer resources were spent for them. During these years, the income generating focus has been mainly on agriculture. Government did put tremendous resources to boost agriculture in many areas but it has land, irrigation, fertilizer and other limitations. Though in the past, it has resulted in green (food crops) and white (milk) revolutions through the villages but this has not been able to boost its economy, rather it has driven people to poverty and underdevelopment. Now the pressing problem is poverty, and larger tally of malnourished, exploited and struggling people and these need to be tackled on war footing. Two-thirds of the populations in rural areas are dependent on farming with limited small patches of land for a large number of family members. It is unrewarding work for most of them and pressure and opportunities to leave the land are growing. Those who remain as farmers or farm labors need support and guarantees from government and society at large.

Economic reforms were initiated in 90s in India to boost urban economy but only with peripheral and trickle down gains for the rural areas. It is only in 2000 decades that importance of boosting rural economy and the villagers at the low end of pyramid is being realized and efforts are being planned accordingly.

Uma Narula (1986) highlights how well meant efforts of the government has underdeveloped the villages, created learned dependency on the government for any problem solving issues, has not brought rural economy to the main-stream economy, rather it has accounted for underdevelopment and low incomes, and low purchasing power.

Uma Narula (1983) study of rural villages and urban slums inhabited predominantly by rural migrant communities focusing on development awareness, motivation and participation highlighted that masses who were most aware of, and most discontented were least motivated to participate actively in development programs. They have acquired 'Learned Dependency' on government—suggesting it is government's duty to address the village issues. They also believed in ethics of proportional efforts suggesting why they should put more efforts which will benefit majority. Second, the development of programs did not commensurate with the efforts that government had expended and did not match the performance expected from contemporary theories of development.

Uma Narula and W. Pearce (1986) interpreted these findings as evidence that masses have acquired 'Learned Dependency' on the government rather than engaged in active participation. Government's development communication efforts included legislation for land reforms and creating wealth in the villages, public works building dams and irrigation canals, development bureaucracy and IEC (information, education and communication) programs. The IEC programs declared that development required initiative from the grassroots and masses deserved a better life and can have it if they participate actively. The legislation, public works, and development bureaucracy of planners and change agents, on the other hand, expressed government responsibility for development and through these; government has disrupted the local community social structures that would have provided the mechanism for local initiative.

As discussed in Introduction chapter, Gandhian Meta Model of development was the strategy of rural reconstruction planned after independence of India in 1947. Gandhian Meta Model was never implemented as such but its various parts were the basis of much of the subsequent development experience in India. It remained a conceptual model. As stated earlier, a re-reading of history of village development since 50s shows an inherent tension between the objectives of socialism and democracy in the context of economic stress but noted that Indian government pursued both.

Dysfunctional Factors in Rural Economic Development Then and Now

Uma Narula (1986) interpreted that the tangible parts of development efforts in India (to create hygiene and health care, to set up village schools) are simultaneously the basis of and symbolize the complex strands of idealism, selfishness, commitment and dismay, planning and bureaucracy, blame and self-justification, and overwhelming discontent that comprise current rural economic scenario.

It is of utmost importance that this local initiative has to be boosted for today's economic growth in 2000 decades. As compared to yesteryears, there is much more awareness to changing lifestyles and work styles world around through media exposures and other globalization factors. These have aroused the aspirations of younger generations and gearing them to appropriate path and through education, employment and other opportunities available will certainly motivate them to achieve higher. Dialogue action strategies are important to break learned dependency, discontent and create self-reliance, motivation and participation of the masses for economic development.

Rural Economic Model

Urban Economic Reforms in 90s focused on 10% of India's population residing in urban areas. By 2000, another 15% were added on the periphery as rural migrants and even people from small towns migrated to bigger cities like Bangalore, Pune, Mysore, and metros of Delhi and its NCR, Mumbai Kolkata and Chennai which were eco growth areas. The focus was economic growth and boosted by expanding growth areas such as development of infrastructure in varied areas, expanding connectivity through telecommunication hardware and software products and services, manufacturing greater number of products and services—all these in global competition and developing world class quality; developing exports markets for these and capital flow from foreign resources for investments and joint ventures. Consumerism was the end objective for economic development and employment generation.

In 2000 decades, we need rural economic reforms to develop rural economy. Can we develop Rural Economic Reforms model as per Urban Economic Reforms of 90s and its extensions? May be to certain extent we can, with some modifications perhaps.

The major focus of Rural Economic Reforms model could be *on income generating rural occupations of rural enterprises in various sectors besides developing agriculture and its allied occupations* and food security for home and export; *developing rural infrastructure to meet challenges* of *Rural Life* in India for providing quality of life for ruralites such as healthy physical environment, education, rural employment and employability, rural healthcare efforts and policies, housing, energy, technology connectivity and the rural Infrastructure development of water, sanitation, and environment. Utmost important is the necessity of building Business Markets for rural economy by development of rural markets segments of Low-end Markets and for the Bottom of the Pyramid through PPP model to encourage consumerism and to build capacity for rural consumerism through rural financials and credit markets.

Currently, 75% population of India resides in rural areas and rural economic model must focus on them.

Rural Economy: Future Growth

The peripheral gains of urban economic boom and globalization is raising expectations of ruralites and for transforming it. It is being realized that both government and public sectors need to focus on development of village and its population; and the business segments and markets needed for them. These will be drivers for developing the rural economy and contribute to future growth of economy of the country. We would explore the extent to which new lifestyles, work styles and changing socio-economic and business scenarios in villages and such opportunities would empower or disempower the ruralites and enhance its economy in general. The key questions in this regard are: How employment, occupational and vocational training will take care of social development, social entrepreneurship of rural population? How rural economic growth will create better environmental growth and do away with peripheral slums?

Changing the way we think about the future of our nation requires a departure from talking about an urban-rural-suburban divide and instead, an exploration of how to best put to work all of our resources for the common good. Rural people and places have a very important part to play in applying resources that will lead to economic prosperity, environmental sustainability, and social equity.

Rural India will continue to have, a vital role in the future of the whole nation and beyond. Sub-divides of urban-rural differences benefit neither city nor rural residents. The emphasis should be on the complementarities and interdependence of metropolitan and micropolitan futures.

Rural contributions: There are four interconnected categories of contribution. ***First***, the growing and processing of food is the most obvious, ranging from large-scale commodity production to local and regional food systems. Agriculture on large and small farms have been productive and innovative over several decades creating the yield, quality, and variety needed to feed our people as well as those in other countries. There has been green revolution and the white revolution. We have to focus on productivity and innovation in these contexts more and more in the future also. In future, we do want to respond to the increasing demands for food that is healthier, more environmentally compatible, and less reliant upon fertilizer and pesticide inputs.

Second, energy independence has gained widespread support. Rural areas should focus on exploring a range of opportunities from wind power to solar power, biogas and producing sugar cane and other crops for producing alternate fuels.

Third, although it is hard to fully grasp the real economic value of the services that rural ecosystems provide, it is clear that wetlands, forests, barrier islands, and other natural systems provide enormous benefits in the form of flood prevention, pollution mitigation, and biodiversity, as well as reducing the impacts of climate change. It will be necessary to harness the resources and ability of rural people to protect and develop our natural endowments that will be critical to the quality of life for all.

Fourth is the protection and management of the wide range of experiences offered by the countryside. These include the enjoyment of natural landscapes and wilderness, participation in active outdoor pursuits, or immersion in rural culture and heritage. Entrepreneurs can create activities and engagement for locals and visitors while preserving what makes the countryside so valuable. It can promote rural tourism.

Rural vulnerabilities: Illiteracy and low education, unemployment and under-employment, low employability generation, low quality of life and poverty are the major vulnerabilities of rural India. They are the consequences of long-term policy neglect that have led to underinvestment in infrastructure, diminishing availability of financial and human capital, and weak institutional capacity. It is also evident that the evils of poverty, casteism, discrimination, and powerlessness are to be found in large measures in many regions of rural India. There are inherent challenges associated with low density and remoteness that lead to diseconomies of scale and high costs of service delivery in many rural pockets especially in hilly areas.

On the development scale, there are many more developed to less developed villages. It is being realized that development of villages has been dependent on the quality and extent of certain State governments' efforts rather than participation of individuals. Therefore, we cannot put them all in one policy basket.

There are other threats over which rural leaders have little or no control but for which they will need all the human, technical, and financial resources they can muster. These include continuing metropolitan expansion, large-scale migrations in and out of rural regions, the growing realization of the effects of climate change, and the continuing impact of global economics that bring shifts in demand and greater competition for resources and products.

***Policy frames for future growth and outcomes*:** These issues have to be incorporated into a policy frame with the main components of regionalism, assets, and entrepreneurship. Regionalism is the antidote to diseconomies of scale, implying cooperation and collaboration across jurisdictions and urban-rural divides, and efforts to identify and articulate common priorities. A focus on assets recognizes the importance of communities and regions being able to build on their particular strengths using strategies to improve competitiveness and sustainability. Entrepreneurship, along with innovation, is the process by which these assets can be converted into economic opportunity and social equity.

Recommended within this policy frame are to enhance institutional capacity, whether for local governance, health-care delivery, or educational opportunity; upgrading human capital at all levels; increasing availability of appropriate financial capital; and rebuilding and improving physical infrastructure.

***Action Plans*:** The outcomes focused for are economic prosperity, environmental sustainability, and social equity. We need to bring the incomes and wealth of rural people to at least the levels of the population as a whole; create optimum employment for them, we need to ensure that while creating economic development, we manage better our rural environment and natural resources; and should no longer tolerate disparities and powerlessness as inevitable byproducts of rural policy neglect.

It is a grand vision, but we can implement it, achieve it through Public—Private—NGO and People's role in rural revival and revitalization to give it new life and energy. It seems there are three main options: (i) to increase the overall scale of resources that flow into rural India, (ii) to find ways of increasing the scale of locally-generated resources from within rural areas, (iii) and to be much more strategic about the nature of investments in rural areas.

There are five suggestions for rural development in these contexts: (i) Encourage initiatives that support regional collaboration focused on micropolitan centers and on their competitive advantage in food systems, renewable energy, ecosystem services, and rural experiences both at the national and regional level. They should ensure that processes are inclusive of community interests and that the above outcomes are central to strategic planning and investment. (ii) Encourage continued exploration of rural-urban interdependence. (iii) Invest in building institutional capacity among planning and service delivery organizations in rural regions. This is needed particularly in the areas of health care, education, and local governance, and there are many different entry points for policy. These might include the use of information technologies for distance learning and interaction as alternatives to consolidation of facilities and institutions; the support of peer learning and exchanges among elected officials and practitioners to expose them to excellent practices; and action research to support innovations in institutional development in sparsely populated regions. (iv) Create healthy communities that could yield major improvements for rural people and places. (v) Invest in entrepreneurship development in a rural context, particularly to help communities and micropolitan regions become more supportive of entrepreneurs and innovation. The scale of resources and programmatic impact are needed to transform rural economies and regions.

NGOs have to be willing to support efforts to shift policy through advocacy and engagement. Rural communities need support in the development of tools to participate and argue their cases so that their voices can be heard alongside those of entrenched and well-funded sectoral interests. NGOs have to be more like venture capitalists and invest capital in rural people and institutions to build their capacity for the long-term so that they are better able to both deliver services and products.

It is time to change the way we think about the future of our nation. We need to cease talking about the urban-rural-suburban divide, but to explore with vigor how we can best put to work all of our resources for the common good. Rural people and places have a very important part to play in the mix and to step up and apply resources in a smart and strategic way that will lead to outcomes of economic prosperity, environmental sustainability, and social equity.

The roadmap for taking rural areas forward is infrastructure and job-oriented. The Indian government has no doubt taken some timely steps to boost rural infrastructure and the rural economy, including the institution of the National Rural Employment Guarantee Scheme. Rural India still needs enormous amounts of money for research, infrastructure, electricity and roads to bring the countryside along with development.

The challenge today, however, lies as much in sustaining this momentum as ensuring an inclusive pattern of growth. Two distinct thrust areas are expected in the Government annual Budget (2009): a focus on social and physical infrastructure, and initiatives to integrate the rural economy with the national economy.

The visions and actions of the head of a country lead to achievements, success and failures; this is true of the village itself also. Therefore, rural democratization depends on the chosen head and his team visions and actions. Therefore, it is of utmost importance for people in the villages to choose right leaders and their teams. Those leaders must be able to hold public discourses for their 'visions ahead' for the villages and villagers must participate in it, and actively carry on, support the implementation and actions effectively. It is equally important that both leaders and people periodically monitor the action plans. If people are discontented they should make demands for change and leaders must plan to change the plans to make them more effective and people demand-oriented.

Moreover, both global economic exigencies and its impact on India's national economy and further on to its rural economy are changing fast, creating more rural economic needs, more resource demands and more strategic actions. There is impact of different learning experiences and changing practices worldwide on Indian villagers' occupations and work styles, and ensuing life styles creating higher impetus for both national political leadership as well rural leaders to improve and push rural economy.

Coordinate Rural economy—past, present, future: The peripheral growth of rural economy discussed in the earlier part of the chapter indicates the past of rural economy. We take this as anchor point for its status in the decades of 90s onwards. Since then, there have been efforts to pull it up and realization to bring it up to mainstream national economy; and the 2000 decades indicate the present growth. In the future growth we highlight visions, plans and action plans for its future growth. These three need effective coordination for growth.

Challenges Ahead

Challenges for rural leaders and policy-makers are to develop and muster all the human, technical, and financial resources to harness rural contributions and its vulnerabilities for future growth. The challenge lies as much in sustaining this momentum as ensuring an inclusive pattern of growth. Visions ahead are for the rural democratization, and effectively coordinating rural economy.

We presume the future rural economic growth will depend on the political leaders' visions and planning for growth of rural economy, entrepreneurs' efforts to develop market forces to set impetus for such growth and ruralites' consumer confidence and consumerism to boost it. Changes in the rural economy such as people moving from agriculture into manufacturing are likely to lead to economic boom. Rural people participation and their growing demand for inclusion in the mainstream economy are the major driving forces for rural economy to grow.

3

Rural Occupations

Rural people and places have a very important part to play in applying resources that will lead to Economic prosperity, Environmental sustainability, and Social equity.

Rural Income: Income Generating Occupations

Agriculture and allied industries, village arts and crafts industries and other miscellaneous enterprises have come up for gainful employment for the villagers in India. Agriculture has been the most conventional occupation of the Indian villagers. Though over time land holdings have dwindled or the land was not adequate for growing population and so could not remain the major livelihood of people who owned land; plus their farm labors who were finding it difficult to get work on farms. Village home industries in arts and craft also have been traditional village occupations but over the years younger generations have lost interest, did not learn the art and also felt they could not get them regular incomes. Slowly, these arts and crafts cottage industries started dying and needed organized revival. Many new enterprises for gainful economic gains have come up because of new technologies, demands of modern ways of doing things differently and new concepts; and globalization.

Agriculture

The future of Indian agriculture in general and the farmer in particular depends on how soon they can become globally competitive.

The performance of the agricultural sector influences the growth of the Indian economy. Agriculture (including allied activities) accounted for 17.8 per cent of the Gross Domestic Product (GDP—at constant prices) in 2007-08 as compared to 21.7 per cent in 2003-04. Notwithstanding the fact that the share of this sector in GDP has been declining over the years, its role remains critical as it accounts for about 52 per cent of the employment in the country. Apart from being the provider of food and fodder, its importance also stems from the raw materials that it provides to industry. The prosperity of the rural economy is also closely linked to agriculture and allied activities. Agricultural sector contributed 12.2 per cent of national exports in 2007-08. The rural sector (including agriculture) is being increasingly seen as a potential source of domestic demand; a recognition, that is shaping the marketing strategies of entrepreneurs wishing to widen the demand for goods and services.

Apart from production, the demand and distributional aspects of the agricultural sector, especially of food availability and food management are important to the economy; the production performance of different segments of agriculture and allied activities covering, inter alia, horticulture, animal husbandry and fisheries as also the developments in the area of food management during the year 2008-09. It therefore emerges that as per the present reckoning from third advance estimates for 2008-09, the production of coarse cereals, pulses, and most commercial crops (in particular, sugar cane and cotton) are lower than the levels achieved in 2007-08.

Growth in the production of agricultural crops depends on acreage and yield. Limitations in the expansion of agricultural land suggest that increase in gross cropped area can come from multiple cropping. In view of this, the main source of long-term output growth is improvement in yield.

Improvement in yield focus on quality of seeds, fertilizers, irrigation facilities of accelerated irrigation program and the integrated watershed development program (AIBP and IWDP), and of course improved variety of crops and multi-cropping.

Oilseeds Production: A Technology Mission on Oilseeds was launched in 1985-1986 to increase production of oilseeds in the country and attain self-sufficiency. Pulses were brought under this Mission in 1990. Before the Mission was launched, oilseed production was 10.83 million tons; during 1995-96, it was estimated at 22.42 million tons, which is a record. Soybean, rapeseed and mustard largely contributed to the increase in production. Production of pulses has seen many ups and downs, which is expected to be checked under the Mission. The country grows mainly nine oilseeds, with groundnut, rapeseed and mustard accounting for 62% of total production. Lately, soybean and sunflower have shown major growth potential.

Agriculture Development Models in India

Agriculture and its other allied sectors of Horticulture, Plantation Crops and Organic Farming, Crop Husbandry, Animal Husbandry and Dairying, Poultry, and Fisheries. These are the major income generating occupations in villages; therefore, the focus is always on enhancing productivity. India is seeking to increase the amount of public investment in agriculture—knowledge, technology, funds and new experts and expertise to enhance productivity. The farmers need this kind of support in addition to the government intervention to revive agricultural growth on high priority, help the unorganized sector and rejuvenate rural economy.

Agriculture Development Model P3: (i) the farmer has the conventional knowledge, expertise and ways of farming and its allied occupations of dairy, poultry etc.; (ii) government off and on gives inputs on farming differently and educates the farming community in new ways, uses new farm products and services, implements and machinery through mass media exposure and interpersonal communication. It provides organized irrigation facilities, and thus contributes financial, technical and human resources; (iii) private investments of financial, technical and human resources; (iv) organized rural markets for the produce and its consumers by industries. This supplements government's limited resources and is being realized as a must for enhanced productivity boost rural markets. Thus the emphasis is on public-private and local community partnerships.

Many people in India are talking of the necessity of a second 'Green Revolution', and white revolution; however, they should not forget that impact of green revolution occurred in areas (Punjab, Haryana, UP) which had already been developed by the British. On the other hand, a very different category of area is the eastern plains of Bihar, Orissa, Assam and West Bengal which have excellent alluvial soil, rain, groundwater and surface water but progress has been very slow due to several reasons including socio-political and economic factors.

In the 21st century, agriculture will continue to be the most fundamental instrument for sustainable development and poverty reduction. Sadly, it has been neglected for too long. The government must implement the report of the M.S. Swaminathan Commission on the farm sector in totality. This is possible only if the government targets a growth rate of 7-8% for agriculture in the next 10 years from the dismal 2.2% currently.

Attributing the rural-urban divide to poor performance in the agriculture sector, the Prime Minister said: "We are faced with a peculiar puzzle whereby on the one side the growth rate is accelerated to more than 9%, but on the other side the share of agriculture in our GDP has dropped to below 20% without any appreciable shift in the proportion of population dependent on agriculture." He emphasized that it was essential to improve basic facilities and infrastructure in rural areas to mitigate impoverishment and prevent large-scale migration. The Prime Minister also asked for several task forces within the current five-year plan panel, in areas like irrigation and agriculture. While the emphasis in agriculture is on ensuring food security and a district-specific agricultural plan, in the case of infrastructure the emphasis is on public-private partnerships (2009).

Agriculture Development Model 2 is supported by policy of improved access to vital inputs for agriculture, private investment and physical rural infrastructure. There's been dazzling agricultural growth in Gujarat this decade, due to proactive policy. It needs to be replicated pan-India, for broad-based growth across the board. Agro-growth in the state is a splendid 9.6% per annum in seven years, since 2000-01. It's over thrice the national average, in what is a drought-prone state. Cotton production has more than trebled—from 3 million bales to 11.2 million bales—during the period; there has been rapid growth in the high-value fruits and vegetables segment, and wheat output has grown over three-fold as well.

The agriculture model that it followed is the policy of improved access to vital inputs like quality seeds, power for irrigation and increased water supply generally, via umpteen check dams, bunds and ponds. About 3 lakh check dams and other watersheds have been created in recent years. Road connectivity too has improved access to markets for agro-produce (almost 99% of villages in the state are now linked by pucca roads).

Public agencies have shored up demand for high-yielding varieties of wheat seeds, and as many as 26 private seed companies have registered no less than 113 varieties of Bt cotton seeds in Gujarat. Extension services like the people-oriented and technology-intensive krishi mahotsav programs have provided information, counseling and farming know-how.

In a milieu where slippages and setbacks on the agricultural front are routinely blamed on the Centre and its policies, the turnaround in Gujarat does underline the fact that sound policy initiatives at the state level can make all the difference.

Heightened water supply from the Sardar Sarovar Project has led to the boost in Gujarat agriculture. Clearly, the way ahead is to step up irrigation and the supply of inputs, and provide for key infrastructure like roads. *What is required is much-needed private investment, skilled resources and institutions for agriculture to take off. Sustained agro-growth would rev up markets, enterprise and overall growth* (Ashok Gulati 7 May 09 ET).

Agriculture Development Model 3: Focused attention has been given by Government to the agriculture sector recognizing that 75% of our population lives in villages. In the period between 2003-04 and 2008-09, Government increased the plan allocation for agriculture by 300 per cent. The Rashtriya Krishi Vikas Yojana was launched in 2007-08 with an outlay of Rs. 25 thousand crore, to increase growth rate of agriculture and allied sectors to four per cent per annum during the Eleventh Plan period. The scheme has encouraged State Governments to take initiatives to develop the agricultural sector.

Food Security: Government is committed to ensure "food security" in the country and meeting the food requirements of the poor under the Targeted Public Distribution System (TPDS). In spite of higher procurement costs and higher international prices during the last five years, the central issue prices under the TPDS have been maintained at the level of July 2000 in case of Below Poverty Line (BPL) and Antyodaya Anna Yojana (AAY) categories and at July 2002 levels for Above Poverty Line (APL) category.

There is relationship between the notion of hunger, poverty and malnutrition. Inadequacy of food is being addressed through the public distribution system (PDS). PDS is a major state intervention to ensure food security to people especially the poor. The Eleventh Five Year Plan has observed that PDS seems to have failed in making food grain available to the poor as is evident from falling levels of cereal consumption over the last two decades. PDS is redesigned as Targeted PDS (TPDS) where higher rates of subsidies were given to the poor and the poorest among poor. However, some major deficiencies are also identified in TPDS. These included high exclusion and inclusion errors, non-viability of fair price shops, leakages and failure in price stabilization. In this situation, it may be useful to introduce food stamps or coupons which may be valid outside the PDS outlets. Food coupons will allow the consumers a wider choice. However, their value needs to be indexed to the food inflation. Multi-application smart cards will also enhance the efficiency of administering various schemes. In PDS system, the smart card will reduce the incidence of bogus ration cards or diversion of food grains. Leakages can also be restricted by redirecting subsidies currently under PDS to better funding of other schemes like Mid-Day Meal scheme or the ICDS.

While poverty rates have declined significantly, malnutrition has remained stubbornly high. It is a matter of concern that despite the country having attained self-sufficiency in food production for nearly three decades, and with mounting public food stocks at its command, there is still hunger in the country and that malnutrition is so widespread. It is time that the various interventions, at the state and at the Central level address this issue.

Government has ensured remunerative prices for the farmers for their crops. Since 2003-04, Minimum Support Price (MSP) for the common variety of paddy was increased from Rs. 550 to Rs. 900 per quintal for the crop year 2008-09. In case of wheat the increase was from Rs. 630 in 2003-04 to Rs. 1,080 per quintal for the year 2009.

Kapila Uma *et al* (2009) have advocated that Indian agriculture has been facing one of the worst crises since Independence. The contribution of agriculture to national income is declining at a faster pace compared to the percentage of population depending on it. The trends in profitability are not consistent across the years, which is a typical character of agriculture. *A number of studies have tried to examine and understand the reasons; important ones include technological, environmental, and policy related.* The poor performance and the declining profitability of agriculture due to one or more reasons have resulted in widespread household indebtedness, which is often identified as the main reason for the farmer suicides. They provide valuable insights into the broader array of issues and problems afflicting the agricultural sector in India.

Other Agriculture Development Efforts

Farmers' Loans: On June 18, 2004, Government has announced a package for doubling the flow of credit to agriculture. The credit disbursements have already gone up from Rs. 87 thousand crore in 2003-04 to about Rs. 2.5 lakh crore in 2007-08 marking a threefold increase. Government will continue to provide interest subvention in 2009-10 to ensure that farmers get short-term crop loans up to Rs. 3 lakhs at 7 per cent per annum.

The Agricultural Debt Waiver and Debt Relief Scheme for farmers, has been able to restore institutional credit to indebted farmers.

Agriculture Loans 2009: State Bank of India (SBI) has announced special drought relief schemes for farmers availing themselves of minor irrigation and crop loans, in view of the weak monsoon and drought conditions, a press release said. The schemes are valid for kharif and rabi season 2009-10, i.e. for loans sanctioned and disbursed till the end of March, 2010.

Rural GDP Growth: The gross domestic product (GDP) growth number for the full year, FY2008-09, came in at 6.7% versus a projection of 7.1%. The GDP growth for the last financial year, FY08, stood at 9%. The numbers for the fourth quarter of FY09 also came in at 5.8% versus 5.3% last quarter and 8.8% a year ago.

Chief Economist at Enam Securities said that the GDP numbers were not totally unexpected. "What has saved the day is agricultural performance and government spending which cannot continue through the year. But both these factors have flown liquidity into the system." Government expenditure puts money into the system that will now translate into a multiplier by the private sector. Similar is the case with farm output—when farmers have money rural consumption will go up. Moreover, the fact is that rural India currently accounts for nearly 36% of organized manufacturing units, 38% of its employees, 43% of output and 41% of net value added.

Rural per capita income has grown by 50% over the last 10 years, mainly on account of rising commodity prices and improved productivity. Development of basic infrastructure, generation of employment guarantee schemes, better information services and access to funding are also bringing prosperity to rural households.

According to an analysis done for *The Economic Times* by Rajesh Shukla, senior fellow at the National Council of Applied Economic Research (NCAER), the combined share of industry and services in rural GDP has risen to 58.4% in the current fiscal from 48.6% in 1999-2000 on the back of strong growth in these sectors in the past five years while the share of agriculture slipped to 41.6%. The contribution of industry, the most robust of all rural sectors, to the rural economy is 30.2% in the current fiscal year while services account for 28.2% (April 2009).

The change of the rural economy into one where manufacturing units contribute bulk of the generated income is also borne out by results of the CSO's Economic Census, 2005. According to it, about a fifth of the non-farm rural workforce is employed in agricultural establishments while four-fifths worked in non-agricultural establishments.

India will grow at a decent clip in 2009-10. Much of the increase in rural incomes is because of four straight good monsoons, high support prices even as inputs prices have remained unchanged through larger subsidies. Also, income transfers through schemes like NREGS and farm loan waiver has added to rural demand. Fiscally strained government may, however, find it difficult to provide such large subsidies or transfers in the future. And monsoons have been low and not timely in summer 2009—as they failed in July-August in North India especially Punjab and Haryana and they could not sow some of the grain crops in time and that could impact the grain stocks and farmers' incomes. Since because of climatic changes, the monsoon has become erratic timewise, it is high time research is done to sowing timetable for different crops.

Since monsoon has not been good in 2009 in North India, the impact of imminent drought can be felt. About impact of likely draught in 2009; Amit Mitra, Secretary General, FICCI said, "One of the biggest challenges that the government faces right now is the drought situation in almost half of the country. Public does not realize that the buffer stock that the government has, to be able to meet these kinds of situations aggregate a record quantum. The challenge before the government is, there may be plenty in one area, there may be plenty of buffer stocks on warehouse in some place and yet may be a 100-200 km from where farmers are committing suicide or at least they are on the verge of doing so. The question is moving the grain to the target entity and that's a very big challenge and we personally feel that the government is taking proactive position. The silver lining is that you have buffer stock enough to be able to meet these contingencies and not to import. The challenging problem is how you get the last mile of delivering to the farmers and persons who are in deficit today. We need to see something positive about the fact that many ministries have taken an extremely proactive position (News, 2 Sept. 09).

Bimal Jalan (09) highlights that whenever you have bad monsoon then the drought affected people lose incomes and you need relief measures and that is an extremely important factor. That would need to kick in if the agricultural incomes fall but the second equally important thing is capital expenditure. So, when you are spending in the agriculture area it is not to boost consumer demand per se, but to make sure that there is poverty eradication and that the impact of drought on the living of the agricultural population is contained. So capital expenditure on agriculture is important from a long point of view.

The Punjab government in a memorandum to the Prime Minister has asked special central assistance of Rs. 1,420 crore for the state for ensuring the power supply to the agriculture sector during kharif 2009. Further, it has also asked for a drought relief of Rs. 100 per quintal for paddy to be provided over and above the MSP (minimum support price). The state government has been demanding for an increase in the MSP for paddy to Rs. 1,350 per quintal for common grade and Rs. 1,400 per quintal for fine grade.

The key challenge before the government now is to mitigate the impact of drought, which has hit many parts of the economy. The government is working to ensure availability of food. Developmental programs are being geared to meet this challenge, and the focus is on making growth more inclusive (News, Aug. 09).

Boosting the Farm Sector comprehensively, the government is likely to come up with a two-pronged program focused on giving a marked push to rural infrastructure and insuring agriculture against the vagaries of the monsoon in rainfed areas. The proposals include provision of additional irrigation funding under all programs for states with a below national average irrigation level (40%) in order to bring it on par with other states; earmarking 50% of Rural Infrastructure Development Fund (RIDF) funding for water management schemes including small and medium irrigation schemes such as small ponds, and granting infrastructure status for processing of agricultural produce. The agriculture ministry has also proposed to the finance ministry that customs and central excise duty-related tax incentives be extended to select agricultural activities such as micro-irrigation components, development of infrastructure for production and distribution of quality seeds, programs for training and extension through the private sector, machinery and tools in agro and horticulture sectors as well as use of environment-friendly bio polymers.

The construction of a beyond-the-monsoon infrastructure has become even more significant in the wake of the poor summer rains in June 09 in parts of the country, making the government rely more heavily on the irrigated regions for agricultural production. It is against this background that the government is considering funding irrigation-shortage states with funds from programs such as the accelerated irrigation program and the integrated water development program (AIBP and IWDP). The current fiscal Budget of the country is expected to allot 50% funding for small and medium irrigation schemes from the RIDF, leaving balance of RIDF funds for financing agriculture, animal husbandry and allied activities.

Given the urgency to boost basic rural infrastructure such as hardware storage countrywide, currently viewed as priority within the farm ministry, the Budget 09 is expected to announce an Infrastructure Status for transport and processing of agricultural produce. That status would make warehouses, cold chains and wholesale and terminal markets eligible for easy credit access by including them in the priority lending bracket by banks.

It would also make them eligible for fiscal incentives such as customs duty exemption for specified imported components, IT benefits such as tax holiday, higher depreciation, etc. and viability gap funding by the government. The setting up of cold storage, controlled atmosphere units and grading and sorting infrastructure is likely to be treated as an agricultural activity. That would allow expediting of land transfer cases and entitlement to other fiscal incentives besides attracting investment from the private sector to this critical area.

Among the gist of proposals being considered is the reduction of excise duty on LDPE, HDPP, LLDP and PP and PVC pipes used in the agro sector alone from the current 10% to 0%, tax on drip and sprinkler system from the current 4% to 0%, and the complete exemption of biopolymers (under the national horticulture mission) from the additional duty on customs (CVD) and special duty of custom (special CVD) on the product. The duties are now pegged at 10% and 4%. Full exemption from duty on all horticultural equipment and machines and income tax exemption for all private sector spending on agro extension services under Section 35 (2) of the IT Act, and full exemption of all customs and excise duty on agro processing equipment and horticulture equipment and machines.

Seeds

The availability of quality seeds (among other factors) makes a critical difference to output growth. In India, more than four-fifths of the farmers rely on farm-saved seeds leading to a low seed replacement rate. The Indian Seed Program includes the participation of Central and State Governments, the Indian Council of Agricultural Research (ICAR), state agricultural universities and the cooperatives and private players. There are 15 state seed corporations besides two national level corporations, viz. the National Seeds Corporation and the State Farms Corporation of India.

Seeds Development: Indian seeds program recognizes three kinds of seed generation, viz. breeder, foundation and certified seeds. Production of breeder and foundation seeds during 2008-09 is anticipated at 1 lakh quintals and 9.69 lakh quintals respectively and the distribution of certified quality seeds at about 190 lakh quintals. Since 2005-06, the Ministry of Agriculture is implementing a Central sector scheme "Development and Strengthening of Infrastructure Facilities for Production and Distribution of Quality Seeds" on all-India basis. The scheme is aimed at making available, quality seeds of various crops to the farmers at affordable price and in time so as to enhance seed replacement rate, boost seed production in private sector and help the public sector seed companies to contribute in enhancing seed production. A major thrust under the scheme is on improving quality of farm-saved seeds through "Seed Village Program", under which more than 25,000 seed villages have been organized during 2008-09 across the country. Certified/quality seed production has increased from 194.31 lakh quintals during 2006-07 to 250.35 lakh quintals during 2008-09.

The seed component of the Prime Minister's Relief Package for distressed farmers is being implemented in 31 suicide-affected districts in four states of Maharashtra, Andhra Pradesh, Karnataka and Kerala under the above scheme. Certified seeds are supplied at 50 per cent of the seed cost to the farmers in such affected districts. During the year 2008-09, an amount of Rs. 445.81 crore has been released under the PM's Relief Package.

Fifty-two proposals for seed infrastructure development were sanctioned for boosting seed production in private sector and nine notified seed testing laboratories and two state seed certification agencies are being strengthened. Financial sanctions have been given for establishing tissue culture facilities in Orissa and Maharashtra for banana and pomegranate respectively. The Biotech Consortium of India Limited (BCIL) has been engaged as an expert agency to execute public awareness programs in nine BT cotton-growing states. The consortium has been provided financial assistance of Rs. 26.65 lakh during the year 2008-09.

The Protection of Plant Varieties and Farmers' Rights (PPV&FR) Authority has been established in November 2005. The Authority has the mandate to implement provisions of the PPV&FR Act, 2001. Fourteen crops, namely, rice, bread wheat, maize, sorghum, pearl millet, chickpea, pigeon pea, green gram, black gram, lentil, field pea, kidney bean, cotton and jute were notified for the purpose of registration under the Act. The Authority has plans to extend its coverage to forestry, aromatic and medicinal plants. The Government of India on January 1, 2008 approved the restructuring of State Farms Corporation of India.

In response to the changes that have taken place in the seed sector, the existing Seeds Act, 1966 is proposed to be replaced by a suitable legislation to (i) create a facilitative climate for growth of the seed industry so as to enhance seed replacement rates, boost the export of seeds and encourage import of useful germ plasma and to (ii) create a conducive atmosphere for application of frontier sciences in varietal development and for enhanced investment in related R&D. The Government moved the official amendments to the Seeds Bill in June 2008, for consideration by the Parliament.

Seeds are a critical input for transferring the latest technology to the farmers for improving productivity. Exemption of income tax to the extent of 50% on taxable income of those farmers is envisaged who produce seeds under contract arrangement since they value add further through processing, packaging, etc. Currently, under the IT Act, income for growing and producing of seeds by farmers are treated as agricultural income, which is exempt from IT Act. However, income from seeds produced on farmers' fields where seed is supplied by companies under contract agreement is not allowed any benefit under the IT Act. The rural economy, therefore, needs to be de-risked and strengthened.

"Providing abundant and accessible food means putting the latest science-based tools in farmers' hands including hybrid and biotech seeds. Monsanto's advanced seeds not only increase crops yield significantly; they use fewer key resources like land and fuel to do it. That is, win-win for the people and the earth itself. Producing more and conserving more improves farmers' lives; and that is sustainable agriculture." The world's farmers would need to double food production by 2050 and bio-technology can help (Monsanto Imagine 2009).

The delayed monsoon has had a substantial impact on the seed sector. A great decline has been seen in crop demand and the quarterly revenue has also been impacted for seed companies. Majority of the sales they do in cotton, maize, sunflower, bajra and paddy. Paddy is down by 6 million hectares compared to last year. The sowing itself has come down. Other strategies such as trying to expand the market in the non-traditional areas where there is still domination by the open polygonal varieties. So, while the projections are that the acreages will come down, but pharmacy is adapting the higher yielding seeds.

***Direct Seeding Venture*:** A recent sustainability initiative by PepsiCo India is the direct seeding venture that ties in with the company's water conservation agenda. PepsiCo India will be "positive water balance" this year, which means that it will generate more water than all that its beverages consumed in India. Direct seeding of paddy fields saves as much as 30 per cent of water (obviating the need for flooding the fields, as traditionally practised) and Pepsi is in the process of patenting the seeder which seeds the soil directly. The company has brought 5,000 acres of paddy across a few States under this kind of cultivation as part of its farmer-outreach program (June 09).

Fertilizers

Fertilizer subsidy is a big deal for the government. About Rs. 50,000 crore a year is spent on subsidizing fertilizer manufacturers. The government wants to transfer that subsidy directly to farmers. They are trying to find delivery mechanism to get the money to the farmers through banks. Banks issued Kisan Credit Card (KCC) to the farmers. Banks decide beforehand how much of money is to be given to farmers using the Kisan Credit Card.

The problem that has come out is that between banks, the Fertilizer Ministry and the Finance Ministry there is a difference of opinion on how effective Kisan Credit Card will be because out of roughly 130 million farmers in India, just about 80 million cards are being issued. The Finance Ministry believes of the 80 million, probably only 40 million farmers have cards. Almost each one of them or quite a few of them have more than one card which accounts for 80 million cards being actually issued to just 40 million farmers. There is simply no way one could use the Kisan Credit Card to make sure all the farmers get their subsidy. As a consequence, government is trying to find solution by which the banks can give money directly to all farmers.

The government will issue *soil health cards* to all farmers in the country detailing the deficiencies in the soil and the amount of fertilizers needed; quality and the normal quantity of fertilizer to be used for a particular crop. For this, setting up of 500 new soil testing laboratories and 250 new mobile soil testing laboratories had been sanctioned in the budget for 2008-09. Studies have found that over-doze and injudicious use of conventional chemical fertilizers and pesticides affect soil fertility, vegetation, human and animal health.

The government is also encouraging use of organic fertilizer and worm compost as overdose of conventional fertilizers has been found to affect fertility of the soil. Land under organic farming has increased from 42,000 hectares in 2003-04 to 464,000 hectares at present. Imbalanced and injudicious use of chemical fertilizers has been observed to have affected soil health and productivity in some parts of the country. Government is encouraging use of organic manure and bio-fertilizers to improve soil health for cultivation. There are 53 fertilizer quality control laboratories in the country. Since bio-fertilizers are regarded as an effective, cheap and renewable supplement to chemical fertilizers; the Government is implementing a National Project on Development and Use of Bio-fertilizers. Under this scheme, one national and six regional centers for organizing training, demonstrating programs and quality testing of bio-fertilizers are to be set up.

It was a challenging decision of the Government to take Bombay High gas through a 1,700-km pipeline to feed fertilizer plants located in the consumption centers of North India. However, the major policy which has ensured the growth of the fertilizer industry is the thrust on accelerating fertilizer consumption by fixing low and uniform price for fertilizers on the one hand, and on the other hand providing the manufacturers adequate compensation through the retention price and subsidy scheme.

Irrigation

The Government of India has taken up irrigation potential creation through public funding and assisting farmers to create potential on their own farms. Substantial irrigation potential has been created through major and medium irrigation schemes. The Working Group on Water Resources for the Eleventh Five-Year Plan (2007-12) has proposed creation of irrigation potential of 16 million hectares (9 million hectares from MMI sector and 7 million hectares from MI sector) during the Eleventh Five-Year Plan period.

The total irrigation potential in the country has increased from 81.1 million hectares in 1991-92 to 102.08 million hectares up to the end of the Tenth Five-Year Plan (2006-07); of the total potential created however only 87.2 million hectares is actually being utilized. To de-risk agriculture, more area has to be brought under irrigation. Accelerated irrigation program and the integrated water development program (AIBP and IWDP) are being encouraged. Better irrigation facilities encourage farmers to invest in agriculture and it is the key to higher production. All efforts continue to increase the irrigation potential in the country.

Flood forecasting has become an important activity over the years. Over 500 hydrological stations collect and transmit data through 400 wireless stations for issuing forecasts for 157 sites. About 5000 forecasts are issued in a year with 94% accuracy. The country also receives international support, with the World Bank as a primary source, for developing the water resources. International cooperation is also envisaged in setting up a National Center for Information on Water and Power. As there is a broad seismic belt in the country, particularly along the Himalayan, the Kutch region and ports of Maharashtra, a scheme is being evolved to collect all data on seismic activity at various dam sites.

Sustainable Agricultural Production: Sustainable Agricultural production depends on the judicious use of natural resources (soil, water, livestock, plant genetic, fisheries, forest, climate, rainfall, and topography) in an acceptable technology management under the prevailing socio-economic infrastructure. Various research studies and policy papers highlight that the Indian agricultural sector faces constraints of resources, infrastructure institutional, technology and policy. To achieve sustainable agricultural development, it is essential to combine natural, capital, institutional and human resources. Sustainable and broad-based agricultural development is critical for raising living standards, alleviating poverty, assuring food security, generating upward market for expansion of industry and services, and making substantial contribution to the national economic growth.

Impact of Economic Reforms Process on Indian Agricultural Sector: Studies show that the economic liberalization and reforms process has impacted on agricultural and rural sectors. Accordingly, of the three sectors of economy in India, the tertiary sector has diversified the fastest, the secondary sector the second fastest, while the primary sector, taken as whole, has scarcely diversified at all. Since agriculture continues to be a tradable sector, economic liberalization and reform policy has far reaching effects on agricultural exports and imports, investment in new technologies and on rural infrastructure, patterns of agricultural growth, agriculture income and employment, food security, and agricultural prices.

Liberalization of agriculture and open market operations will enhance competition in resource use and 'marketing of agricultural production', which will force the small and marginal farmers (who constitute 76.3% of total farmers) to resort to "distress sale" and seek for off-farm employment for supplementing income.

Salient Agriculture Programs to Boost the Agro Production

Safe Drinking Water and Sustainable Agriculture: It is estimated that for every random sample of 100 people in the Bengal Delta, at least one person will be near death as a result of arsenic poisoning, while five in 100 will be experiencing other symptoms.

In 2008, Queen's University Belfast scientists created low-cost technology that provides arsenic-free water to affected areas. The technology was developed by a team of European and Indian engineers led by Dr. Bhaskar Sengupta from the University. Queen's has now been announced as a provider of training to thousands of people who will learn how to use the equipment and improve environmental conditions.

Dr. Harold Johnston, Director of Education of Civil Engineering at Queen's, also helped develop the training program in Kolkata and Jamshedpur. The program is supported by the British Council under the Development Partnerships in Higher Education Program (DELPHE).

Dr. Sengupta, who is co-coordinating the project, said: "This initiative will help to train more than 1,000 people over the next three years in Eastern India in a novel chemical-free arsenic removal method".

Arsenic poisoning is behind many instances of ill-health in Asia, including a number of cancer cases. Developing a low cost method of decontaminating groundwater that is laced with high levels of arsenic is a key challenge for sustainable agriculture in the region.

The training program developed by Queen's is the only method which is eco-friendly, easy to use and deliverable to the rural community user at an affordable cost.

Dr. Satish Kumar, Director of the India Initiative at Queen's said: "The theory behind community-based natural resource management argues that the best way to manage natural resources is for the local people to use their knowledge and technologies. The issue of deeply entrenched arsenic contamination of groundwater in Kolkata and in large parts of West Bengal calls for an approach where the local population is empowered to engage with this new technology" (Source: Anne Langford Queen's University Belfast 2009).

The Field Fresh Agri Center of Excellence is set up in India for collaborative farming by Field Fresh Foods Pvt. Ltd. for land under cultivation in Punjab and its growing partnerships in Rajasthan, Uttarakhand and Maharashtra. The Center will showcase advanced technologies and agricultural best practices and serve as the hub to impart knowledge and training to the grower partners of Field Fresh. The focus is on early adoption of best practices across the fields to enhance agricultural productivity in an environmentally sustainable manner. "Link Indian farms to the world, by creating the country's first global outsourcing opportunity in fresh produce. The Agri Center of Excellence with its state-of-the-art infrastructure will play a vital role in ensuring that our partner farmers get access to the latest agriculture practices resulting in the world-class fresh produce from India for global markets."

According to Lady Lynn Forester de Rothschild, Director, ELRO Holdings, "The international food market offers a great opportunity for quality farm produce from India. This state-of-the-art facility is an important step towards creating linkages between Indian farm sector and the world."

The Field Fresh Agri Center of Excellence has 211 acres of open cultivation and micro-irrigation test and control facilities in 50 acres. The center houses India's largest protected cultivation spread over 42 acres that includes poly-houses, glass and green houses and net houses. The Center also has an extensive area under nursery trials and 20 different crops under cropping cycle with 200 varieties being currently tried. A pack house and cold storage facility will soon be ready at the Center to maintain the quality of the fresh produce. In addition to this, the Company is working in close partnership with Punjab Agriculture University on several R&D projects for development of world class produce for international markets. "R&D will be one of the strategic drivers for ensuring delivery of superior, innovative products to our global customers."

The Company plans to bring a total of 20,000 acres under cultivation in the near future. All growing facilities will be supported by appropriate facilities such as modern pack houses and cold storages, thus creating the backbone of the produce supply chain—delivering safe, consistent and competitively priced produce, through the year. The Company is also ensuring the welfare of its workers and local communities. Bharti Foundation has set up welfare shelters, crèches, and medical facilities at the Field Fresh Agri Center of Excellence to ensure the well-being of workers. The Center also houses a 'Satya Bharati School' for children from local community.

The Low-cost Agro-animal Technologies Developed by the Defence Institute of High Altitude Research (DIHAR), Leh, have found wide acceptance among farmers in Ladakh. Adoption of these technologies by farmers has not only boosted the availability of fresh food in that region but also helped in socio-economic uplift of the people there. Stating this during the 17th Ladakhi Kisan Jawan Vigyan Mela organized by the institute, local farmers have been generating income amounting to several crore by selling vegetables to the Army formations deployed in that sector. Jammu and Kashmir Chief Minister Omar Abdullah, who was the chief guest at the two-day event, emphasized the need for self-reliance in the region. He advised farmers to develop their own small-scale industries keeping in view the concept of high value-low volume products. Appreciating the role of the DIHAR, he said the institute should play a lead role in boosting the agriculture sector in Ladakh (August 9, 2009).

ITC e-Choupal program and such programs by many other companies in India have helped increase the income and productivity of millions of farmers by giving them more direct access to markets, as well as pricing and product information, via village-based Internet kiosks. e-Choupal is now expanding its service to include education.

Expanding the Food Products Supply: In 80s and 90s, there was food scarcity actual or created in urban areas (Delhi) for bread and milk. Milk and bread were rationed per family and there used to be long queues seen to get them as some days the supply of these will be erratic also. During Rajiv Gandhi's time, this was handled by expansion, competition from private businesses to supply both bread and milk. Government monopoly was broken and the supply became more efficient and both bread and milk was in abundance and available in different varieties and byproducts and thus even expanding the business base of these two products.

Similarly, we can expand the food products in villages by expanding the supply chain of vegetables and fruits grown around the villages. That gives them to eat different stuff as well to have whatever is not available in their village. Supply from villages around will be cheaper and fresher as compared to supply from urban areas, they will enjoy diversified food products and staples also. It will create business for surrounding villages as well for the village itself. True, consuming more than grown will be to make supply chain efficient.

Food prices must be under control and regulated. Availability and competition should not increase or exploit them. The poor are more vulnerable to high food prices.

National Food Security Mission Information Availability: Timely availability of reliable information on agricultural output is of great significance for planning and policy making. The existing system of agricultural statistics, in spite of established procedures and wide coverage, has inherent limitations in the matter of providing an objective assessment of crops at the pre-harvesting stages with the desired spatial details, which are essential to identify problem areas and the nature of required interventions in terms of spatial, temporal and qualitative inferences. Capabilities of the existing system of crop forecasts and crop estimation can be enhanced with the introduction of technological advancements and their adoption. ICTs applications discussed in later sections will be useful.

Research and Extension Agriculture Development Model: R&D plays important roles in the enhancement of agricultural productivity. Research, on the one hand, generates improved technologies and practices that help to raise crop yields and incomes, particularly of small farmers. Extension, on the other hand, provides the mechanism by which those technologies and practices are disseminated for adoption by farmers. For the technology transfer process to be successful, however, these two vital support services need to be effectively linked. The strategies and mix of mechanisms employed depend on the policy, institutional, and resource context of a particular country: (i) viewing research and extension as an integrated knowledge and technology system; (ii) focusing on research and extension functions, rather than simply on organizational structures, to broaden dialogues among all stakeholders; (iii) strengthening crucial linkages under a pluralistic approach and system; (iv) promoting informal networking at many levels with an incentive system for improving linkages; and (v) empowering farmers' groups for more demand, and farmer-driven research and extension services.

The apex body for education, research and extension education in the field of agriculture is the Indian Council of Agricultural Research (ICAR). India's transformation from a food deficit to a food surplus country is largely due to ICAR's smooth and rapid transfer of farm technology from the laboratory to the land. ICAR discharges its responsibilities through 43 research institutes, four national research bureaus, 20 national research centers, nine project directorates, 70 all-India coordinated research projects, and 109 Krishi Vigyan Kendras (farm science centers). Besides, the program of Agricultural Education is coordinated by ICAR with the curricula and other normative guidance given to the 26 Agricultural Universities and four National Research Institutes.

Emerging Trends in agricultural research and extension is that the clients are now becoming partners. Market and environment considerations are driving the innovation process and development potentials are being defined in the international arena. Information science and biotechnology are also greatly influencing agricultural research and extension. Research and extension, for instance, are depending more and more on communication and information tools. Innovations are being generated in networks. What is emerging is a public-private co-innovation system.

Agricultural Knowledge Initiative (AKI): On July 18, 2005, US President George W. Bush and Indian Prime Minister Dr. Manmohan Singh announced the U.S.-India Knowledge Initiative on Agricultural Education, Teaching, Research, Service, and Commercial Linkages (AKI). Recognizing the long history of cooperation in agriculture and the success of India's Green Revolution launched 40 years ago with U.S. assistance; the AKI addresses new challenges and opportunities of modern-day agriculture. It will help to facilitate technology transfer, trade, and investment and bolster agricultural research, education, and extension through public-private partnerships. In pursuing these objectives, a critical component is cooperation on development of effective policy, regulatory, and institutional frameworks. These, in turn, will contribute to increased prosperity for farmers and agricultural growth.

Since its inception, the AKI has made notable progress. Both countries created a board comprised of academia, government, and private sector representatives from the United States and India. The board agreed to a three-year work plan that supports the "Evergreen Revolution", which is based on environmentally sustainable, market-oriented agriculture. To jump start the Initiative, the United States secured funding of $8 million in fiscal year 2006, with a total of $24 million pledged through 2008.

A number of activities have been accomplished in each of the four key areas identified by the board for cooperation: Food Processing and Marketing, Bio-technology, Water Resources Management, and University Capacity Building and to develop a plan to strengthen India's agriculture library and information systems.

The U.S.–India AKI has the potential to raise agricultural productivity, strengthen food security, increase technology transfer, expand U.S.–India trade and investment through policy and regulatory capacity building, ensure key roles for the Indian and U.S. private sectors, and reinvigorate the U.S.-India university partnerships programs in Agricultural Education, Teaching, and Research.

Agricultural Resources Information System

Information Technology can play an important role in the rapid economic growth and social transformation, facilitating sustainable agricultural development in India. It suggests the need for development of metadata and application of Open GIS model for optimal utilization of agricultural resources in India through technology.

Ministry of agriculture has implemented Information Technology Plan, in collaboration with NIC, to implement "NICNET based Agricultural Informatics and Communication (AGRISNET)" in the country, to achieve higher sustainable agricultural productivity and also to make "Indian Agricultural Sector On-line". This is likely to be the largest sharable Internet Portal in the world, for agricultural sector in India, on NICNET having more than 10,000 nodes to government itself.

AGRISNET will have data and information on basic resources such as soil, water, and climate; and other data sets (collated from Remote Sensing as well as conventional means) such as basic data on crops, animal husbandry and fisheries, genetic (plant, animal & fisheries) materials, land ownership, socio-economic data, infrastructure for agricultural development.

For increasing production at micro level, an inventory of currently used, potentially available, as well as an evaluation of the quantity and quality of all resources is required. This requires design and development of agricultural resources information system using state-of-the-art IT Tools to facilitate effective agricultural planning and development; such as Data warehousing (Data Bases & Model Bases), Expert Systems & Knowledge Bases, Networking (Internet, Intranet and Extranet), Geographical Information System (GIS), Application of Remote Sensing Data, Multi-media Information System, Decision Technology System, e-Commerce & e-Governance, and Digital Library.

Agricultural planning and development require (i) knowledge about recent progress in agriculture, (ii) the existing situation (especially the main problems impeding development), and (iii) the potentialities for achieving agricultural objectives. This information is needed for re-assessing current investment and other development activities as well as for planning new measures, setting benchmarks against which to monitor progress. Proper analysis of the agricultural sector should be inter-related and inter-dependent on elements of a system of functionality, each of which contributes to the existing and potential level of performance of the sector.

Remote Sensing has provided a new impetus for the earth resource and environmental scientists. Increasing population and diminishing resources have compelled us to consider better ways for management of natural resources. Soil survey and preparation of soil maps are being carried out by State Departments of Agriculture, State Soil Survey Units, State Agricultural Universities, State Remote Sensing Application Centers, etc.

A review of the soil mapping and land degradation mapping was conducted by an Inter-Agency Expert Committee constituted by the Ministry of Agriculture and the Department of Space, and on the basis of the recommendations, a National Mission on "Mapping of Soils and Land Degradation at 1:50,000 Scale" with the major objective of creation of uniform soil and land degradation database for the entire country is being contemplated. Also for creating "resources databases" using ground truths and applications of remote sensing data (Source: AGRISNET 09).

Application of Geomatics Technology

Internet Technology based applications (Portals) on agricultural resources are expected to facilitate agricultural development, rural development, and backward area development in the country. Design of agricultural resources information system is to support the various management systems at National, State, District and Village level vis-a-vis catchment, watershed and micro watershed level. MOA has established AGRISNET nodes in districts during the Ninth Plan Period and extend to block levels during the Tenth Plan Period and in Eleventh Plan.

Geomatics technology is the synergy of multiple disciplines, Geographic Information Systems (GIS), Remote Sensing, Image Processing, GPS, Cartography, Database Technology and other Geo-related sciences. This offers an integrated and holistic approach for an efficient and effective planning and development of watersheds, and other natural resources management.

Indian remote sensing satellite data in conjunction with the GIS technology is being applied to prepare updated inventory of all the natural resources of the block at the village level which prove an invaluable input to area specific government development schemes.

Salient Projects: The Agriculture Geo-Capacity Network (AGCN) for the state of Punjab (India) is a project initiative between Canada and the state of Punjab to facilitate the Indian agriculture sector to improve their fundamental decision making processes with advanced image-centric enterprise technology. In partnership between the Punjab Remote Sensing Center, PAU, Info-Electronic Systems (Montreal and New Delhi), the Canadian International Development Agency (CIDA Inc), and PCI Geomatics, the AGCN phase I of the project provided a feasibility study, complemented by a Proof of Concept (PoC) to illustrate how information on crop yields and trend analysis can automatically be generated and delivered to government officials and the general public via a simple web browser.

PCI Geomatics' solution is based on a central data repository, providing automated geospatial data processing workflows and multiple channels for geospatial information to be delivered. The AGCN solution is based on industry standards and an open architecture with the spatially enabled database Oracle.

India's current methodology for calculating yield forecasts relies heavily upon labor-intensive desktop solutions. Currently, all data is ordered, acquired, and processed manually. The geo-correction processes, agriculture modeling and yield and trend analysis use desktop GIS/ Remote Sensing applications on a file-based architecture. Their reports are generated externally and printed in a hardcopy format (paper and reports) for distribution. The disconnect that exists between the data, users, and reports promotes a reliance on human resources, thus adding to the delivery time of critical information and increasing the risk for human error. The current agricultural issues that exist in monitoring and crop yields are: Difficulty in efficiently and effectively accessing information from the file-based data management system for generating geospatial products and reports (source PCIGEOMATIC.com).

PROJECT: *C-DAC has developed an Online Monitoring and Management System (OMMS)* to effectively monitor and manage various activities under PMGSY. The main goal of the GIS component of the project was to develop and operationalize a computerized database for rural roads in GIS environment for PMGSY and various state level programs in Rajasthan and Himachal Pradesh. The spatial database has been linked to the OMMS and a standalone GIS interface, named as GIS-enabled Road Information Management & Monitoring System (GRIMMS), has been developed. It contains user-friendly menus for data query, analysis and report generation. The Web GIS version of GRIMMS provides citizen-friendly access to PMGSY for online dissemination of selected information, maps and reports.

PROJECT: *Design, Development and Implementation of GIS-based MIS in Integrated Watershed Development Project (IWDP)*, Hills II, Himachal Pradesh. The World Bank funded project aimed at developing a GIS-based Management Information System (MIS), which will help accelerate the pace of local processing and transmission of data to central and head offices and the dissemination of processed information to all work-sites in a near real-time environment. Under the project, commercially available off-the-shelf GIS were customized to develop the Decision Support System for IWDP-HP, which serves to monitor key project performance indicators. C-DAC also provided customized training to officials of the IWDP to handle the package.

GIS helps to visualize queries about database and statistical analysis. A geographical analysis with regard to GIS assists us in explaining events, foreseeing outcomes and planning strategies. India has an exploding population with inadequate resources; so successful planning of resource management and monitoring and its deployment is absolutely necessary so that GIS can play a crucial role in government and private sectors. Government is the biggest initiator and consumer of GIS data and its applications: *The areas where GIS information is utilized by the government are environment, water management, forestry, defense, urban development, agriculture, etc. and in "Reaching-the-Unreached", and "Resource-Poor-Farmers", through Information Technology applications.*

The central issue in agricultural development is the necessity to increase productivity, employment and income for poor segments of the agricultural population of whom, the small and marginal farmers constitute a sizeable portion. Information Technology tools facilitate the farmers to know the "agricultural situation" in India as well as abroad and accordingly undertake agricultural production. This IT-led globalization will certainly benefit the medium and large farmers who can invest on IT, as has happened during "green revolution". The agricultural development strategy has been mostly "growth-oriented" and therefore had a "built-in bias" in favor of big farmers over small farmers. The big farmers can invest on computers to get access to Internet, but it is not possible for them to invest on "agricultural informatics" with decision support system using geomatics technology.

Agriculture is a "state subject" and a primary sector which accounts for about 27% of GDP, 65% of labor force, and 21% of total exports, the Central Government implements agricultural resources development schemes under both central sector and centrally sponsored sector. These schemes generate voluminous information, spatial and non-spatial, related to agricultural resources, using conventional, remote sensing and GPS technology.

Information Technology facilitates data support for better research, better results, and sustainable planning; bridging the gap between knowledge and practice; and judicious land use, resource surveys, efficient management practices and sustainable use of natural resources, AGRISEN can reduce the process of marginalization of small farmers and evolve small farmer development strategy making full use of information technology and bio-technology and ensuring the linkages between research, technology, and production on one hand, and on the other hand, effectiveness of the delivery system and extension network to carry the benefits of S&T to the farmers.

Effective Networking of Research and Extension: Information Technology

Rita Sharma (09) highlights the role of varied and ever growing new Information Technology for Agriculture research and extension. In the 21st century, agriculture will continue to be the engine of economic growth for many developing countries and it will provide sustainable livelihoods to the majority of rural populations. However, the nature and scope of the demands of the rural community to improve their quality of life—social, economic and political—are undergoing significant changes. No longer are the farmers today content with production technologies of foodgrain crops embodied in the Green Revolution era, as technologies for these crops are already well-known to farmers, who are well-served by seed and input suppliers.

More varied research and extension services are demanded by farmers to remain competitive and profitable, diversify production, and produce for niche markets, and move to higher-value products and more value-added production. Effective linkages of production systems with marketing, agro-processing and other value-added activities have acquired greater importance. In this competitive environment, research and extension services must be oriented to markets and must overcome the exclusive focus on production that ignored market demand and profitability in the past.

Knowledge & Information Focus: Agricultural growth in the new millennium would largely accrue from improvements in productivity of diversified farming systems with regional specialization and sustainable management of natural resources, especially land and water. Furthermore, increases in productivity are likely to come from more efficient use of inputs. Technology recommendations will be tailored to specific groups of farmers and more narrowly defined production environments. Innovation will require more knowledge and information input from research and extension services which will have to respond to specific farmer requests for information in demand-driven mode.

Multi-agency Research and Extension Providers: The diversified nature of farming demands, against a background of economic liberalization and globalization, is radically changing the spectrum of service providers to the rural community. No longer are public research and extension systems the sole providers of agricultural services to the farming community. Private sector, farmers' organizations, cooperatives, self-help groups, para-professionals, NGOs, input suppliers and small agro businesses are engaged in both generation and dissemination of technologies, information, and services. The focus is now shifted to demand-driven, location-specific, customized and tailor-made technologies and services to serve different categories of farmers.

NARS & NAES

In India, radical policy reforms and institutional restructuring is taking place to modernize the National Agriculture Research Systems (NARS) and the National Agriculture Extension Systems (NAES) to make the technology generation and technology dissemination system more farmer-driven and farmer accountable.

Under the National Agriculture Technology Project (NATP) supported by the World Bank, one of the objectives is to strengthen research-extension-farmer linkages. Using both the traditional inter-personal mode, group mechanism, as well as the modern instrument of Information Technology (IT), effective linkages are being forged between research, extension and farmers.

Information Technology is important for *integration of research-extension-farmer*. It has become vital not only because the farmer is a client and recipient of technology, knowledge, and information and provides crucial feedback to the service providers; but it is important for him as an individual farmer, as a member of community-based organizations, cooperatives, farmer interest groups and self-help groups. ICTs (telephone, computer, Internet, email, video conferencing, satellite, TV, radio) have the potential to reach out extensively and rapidly.

Some Major Sectors in Rural Economy of India

Rubber Business: Rubber is one of the significant commercial crops in India. Rubber Industry in India has accounted for a production of 6.49 lakh tons for the year 2006. Places in India where rubber is cultivated include areas of southwest Konkan and Malabar Coast in Kerala and in some areas of Tamil Nadu.

Fisheries in Rural India: The fish production rate in India has witnessed a remarkable growth since 1995-96. The National Program of Developing Fish Seeds, Fish Farmers' Development Agencies and Brackish Water Fish Farmers' Development Agencies have been the major contributors to the growth in fisheries in rural India. A diversified range of fishing methods along with processed fish products have been introduced in the Indian rural market through an Integrated Fisheries Project.

Poultry Business: Poultry Business is one of the major contributors to the growing economy of rural and semi-urban India. India has witnessed a remarkable growth in the egg and poultry meat industry in the recent period. States of Andhra Pradesh, Karnataka, Kerala and Támil Nadu contribute to around 45 per cent of the total egg production in India whereas the eastern and central parts of India contribute to around 20 per cent of the same.

Tobacco Business: India is one of the most predominant producer as well as consumer of tobacco. It ranks third in terms of tobacco production around the world. Tobacco leaves are highly exported in the overseas countries which has accounted for a 99 per cent increase in the revenue from exports.

Jute Business: Jute is one of the most prime products in terms of exporting to the overseas nations and it brings in maximum foreign exchange earnings. River Ganges delta in West Bengal is perfect for jute cultivation. A wide range of gunny bags, shopping bags, handicrafts, carpets, and many more other items are made from Jute.

Horticulture: India has a diverse soil and climate which provides a promising opportunity for horticulture. Some of the crops cultivated in the horticultural sector comprise of fruits, vegetables, root and tuber crops, flowers, ornamental plants, medicinal and aromatic plants, spices, condiments, plantation crops and mushrooms.

Sericulture: Sericulture is one of the rural-based agro industries in India. Silk production activity has accounted for a total income from export production of more than US$ 600 million. Sericulture offers agro based, ecologically and economically sustainable activity for the poor, small and marginal farmers which also include women. 60 per cent of the pre-cocoon and post-cocoon sector activities are carried out by women.

Tea Business: The tea business has been ruling Indian economy for the past 170 years. The chief areas of tea production in India include rural hills and plantation areas of North-eastern like Assam, West Bengal and southern states, Tamil Nadu and Kerala. India mainly manufactures tea variants such as CTC, orthodox tea and green tea.

Biogas Production: Rural India has a vast potential of biogas generation and application. During the past two decades, biogas has been promoted mostly as a cooking fuel in the rural areas. According to the prevailing practices in these areas, fuel for cooking is not being purchased but collected by the users from the farm fields and surrounding areas. Majority of rural population feels that biogas generation does not offer them direct monetary benefits, and therefore, many of them are reluctant to accept it. However, biogas, when used for production activities, in small-scale rural industries, may be able to fill the gap in energy availability and demand in the rural areas. Being a renewable source, biogas, when utilized properly, can replace the commercial and non-renewable energy sources to a considerable extent in a variety of production activities. Biogas application in the above context has been found to be self-sustaining, while fulfilling the rural energy demand. There are other important aspects such as employment generation, socio-economic and environmental impacts.

In India, solar and wind power has still to be promoted widely for rural use in rural and remote hilly areas as electricity generation is not fully productive and accessible in these areas so far.

Village Enterprises

Rural-based products and services of rural industries can change the rural landscape and occupational scenario. Impact of these industries is favorable on communities as new jobs are created, but these may be limited to younger generation who have better level of education and have or are capable of acquiring vocational skills. Creation of community workshops also helps for lack of job opportunities in the industries. The economic benefits gained through employment in industries are sufficiently attractive to engage the better educated younger male and female. Strong services industry has a huge potential for rural economy as services account for over 28% of rural GDP. The share of industry in rural areas has grown at a faster rate to over 30%. However, capital intensive manufacturing, largely a response to cheap capital and inflexible labor laws, would not be as equitable as labour intensive services in distributing the gains of growth.

Recent interest on rural industries derives from recognition of the limits of agriculture and organized manufacturing sector in employment generation especially during the post-liberalization period in India. Historically, industrial development of the West and the East presents contrasting pictures of rural industries. One, the linearity model founded on the historical experience of the West, holds that development implies a movement away from traditional subsistence production in rural areas to modern industrial production in urban centers. The other, the South-east Asian

Experience has shown that the growth potential of rural industries is considerable given the under-utilization of the physical labor and the entrepreneurial ability of rural people. A combination of putting out system and sub-contracting system along with modern factory and industrial cooperatives has persisted in the rural manufacturing sector even in the era of economic liberalization. We find differential capital endowments and socio-economic constraints of rural artisans reflecting extensive division of labor, specialization and fragmentation of the labor process. These do not satisfy the requirements of the linearity model founded in advanced capitalist countries.

The Ministry of Agro and Rural Industries (MoARI) in India was established in September, 2001 with the aim to develop the Rural Industries in the Indian Economy. The main objectives of this initiative were to ameliorate the supply chain management, upgrade skills, introduce innovative technologies and expand markets of the entrepreneurs and artisans. A wide range of programs, schemes, projects and policies have been formulated to carry out various activities in the rural sector in India.

Village jobs can be created in food processing, cold storage of food, Handloom, Handicrafts, Power loom, Sericulture and Wool, micro and small enterprises (MSE) sector, consisting of the traditionally defined small-scale industries and small-scale service and business entities, such as khadi, coir and bamboo industries. Employment generation in the areas for production, distribution and marketing, technology upgradation and exports can be created in these areas. It would need supportive credit policies and practices, marketing support, and training needs of entrepreneurs. Self-employment opportunities can be expanded through these enterprises. We have discussed details of Employment generation in these areas in Chapter 3—Rural Industries and Chapter 6—Rural Markets.

Village Industries are employment intensive and require less capital. However, the earnings per worker are low and hence they require to be upgraded so as to compete in the highly competitive and constrained market. The village industries boards have been promoting Village Industries by establishing production centers in different districts, organizing Cooperative Societies and granting margin money to entrepreneurs for establishing Village Industrial Units.

Micro and small enterprises in India has a special significance with regard to bridging up the disparities between urban and rural sectors of the economy on the one hand and the more industrialized and the less industrialized states on the other. It would also channelize to the mainstream, the forces of development in the rural and remote areas presently strewn with the immense possibilities of manufacturing and service activities. Micro, Small and Medium Enterprises Development Act, 2006 reflects the relevance of small enterprises and action taken.

Rural Art and Crafts Industries: Rural art and crafts industries in rural areas in different States all over India have developed differently according to their product specialization. For example, Southern states of Tamil Nadu and Karnataka, and Northern states of Rajasthan and UP have richer cultural heritage. Eight states of the North-Eastern Region (NER) of India: Arunachal Pradesh, Assam, Manipur, Meghalaya, Mizoram, Nagaland, Sikkim and Tripura, are all well known for their handicrafts. The Scheduled Tribes form the majority of population there. Most of these states are hilly and have remained agriculturally as well as industrially backward. Promotion of small enterprises is most suitable for their timely development.

Khadi and Village Industries Commission (KVIC): It is the national nodal agency. At the state level, the scheme is implemented through State KVIC Directorates, State Khadi and Village Industries Boards (KVIBs) and District Industries Centers (DICs) and Banks.

To support the khadi sector, two new schemes have been launched. Under *Work- shed Scheme* for Khadi artisans, it has been targeted to provide 38,000 work sheds to khadi spinners and artisans. The 'Scheme for Enhancing Productivity and Competitiveness of Khadi Industries and Artisans' aims at increasing productivity of khadi artisans through 200 selected khadi institutions by assisting them with quality raw material, capacity building, value addition and marketing linkages. A scheme to rejuvenate, modernize and technologically upgrade spinners and tiny household sector in coir production has been launched. Under the scheme, outdated ratts and looms would be replaced and work-sheds would be provided. Financial aid has been tied up with the Asian Development Bank funding amounting to US$ 150 million over a period of three years for implementing a comprehensive Khadi Reform Program. Under this, the khadi sector would be revitalized with increased incomes, employment, sustainability and artisans' welfare and KVIC would be enabled to reduce dependence on government grants. Initially, program will be initiated in 300 khadi institutions (The current scenario in 2008-09).

The focus would be needed on schemes, programs for increasing the productivity of individual workers, artisans, entrepreneurs as well as their groups and clusters through training, better access to improved tools, equipment and processes, and provision of common facilities for compliance with prescribed quality standards, etc.

Among the village industries scheduled for development by KVIC, are the forest-based industries: collection of forest plants and herbs for (mostly medicinal purposes); cane and bamboo processing; gums and resins; khattha manufacturing; and shellac industry. These industries utilize minor forest produce which are under the control of State Forest Departments. Cane and bamboo industry is widespread in India since the raw materials occur everywhere and are associated with many aspects of rural activity. The availability of canes in India is meagre compared to its requirements. The chief uses are for making furniture, baskets, handles for umbrellas, and mats. Industries based on gums and resins, and khattha (a medicinal extract of Khair tree) are relatively minor to cane, bamboo and herbs collection; Shellac, which employs over a million people, is more prominent. There are nearly 8,000 units producing wood products in the small-scale sector employing 0.29 million persons or about 1 per cent of the SSI employment total.

The major Village industries supported under the Tamil Nadu Khadi and Village Industries Board, for instance, are Leather, Bee-keeping, Non-Edible Oil & Soap, Pottery, Hand-Made Paper, Palmgur, Carpentry and Blacksmithy and Palm Products Development. The Palm Products Industry is also one of the major cottage industries under the Village Industries Sector in the State. It is pioneer in development of Palm Products Industry in India. Out of the estimated 8.59 crore of Palmyrah trees in India, about 5.20 crore of Palmyrah trees are in Tamil Nadu. Palmyrah is declared as the "State Tree" of Tamil Nadu. The State also earns foreign exchange by export of Palm Products.

The Tamil Nadu Palm Products Development Board is functioning since 1995 and is engaged in initiating modern concepts to promote research for the development of Palm products industry and better utilization of Palm products with the social objective of uplifting the economic condition of rural palmgur artisans. Edible products such as Neera, Palm Jaggery, Palm Candy, Palm Sugar, Palm Fruit Jam, Nungu preserve and other confectionary products as well as non-edible items like Palm Fiber and Palm Leaf products, brushes and baskets are produced and marketed. Six lakh artisans, both men and women, are currently engaged in the Palm Products Industry in the State both directly and indirectly. This includes 30,000 Scheduled Caste artisans who are directly engaged in activities related to the Palm Products Industry such as tapping of Neera, manufacturing of Palm Jaggery, Palm Fiber and Date Palm Baskets.

The Khadi Rural Spinning Centers provide employment to such categories of people to help them to earn subsidiary wages so as to lift them above the poverty line. The main products that are being produced under Khadi sector are Cotton, Poly vastra and Silk varieties. TNKVIB has established its production centers for Khadi cotton and Poly vastra fabrics in different parts of the State. TNKVIB is also known for its exquisite Khadi Silk Sarees, made especially from original Zari, using eco-friendly and natural dyes.

Institutional Support: This support is meant for small-scale rural processing enterprises. Village and small industries have been grouped broadly under six different areas. Each area comes under the overview of one of the following organizations set up by the Central Government: (i) The Small-Scale Industries Board, (ii) The Khadi and Village Industries Commission, (iii) The All India Handicrafts Board, (iv) The Central Silk Board, (v) The Central Coir Board, and (vi) The All India Handloom Board.

All-India Handicraft Boards are a third set of national institutions which oversee implementation of small industry programs. Some states have also set up Handicrafts Development Boards to supplement the activities of the All India Organizations. Research and Development Centers, Design Centers, etc. are also established for particular handicraft items. Boards also give assistance in expanding markets, through the network of corporation showrooms which provide direct marketing assistance to the artisans for the sale of their products. In addition, the Corporation also organizes exhibitions throughout the country to explore more marketing avenues for the handicrafts produced by the artisans. It assists in supply of essential raw materials, providing (and subsidy on cost) finance for investment and working capital and giving technical assistance and other advisory services. They implement various schemes for the development of the crafts and craftsmen in the state.

In rural industries, special focused 'Product Clusters' are developed in the specific areas under SFURTI Scheme. For example in Tamil Nadu rural areas six clusters are being developed viz., Tamarind processing rural cluster at Erode, Wood Carving Cluster at Villupuram, Arecanut Leaf Cup Cluster at Salem and Namakkal, Brass Utensils Making Cluster at Tirunelveli, Bell Metal Cluster at Nachiarcoil and Thanjavur, and Sea Food Preservation, Processing, Packaging and Marketing Cluster at Nagapattinam. Under SFURTI, during the Eleventh Plan period, a Central share of Rs. 6.15 crore and a State share of Rs. 0.88 crore and during 2008-09, an outlay of 16.56 lakh is proposed to implement this scheme.

Similar cluster schemes are being developed in rural areas of different states according to areas product items specialization.

Rural Backward Area Subsidy in Specific Identified Areas: A Committee has been set up for identifying the backward areas in rural areas in the State to extend Capital Subsidy for Industrial Units set up in these areas. An outlay of Rs. 100 crore is approved during the Eleventh Plan for the scheme, which seeks to encourage setting up of industries in the identified backward areas. A sum of Rs. 20 crore has been allocated for the year 2007-08 and expenditure for the same will be incurred by the end of the year. In the year 2008-09 an amount of Rs. 30 crore is proposed to be incurred for this scheme.

Assistance for 'Technology Upgradation and Modernization: The existing schemes for providing interest subsidy for technology upgradation did not have a good response, because the 3% subsidy was linked to the Prime Lending Rate (PLR) of banks. Further, the scheme was partitioned into four parts affecting its flexibility and there was low awareness regarding the benefits. It is proposed to extend the interest subsidy at a flat rate of 3% for the loan obtained from the banks and financial institutions without reference to Prime Lending Rate (PLR). With the investment ceiling on Plant and machine being increased from Rs. 1 to Rs. 5 crore, it is expected that the interest subsidy scheme will be energized and reactivated. A sum of Rs. 50 lakh was allocated for the year 2007-08 and the same is expected to be incurred by the end of the year. For the year 2008-09, a sum of Rs. 50 lakh is proposed to be allocated for this purpose.

Handlooms and Textiles: The Tamil Nadu Textile Industry is the forerunner in the rural industrial development as it provides large scale employment for the rural people, weavers next to agriculture. The various sectors of the textile industry in the state comprise of handloom, powerloom, spinning, processing and hosiery and garments sectors.

Out of the total handlooms in Tamil Nadu, 2.19 lakh handlooms are functioning with 1117 Handloom Weavers' Cooperative Societies and the remaining 1.94 lakh looms are outside the cooperative fold. All the developmental and welfare schemes of the state Government intended for the handloom weavers are being channelized through these Weavers' Cooperative Societies. The power-looms in Tamil Nadu are mainly cotton oriented. Out of 3.66 lakh power-looms only about 5000 powerlooms are sophisticated. There are 19.03 lakh registered power-looms in India.

Sericulture: It is a unique combination of both agricultural and industrial activities. On the agriculture side, it involves cultivation of mulberry to feed the silkworms. The industrial activities involve reeling of the silk filament from the cocoons and value addition such as processing and weaving. Sericulture is a labor intensive industry in all its phases, viz. cultivation of mulberry, silkworm rearing, silk reeling and other post-cocoon processes such as twisting, dyeing, weaving, printing and finishing.

Handicrafts Development: The handicrafts sector is of special significance in the country's economy due to its contribution to employment generation and foreign exchange earnings through exports. Handicrafts of a State reflect rich cultural heritage. The State Governments in collaboration with the Government of India have been implementing various schemes to preserve and nurture the ancient crafts of the state while at the same time ensuring the welfare of the artisans who make these beautiful artifacts. These handicrafts are in bronzes, stone sculptures, artistic brass lamps, intricately carved art plates and woodcarvings from the craft pockets, appliqué & chikenkari work, and Zari work.

Rural Outsourced Production Enterprises (ROPE): This enterprise focuses on outsourcing or contracting production to villages in select sectors and using ICT tools and applications for efficient production organization. Based in Chennai, operations started in March 2007. The mission of ROPE is to integrate domestic and international markets with informal sectors of rural India and generate value for the skills and resources available in these sectors through production outsourcing. ROPE has so far supplied its products to more than thirty big and small clients both within and outside India.

Some of its prominent clients include IKEA, Chennai; Industree Crafts, Bangalore; CwithCo, New York; TiE, Chennai and IIT Madras.

ICT Applications and Rural Cyber Cafe: NGO sector also came forward to provide ICT services in villages across the country. Some of the prominent ones are n-Logue, Tarahat, MS Swaminathan Foundation, Byrraju Foundation and Drishtee. NGOs are playing a very proactive role and some of them are helping youth entrepreneurs setting up their own cyber enterprises in villages. Thousands of cyber enterprises are set up and entrepreneurs are promoted by such NGOs. This also enables handicrafts and rural-village enterprises to market their products and get wide exposure.

Rural Business Hubs for Village Arts and Crafts, Industries

The village arts and crafts, industries are dying; to revive these and make them viable for income generating occupations, two-pronged effort is being made by the MoPR (Ministry of Panchayati Raj) and confederation of Indian industries in 2008-09: (i) to encourage organized revival and promotion of these industries, (ii) to market these products both in domestic and international markets.

The project will encourage rural people in every block panchayats, to develop their local arts and crafts products, and household industries to generate income. RBH has been conceptualized to synergistically link rural products, skills with the marketing and professional skills of the industry. It is a unique concept of P4 model partnership to involve industry to improve and refine locally available resources and produce goods of international quality and standards and to address this lacuna in the market structure.

The RBHs indicate a group of entrepreneurs including farmers and artisans working together under the aegis of a block panchayat to enhance value of their products with private sector participation for greater market access and prosperity.

The RBH is aimed to allow people living in communities to use their skills in manufacturing products while the

Government and the private sector would render assistance on developing the products. Direct linkages will be between industry and local community.

Since there are about 6,097 blocks and intermediate panchayats all over the country, the MoPR—CII and RHB Council will select only the products that are export-ready and of outstanding quality to promote at the national and international levels.

RBH will provide members of Indian industry a unique opportunity to participate, learn and profit from sustainable rural ventures. Each RBH venture will seek to improve the quality of local arts and crafts products in handpicked rural business hubs (approximately the size of a village block) by using modern training and production processes. Both large and small industries will come together with farmers or local artisans to enhance the market value of a selected product. The objective is to improve market access and ensure profitability across the value chain. Creation of RBH will bring economic prosperity to the Rural India. RBH scheme and its process of setting up is discussed in chapter 6—Rural Markets, and in Appendix 3.

Challenges Ahead

There is increasing importance of Information Technology, Bio-Technology, and Geomatics technology for developing agriculture and sustainable agriculture. More varied research and extension services, diversify production, and effective linkages of production systems with marketing, agro processing and other value-added activities oriented to markets and market demands, and profitability will improve returns of agriculture based rural occupations. It is a challenge how best to achieve it through PPP model and community initiatives.

Our challenge ahead is to revive village industries and make them viable business propositions and profitable as being initiated through rural business hubs and PPP model.

Many new enterprises for gainful economic gains have come up because of new technologies, demands of modern ways of doing things differently and new concepts; and globalization.

There is growing consensus that higher occupational incomes of ruralites can grow rural economy. Our discussions highlight that the focus of generating higher incomes for rural occupations—primarily agriculture and its allied occupations and village industries can be enhanced by organized efforts by P4 model. What is required is much-needed private investment, skilled resources and institutions and people initiatives.

4

Human Development: Ruralites

Innovate today for tomorrow's villages;
Creating Ideas means creating jobs

We assume people play the most significant role to maintain clean and healthy environment for themselves. All depends on their top priority efforts.

It is not whether the villagers have money to spend or not, rather what is more important is what they think of themselves—powerless, helpless, or ignorant. What matters is their self ID and self-esteem. Equally important is, how others—the government, bureaucracy, urban civil society—think of them—as dependant, naïve, ignorant and to be ignored and bypassed. Both, self ID and other ID are important and these can be boosted by giving villagers quality of life through education, employment, health, clean environment and connectivity. *The bottom level of the society needs to be strengthened by developing the people and they can be the drivers of rural growth.*

We advocate that we need development of Rural Infrastructure by focusing on developing Human dimensions. We need to give quality of life to people on personal and occupational fronts to create better rural economy.

Education and employment will develop them, they need to be healthy and the focus should be on rural health care, safe drinking water, sanitation, clean environment and housing. To facilitate and achieve these objectives, we need to focus on rural electrification, and rural roads.

Rural infrastructure development focus will be two ways: (i) Education—setting up village schools for education, employment and creating employability by boosting agriculture and village enterprises; rural health care infrastructure by developing the medical facilities, safe drinking water, sanitation and clean physical environment. (ii) Develop infrastructure for rural electrification and rural roads. We will be highlighting these focuses and advocating these will be drivers of rural economy.

We need to give quality of life to people on personal and occupational fronts to create better rural economy. We presume the development of these human dimensions: quality of life for villagers, healthy physical environment, healthcare, education, occupational and vocational education and training, employment, and teleconnectivity will create economic gains for ruralites and hence create healthy physical environments conducive to quality of life, both through physical and psychological well-being. We reiterate it needs the collaborative efforts of people, local, state and central governments, entrepreneurs' business plans and social responsibility programs, NGOs, and social entrepreneurs' involvements and inputs.

Narula (2006) points out that poverty from the economic perspective, commonly implies lack of resources—money or material possessions that are necessary for individuals or households to consume goods and services above a certain subsistence level; but generally, the minimum level of goods and services that comprise the subsistence level is subjective. Although we agree that there has to be basic minimum needs (BMN) for subsistence such as food with certain nutritional value, housing that meets certain minimum standards, some level of health care, clothing, education, and such other basic goods and services. Yet, there is no agreement as to what quantities and qualities of these items comprise the subsistence level of living. The particular subsistence level needs to be socially acceptable also.

Yunus (2006) points out that being in poverty means that you are not contributing your talent, your energy, your creativity into the marketplace to benefit everybody else. "We should be removing poverty not for the person himself or herself. It is for us too. Because denying ourselves the brilliant ideas and productivity and ingenuity of all those one and a half billion people is a terrible loss."

From these points of view, currently more then 95% of the villagers may not have even subsistence level of living; they lack in one or the other BMN. If they have food, it may not be enough in nutritional value or healthcare and so forth. *They thus are not able to contribute their talent, energy, creativity for development of self, their village community and society at large.*

Hence we need to create sound policies to achieve these for the rural strata. Right on, we need special rural policies in these areas to bring them at par with urban and national mainstream economy as there is wide lag for it. Development of these rural infrastructures by human dimensions will drive rural economy.

In order to demonstrate its commitment towards the people of India, the government is emphasizing currently (2008-09) on social sector welfare schemes such as Sarva Shiksha Abhiyaan, mid-day meals, secondary education, health sector spending, National Rural Employment Guarantee Act, Rajiv Gandhi Drinking Water Mission and women empowerment specific programs. More and more is being allocated for social sector spending by government.

"Social welfare aimed at human development or improvement in the well-being of the people is an important objective of development planning. While economic growth is extremely important, it has to be accompanied by improvement in the quality of life of the people for the development process to be sustainable in the medium to long run. More importantly, it has to be inclusive in nature. The notion of inclusive growth relates essentially to equality of opportunity to all for a productive and meaningful life with freedom and dignity. It is much broader than the objective of poverty alleviation. It encompasses human development and economic and social mobility for all sections of the society, and in particular, for the disadvantaged and marginalized population groups of the society. These population groups have not only to be brought into the economic and social mainstream but made active participants and legitimate beneficiaries of the development process. Ultimately, *a healthy, educated and an empowered population contributes to improved productivity which, in turn sustains economic growth*" (Eleventh Five-Year Plan document).

The programs for educational development, economic and social empowerment of socially disadvantaged groups and marginalized sections of the society are implemented through the close participation of State Governments, Union territory (UT) Administrations and non-governmental organizations (NGOs). Public-private partnership (PPP) approach is also one of the strategies for attaining the objectives of development of the targeted groups.

While some innovative steps taken in the implementation of these programs have brought in some transparency, much more needs to be done in this direction. More emphasis is required on better governance and improved service delivery so that the targeted groups of people are actually benefitted from the schemes implemented by the Centre and States. There is also a need to involve local communities and Panchayati Raj Institutions to the maximum possible extent so that local people have a stake in planning for their welfare and upliftment. This will also help in preventing leakages as well as wastages in the form of implementation of schemes with overlapping objectives and beneficiaries.

The Central Government expenditure on social services and rural development has gone up consistently over the years. The share of Central Government expenditure on social services including rural development in total expenditure (plan and non-plan) has increased from 11.23 per cent in 2002-03 to 19.44 per cent in 2008-09 (RE). Central support for social programs has continued to expand in various forms although most social sector subjects fall within the purview of the States. Major program specific funding is available to the states through the Centrally-sponsored schemes. However, the reach of public and quasi-public goods and services supplied by the state to people still leave a lot of scope for improvement. There are still leakages in the schemes and the benefits in full do not reach the intended target groups of people.

The public has given a great mandate to the political leadership in the National Elections of 2009. There are three concerns that need to be addressed. One, are we going to have government ministers who will provide effective governance and carefully look after implementation? Two, will the Finance Ministry on a quarterly basis carefully look at schemes and programs where expenditure is being made from taxpayers' money? Three, are the benefits actually going to the intended end-users? The government should regularly conduct an audit to check deliverance on the effectiveness of expenditure; operational control and review on a monthly or quarterly basis on accountability and transparency of schemes to avoid any corrupt practices. So we should look forward to new mechanisms of controls for projects and delivery, and effective spending.

As highlighted by Finance Minister, the combined expenditure on social services in 2008-09 was Rs. 257 per month per person roughly. "The total combined expenditure of the Centre and the state governments on social services in 2008-09 was 6.72 per cent of the country's GDP. The Government is fully committed to inclusive growth and is making all efforts to provide sufficient funds for social security, especially for the disadvantaged sections of the society," he said. Social services include education, sports, art and culture, medical and public health, family welfare of SCs, STCs and OBCs, labor welfare, social security and welfare and nutrition, relief on account of natural calamities (Aug. 09).

Challenges of Rural Life in India

Optimum development of rural segment will pose ongoing challenges. In the 2000 decade, rural India is getting special attention for development in various sectors; but we all realize, in the coming years, rural segment needs greater and exclusive plans and programs to develop it. Its present development is only a drop in the ocean. It has become segregated segment which will need special plans and programs for being brought closer to the mainstream of society, and as such, benefit from programs planned for the whole society. How do we bring it closer to mainstream society? We need to focus on particular strategies, why it is lagging behind despite the fact rural segment has been the priority sector for development since 50s.

Connecting roads, electrification, safe water and sanitation should have been the first priority even in 50s; but we failed. There have been efforts to provide good healthcare through primary healthcare centers and dispensaries tiers and barefoot doctor schemes in 70s. We had initiated excellent program of Panchayati Raj to the lowest tier of village level workers. Villages had always been the focus of new agricultural training. Even NABARD—rural bank was set up to microfinance. Many other development schemes were initiated from 50s to 70s; although schemes were ideal, their implementation was poor and villagers' motivation was low. Resources were not spent effectively. So, efforts made did not commensurate with the progress and development expected.

India can no longer afford to ignore the "dualism in the society" wherein the urban areas surge ahead on the path to progress while the rural India lags behind. There is an India which wants to move stronger while there is another which is trying hard to catch on with it. We need to think hard to give rural India a better deal. No government can ignore either challenge. Consistent efforts are needed to upgrade rural communities, and they need better deal.

Currently, the challenges of rural life in India is to provide better education, provide access to health, safe drinking water and water for irrigation and other purposes, sanitation and a better environment to people residing in rural areas. To develop rural road connectivity is very important. The physical and social infrastructure in rural India must catch up at least with that of semi-urban India within the next decade. The other major challenge is to provide employment within the rural areas so that flux to urban areas is controlled. Developing business bases, BPOs, and outsourcing outlets in the villages, and expanding rural retailing may create more jobs.

Finance Minister (June 09) said economic growth is critical for employment as well as going back to the trajectory. The government's focus should shift from expenditure to effectiveness of expenditure *and action to delivery and implementation.* Actually, what they are doing in terms of focusing on rural, social sector inclusive growth is very much in keeping with what they have been doing. But it is back to execution and implementation that is going to determine how fast we progress. *Be it sanitation, education, public health, electricity, roads, public spaces and environment, whatever are the criteria, rural India needs special strategies.*

Quality of Life for Villagers

Healthy Physical Environment: Let us first focus on promoting for them healthy physical environment through cleanliness of their surroundings, houses, and personal hygiene. This has to be the collaborative efforts of local people, local agencies and NGOs to create awareness, motivation among people and people to enact and understand the value of clean environment by proper hygiene and garbage disposal.

For further healthy physical environment, sanitation and water availability is essential. Providing community toilets requires both state and local efforts. State should be willing to provide space and technology of *sulabh shochalya* and people collectively willing to spend resources of money, labor and efforts as well willing to adopt the use of toilets and keep them clean which is very important. Of course, sanitation requires water availability for which both state and central governments have to plan and supported by entrepreneurships' social responsibility programs and by NGOs.

Safe and clean potable drinking water is necessary and it requires both private and public efforts; efforts of local, state and central governments on one hand and most importantly for the people to use water cleanly, both at its origin i.e. taps, wells, and rivers; at storage in tanks, bins and pots and while drinking. So, pollution of water has to be checked at every level that needs NGOs to create awareness for clean water for healthy living, and people to use clean water. Both of them need to keep checks and monitors for the clean water facilities.

Providing basic facilities of clean environment, sanitation, water facilities lead to better health care and disease control. Resources spent on providing these basic facilities will equal to the money spent on providing basic health care facilities.

Education for people is a significant facilitator for creating awareness, motivation, adoption and handling clean physical environment and its side issues. Education motivates and stimulates people to achieve for better QOL and how this can provide a mindset for employment and economic gains.

In later sections, we highlight the significance of education, employment and health care for people achieving QOL. The focus on sound education, employment and health care policies can drive the rural economy to economic growth.

Education Model in India

It has been said that literacy levels are a measure of a nation's degree of commitment to social justice. A literate environment is essential for ensuring universal elementary education, reducing child mortality, curbing population growth, ensuring gender equality and acquiring essential livelihood skills. This is equally true for rural education.

According to the 2001 Census, 65 per cent of Indians are literate. And almost every child now has access to a school, with around 95 per cent of our rural population having a primary school within one kilometer of their habitation. If one were to identify the single most important achievement in the field of education by the government in the post-Independence era, it would have to be putting a school within the reach of almost every child. But what is important is the viability of that school for the child in terms of education.

Broadly, the vast majority of the population, both rural and urban, sends its children to government-run schools, as these are free, i.e. they do not charge fees. However, given that the quality of education in these schools is usually quite poor, the fast-increasing middle class in urban areas prefers to send its children to the government-aided, privately-run schools. The private schools even cater to the elite upper-class population. But rural child has no other choice but the government-run village school. Therefore, it is important that such school should impart quality education; otherwise it is not effective expenditure by the government.

The big questions are: does the socio-economic condition of rural children allow them to go to schools? How many drop-outs within a year or two? And what is the quality of education available at these schools? Thus, *social context* of rural education is significant and needs consideration when planning rural education.

Nandan Nilkeni (2009) comments on the Indian government's education approach which has been clumsy and unyielding; the focus of government in education has been on building infrastructure with a little emphasis on teacher's training, educational achievements and performance measurement. Education policies have funded schools and not schooling. Such an education approach has affected the rural education scenario badly, that needs drastic and innovative change. Ideas for a new century, perhaps captures the current crisis in our classrooms. Public expenditure on education increased four-fold in the Eleventh Five-year Plan, but the solution to this crisis is not political attention and funding, but liberalizing and de-control. So, are we ready for reforms in education?

We have to look at three issues for educational reforms: access, equity and quality. Access means expansion, equity suggests inclusion and third issue of quality suggesting excellence. Equity is important. Unless we are able to provide to the ordinary people, the marginals and the ruralites the kind of quality education that we provide to the elite, this is not going to work. We have to have a model to do that. Expansion, inclusiveness and excellence and more forward within that framework is important.

Human Resources Development Minister Kapil Sibal said (09) that the Right to Education Bill is planned to incentivize private sector investment into education. He also said that HRD Ministry would reform current regulatory bodies and would push for a SEBI-like regulatory body for the education sector as well for FDI (foreign direct investment) into education. Education bill will open up the entire education sector, to greater investment and to allow children to go to the school that they want without any concern about where the money is going to come from because we will have to put in place a loan scheme, both in higher education and public education. The government school education is going to be free but even for private schools, if someone wants to go to a private school, he should be entitled to go as long as he gets a loan.

Education Bill: The passage of the Right of Children to Free and Compulsory Education Bill in 2009 indeed is a historic moment and the flagship program displays the commitment towards transforming the education system. The Bill is the right step in its broad parameters. But only integrated visions encompassing the whole spectrum of issues from teacher's pay to curriculum to infrastructure can effectively achieve the objectives of the fundamental right to education.

However, there are a few immediately discernible grey areas on implementation. Funding is a key issue, with the Centre-State arrangement yet to be worked out. There are also valid concerns on quality and whether the Bill could lead to an entrenching of inequitable schooling. The legislation has missed out a larger vision of integrated education; a linkage between primary, secondary and higher education. It is in a broader integrated vision where the question of employability, for instance, can be better addressed. For example, letter-of-law definition of primary education as until class VIII, while a matric or 12th is essential for employment. Absenteeism and dropouts are linked to a lack of foreseeable employment, social needs must be integrated into policy on education. An instance of the latter would be to bring child labor policy within its ambit.

There is overwhelming dependence, particularly in many towns and rural areas on government schools, the focus should be on upgrading the government school system. There is the issue of producing adequately trained teachers so that they can contribute more to the education system. A greater community involvement in the management of local schools, can address issues like widespread government school teacher truancy. This has worked well in states like Kerala and Nagaland and can be replicated in other parts of the country (News item 6th Aug. 09).

Investment and expenditure on education, have gone up significantly from the 10th five-year plan to the Eleventh Five-Year Plan almost from 7.5% to 19% and perhaps for the first time in India's history that we are seeing this kind of money being pumped in, but it is not just a question of money but it is also a question of implementation and execution, how do you monitor, and how do you make this accountable?

Over the last five years, we have employed around 9 lakh teachers, lots of schools are being built, but we need to have a long-term solution and there are different issues at different levels. So we need to first have a national roadmap for education. The issues of primary, secondary, and higher education, teacher training, education research, skill development, educational reforms and usefully and effectively spending of education allocation need to be handled effectively. If expenditure in education allocation is usefully and effectively spent, then half the problem would be solved.

How do we incentivize private investment, there is a Supreme Court order that says education cannot be for profit. Private investors need not necessarily make money out of this but they need to have sustainable and viable businesses. But they should not hive off the profits into other businesses and what we need is a rational approach; let institutions make money but that must go back into education. For instance, if somebody sets up an ordinary private school and then he wants to build a vocational training center from the profits that he makes from the that school, he is entitled to do it.

In the Eleventh plan document, for higher end technical education, the estimated need is around Rs. 250,000 crore and the outlay is about 30,000 crore so this tells us that there is a huge need and irrespective of how much allocation we want from the government, there is a big gap, so we need to identify these gaps which are different at different levels. So, gaps in

Rs. 250,000 crore will be bridged if we have the appropriate polices in place (News item, June 2009).

It is observed that most private educational institutions across the country saw the slowdown as an opportunity and were in expansion mode. Most private universities across the country had reported a surge in demand among students for academic courses, be it short-term or long-term. There was also an increase in the demand for short-term skill enhancement courses. So, we must effectively regulate this expansion mode by private funds. In this respect, *Public-private partnership (PPP) in school education* is *important to fill the gap in finances*.

Experts say HRD ministry will encourage private players to come forward. The Public-Private Partnership (PPP) Education Policy and guidelines would be announced soon. What could this mean for education companies? The companies such as NIIT and Everonn Systems, Educom, etc. that are into this area perhaps may find some benefits. Government would also formulate a policy framework for foreign investment in school education (Aug. 09).

In education sector in general, government has got three types of funds; Sarv Shiksha Abhiyan, Madhyamik Shiksha Abhiyan and the ICDS schools—and probably Rs. 2,000-3,000 crore will come into this line for public participation over the next two years.

Public-Private Partnership Model in School Education: PPPs have clearly defined goals of delivering high quality services to the citizenry, ensuring that the public interest is served and that public resources are efficiently and equitably employed, and at the same time, sufficient profits are earned by the private entities to enable them to sustain and continue as participants in such ventures.

PPPs have been used in all sorts of sectors including roads, hospitals, schools, information technology infrastructure and general governmental administrative tasks. In PPP schemes, the public sector asks the private sector to fund, provide and take some of the risks inherent in the project, in return for the possibility of making a profit. The idea is that the public body purchases a service. In a hospital scheme, for example, the services being purchased will be the use of the hospital, equipment and the provision of ancillary services (such as cleaning and repair)—the doctors and nurses are still trained and employed by the government. This switches the role of the public sector from a provider of services to a guardian of services.

Currently, most of the educational institutions are run under trusts, and these are not allowed to come out with public issues. Also, the concept of profit does not come in a trust. So long, the surplus resources generated are not taken out of education, there should be full leeway to allow that to go into any kind of education and institutions. However, with these initiatives, there will be more transparency and more private players will come forward under the PPP model. The Eleventh Plan also includes a policy framework for PPP model in school education. If it can be implemented effectively, it will help in reducing the huge gap between demand and supply.

Recently in June 2009, there were two major private equity deals in the education space: Pearson UK invested around $12.5 million in TutorVista, which is into online tutoring. Also, Educomp and Pearson set up vocational training venture. The joint venture is a 50:50; where Pearson invested around $17.5 million. Besides, Helion Venture Partners and Navis Capital Partners invested in Global Talent Track Company and Edutech respectively in education industry. HNIs perhaps have been the earliest to catch on. HNIs have been increasing their stake continuously in these companies since September 2008. Several new initiatives are set to follow. Under the legislative initiative, the ministry is going to put in place a law, which can regulate foreign education providers. Several initiatives are being taken to attract talent beyond the political borders under 'Brain-Gain' policy.

"Such steps of the ministry will bring transformational change in the education industry. It will also help develop newer methods of learning. Many players see a huge opportunities in near future."

Expressing their views about PPP model in education in an interview with a correspondents of *The Economic Times*, Rajendran, CEO of NIIT appreciates government and private companies PPP efforts. "Let's take it into two pieces; first is, how to do the Public-Private Partnership (PPP) with the government and second is, who will be the players. I just want to cite one background information—1999 was the first time when we worked with the government for a PPP model for introducing IT in the government schools. Over ten years with 8 million children who have gone through this, we had seen some tremendous impact of this, one is in terms of subject, second is in terms of their ability to grasp even the other languages and third, of course, is their employability when they either dropout of the school or graduate and get on to the university. For us, that has been a terrific experience in creating a viable model of course in that case children were not paying fees, so government had to fund the whole project. Coming from there, we introduced IT in teaching other subjects. Today, if the government is putting together a plan for 2,500 schools in a PPP model, then what exactly the model will be; there will be some viability gap till which time the government will have to fund it because the fees from the students will get regulated somewhere. But government must ensure in general that these private companies in education space must deliver quality and should have right kind of faculty. "I think PPP model is going to take us at least a year or two of running to figure out how exactly the bottom line has to be managed," he said.

The Managing Director of Everonn Systems India said, the margins were much higher in the private schools but the government had also been equally rewarding. "I understand the government will provide the land and then private participation will come in infrastructure and the content. So, there could also be a system where they could pay by vouchers up to standard 6th and up to standard 12th by another vouchers," he added. Education companies are doing a tremendous job, for example, Everonn does this in Jharkhand, There are about 110,000 students studying in 216 schools. More than in 50% of the school; I actually had to shift this infrastructure by bullock cart. I think we are doing a great social work, we are also adding good value to our shareholders".

To ensure quality higher education in rural areas, Punjab Government has decided to open degree colleges in all rural development blocks in the state under the next two five-year plans.

Besides, a National Curriculum Framework for teacher education would be evolved in consultation with stakeholders and in accordance with NCF-2005. Sibal (09) also announced that the National Literacy Mission would be recast to focus on women. He said the Government would explore the possibility of setting up an independent accreditation body in the area of school education to ensure quality.

The ongoing *Sarva Shiksha Abhiyan* (universal education) program may have increased the number of students but we need to do qualitative improvement in education. Now the government wants to focus on to *Madhyamic Shiksha* going for the higher classes till eighth standard. These are opportunities and challenges that train lots of kids coming into middle school. This is the second big area for which we have to gear up like we did for Sarvasiksha Abhiyan. Further on, it is going to move ahead into higher education, so all areas need to be dealt with.

The *right to education* means to get a child literate is the responsibility of the government to elementary level, to middle level and to higher secondary level. And as the child grows and becomes more conscious of choices and reaches either the vocational level or higher education level, it is possible to assign an economic value to that education. So the economic equation can happen at higher education and therefore, the liberalization at higher education can be much more of involving non-government actors because the economic model can work. There is a rationale that educated person is better informed person also.

Government cannot look after people at the bottom for education all alone; we need to open elementary, higher and secondary education to private sector participants in a big way thus bridging the investment gap.

The area where you have the greatest drop-out rate is not at the primary level but as you reach class VII—the *Madhyamik stage;* the children start dropping out. There is not much dropping out between class X and class XII. Now how do you stop that? What's the reason for that drop-out? We have to first examine that before we move forward. In higher education, it is easier because you can liberalize the system and those at the top will have much greater choices and you will get that investment in but the real problem is at the bottom. We need structural reforms both at the school level as well as the higher education level.

Fundamentally, the supply side for education has been hugely constrained. So we need massive doses of reform to open up this sector. We need more new bodies for regulation and accreditation. The regulatory framework and regulatory institutions for higher education should focus on providing honest and transparent quality rating and information on financial costs. A National Council for Higher Education will be set up to reform regulatory institutions.

It indicates the stellar role that the National Knowledge Commission will command stellar role in the policy and framework formulation in the education sector. This will be particularly true of the higher education segment. "Government's strategy for higher education will be formulated around a three-fold objective of expansion, inclusion and excellence. The suggestions given by the National Knowledge Commission will guide the formulation and implementation of the strategy." Skill development will be another focus area. The challenge, according to the government, is "*to invest in education, employability and employment*". The focus would be to provide education that provides employable skills. Vocational training is a much-neglected area that has got little or no attention from the government and the private sector. Only 10% of educated young people in India are equipped with vocational skills.

Higher education and skill development are the focus areas, especially as the government would like to "realize the demographic dividend." The government, however, is not unmindful of the other end of the education spectrum. With an eye on the relatively low level of female literacy (54%), the government will recast the National Literacy Mission as National Mission on Female Literacy. It also indicates the understanding that female literacy has a multiplier effect, especially when it comes to social development.

This brings up the question of government schools versus private schools. Private schools are accountable, people know the sort of quality that they are going to get at the end of the day. Government schools provide compulsory free education in most of the cases. It is state run. But it imparts bad quality education ***It is such bad quality that even bottom of the pyramid who are getting aware of merits of educating their children are not willing to send children to government schools but they are helpless, they have no financial means to support schooling.***

The government teachers are either not adequately trained or they are unwilling teachers. They are even sub-contracting their jobs to poorly educated persons especially in rural schools. Over and above, there is the problem of teacher absenteeism and truancy. How such teachers can motivate students for education, even *when students may be lacking motivation on their own or from their parents who may not be educated; but only cherishing a dream of an educated child who would earn more if educated.* It is also becoming a class issue because only a certain class of people can go to the private schools and a certain class of people is left with no choice but to go to the government schools.

How to improve the quality of these government schools? We need to improve the quality of government schools and we need public-private partnership (PPP) to be able to do that—to get those teachers, train them properly and make sure that students are educated properly. Private schools are few and far between and they are quality schools and with the Right to Education Bill, 25% of the intake in private schools is also going to be from the local area of the less privileged. So that also will give an element of inclusiveness in private education institutions. We do hope that PPP in school education can improve the government run schools.

One area where in government schools the PPP model has worked, is in IT education in rural India. It started with Tamil Nadu and now most states are doing it and that model is working very well. The model works as: the IT education part is contracted out in a competitive way to the companies and they have responsibilities to set up the schools, the room, to put the computers, to get a generator and give a certain outcome. So, that is the little center of excellence where the classes start on time, students and teachers are motivated to learn and achieve; it is becoming a point of transformation. Actually, in the last ten years, we had evidence that PPP model is working effectively. But it is a vocational training area, it is an unregulated area. It is not part of the mainstream education. But we can apply this model to mainstream education.

Thus, there can be a multiplicity of educational models: government run schools, government-aided schools, private schools run by trusts, foundations, and corporates; schools under PPP model. There are schools run by the charitable institutions and they have some other constraints; and also religion based schools, and minority based schools. All these have some limitations.

The major point is that these have to be regulated and monitored by higher well set-up agencies. As far as inclusion is concerned, under the right to education, everyone has right for free education up to elementary so far and may be later to middle level. From the perspective of the student or the parent, if the choice is available for a government school, then we must certainly improve government schools for better quality delivery of education and regulate the functioning of others. Moreover, government should allow foreign money and private equities willing to come in the education ecosystem.

Huge effort is needed for capacity building and quality improvement. It doesn't matter who is spending on education, whether it's the private sector or the government or the charitable sector, we must be able to demonstrate that it is delivering quality value, value in the minds of student. *We must monitor periodically, consistently that there is effective expenditure and implementation and quality of education is imparted to all strata without any social bias.* A targeted and outcome oriented review and reform of elementary education should be undertaken in this context.

Rural Model of Education

"If every rural child who goes to school and every one of them who wants to study has accessibility to higher education; it will truly represent the way forward for rural India. If we can get a roadmap for that way forward, which is constructive and job-oriented, and if we break out the mindset of the past; we can do a lot with driving ahead the rural economy."

Initiatives for Village School Education

Children living in rural areas continue to be deprived of quality education, because of quality of poor education in government run schools as highlighted above. Moreover, part of the reason is large number of teachers refuse to teach in rural areas. Those that refuse to teach in rural areas cite distance and lack of interest by students as problems. Many of the teachers also lack the enthusiasm to teach because of their meager salary. Those who teach are usually under-qualified. There is more emphasis now on the training of rural teachers, whose educational backgrounds are generally not as sound as their urban counterparts. In recent years, the number of qualified teachers has increased because of increased efforts by the government and private groups to improve the general education and professional training of teachers. Another obstacle faced by the rural schools to get more teachers is because of state guidelines that approve of high student-to teacher ratios.

As the lack of teachers creates many obstacles for children in rural schools, another setback is the lack of resources which becomes detrimental to the learning process. Lack of books and other reading materials seem to be a widespread problem. The use of high-tech devices such as computers is very rare.

There are inadequate facilities in the classes. Some schools are located in warehouses while others in small houses or even in shed which drip water in rains. Even many of the rural schools operate without electricity, drinking water and toilets.

While many rural schools search for the proper resources, the distribution of government funds is major hindrance to the educational system. According to a recent study done by the World Bank, thirty per cent of the total educational funding goes toward higher educational institutions. This is an important issue because the number of students enrolled in these types of institutions represents such a small per cent of India's students. *In earlier years, the primary education of rural area children was a low priority in budget outlays but no longer, government is giving high priority to it in the budget 2009 and plan outlays.*

When villagers exercise their 'right to accountability' and community participation for village school, they get better results. Here is a recent example (2009). Villagers of Parsai, 60 kms north-west of Chindwara, were inspecting how their primary school is being run. They observed the teacher truancy problem as one factor besides poor quality of learning. The villagers withheld the salary of teachers for two months for not coming to school on time and being unsatisfied with the learning progress of students. After that, the teachers reported on time and would frequently brief villagers on performance of 90 odd students.

Social Political Contexts: Social context is the socio-eco-cultural environment and demographic factors that predominate for village education. Socio factors such as community, family and kinship, caste and class; economic factors of cost of schooling, poverty, child labor; and socio-cultural factor—marriage of girl child, gender case disparities play significant role in village education delivery. Demographic factors such as health status of child, and family size are equally important. These can hinder or promote universal elementary education in villages, and quality of education as well as level of learning. *Social context can significantly govern access, retention and achievement of school going children.*

Political context is equally significant in India for delivery of rural education.

It is desirable to promote village community participation and also involve those who are affected by education and school learning in villages such as parents, teachers, members of Village Education Committee, NGOs and activists associated with the village programs. They can also give their inputs on which learning products and subjects would interest children, and what teaching techniques they would like and would benefit most and are effective techniques as assessed by the teacher.

We are still at a stage where primary school in every village may exist, but a middle school or high school in every village is a far-off dream. The major concern is of quality of education—which is missing in most of the schools, rather than numbers. We have a unique challenge here. We need more schools to cover larger number of children in the country and at the same time, the quality of education in terms of school infrastructure, class room process as well as teacher support system. Since the launch of the Sarva Shiksha Abhiyan program, there has been an improvement in the access to the school for the children in the rural areas. Today, close to 90% of the children have access to an elementary school within a distance of 3 Kms from their homes. However, in the process the quality of education has taken a beating.

One of the main reasons for the higher school drop-out rate as well as low learning in the elementary schools is the quality of class-room process, curriculum design and teacher support system in addition to other socio-economic factors. The good news is, there is an increased awareness on these issues and there is a good focus from all concerned including NGO's, Educational Foundations, Ministry of Education in the Center and in the State government to address these issues. It is a slow but a definite process towards improving the quality of education in the elementary schools.

A plethora of government initiatives, private initiatives and community initiatives to provide access to primary education in village schools may be underway, but issues of equity, quality and access remain areas of concern.

Government Initiatives for Village School Education

So far, it has been totally government efforts not even people's own efforts to run a school and provide basic facilities, to volunteer teaching efforts by educated girls and boys in the village itself. Government should make it compulsory for teachers' training program degrees to teach in village school for a specific period. This would expose the village school teacher and children to new teaching techniques. Government has been putting more emphasis and sanctioning higher spending on village education, monitoring on transparency, accountability and quality of education delivered. They are emphasizing on girl education, vocational skill training and paving way from primary to middle level education in villages. It is making concerted efforts to control social and political contexts for education in villages.

Gender gap persists in rural primary education; there are more girl drop-outs also. Empowering the girl child through education is important. Talking about the philosophy and success of Kasturba Gandhi Balika Vidyalaya (KGBVs)—a scheme for girls from rural and disadvantaged groups from educationally backward blocks (EBBs)—"The scheme is aimed at realizing the constitutional commitment of providing free and compulsory education to all children in the age group of 6-14 years. The program also aims to bridge gender and social gaps in education, which is an important objective of SSA." Currently, the scheme is operational in over 3,000 EBBs in 24 states, where rural female literacy is below the national average and the gender gap in literacy is more than the national average. At present, there are 2,578 KGBVs, of which 2,383 are operational and the total number of girls enrolled is 1,76,713.

Similarly, the Mahila Samakhya Programme (MSP), working in the field of women empowerment through education, aims to promote 'skill-development' and 'entrepreneurial skills' to make women self-reliant "We are not into imparting skills like sewing or tailoring. Instead, we impart skills like plumbing, repairing and so on to break gender stereotypes and empower girls. So, when flooring has to be done in classrooms or taps are not working, our students are in a position to handle the situation."

The Annual Status Education Report on rural India 2009 released by NGO Pratham about the success of the government's flagship Sarva Shiksha Abhiyan program. The report on the state of learning in rural areas shows that enrolment rates are rapidly rising, but the quality of learning has actually got worse. There is a steady increase in school enrolment and attendance, but not much (if any) improvement in the level of education attained. Drop-out levels remain high, and the majority of students in Class V are unable to do the work that they should have mastered three classes earlier. These are decidedly not very encouraging results, when there has been massive recruitment of teachers, and more money being spent under a variety of schemes, including for building the physical infrastructure for schools.

The NGO's survey in 2007 had put the proportion of out-of-school children in the 6-14 years age bracket at 4.2%. In 2006, the figure was 6.6%. Though the changed age bracket in the 2008 survey makes comparisons with past years difficult, the figures do indicate a continuation of the downward trend.

Sarv Shiksha Abhiyan (SSA) has a very varied picture in different States. In certain States, it has made very good progress. Especially in States where the Panchayati Raj system is in good health and the Village Education Committees are working properly, SSA has come close to attaining its major goal of bringing every child to school. In States where village-level bodies are sluggish, the picture is poor. However, the question of quality applies uniformly to the entire country. SSA was envisaged as a movement, and it has indeed generated an enormous amount of social and professional energy by awakening.

Private Initiatives for Rural School Education

Private initiatives by domestic and international organizations are making efforts to run schools in villages. We pose two salient questions in this context: Can we have PPP model to run village schools like in urban areas? Looking at the rising enrolment in private schools in rural India, Planning Commission Deputy Chairperson Montek Singh Ahluwalia has pushed for the PPP model in elementary schools. But this has found few takers in rural areas. (Jan 09). Can we get foreign investments for village schools? So far, PPP model has not evoked much interest though it is assumed that would streamline and make village education more efficient. Government is recently opening foreign investment in education; there has been interest in urban and higher education so far. But there have been few private initiatives for village school education both by domestic and international NGOs and individuals. Few of such efforts are cited.

International NGOs: John Wood of Microsoft foundation, is opening schools and libraries in the villages through his 'Room for reading initiative'. Harvard University Boston students visit Indian village school at regular periods. They demonstrate to the village teachers' new techniques of teaching and new methods of learning to students. Then there are village schools set up by Expats, mostly in the villages or surrounding ones where they were born or have family roots. They put fair amount of money to set up village schools either for girls, for vocational training and even for imparting education and training in Information technology. Even some of the philanthropic trusts also run village schools and vocational training centers for youth, women, girls, etc. Then there are specific organizations interested in specific aspects of schooling in villages, such as schools just to teach basic hygiene to children, or Anganbari program or other school supporting projects of UNICEF in many villages. Some organizations run special training program for rural school teachers in villages. These specific aspects of schooling efforts become part of the village school system. Such efforts are commendable and efficient but very few village schools are beneficiary of these efforts. These can be turned into PPP model by initiatives from both government and of these organizations.

Domestic NGOs: Pratham is the largest domestic NGO working to provide quality education to the underprivileged children of India in slums and rural areas. They reach out to millions of such children through a range of interventions. Pratham team comprises of educationists, development professionals, media persons, corporates, workers, activists, PhDs, MBAs, CAs, civil servants, bankers, corporate professionals, consultants, who all bring their experiences and perspectives to the organization and are unified by the common vision of improving the future of these children.

Azim Premji Foundation is focused on Rural Government Schools in the states. They work along with the State Governments in executing some of their priorities. Karnataka has over 45,000 Elementary Schools and 8,000 Education functionaries. However, the learning levels in these schools are very low. The key objective of the Azim Premji Foundation is to significantly contribute to the universalisation of Elementary Education in India that facilitates a just, equitable and humane society. After 7 years of operations driving this goal, the foundation has now identified *teacher, education functionaries as well as examination reforms* as the three pillars for the major programs to pursue.

Career Launcher chain of schools and SKS Microfinance has jointly launched SKS-CL Academy to set up English medium schools in rural Andhra Pradesh in 2008-09. The Academy would set up 10 schools in Nalgonda, Khammam, Rangareddy and Medak districts in the State in the pilot phase to provide primary education till third standard using the National Open School syllabus with special emphasis on technology.

Likewise, the 'Pehchaan' project is a model that attempts to ensure that out-of-school girls (9-14 years) are provided with educational opportunities and brought on par with the other children of their age in schools. The project is collaboration between UNICEF, NGOs Digantar and Culp and the community.

Community Initiatives

Community participation is being recognized as one of the effective strategies to improve access and quality in education, "A rural school of Surat owns an LCD projector through community funding and children of 9-10 years of age can use it effectively for teaching-learning processes." Similarly, "There is a government school in Gujarat with 70 herbal plants that involves students in activity-based learning like planting seeds, encouraging concept learning like the germination process, and so on. It turned out to be such a successful venture that four private schools in the vicinity had to close down, with students from the private schools moving to the government school." It is the devotion of individuals, innovative practices employed, the joint efforts of the school and community that works wonders.

Participatory videos can best be used to empower underprivileged students from rural areas. Breaking away from producing educational videos for children, a participant believes that innovation and creativity of children should instead be tapped to enable maximum learning. Thus, she conducted a study on class VIII and IX students where students were imparted lessons in script writing, video-shooting and editing, using various formats. Today, her students are creative individuals producing video clips on concepts like force, pressure, covalent bonds, and so on.

Even Community Initiatives in monitoring the management of school, quality of education being imparted, and teacher truancy and teaching quality can improve village schools. Community feedback and checks are bound to create accountability from the concerned authorities.

There is another unique kind of community participation through 'People's participation in getting children out of work and into School' program. This is funded by UNDP—Supported by NORAD, CREDA. Problem in rural areas is that children are not being allowed to receive education as they have to work to support their parents' income. Child laborers are helped by Network of grassroots NGOs and CBOs created for advocacy on sustainable approaches of eliminating child labor through education and social mobilization.

Rural Tele-centers Educational Initiatives: There are many rural ICT to supplement the rural school education. Tamil Nadu and Pondicherry have many rural ICTs programs. Among these, the n-Logue's Rural Information Kiosks and M.S. Swaminathan Research Foundation's Village Knowledge Centers (VKCs) are pioneers in disseminating the educational related information and syllabus-based educational program to the rural students. They also provide basic computer training. It is to be noted that the rural students not only need educational development but also require economic development to balance their economic condition and obtain higher level in education. So, they need some kind of vocational skills to earn money and to continue their studies. This will reduce the dropout numbers from rural schools. It will thus be very beneficial if such trainings are given through the rural information centers.

With regard to school education as such, the rural information centers are creating some impact in the educational performance of rural students like—creating confidence in subjects, higher marks in exams and increased pass percentage. But their impact has not been as phenomenal as to address the over-all literacy problem.

Some of the challenges and limitations faced by the rural tele-centers educational initiatives are: Most of the time, male adults or male students occupy the computers; therefore, access to girl students is minimal. There is a general notion among rural people about the Internet-based computer centers that they are used for some illegal activities like watching pornographic movies. Therefore, the parents do not allow girls to go there. The rural community has deeply embedded caste prejudices. If the kiosk is located in Dalit (Lower caste) hamlet, the other caste students are disinclined to go and use the facilities and vice-versa. To teach the educational related program through the computer, the operator must have some basic subject knowledge. But many of the operators have minimum educational qualification and operational knowledge;

so they are unable to explain the course materials effectively and create interest in them, because they are not trained in such a way.

The Internet-based educational program is an integrated approach. It should have better cooperation with the local school teachers. But the school teachers do not encourage the students to attend the rural ICT center's educational program. The infrastructural facilities like space of the center, the Internet connectivity and number of computers are not sufficient to engage many students at the same time. The operational time of the tele-centers (normally from 10 am to 5.00 pm) is not suitable for the students.

I-Slate initiative between Rice university computer scientists and Indian educators. Computer scientist Palem says schools in rural India will benefit from the low-energy computer chips invented by him creating a slow powered electronic slate, the electronic version of black slates used by children. In I-slate the significant goal is energy and environmental sustainability. It works on PCMOS (probabilistic CMOs) principle and work on 1 solar cell. I-slate team of developers is working with International Institute of Information Technology Hyderabad (IIIT) to develop a visually based mathematical curriculum that allows children to learn by doing regardless of their grade level or whether teacher is there or not. The program is called 'Rural IIIT', starting in Hyderabad villages with 10th grade students. "Learning-by-doing" philosophy behind it allows students to learn complicated concepts by trying an developing models by repeated trials rather than having a teacher focus the instruction through fixed rules and exercises.

The power of ICTs can help in a considerable way to address the challenge of rural education.

Suggestions: Improve infrastructure facilities in the rural schools to facilitate the maximum utilization of the ICTs facilities. Motivate school teachers and tele-centers operators to deliver the computer-based education effectively to the rural students. Frequent visits by educational authorities and Internet service providers to the rural schools to evaluate the computer education based performance of the students and teachers. Organize committees with parents, schools teachers and tele-centers operators in the villages and conduct frequent meetings to improve the educational performance of the students as well as the development of tele-centers. Motivate all community students to use the computer and Internet facilities in the tele-centers. Set up rural tele-centers in places that can be easily accessed by members of all communities. Provide value added information in the field of education and ensure it will provide employment opportunities to rural aspirants. Make the students and their parents understand the realities of the computer-based education and utility of Internet to improve educational performance. Provide special training to rural schools teachers and operators of rural tele-centers on new educational developments, availability of new courses and information about institutions. Government and Non-Governmental organizations should provide incentives to the students as well the tele-center operators.

Corporate Social Responsibility Initiatives

CISCO National Institute of Open Schooling (NIOS) is on PPP model, between CISCO and NIOS that offers CISCO Networking Academy Program in 10 accredited vocational institutes to begin with across the country, including in north-east India. Each of these institutes, called a CISCO Local Academy, provides PC hardware and networking information technology (IT) essentials to students. CISCO NetAcad focuses on teaching students how to design, build and maintain computer networks and prepares students for the 21st-century workplace while serving as a valuable model for online learning. This program is unique in many ways including its vocational focus, job-oriented curriculum, and inclusive nature (this course is offered to everyone including school drop-outs, mid-career professionals, etc.). CISCO believes that working in conjunction with the Indian government gives this partnership great reach and potential. NIOS is part of the Ministry of HRD and plans to scale this program to over 100 accredited vocational institutes spread across the country. In addition to imparting IT knowledge and networking skills, NetAcad also aims to bridge the 'digital divide' as it takes technical education to rural India including technologically backward states like Kashmir, Orissa and Tripura.

The Rajasthan Education Initiative in India's largest state that seeks to improve social and economic conditions by developing IT skills in what is a predominantly agrarian region. Targeted at girls, rural children, urban under-privileged children, and children with special needs, the initiative aims to accelerate IT education in 32 government District Computer Education Centers (DCEC) across Rajasthan.

The Dilemmas of Rural Education

Quality of rural school education is poor and affordability of time for children to attend school is not conducive. Closing gender gaps in rural education is essential. Girls' education focuses on women as active agents of transformation of education system that discriminate against gender. The moot question is, are girls in rural areas getting into schools? The parents are motivated to send them not only through success stories of being economically independent. But in practice, providing security for the girls such as toilets in the school especially in mixed schools was necessary to let them send girls to schools. Grown-up girls were being withdrawn from schools for the fear of not having privacy in this respect. Setting schools in the vicinity of the village also motivate parents to send grown-up girls to school.

There is dilemma for rural parents. The quality of rural education imparted is poor, because there is no accountability by the teachers and parents cannot afford to send them to urban schools outside the village especially girls and even as such the quality of education is equally poor in the urban government run schools though affordable.

Of course, a school within reach is not the end—it is only the beginning. The significant questions are: Does the socio-economic situation makes it possible for that child to actually go to school? What happens in school is that attractive and relevant enough to keep that child in school for at least eight years? In these eight years, does the child gain anything of significance and value in her/his life? Does schooling prepare students for certain level of employability? While there is an increasingly apparent focus on these issues, both in government and in civil society, the answers to these questions are at present an alarming but definite NO.

To really provide equity in basic education, what is needed is a combination of the best of both, relevant and appealing educational structure for the rural child; on the solid framework of child-friendly core curriculum. The government has been making great efforts in the past few years to improve this situation by trying to develop a core curriculum, or minimum levels of learning, which will ensure a basic equity in learning, and which can then be adapted locally and made more meaningful. Government-initiated teacher training programs also emphasize 'child-centered, activity-based' learning. New and better textbooks have been developed by most states. However, these efforts have by and large been only theoretical. The vast majority of schools continue to burden the child with vast amounts of useless information, resulting in a crisis in confidence among rural and urban learners from poor families.

The issue to be addressed is that the *system, though well aware of the problems and the solutions, remains unaccountable*. Teachers and the school are simply not held responsible for what the average rural child actually learns. Of great importance in this situation is the increased awareness among parents, especially among poor parents about schooling and learning, and they are being shortchanged. A climate is slowly developing in which parents feel that they can demand accountability from the system that promises to educate their children, and can have a say in what and how their children are taught. *This is the most hopeful sign of change, and is being greatly helped along by community-based organizations and NGOs.*

The ongoing process of decentralization, which puts increasingly more power in the hands of local bodies, is a step that can only help this process. For example, the Village Education Committee is now a statutory body, consisting of members of the village *Panchayat* (the elected local government in a village), the village primary school, and local women's group. Parent-Teacher associations at the village level are also mandatory. Of course, community involvement can also serve to perpetuate existing casteist and patriarchal attitudes. It is not enough to put control of education in the hands of existing local hierarchies; it must be truly in the hands of the people.

The National Council of Educational Research and Training (NCERT) has set up a *Rural Education Cell* in 2009 to figure out the problems that plague rural schools and to strengthen their overall performance. It will make a deep analysis of the all-India education survey data to assess the condition of rural schools. "We will segregate the rural data gender-wise and age-wise to look deeply at patterns that emerge. We will try to get to the heart of the problem of rural education in terms of working conditions, infrastructure, teachers, poor performance and high drop-out rate of students, The cell will also conduct case studies in different States and organize conferences for rural teachers to help evolve a policy for rural schools. The rural-urban divide in the field of education in our country is something which we would very much like to study and bridge." In view of such concerns, the recently constituted Rural Education Cell, department of educational surveys and data processing, NCERT, organized a national seminar on 'school education in rural India' at its Delhi headquarters (2009). The seminar provided a platform to policy analysts, administrators, researchers and practitioners to analyze the current scenario in rural education, identify problems and come up with recommendations to improve the situation. The deliberations of the seminar highlighted significant trends in rural education model.

***A smarter education strategy*:** Research studies highlight the Initiatives that bring positive progress for rural schools and taught. It suggests that good working conditions in school, a different work ethic and social ethic is needed—which support 'collective responsibility' not 'narrow accountability' for improving schools. Strong schools do not compete against weak ones rather they help them instead. This will make smallest achievement gap between students based on their social background. Education leaders built ties with local community groups, bring the community inside the schools as classroom aides, translators and social service providers. School set their own improvement targets, if it fails, all (community, education leaders) rally around to help. This reverses high truancy rates. There are schools they would design their own local innovations and solutions to educational problems.

Rural Employment

In any geography, at any time, this farm-to-non-farm journey has never been easy, particularly so in India. The contrast between rural and urban life is dramatic. Government has been working on basic job security to high level job generation in rural relevant areas which are likely to boost the economy. According to the 61st round of the NSSO (National Sample Survey Organization) survey, rural unemployment rose by 3.69% per annum. During the first three years of the Tenth Plan, the employment elasticity of GDP growth was 0.16%. Thus, the addition to the workforce was 1.2% per annum while the rate of growth of the workforce was around 2.5%. Thus, unemployment added every year is between 1% and 1.5%. This means the fruits of reform have not reached the grass roots level of society.

The *Prime Minister's Employment Generation Program (PMEGP)* has been launched by merging the erstwhile Rural Employment Generation Program and Prime Minister's Rozgar Yojana. Its objectives are to generate employment opportunities in rural and urban areas by setting up new self-employment ventures, projects, and micro enterprises, bring together dispersed traditional artisans and unemployed youth and give them self-employment opportunities, provide continuous and sustainable employment to them to prevent rural-urban migration and increase their wage earning capacity.

Rural employment is generated through development of rural enterprises, when rural marketers create retail rural hubs, when telecom facilities are set up in the villages such as computer hubs, cyber café, telephone operating kiosks—both for landline and cell; both for people to use as well to use them for other uses such as money transfers etc. Managing microfinance in the villages also create jobs. Many corporates are now focusing on starting BPOs closer to villages because of low cost. This could create ancillaries jobs for the villagers.

Not only people are in jobs of tending to farms and food crops but jobs related to the technology of food production from tractor running to tending irrigation canals, technology for food distribution and supply chain and storage facilities, etc.—all these need skill development.

Other village jobs can be created in food processing, cold storage of food, Handloom, Handicrafts, Power Loom, Sericulture and Wool, micro and small enterprises (MSE) sector, consisting of the traditionally defined small-scale industries and small-scale service and business entities, such as khadi, coir and bamboo industries. Employment generation in the areas for production, distribution and marketing, technology upgradation and exports can be created. It would need supportive credit policies and practices, marketing support, training needs of entrepreneurs. Self employment opportunities can be expanded through these enterprises. We have discussed details of Employment generation in these areas in Chapter 3—Rural Industries and Chapter 6—Rural Markets.

A greater number of jobs are also created when industries are set up closer to villages such as Tata's Nano car in Gujarat, steel plants of Arcelor Mittal and Porsche in Orissa, Reliance group of industries and Birla group companies in villages closer to Mumbai and Kolkata. Almost all the industries in India set up their industrial hubs closer to the villages where more land is available. The industries develop the areas around such as connecting roads, transportation, schools, dispensaries and mini hospitals, parks, etc. as social responsibility to the community of those surrounding villages. They also give vocational training to the people for jobs in those industries.

Employability generation is important by imparting vocational skills, technical skills and training in different sectors. It has to be two tier: skill and capability enhancing training for higher age groups and even on the job; and in-built in the education pattern and structure of village school core curriculum. There should be no gender differentiations.

On one hand, the employability generation efforts have to be by government and industries and business enterprises; and on the other hand, creating awareness of opportunities and developing capabilities of people is NGOs' task; though government, industries and business enterprises also contribute for these efforts. Moreover, people have to be willing and achievement motivated for jobs thus being created.

Skill development program for ruralites: As an integral part of the coordinated action plan for skill development, the Government created the National Skill Development Corporation in July 2008 with an initial corpus of Rs. One thousand crore to stimulate and coordinate private sector participation in skill development. A rural focus of skill development for ruralites can be incorporated. Any skills development initiative of the government would play an active role in creating employability and employment.

Rural Employment Programs

The major employment program is National Rural Employment Guarantee scheme (NREG), and Self-Help groups scheme.

NREG was launched in February 2006 that covers 596 rural districts, which has benefited almost 36 million households so far, as it guarantees one member of each family employment for at least 100 days a year. It has now been extended to all the districts of the country. During the year 2008-09, employment of 138.76 crore person days, covering 3.51 crore households, has already been generated. The implementation of this program has resulted in increased wage employment, enhanced wage earnings, and improved equity with significant benefits flowing to SC/ST and women. This has also led to increased demand for and consumption of wage goods. Government has now proposed an allocation of Rs. 30,100 crore for this Scheme for the year 2009-10.

Rahul Gandhi said the NREG gave the poor support in the labor market by not letting them fall below a certain level. No matter who you are, you can get 100 days of work at a particular salary, he said. "This has changed completely the dynamics in poor States like Uttar Pradesh, in areas where it has been used effectively, which frankly are limited." In States like Andhra Pradesh, it has "revolutionized the system", he said.

Touching on the gulf between rich and poor India and the Congress approach towards bridging it, he said, "The central thrust of what the Congress does and is going to do for the next couple of years is try and recreate that one India but ensure that it is an India of opportunity for all. Underscoring the redistributive nature of welfare policies adopted by the UPA government, the idea is that you take the India of opportunity, you grow that India. Then you take some of the benefits and put them into the villages and thus engage and integrate that India into the first India. NREG is one such weapon we are using in the effort to bridge the gap between the poor and the rich Indians. Massive expansion of the education system is another weapon. Massive expansion of the health system is the third. Universal ID is the fourth weapon" (Oct. 2009).

Despite the risk of corruption by the officials administering it, an employment guarantee could give the poor something to fall back on. This might encourage farmers to take productive risks, such as experimenting with high-yielding seed varieties. It might spare them from distress sales of draught animals, keep them from pulling their children out of school and stop them from migrating to city slums. NREG is a great program but 85% of funds spent for the public do not reach the targeted people—so the government should audit that process and implementation results of NREG. This governance reform is necessary.

At the same time, some innovative measures have been initiated in NREG to bring in more transparency in disbursements of funds and prevent leakages. However, it is necessary that for every program, an Internet accessible public accountability information system (PAIS) should be available. This system would provide information about the funds allocated and the expenditure made along with the name of the beneficiaries. This system should be accompanied by an integrated smart card system which empowers the citizen to demand approved and budgeted entitlements as right. Government is in the process of working out Unique Identity card (UID).

States such as Rajasthan and Uttar Pradesh have sharply raised the pay for workers under the flagship rural job guarantee scheme in the last one year (2008-09), making the Union government fear that such populist moves may disrupt the rural economy. The Centre is thinking of limiting the annual pay raise for workers so that there is no sudden surge in income under the largest job guarantee scheme in the world that could keep commodity prices high in rural areas and deprive workforce for projects outside the scheme. Officials in the ministry of rural development and the ministry of finance say that a sudden rise in wages may keep rural inflation high. An official executing the NREG scheme said that states such as Rajasthan raised the minimum wage from Rs. 70 to Rs. 100 in the last one year while some others doubled it during the period.

Ahluwalia (May 09) said the central government may soon change the guidelines of its flagship social welfare programs, including the National Rural Employment Guarantee Act (NREGA), to better suit the needs of individual states. I understand states have genuine problems. But they need to come out with specific proposals. Present guidelines under the NREGA prohibit the construction of permanent assets like hospitals and check-dams. In spite of funds being available, such restrictions constrain states from spending the money. The government would further hike spending on NREG scheme in November 2009. The government is expected to further expand the scope of NREGA.

Vice-Chairman of Planning Board, Madhya Pradesh, added that the states have demanded an increase in the 100 days job guarantee to at least 150 days every year to each rural household that needs work. Commenting on the plan document, "The plan document has failed to resolve the issue of increasing rural unemployment."

Rural development (RD) ministry organized a national workshop on NREG in Aug. 2009 to commemorate Rajiv Gandhi's birth anniversary and had Rahul as chief guest. The RD minister announced a clutch of programs under NREGA, important being construction of offices for all 2.52 lakh panchayats—Bharat Nirman Rajiv Gandhi Sewa Kendra.

Joshi, another participant was critical about NREG functioning. He said, "Job cards are not reaching beneficiaries, sarpanches are supposed to make plans but that is not happening and funds for material components are not being used properly." He, however, sought to assure Rahul that use of IT and a proper mechanism would make NREG the new mode of governance.

Nilekani announced collaboration with NREGA for UID project. He said UID was about providing an identity to the poor. UIDs will be based on biometrics and would "remove the ghost of duplication in the system" and ensure that valid job card holders were given work and wages.

Aiming to root out corruption in implementation of the NREG in Bihar, the state government has decided to cover one million beneficiaries under the e-shakti scheme by March 31, 2010. "In the very first year, the project, with the help of service provider Smaartech Technologies Limited, will cover beneficiaries from Patna district. This will entail issuing 10 lakh e-shakti cards in over 1300 villages spread over 23 blocks in the district," Smaartech Director (Bihar) B.K. Mishra told the news agency. He said subsequently over the next four years, the project would be set up in the remaining 37 districts to cover 24 million NREG beneficiaries in approximately 39,000 villages spread over 534 blocks. In total, about three crore e-shakti cards would be distributed under the state pilot project in Patna which was in the process of being implemented early.

There had been allegations that the NREG is beset with corruption and there is no proper method of work measurement, taking attendance and disbursing wages. The ICT applications are being introduced to bring effective coordination in execution, better targeting of beneficiaries, establishing transparency and accountability, e-based grievance redress mechanism and establishing state of art financial management systems. This is likely to provide technological solution for NREG schemes.

The e-shakti cards would also facilitate registration process of individuals which includes recording of personal information as well as biometric information (photograph and all 10 fingerprints). A separate bank account is being opened for each adult member of the household (Oct. 2009).

Mishra said, "Bihar thus became the first state in the country to start a call center in Oct 2009 under e-shakti project dedicated exclusively to redress NREG schemes corruption charges." The project, when fully functional, would empower the rural economy of the state.

"Recession is an opportunity for India to rethink the structure for future and the future for India is in green jobs. We are in consultation with ministries of Environment and Forest, Medium and Small Industries, Labor and Employment, Agriculture and others to arrive at certain common policy platforms on this," Campbell said.

Self- Help Groups Scheme

The major areas in which SHGs have been formed are agriculture, pisciculture, handloom, poultry, and dairy. Over 25 per cent of the SHG members earn in the range of Rs. 2000 to Rs. 3000 per month; while 18 per cent earn an average of Rs. 5000 per month and another 18 per cent earn less than Rs. 2000 per month.

Assam's rural economy is undergoing a silent revolution with more than 85,000 Self-Help Groups (SHG) playing the role of a vital catalyst. Chief Minister Tarun Gogoi said that already 85,000 SHGs have been set up throughout the state generating considerable level of self-employment but there was, however, scope for more such SHGs. "The spark of a silent revolution has already been ignited by mobilizing a sizeable section of the rural populace and motivating them to march on the road to economic emancipation through capacity-building measures and setting up of SHGs", he said. "The primary aim of setting up SHGs was to address the problem of rural unemployment which had led to disillusionment among the youth who took the path of militancy but now even educated unemployed rural youth and women are equipping themselves to take up income generating activities by organizing themselves into SHGs," Gogoi said (2009).

Priyadarshini Project is a Rural Women's Empowerment and Livelihood Program of the Ministry of Women and Child Development and funded by International Fund for Agriculture Development, (IFAD) in the Mid-Gangetic Plains. The program will be implemented as a pilot project in the district of Madhubani and Sitamarhi in Bihar and Shravasti, Bahraich, Rai Bareli and Sultanpur in Uttar Pradesh. Gender Budgeting Cells (GBCs) have been put up in ministries and departments.

It would be useful to set up a sophisticated, IT-based, employment information system for unskilled, semi-skilled and skilled labor; that can reflect demand and supply across the rural-urban divide, across education-income categories and across different states. The PPP model can be used to ensure that both public and private good elements are accounted for.

Most of the workforce in the unorganized sector is left totally uncovered by any safety net in case of loss of jobs or livelihood. Details of Social Welfare schemes for the ruralites are given in Appendix 3.

Rural Health Care Efforts and Policies

Government has accorded highest priority to rural development. A number of programs have been designed to help improve the living conditions of rural population. India spends a mere Rs. 37 per head every month to provide healthcare facilities for its one billion plus citizens, a reply tabled in the Lok Sabha has revealed. "The per capita expenditure for the years 2006-07 to 2008-09 is in the range of Rs. 300 to Rs. 450," Commission of Microeconomics and Health set up by the World Health Organization (WHO) had estimated that the minimum expenditure for essential health interventions for one person should be at least $34 (Rs. 1,600) per year. Though India's health budget for fiscal 2009-10 has increased from Rs. 19,534 crore to Rs. 22,641 crore, the allocation constitutes a little over one per cent of the GDP. Public health experts believe that government must provide around three per cent of the GDP for health related expenditure.

A demand for more outlay on rural health and health in general is necessary. The industry wants the government to increase its spending on healthcare from 0.9 per cent of GDP to at least 2%, along with the private sector's contribution of 5%. It also wants a higher outlay towards health insurance schemes to achieve universal health insurance coverage.

The health scenario of India has changed significantly in the past few years. While the communicable diseases continue to be the leading cause of morbidity and mortality, the changing lifestyles, urbanization, industrialization and shift in demographic pattern towards aging population as a result of increased life expectancy have contributed to the emergence of non-communicable diseases like cardiovascular, cancer and diabetes assuming larger proportion in terms of morbidity and mortality. To tackle the menace of these diseases, various disease control programs are being vigorously implemented.

The major initiatives taken by the Department of Health are implementation of National Health Programs throughout the country to control communicable and Non-communicable diseases like Malaria, T.B., Leprosy, Blindness, AIDS, Cancer, etc. Schemes are also under implementation for strengthening surveillance and epidemic response system to prevent outbreak of infectious diseases.

Primary Health Care System in Rural Areas

A Perspective: The focus on rural healthcare in India started in 50s, from First Five-Year Plan (1951-56) with the priorities of providing safe drinking water and sanitation and control of malaria, health services for mothers and children; training and health education; family planning and population control. The broad objective was to bring about progressive improvement in the health of the villagers by ensuring a certain minimum level of physical well-being and to create conditions favorable for greater efficiency. There was a shift in focus from promotive, and preventive to curative health services and family planning.

Health Survey and Planning Committee (Mudaliar Committee 1962) focused on the development of the health services infrastructure and the healthcare at the primary level. It suggested that infrastructure needed radical transformation and investment of funds for growth. Another major shift came in the Third Plan (1961-66) when family planning received priority for the first time. Increase in the population became a major worry and was seen as impediment to development.

During the Fourth Plan (1969-74), efforts were made to provide an effective base for health services in rural areas by strengthening the PHCs. The vertical campaigns against communicable diseases were further intensified. During the Fifth Plan (1974-79), policy-makers suddenly realized that health had to be addressed alongside other development programs. The Minimum Needs Program (MNP) promised to address all this but became an instrument through which only health infrastructure in the rural areas was to be expanded and further strengthened. It called for integration of peripheral staff of vertical programs but the population control program got further impetus during the Emergency (1975-77) and most of the basic health workers got diverted for the family planning program.

The plan documents henceforth emphasized on restructuring and developing the health infrastructure, especially at the primary level. The Seventh Plan (1985-90) restated that the rural health program and the three-tier health services system need to be strengthened and that the government had to make up for the deficiencies in personnel, equipment and facilities. The Eighth Plan (1992-97) distinctly encouraged private initiatives, private hospitals, clinics and suitable returns from tax incentives. With the beginning of structural adjustment programs and cuts in social sectors, excessive importance was given to vertical programs such as those for the control of AIDS, tuberculosis, polio and malaria funded by multilateral agencies with specified objectives and conditions attached. Both the Ninth (1997-2002) and the Tenth (2002-2007) Five-Year Plans start with a dismal picture of the health services infrastructure and emphasized to invest more on building good primary-level care and referral services.

The health reports and plans mostly concentrated on building the health services infrastructure and even this lacked a sense of integration. Most of the policy reports missed out on the importance of a strong referral system. Instead, there has been more emphasis on building the primary-level care and even that has lacked proper implementation. The Bhore Committee report and later, the Primary Health Care Declaration discussed the operational aspects of integrating the other sectors of development related to health. The multi-sectoral approach that is much needed and the inter-sectoral linkages that are essential for a vibrant health system have not been well thought out, and there has been no plan drawn out for it later. It is important to question whether it is only the low investment in health that is the main reason for the present status of the health system or is it also to do with the framework, design and approach within which the policies have been planned.

The rural public health care infrastructure has recorded an impressive development during the last 50 years of independence. The network consists of 1,45,000 sub-centers, 23,109 primary health centers and 3222 community health centers, catering to a population of 5000, 30,000.

Primary Health care range of services individuals and communities receive on a regular, ongoing basis in order to stay healthy, get better, manage ongoing illness or disease, and cope with end of life. In India, Primary Health Centers (PHCs) are the cornerstone of rural healthcare; a first port of call for the sick and an effective referral system; in addition to being the main focus of social and economic development of the community. It forms the first level of contact and a link between individuals and the national health system; bringing healthcare delivery as close as possible to where people live and work.

The Public Health care infrastructure in rural areas has been developed as a three tier system: Sub-Center, Primary Health Center and Community Health Center. The Sub-Center is the most peripheral and first contact point between the primary health care system and the community. Each Sub-Center is manned by one Auxiliary Nurse Midwife (ANM) and one Male Health Worker, one Lady Health Worker (LHV) supervises six Sub-Centers. Sub-Centers provide services in relation to maternal and child health, family welfare, nutrition, immunization, diarrhea control and control of communicable diseases programs and focus on interpersonal communication in order to bring about attitude behavioral change for health. The Sub-Centers are provided with basic medicines for minor ailments, and basic health needs of men, women and children. The Ministry of Health & Family Welfare is providing 100% Central assistance to all the Sub-Centers in the country since April 2002.

Rural Public Health Care was ideally conceived in 50s but it did not function efficiently for delivery of health services due to social, structural, political and lack of full implementation reasons as many research studies and periodic evaluation of the system have pointed; even one mentioned in introduction chapter. To make the system more effective and commensurate with the funds spend it needs revamping.

Revamping Primary Healthcare Infrastructure: Primary healthcare services substantially affect the general health of a population, however many factors undermined the quality and efficiency of primary healthcare services in India. To some extent, the deterioration in health status in rural areas is attributed to inadequacies in PHC implementation, neglecting the wider factors that have been responsible for this deterioration such as lack of commitment, inadequate medical and paramedical personnel in position, corruption, social impediments and lack of community participation. In Introduction chapter, the research findings of a five years experiential studies in 1972-1977 highlight the reasons for

PHC being inadequate health delivery system, and even those failings have not been addressed to a greater extent till now. Commenting on what ails the National Rural Health Mission, it needs far greater strengthening in terms of several of its components in order to yield the expected outcomes. "We require greater strengthening in terms of the human resources for health. We need more doctors, nurses, and auxiliary nurse midwives." The shortage of the medical staff in the public hospitals is a painful affliction for poor countries. Beside these reasons for poor PHC performance, accessibility is one of the major obstacles; hopefully current planned improvement in road transport infrastructure would take care of this.

Planning Commission's sample study of Andhra Pradesh, Rajasthan, Bihar, and Uttar Pradesh done as recently as May (09) by Kaveri Gill found shortage of the medical staff. Absenteeism was a norm among doctors and specialists which aggravates the scarcity of skilled medical personnel. Scarcity and non-accountability is one reason why Gujarat is trying out a partnership with private gynaecologist.

The current outlay for the health sector, which is somewhere between 2 to 3 per cent, needs to be enhanced to at least 5 per cent to ensure adequate supply of equipments, drugs and other wherewithal to help District Hospitals, Primary Health Centers and Sub-Centers to attain optimum levels of efficiency. The current situation of 80% of funds being spent on salaries and building and only meager balance available for medicines, equipments and other necessary supplies is deplorable. If we do not urgently improve the situation, we will end up as a nation full of sick people, requiring extraordinary amount of resources to cure them from various ailments.

Further, active participation of the people in managing their own health and that of the communities should be encouraged. There should be optimum utilization of existing primary health care infrastructure to remove the current inertia and to gear them up to meet the present and future challenges of healthcare; active participation of voluntary organizations in the planning, monitoring and implementation of health programs, particularly in the vulnerable areas. Ensuring a disciplined and responsible growth of the private sector both in curative as well as preventive and promotive care. Revitalization of local health traditions and strengthening of local practitioners so that they can play important roles in health promotion, throughout the country. Decentralized district level planning with flexibility to cater to the local needs and constraints. Handing over the responsibility of health services gradually to Panchayats and Zila Parishads with technical support, guidance and leadership from State Health Services. Special Sub-plan to uplift the health status of the vulnerable people.

Suggestions

1. Greater importance shall be attached to the development of the healthcare in rural and remote areas. The government shall include the rural areas as a whole and promote an equity-oriented health policy. A health funding mechanism with preference being given to the rural and remote areas shall be set up to provide guarantees for the sustainable development of the primary healthcare to provide safe, efficient and accessible medical and health care services.

2. Priorities shall be given to the development of human resources for the rural and remote areas. Investment in human resources shall be increased to develop a sizable pool of talents. And an effective mechanism to attract and retain quality health workers in rural areas shall be established.

3. The rural medical insurance system shall be improved. A medical insurance system that covers all rural residents shall be established to effectively reduce the farmers' burden of medical expenses and secure their access to the basic medical and health services.

4. Feasible health technologies shall be extended and applied. Reliable, cost-effective and popular health technologies shall be promoted in the rural and remote areas, while giving full play to the advantages and roles of the traditional medicine in the primary prevention shall be stressed.

At Community Level

Traditional health functionaries can contribute towards taking care of people's health at low-cost in their own community settings; but for this, department of Indian Systems of Medicine should be encouraged to work out a program for upgrading the skills and knowledge of these practitioners as well as weeding out malpractices. Local health practitioners should be further strengthened with the introduction of 'Community Health Workers' throughout the country. The nucleus of this scheme should be a motivated social person from the village itself, as the Panchayat Swasthya Sahayak (PSS) and be selected by the village Panchayat. He/she has to assist the Panchayat in meeting the basic health needs and act as a strong link between the Government Health Agencies and the people. There should be one PSS for every 1000 population in plain areas, and one PSS for around 700 population in hill tribal and/or difficult areas. The entire country should be covered in a phased manner. There should be a massive effort in health education in the entire country, through school teachers, panchayat members, youth clubs, Mahila Mandals and health workers to help people inculcate a more rational and scientific understanding of health.

At the District Level

There should be a District Health Plan for all the districts of the country done at the district level itself. This should be supplemented by a Panchayat Health Plan. In the district level plan, there should be adequate flexibility for specific areas like the Desert and the Hill areas where a strong base-hospital supported by a mobile service must be provided.

Given the fact that lack of safe drinking water is a major cause of morbidity, it should be ensured that every citizen of this country has access to a reasonable quantity of safe drinking water. This program should be implemented in collaboration with the Ministry of Rural Development and Employment. To ensure that the sources of safe drinking water are maintained properly, communities should be involved right from the beginning, from the installation to maintenance of these sources.

Health Impact of Developmental Projects: Many of the emerging health problems of rural areas are related to the development processes. It is essential to look at the health impact of these projects during planning. Incidence of pesticide poisoning, pollution and gradual degradation of ground water and emergence of malaria in desert areas are examples of some of the problems which are directly linked with developmental projects. We should ensure that health hazards of development projects are properly looked at before implementing them.

Similarly, serious efforts should be made to educate and diagnose sexually transmitted diseases including AIDS in the rural areas. With the very large migration of workers from rural to urban areas, health problems from these diseases are gradually taking alarming proportions.

Health Care for the Vulnerable Population

As mentioned earlier, approximately one-third of the people of our country, particularly living in the tribal, hilly and arid as well as feudal areas have a critical health status. Their health problems are very much associated with the issues of food security and underdevelopment. The health of this population is directly linked to their economic, social and political status. It is quite clear from the findings of all social development ministries that there is a need to think of a Sub-Plan for the vulnerable and deprived regions. This will ensure food security and health security for the most vulnerable population of the country.

The voluntary sector should be involved in providing primary health care in a more effective manner, particularly in the neediest areas. A special fund like CAPART should be set aside for this purpose. They will also play a very important role in imparting health education through schools and other fora. The services of qualified voluntary organizations should be utilized for training of community health workers as well as for giving continuing education to other health personnel of the government. Similarly, they should be partners in the program of eradication of TB and malaria throughout the country. Given the growing professional competency of the voluntary organizations and their successful experimentations on various aspects of healthcare, they should be involved in the process of planning and monitoring of health services both at the central as well as at state levels.

Rural Health Systems Research: This is important for monitoring and checks and to find out successful approaches to implementation of key programs of public health. The research can focus on Community Participation, Integration of Indian Systems of Medicine in PHC, appropriate and low-cost health management information systems for rural healthcare and financing of rural health systems. Effective methods of health education, Inter-sectoral coordination and mechanics of convergence of social development work in rural areas and effective epidemiological surveillance at the district level.

National Rural Health Mission

Under the mandate of National Common Minimum Program (NCMP) of Government, health care is one of the seven thrust areas of NCMP, wherein it is proposed to increase the expenditure in health sector from current 0.9 % of GDP to 2-3% of GDP over the next five years, with main focus on Primary Healthcare. The National Rural Health Mission (NRHM) has been conceptualized and the same is being operationalized from April, 2005 throughout the country, with special focus on 18 states which includes 8 Empowered Action Group States (Bihar, Jharkhand, Madhya Pradesh, Chhattisgarh, Uttar Pradesh, Uttarakhand, Orissa and Rajasthan), 8 North East States (Assam, Arunachal Pradesh, Manipur, Meghalaya, Mizoram, Nagaland, Sikkim and Tripura), Himachal Pradesh, and Jammu and Kashmir.

The main aim of NRHM is to provide accessible, affordable, accountable, effective and reliable primary health care, especially to poor and vulnerable sections of the population. It aims to bring about uniformity in quality of preventive and curative healthcare in rural areas across the country and improve upon the earlier primary health care system. An allocation of Rs. 12,070 crore for this program is proposed during the year 2009-10. Although healthcare in India has come a long way, a large number of people still suffer from diseases which could be prevented by better medical care. The weaknesses of the health system hit the poor hardest, especially poor women and children.

It also aims at bridging the gap in Rural Health Care through creation of a new cadre of Accredited Social Health Activists (ASHA) and improving hospital care, decentralization of program to district level to improve intra- and inter-sectoral convergence and effective utilization of resources. *Decentralisation is the key to the rural health mission and a large number of Rogi Kalyan Samitis and village health and sanitation committees, and Vaccine Healthcare Centers (VHC) are set up. This suggests community participation and positive move.*

The NRHM further aims to provide umbrella to the existing program of Health and Family Welfare including RCH-II, Malaria, Blindness, Iodine Deficiency, Filaria, Kala Azar, T.B., Leprosy and Integrated Disease Surveillance. Further, it addresses the issue of health in the context of sector-wise approach addressing sanitation and hygiene, nutrition and safe drinking water as basic determinants of good health in order to have greater convergence among the related social sector departments i.e. AYUSH, Women and Child Development, Sanitation, Elementary Education, Panchayati Raj and Rural Development.

The Mission further seeks to build greater ownership of the program among the community through involvement of Panchayati Raj Institutions, NGOs and other stakeholders at National, State, District and Sub-District levels to achieve the goals of National Population Policy 2000 and National Health Policy.

Under the strategy of NRHM, in order to fill the gaps in the existing rural health care infrastructure available in the country, the key components, inter-alia, of the Mission are: (i) Creation of ASHA in 2.5 lakh villages in four years—8 EAG States, J&K and Assam. (ii) Creation of village health scheme and preparation of village health plan in 18 + states.

(iii) Strengthening sub-centers with untied funds of Rs. 10,000/- per annum in 18+States. (iv) Raising 2000+CHCs to the level of IPHS. (v) Codification of Indian Public Health Standards (IPHS) in 18+states. (vi) Integrating vertical health and family welfare programs under NRHM at National, State and District level in all states. (vii) Strengthening Program Management Capacities at National, State and District level in 18 states. (viii) Institutionalizing district level management of health in all districts. (ix) Supply of generic drugs (both Allopathic and AYUSH) in 18 states. (x) School health check up program in 18 states. (xi) Promotion of multiple health insurance model in all states. (xii) Supplementing Vitamin 'A' and Iron Folic Acid to deficient children at Anganwadi level in 18 states. (xiii) Promotion of private sector for achieving public health goals in all states. (xiv) Setting up of comprehensive Health and Family Welfare clinics in 5 states+select districts. (xv) Services of ANM and medical officers, PHCs to be ensured at fixed days at Anganwadi levels. (xvi) Mainstreaming ISM, exploring new Health Financing Mechanism, Policy reforms in Medical Education and Public Health Management.

The National Rural Health Mission is being launched for a period of seven years (2005-2012) i.e. 2 years of Tenth Plan and full Eleventh Plan from April 2005. It will cover entire country, with focus attention on 18 states having weak demographic indicators and infrastructure. It is a broad-band program, and all other programs would be sub-components, retaining the sub-budget heads wherever required for vertical programs; RCH-II, including National Family Welfare Program (NFWP) and Empowered Action Group (EAG) are subsumed into NRHM.

The emphasis under NRHM is to improve primary health-care, decentralization, intra- and inter-sectoral convergence and community ownership. It provides broad policy guideline, but states have flexibility to draw their action plans to attain the goals of NRHM.

Strengthening of Rural Health Care Infrastructure: Since the early rural health care plans initiated since 50s have not delivered the health care efficiently, so, NRHM planned to revamp that system with additional components and further strengthen the existing ones. Every village/large habitat will have a female ASHA chosen by and accountable to the panchayat—to act as the interface between the community and the public health system. She would act as a bridge between the ANM and the village. She will be an honorary volunteer, receiving performance-based compensation for promoting universal immunization, referral and escort services for RCH, construction of household toilets, and other health care delivery programs. ASHA will be provided a medicine kit containing generic AYUSH and allopathic formulations for common ailments. It will be replenished from time to time.

The government has trained six lakh ASHA who are to go between the auxiliary nurse midwives and the expectant mother. In the process, the government says that there has been a seven-fold increase in hospital deliveries because of which deaths of infants and mothers have come down. We are seeing an increase in institutional deliveries. But until we integrate Dai's firstly into the system more than point of call, and secondly, improve quality in hospitals such that women naturally want to go to a hospital for a delivery as opposed to for an incentive, we will see it work effectively.

ASHA are an important contribution to social mobilization and are increasing the referrals for institutional deliveries by both increasing awareness plus motivating the women to seek that kind of care. ASHA have other functions to deliver as well. They are involved in motivation for immunization and now some additional activities are also being added to their portfolio, so *that they will actually become health motivators in the village not merely for a few confined functions but for several other broadband ranges of health functions.*

SEWA, a trade union of self-employed women in the organized sector, has 1.1 million members across 9 states. For the rural health mission, it has been training ASHA, setting up village health and sanitation committees and persuading women to do deliveries in hospitals under the Janani Suraksha Yojana.

ASHA will be trained in teaching of public health; developed and mentored through a Standing Mentoring Group at National level incorporating best practices and implemented through active involvement of community health resource organizations. The Government of India will bear the cost of training, incentives and medical kits. Induction training of ASHA will be for 23 days, spread over 12 months. On the job training would continue throughout the year. Training would require partnership with NGOs/ICDS Training Centers and State Health Institutes.

ASHA will facilitate preparation and implementation of the Village Health Plan along with Anganwadi worker, ANM, functionaries of other Departments, and Self-Help Group members, under the leadership of the Village Health Committee of the Panchayat.

Thus, ASHA becomes an important component of Rural Health Care at the first level—at village contact. Therefore, it is important she should be well selected and well trained as well actively monitored for her performance.

Strengthening Sub-Centers (SC): Untied Fund for local action @ Rs. 10,000 per annum. This fund will be deposited in a joint Bank Account of the ANM and Sarpanch and operated by the ANM, in consultation with the Village Health Committee. Essential medicines both, allopathic and AYUSH will be supplied to the Sub-centers. In case of additional outlays, multipurpose workers (male)/additional ANMs wherever needed, sanction of new Sub-centers as per 2001 population norm, and upgrading existing Sub-centers, including buildings for Sub-centers functioning in rented premises will be considered.

Strengthening Primary Health Centers (PHCs): This is to provide for quality promotive, preventive, curative, supervisory and outreach services, through adequate and regular supply of essential quality drugs and equipment (including Supply of Auto Disabled Syringes for immunization); providing 24 hour services in at least 50% PHCs by addressing shortage of doctors, especially in high focus States, through mainstreaming AYUSH manpower. Upgradation of 100% PHCs for 24 hours referral services may be undertaken, and provision of 2nd doctor at PHC level (1 male, 1 female) would be undertaken on the basis of felt need for ongoing communicable disease control programs, and new programs for control of non-communicable diseases.

Strengthening Community Health Centers (CHCs) for First Referral Care: Operationalizing 3,222 existing Community Health Centers (30-50 beds) as 24 hours First Referral Units, including posting of anesthetists; promotion of Stakeholder Committees (Rogi Kalyan Samitis) for hospital management; and developing standards of services and costs in hospital care. In case of additional Outlays, creation of new Community Health Centers (30-50 beds) to meet the population norm as per Census 2001, and bearing their recurring costs for the Mission period could be considered.

Another important intervention under NRHM is the provision of a Mobile Medical Unit at district level for improved outreach services.

The current position in 2008 of specialists manpower at CHCs reveal that out of the sanctioned posts, about 59.2% of Surgeons, 46.4% of Obstetricians & Gynecologists, 56.6% of Physicians and about 51.9% of Pediatricians are vacant. Overall, about 50% of the sanctioned posts of specialists at CHCs are vacant. Moreover, there is a shortfall of 64.8% specialists at the CHCs as compared to the requirement for existing infrastructure on the basis of existing norms.

Revamping Primary Health Care Infrastructure: Primary healthcare approach, if implemented in its true spirit, improves the performance of primary care. The comprehensive and integral nature of services prevents and controls many illnesses. Early diagnosis and appropriate treatment of ailments ensures that the patient does not land up in complications. Good quality of services encourages the community to seek treatment at the primary level itself. Thus, only patients referred from the primary level or those with complex health problems needing specialized care will seek treatment from the hospitals and at higher levels. This will prevent overcrowding at the hospitals.

Primary healthcare services substantially affect the general health of a population, however many factors undermined the quality and efficiency of primary healthcare services in India. To some extent, the deterioration in health status in rural areas is attributed to inadequacies in PHC implementation, neglecting the wider factors that have been responsible for this deterioration such as lack of commitment, inadequate medical and paramedical personnel in position, corruption, social impediments and lack of community participation.

Commenting on what ails the National Rural Health Mission, it needs far greater strengthening in terms of several of its components in order to yield the expected outcomes. "We require greater strengthening in terms of the human resources for health. We need more doctors, nurses, and auxiliary nurse midwives." Hopefully current planned improvement in road transport infrastructure would take care of this.

The health infrastructure in India is based on the primary healthcare approach. Over the past years, there has been a significant reduction in crude birth rate, crude death rate, infant mortality rate and an increase in life expectancy. The country has an extensive network of health centers. Yet, the geographical and quantitative availability of primary healthcare facilities is far less than the guidelines laid down by the government. Studies have shown that only 20 per cent of those seeking outpatient services and 45 per cent of those seeking indoor treatment avail public services.

Primary healthcare is as much of a pressing priority now as it was before. Social, demographic and epidemiological transitions along with globalization, urbanization and an ageing population pose challenges of a magnitude not anticipated earlier. Primary healthcare is an ideal approach to deal with this complex situation of great magnitude.

In addition, in this scenario, many persons are likely to present with co-morbidities which underlines the importance of dealing with the person as a whole which is possible with this approach.

As societies modernize, there will be a rise in expectations regarding health and healthcare. A people-centered approach like primary healthcare is likely to satisfy such expectations of a knowledgeable society.

It has also been observed that focusing only on priority diseases through vertical programs leads to fragmentation of health services and short-term gains while the holistic and person-centered approach in primary healthcare provides long-term gains. Primary healthcare in urban areas is the need of the hour. Apart from urbanization, the enormous social and economic stratification within the urban areas leads to extreme marginalization in the form of slums and street dwellers.

Overall, there is a shortage of all cadre of medical and para medical staff. In the present circumstances, medical personnel in general do not want to relocate to rural and remote areas.

Attempts have been made to bridge this gap but have met with limited success. Appointments on contract basis, posting interns and graduates and postgraduates after their degrees in rural areas have been tried. However, concrete steps need to be taken to tackle this problem.

The misconception of primary healthcare amongst policy makers and field workers is that it is cheap, low technology, non-professional care for the rural poor and deals with few priority diseases. It is important to understand that primary healthcare requires adequate resources and investment. It gives much better value for money than other alternatives.

The community-level health workers can only complement the team at the health centers and cannot be an alternative for them. It is important to focus on the team approach; a team of trained, motivated workers who are able to establish ongoing relations with the community to ensure continuity of care, a team which has the capacity to provide integrated services in response to the community needs.

Primary healthcare is not the antithesis of hospital care nor can this care be isolated care provided through isolated centers.

Currently, the referral system is ineffective and the health centers hardly coordinate with other departments and organisations. Ideally, primary healthcare should serve as an entry point for the individuals, which ensures continuity of care by coordinating a comprehensive response at all levels of care.

The problems of manpower shortage and universal coverage are major challenges. Community participation and inter-sectoral coordination are aspects which will require special efforts. Effective leadership and administrative skills are required to implement these principles on field which appear simple on paper.

Public private partnerships in provision of primary healthcare are interesting avenues which should be tapped. Non-governmental organizations and corporate sector should show interest in contribution to primary healthcare.

In the last five decades, there has been a significant progress in various aspects of health in the country. It is imperative that in the coming Five-Year Plan, sufficient emphasis is given to healthcare needs of the people living in vulnerable regions, by ensuring that the pockets of darkness in the advanced states are adequately taken care of and a healthy nation, therefore, is possible only if there is total participation of its citizens, communities and the government in this goal.

The systems and infrastructure available in the country are totally revitalized to competently deal with the newer challenges in the healthcare. This task cannot be done just by the government and its functionaries alone. It requires enthusiastic and sustained participation of all the citizens of the country in taking responsibility for their own health as well as that of their communities. We also need to ensure active and responsible participation of the private and voluntary sectors.

There is a considerable challenge for optimizing the existing rural health infrastructure throughout the country. Keeping in view the potentiality of the Panchayati Raj, it is proposed that health infrastructure in the rural areas is gradually but surely made accountable to village panchayats, panchayat samitis and Zila Parishads at their respective levels. There are good examples of this approach from Maharashtra, West Bengal and few other states. This will considerably improve the functioning of the infrastructure and will ensure participation of the people.

The rural health mission has set a target of spending 2-3% of gross domestic product (GDP) on public healthcare. The current outlay for the health sector, which is somewhere between 2 to 3 per cent, needs to be enhanced to at least 5 per cent to ensure adequate supply of equipments, drugs and other wherewithal to help District Hospitals, Primary Health Centers and Sub-Centers to attain optimum levels of efficiency. The current situation of 80% of funds being spent on salaries and building and only meager balance available for medicines, equipments and other necessary supplies is deplorable. Overall spending now is 0.89% of GDP with increased Central spending making up for the decline in state spending, though health is a state subject. This raises doubts about the ability and willingness of states to make the required 10% of contribution. The Centre's outlay has increased from Rs. 7,200 crore to Rs. 12,050 crore over a four year period but four states evaluated recently in a Planning Commission Sample Study were found not to have spent over a third of the money allocated to them. Local health traditions and strengthening of local practitioners should be revitalized so that they can play important roles in health promotion, throughout the country. District level planning with flexibility to cater to the local needs and constraints should be decentralized.

While the NRHM does provide substantial amount of revenues to various states to improve health services, the states too need to pitch in with greater contributions to primary healthcare. Till states take ownership of these programs, we are not going to see an effective delivery at the state level.

A few more suggestions through research studies on NRHM to revamp the primary care system:

A health funding mechanism for the rural and remote areas shall be set up with government leadership, public funding and individual's participation to provide guarantees for the sustainable development of the primary healthcare to provide safe, efficient and accessible medical and health care services.

Priorities shall be given to the development of human resources for the rural and remote areas. Investment in human resources shall be increased to develop a sizable pool of talents. And an effective mechanism to attract and retain quality health workers in rural areas shall be established.

The rural medical insurance system shall be improved. A medical insurance system that covers all rural residents shall be established to effectively reduce the farmers' burden of medical expenses and secure their access to the basic medical and health services.

Feasible health technologies shall be extended and applied. Reliable, cost-effective and popular health technologies shall be promoted in the rural and remote areas, while giving full play to the advantages and roles of the traditional medicine in the primary prevention shall be emphasized. Strengthen health promotion and advocate a healthy philosophy of life through enhancing the health awareness and self-healthcare capabilities of the residents.

Quality of pre- and post-contraception care through PHC is poor. The predominant contraception method among both tribal and rural areas is female sterilization, i.e. tubectomy. The government institutions were the main source of contraception in both tribal and rural areas. Though, the quality of pre- and post-contraception care among the community is very important, the perceptions of the community on post contraception care is not at desirable levels. These findings emphasize the continuing need to strengthen post-operative care and counseling for sterilization acceptors.

It is also necessary that all PHCs are equipped with modest lab facilities for doing simple pathological tests. We should ensure that every PHC, CHC and Sub-centre of the country is properly equipped and manned.

Rural service should be made mandatory for all medical graduates before they can seek admission for post-graduation. To encourage motivated and bright young professionals to join

Primary Health Care Services, it is proposed to introduce an 'Indian Health Services', so that health care management of the country is done by competent people. Administrative Services, health personnel, including nurses, should be given adequate orientation and training in rural contexts before joining services. This should be further strengthened with compulsory continuing education for health personnel at all levels.

Health management information system for the country would ensure good quality, uniform national health data, based on epidemiological findings from the villages.

To avoid duplication of efforts, all health, population, and women and children related welfare programs at the rural level should be converged to ensure optimum resource utilization of funds and efforts. This suggests that uni-purpose workers will gradually become multi-purpose workers. If adequate and competent services are available at the primary level, then enforcement of strict referral services will be possible. This will help avoid overcrowding at the sub-divisional and district hospitals.

The current growth of various vertical intervention programs like TB, Malaria or special program on Sexually Transmitted Diseases and AIDS should be gradually curtailed and brought under the Primary Health Care, in order to stop the lopsided management of health problems. Serious efforts should be made to educate and diagnose sexually transmitted diseases including AIDS in the rural areas. With the very large migration of workers from rural to urban areas, health problems from these diseases are gradually taking alarming proportions.

A dentist and ophthalmologist for eye care is must in PHC for routine checkups and early detection of problems.

At Community Level: Traditional health functionaries can contribute towards taking care of people's health at low-cost in their own community settings; but for this, department of Indian Systems of Medicine should be encouraged to work out a program for upgrading the skills and knowledge of these practitioners as well as weeding out malpractices. Local health practitioners should be further strengthened with the introduction of 'Community Health Workers' throughout the country. The nucleus of this scheme should be a motivated social person from the village itself, as the Panchayat Swasthya Sahayak (PSS) and be selected by the village Panchayat. He/she has to assist the Panchayat in meeting the basic health needs and act as a strong link between the Government Health Agencies and the people.

There should be a massive effort in health education in the entire country, through school teachers, panchayat members, youth clubs, Mahila Mandals, NGOs and health workers to help people inculcate a more rational and scientific understanding of health. The services of qualified voluntary organizations should be utilized for training of community health workers as well as for giving continuing education to other health personnel of the government.

At the District Level: There should be a District Health Plan for all the districts of the country done at the district level itself. This should be supplemented by a Panchayat Health Plan. In the district level plan, there should be adequate flexibility for specific areas like the Desert and the Hill areas where a strong base-hospital supported by a mobile service must be provided.

Lack of safe drinking water is a major cause of morbidity, it should be ensured that every citizen of this country has access to a reasonable quantity of safe drinking water. This program should be implemented in collaboration with the Ministry of Rural Development and Employment. To ensure that the sources of safe drinking water are maintained properly, communities should be involved right from the beginning, from the installation to maintenance of these sources.

Health Impact of Developmental Projects: Many of the emerging health problems of rural areas are related to the development processes. It is essential to look at the health impact of these projects during planning. Incidence of pesticide poisoning, pollution and gradual degradation of ground water and emergence of malaria in desert areas are examples of some of the problems which are directly linked with developmental projects. We should ensure that health hazards of development projects are properly looked at before implementing them.

Approximately one-third of the people of our country, particularly living in the tribal, hilly and arid as well as feudal areas are vulnerable and have a critical health status. Their health problems are very much associated with the issues of food security and underdevelopment. The health of this population is directly linked to their economic, social and political status. It is quite clear from the findings of all social development ministries that there is a need to think of a Sub-Plan for the vulnerable and deprived regions. This will ensure food security and health security for the most vulnerable population of the country.

The voluntary sector should be involved in providing primary health care in a more effective manner, particularly in the neediest areas. A special fund like CAPART should be set aside for this purpose. They should be partners in the program of eradication of TB and malaria throughout the country. Given the growing professional competency of the voluntary organizations and their successful experimentations on various aspects of healthcare, they should be involved in the process of planning and monitoring of health services both at the central as well as at state levels.

Rural Health Systems Research is important for monitoring and checks, and to find out successful approaches to implementation of key programs of public health. The research can focus on Community Participation, Integration of Indian Systems of Medicine in PHC, appropriate and low-cost health management information systems for rural healthcare health education, Inter-sectoral coordination and mechanics of convergence of social development work in rural areas and effective epidemiological surveillance at the district level.

PPP Model for Healthcare

Public-private partnership is important and necessary for healthcare in India. It needs P4 model of Public—private—NGOs—community to make it successful; more so in rural areas. There is lot of private investments and operations of health care facilities of excellence in urban areas but very negligible in rural areas. A few philanthropic and corporate trusts have organized excellent facilities in different health areas to cater to rural people. But they are negligible. Thus core rural health services such as promotive and curative happen to be government's responsibilities and it is the main guarantor. It has to put major resources for it. Currently, government is spending more on public health than on urban healthcare. In preventive healthcare such as about safe drinking water, sanitation, nutrition, and environment private sector may contribute sufficiently and also contribute for the awareness and education for adoption when they do the product marketing campaigns. Government has to spend resources for urban poor and slum dwellers healthcare—who are 15% of the urban population as they cannot afford the expensive urban healthcare offered by private sector health facilities.

Government does run big hospitals in the cities so that both urban and rural poor can get free advance level curative care. Though government does make mandatory on private health facilities to treat 5% of their poor patients free in lieu of other facilities provided to them by the government. There are urban community hospitals run by philanthropic and corporate trusts that treat poor patients either free or on nominal charges. But there are no government dispensaries run on rural PHC model as first contact point for promotive, curative and preventive health treatment.

NGOs role in both rural and urban preventive healthcare is both important and necessary to create health awareness, educating them about health measures, and motivating them to adopt them for preventive care. NGOs work with communities to create social consciousness among individuals, of being responsible about their own health as well as of their communities. Thus these small steps taken by the individual and community help each one of them in a big way.

NGOs role is also important as go between the government, other stakeholders and private sector to get the required health facilities in the specific geo areas. They also make efforts to create social consciousness for providing health care among medical and para medical staff in rural areas where truancy, neglect of duty and other social impediments of castes affect public health care quality.

Government has mainly to take all roles of—planning, financing, providing manpower, administering and monitoring the rural public health care in particular and healthcare in general. Private sector contributes to financing and training medical manpower, urban healthcare facilities and some selected rural facilities, research, development and financing medical breakthroughs, particularly pharmaceutical companies in the field of developing medicines and treatments of various ailments. As stated earlier, private sector does contribute in a big way for preventive health measures.

NGOs contribution is voluntary but very significant for the effective implementation of health services. Efforts from all these stakeholders are consistent but not enough. We need more aggressive contributions from individuals and local communities to make their own healthcare a success by adopting vigorously the preventive measures at least and stay healthy.

Where necessary and where useful, PPP can extend the outreach of services and enhance the efficiency as well to some extent. In Gujarat particularly, the *Chiranjeevi model* has been successful and where you do not have adequate facilities for immediate provision of services in the public facilities co-opting people from the sector through PPP would appear to be useful modality.

Ultimately, the state has to be the main provider or at least guarantor of health services in this country. The private sector and the voluntary sector also have useful complementary roles to play, but unless you have a strong and efficient public health system, you are not going to see improvement in health gains; particularly you will not see reduction in health inequities. You must ensure that universal healthcare especially of essential health services is available.

The planning of community health schemes by non-governmental or faith based organizations in rural areas from both top-down and ground level is significant. Both types of planning approach are valid and necessary for sustainability of public healthcare.

Health Minister pointed that "for the development of healthcare in rural areas, the government is also looking at a public-private partnership (PPP) model. Under the proposal, the private players would be allowed to set up medical colleges with the district hospitals as the nodal centers in rural areas. These policy decisions have been taken by the ministry as part of the 100-days program in early 2009 of the government. The government would also provide special incentives to doctors practising in rural and remote areas. In hilly and backward areas, we have given a lot of priority and concession to public-private partnerships. This has been done in order to increase human resource in the health sector. The private sector can play a pivotal role in augmenting government's efforts towards providing healthcare to all, but on the flip-side it can be seen that the private sector costs are high and its penetration in rural areas is poor.

The government has shown keen interest in finding private partners to revitalize the PHCs. To this end, The George Foundation, in collaboration with the Government of Tamil Nadu, has initiated a pilot project involving one PHC covering some 79,000 people in the Dharamapuri District. Five more PHCs will soon be included in the pilot project. The goal is to build on the existing "infrastructure" at these PHCs, make them functional and enhance their capability. The George Foundation will coordinate and manage this proposed project.

A convergence approach to healthcare is a must to make it effective, that in rural healthcare, the determinants of many other sectors which operate outside of the health system influence the healthcare. Whether clean water supply, sanitation, agricultural nutrition, environment, urban transport, all of these have a tremendous influence on health. So, all of those policies also must become more aligned, sensitive to, and responsive to public health concerns. States must align their policies and programs within their domain in the interest of public health.

Public health is not just about cure it is also about prevention. Has the rural health mission created enough awareness, has it enabled people or has it changed attitudes and behavior towards sanitation, safe drinking water, cleanliness—clean physical environment and personal hygiene? In terms of prevention, the key issue is investing in water and sanitation. We have not seen the level of investment we need such that every family has a toilet, every family has access to clean water and drainage. If those three issues are addressed, in depth, then we'll see definite public health gains. In terms of awareness, that is certainly an issue that needs a lot more work because health education and awareness and attitude and behaviour change towards health can be done by both mass-media and interpersonal communication channels. As we have learnt that it also requires a level of one on one contact to be effective which could be a role for ASHA's and other community health workers like Dais if the appropriate training is given; and for volunteer workers from NGOs. Moreover, even delivery of medicines and the scarcity of trained medical paramedic personnel and willing doctors are the big gaps in rural healthcare areas. Has the rural health mission been able to address these intractable issues?

We consider the planning of community health schemes by non-governmental or faith-based organizations in rural areas from both top-down and ground level viewpoints. We conclude that both types of planning approach are valid and necessary for sustainability of such developments. With top-down planning in mind, we describe our hierarchical models especially designed for location of community health facilities, with objectives pertaining to both efficiency and equity of provision. From a ground level approach there are maximal numbers of self-sustainable primary healthcare workers in rural regions.

Commenting on current healthcare status in rural India, Oxfam CEO said, India urgently needs to spend more on healthcare and save its poor population from poverty and hunger or face the risk of slower economic growth, leading health experts said in a report released. India is home to more than 230 million undernourished people, more than any other country. While the proportion of malnourished has fallen, the absolute numbers are rising with the population.

"A sick and vulnerable population cannot contribute to the growth and India will continue to see a pattern of growth that is leading to growing inequalities and low rates of poverty reduction." The Indian government spends only 1 per cent of its Gross Domestic Product (GDP) on healthcare facilities, forcing millions of people to struggle to get medicines, Oxfam and 62 other agencies said in a report called: "Your Money or Your Life".

"Poor people will continue to be denied their right to basic healthcare, leading to very high rates of infant and child mortality...," Agrawal said. India's maternal mortality rate (MMR) stands at 450 per 100,000 live births—against 540 in the 1998-99 period, which is way behind the MDGs which call for a reduction to 109 by 2015. To improve on the dismal record, aid agencies say India needs to increase public expenditure and ensure better healthcare facilities. "Without that, India will continue to be off-track in attaining the MDGs, especially in the healthcare area and will continue to lag behind its peers in these basic indicators of welfare," Agrawal added (Sept. 09).

Salient Rural Health Programs

Population Control in Villages: Population is positive demographic dividend, but with limited resources available to rural areas for creating employable work force, education, promotive, preventive, curative and rehabilitative health facilities; there is concern about the population explosion and called for fighting it by reaching to the grass roots level and creating awareness.

"Demography is in India's favor as the country is young in comparison to other countries. But to take advantage of this situation, there is a need to promote education and awareness and population control." "Go to the village level, block level and district level where the problem is real. Make family planning reach every household. There is no need of using force (for family planning) but we have to keep our focus intact," so say must development functionaries.

"Population forecast in our country is really scary. Unless population stabilizes, all our efforts will fail. We need to do at least three things to stabilize population—*awareness generation, people's participation* and *incentives to people,*" he said, adding that the central government must hold meetings with states where the population growth rate is high. States like Uttar Pradesh, Bihar, Rajasthan and Madhya Pradesh where the population growth is far higher than in other states. National Population Stabilization Fund executive director Amarjeet Sinha said there is a huge unmet demand for services in the most problematic states of Bihar, Uttar Pradesh and Jharkhand. Family planning can be success if the private sector steps in a desired way.

We are also equally eager that every Indian citizen enjoy good health as well. In order to make sure that health is available, affordable, and is of an appropriate nature to everybody including in those who are living in the rural areas, we need much greater strengthening of our health services and family welfare schemes vis-à-vis controlled families. Controlled families have to be a concerted effort with a convergence program approach to make it effective

Rural Dental Health Programs

Dental hygiene in villages especially for children is badly neglected and the effect of brackish water in many villages in North India also affect the teeth and its falling premature in adults as well as children. There are no dentists available in the village PHCs even to look after the normal wear and tear and care of teeth; and even no dental hygiene education through the sub-centers in villages or even village schools. According to WHOs' recent report, 90% villagers in India are affected by dental diseases and good number suffer from oral cancer related deaths. Oral cancers account for 40% of all diagnosed cancers in the nation. In India, one oral-cancer related death occurs every 7 minutes and the mortality rate associated with oral cancer has not improved in the last 40 years. WHO has determined oral cancer to be an epidemic in India.

One of the causes of this poor dental situation is the lack of dental health awareness and the small number of dental professionals in the nation. In India, there is only one dentist for every 10,000 people in urban areas and an estimated 250,000 people in rural areas. And still, negligent number of dental surgeon for the burgeoning population both in cities and rural areas. In rural areas, the average 16 year old has 4 decayed, missing, or filled teeth and the older population will have many missing teeth without denture provisions, they do suffer from many stomach related diseases as they are not able to eat and digest well.

Dental HygIndia is working to reduce the number of people afflicted with dental diseases. To spread awareness and provide free dental care in order to foster the development of oral health conditions in rural India is a must. Dental health-care awareness camps around villages should be set up frequently and IEC campaigns should create awareness and education about dental hygiene and spread a greater understanding of oral hygiene. Even mobile dental vans catering to small cluster of villages will be useful. Through school programs and mobile dental clinics in rural areas and slums, Dental HygIndia is working towards increasing oral care awareness and preventing the deterioration of dental health. It conducts dental programs in rural areas in partnership with dental professionals and local schools. It provides free dental care to low and moderate income families through mobile clinics.

It is imperative to provide preventive dental care education to prevent cavities, gum disease, and other dental problems by proper brush and flossing daily by using right kind of dental products; proper diet and fluoride content through water or dental products and educating them about the ill-effects of smoking, pan parag, Pan Masala, tobacco chewing, etc. on teeth as well for oral Cancers.

In villages and remote areas, the lack of dental treatment facilities and proper dental care has led to an overall lack of oral hygiene awareness and the disastrous percentages of dental afflictions. Many school children suffer from dental caries, scaling problem, irregular teeth, and bad teeth due to nutritional deficiency. A few suffer from even cleft lip—cleft palate, skeletal deformities. Therefore, periodic dental school programs are a must. In the camps/check up programs, they have been providing free dental kits containing tooth brushes, tooth pastes and mouth washes to the children every 3 months to encourage daily dental care and supply nutritional supplements for nutritional deficiencies; nutritional supplements and vitamin supplements are supplied along with the necessary antibiotics and pain killers for school children.

Even Dental HygIndia takes care of surgical treatment for cleft lip and cleft palate, orthodontic correction of teeth, skeletal deformities treatment, speech therapy, and complete oral rehabilitation.

Dental HygIndia is active for Andhra Pradesh villages. But there are many other NGOs which are actively working in villages and remote areas in many parts of India and their efforts are commendable. PPP model should work for rural dental care in the long-run.

Rural Eye Health Care

Eye diseases in rural areas are common, and need frequent attention for all. Beside minor ailments, there is incidence of childhood blindness and in other age groups also due to lack of care for these minor ailments. In India, nearly 12 million people are blind, the major proportion of which remain in rural, remote and underserved areas. A major proportion of aged population in rural areas also suffer from cataracts, glaucoma and other eye ailments, as they have poor access to eye care facilities. The poor nutritional status of mothers and young children predisposes the pre-school children to nutrition blindness. Adverse environmental conditions and domestic unhygienic conditions also predispose to high eye infection rates. Many times the prevalence of myths and misconception about surgeries hamper the achievement of program objectives.

Eye Care Efforts

IEC campaigns should create awareness and education about eye care and eye diseases and about promotive, preventive and curative eye care is necessary. Eye care awareness camps around villages should be set up frequently. But eye care is needed since the child's birth to the old age, and this is an area which is badly neglected and many lose their eyesight.

The greatest prevalence of blindness in India is among the ruralites because they have least access to eye care services in particular and health care services in general. Control of blindness in India has neither been effective nor efficient. The focus has primarily been on cataract surgery in make-shift environments in rural India. Many hospitals and NGOs set up cataract operation camps around the villages. This does help the villagers to some extent rather than no service. Even some of them also provide mobile eye vans catering to small cluster of villages. But you need more of them with more frequency. The quality of eye care available to the people in rural India is sub-optimal because of the lack of infrastructure and of human resources, i.e. capable and well-trained personnel for providing quality eye care.

A public health strategy that addresses the issues of availability, accessibility, and affordability of eye care services is needed to address current problems and to meet long-term plans for reducing blindness and other eye diseases. In order to develop good quality, permanent and affordable eye care for rural India, efforts should be made to plan new facilities and improve the existing ones. There have been few initiatives by private hospitals with higher resources to provide high quality eye care to ruralites. They also provide good eye care models which government hospitals can emulate. There are NGOs with low resources but zeal to serve the rural eye care and they do adopt a village or two to provide eye care education, contribute to IEC campaigns and some with even better resources do set up eye cataract camps around the villages and send mobile vans to follow such cases. In the past government has made efforts for preventive and curative programs for blindness under National Program for Control of Blindness, but they have not been enough and there have been resources constraints. Government is getting sensitized to major eye disorders and eye care problems in rural areas which need utmost attention, more financial and human resources and good strategies. They have planned for these in the current five-year plan and health care budget for 2009-10. The good point is they would be emulating good eye care models from private hospitals, plus their collaboration to deliver quality care and timely care to check deterioration of eye health. Equally necessary is community and individual participation. A PPP model is a must and government is working towards that in its new approaches and strategies for rural eye health care.

PPP in Health Care

Elder Pharmaceuticals has earmarked Rs. 40 crore investment for a rural thrust and set up a dedicated division called 'Elvista' to spread its network to villages, towns, sub-urban and periphery markets and hinterland districts. The initial targets are Class II-IV towns and rural markets with a dedicated sales force of 240, a company press release said. "Elvista is targeting therapeutic categories which have greater relevance in rural areas and are preferred by doctors like anti-peptic ulcerants, anti-malarials, anti-infectives, quinolones and cough preparations, among others" the release said. The division has been launched with 16 brands including Eldervit injection and a few niche brands.

Elvista has already penetrated the rural markets of Uttar Pradesh, Maharashtra, Andhra and Bihar and will soon enter the south, the release said. It will expand the range and reach of social safety nets by providing direct assistance to vulnerable sections; and strengthen the delivery mechanism for primary health care facilities with a view to improve the preventive and curative healthcare in the country (2009).

Private Initiatives: Eye Health Care

LV Prasad Eye Institute Focus: The International Center for Advancement of Rural Eye Care (ICARE) was established at the LV Prasad Eye Institute, Hyderabad, India. ICARE is working to develop a comprehensive approach to eye health in India by providing and coordinating training efforts for the development and management of eye care facilities in underserved areas particularly rural areas. They have developed ongoing projects and programs on: Village Vision, Community Assisted and Financed Eye Care, Eye Screening Programs for school children, community disorder surveys and community screening programs, IEC campaigns, Community Based Rehabilitation, Pediatric Ophthalmology, Community Linkage for Integration of Primary Healthcare, and its Eye care Pyramid model.

All the rural outreach and community eye health programs are carried out by ICARE under the banner of *Village Vision* programs. These include service delivery, training and operations research projects. So far, the programs have been confined to Andhra Pradesh. However, with the experience gained from such projects, the programs will be extended to other parts of the country and to other developing countries.

The Community Assisted and Financed Eye Care (CAFE) project is conceptualized as a pilot project to explore the modalities of delivering community assisted and financed eye care, and to find an entry point for the delivery of other health-care services and programs to an adopted community, based on the principle of a self-payment scheme. Under the scheme, the whole community makes a nominal contribution of Re. 1 per person, per month, and the entire family is registered under the scheme. This money goes into a fund to serve the whole registered community. Whoever requires eye care is given the benefit of a package of services, including a secondary level of eye care free of cost.

Eyesight International, Canada has provided the support for CAFE, while LV Prasad Eye Institute is the implementing agency. Smt. Rajeswari Ramakrishnan Lions Eye Hospital, Nidadavole, is the service provider.

This project serves to train eye care workers at every level required in these areas; to act as consultants providing information, training, and the benefit of experience in the field to local, governmental, private or international organizations working to develop eye care in Andhra Pradesh; and to participate in planning eye health in the developing world on the basis of reliable epidemiological research and bio-statistical information.

It undertakes *School Eye Screening Program* in the catchment population of all its partner secondary level eye facilities and vision centers. School Eye Screening is meant for generating awareness regarding eye health among the children, parents and the school teachers. Free services for treatment and surgery are provided to those who are underprivileged and cannot afford payment. Moreover, teachers in the schools would be trained in measuring vision and would be provided with a referral book. They would refer children suspected to have decreased vision or an obvious ocular abnormality to CSP. A field worker would always assist a teacher in the screening. Teachers would also be taught about the basic prevention to maintain good ocular health and would be required to check the compliance of the children with glasses.

Approaches and Strategies for Eye Care

Community Screening Program (CSP): Community Eye Health workers conduct door to door survey for the entire village population and would refer those with the eye problems for community screening program. Community Screening Program (CSP) would be conducted twice a week in the areas where the door-to-door survey has been completed. The ophthalmic technician at the CSP site would do ocular examination. Those in need of glasses would be prescribed glasses and those in need of further management would be referred to the base hospital. Those referred would be examined at the base hospitals by an ophthalmologist and the necessary treatment and surgical management would be provided.

Public awareness campaigns to create awareness in the public regarding the eye disorders and their prevention would be conducted once a week and along with every CSP twice a week. Posters, banners, pamphlets, dramas, and personal communication are a few of the methods for awareness. A link would be established with the existing health care workers, school teachers and community leaders to make the community aware about preventive and curative aspects of eye health in a manner that is long-term and sustainable.

Community Based Rehabilitation (CBR): Those identified as incurable blinds would be taken up as clients by the field workers and would be trained according to their needs and environment for better living and positive contribution to the community. The inclusion of visually impaired children in the local regular schools is one of their strategies in target area.

The field workers would counsel the visually impaired and blind individuals and their family members assess their potentials, interest of the clients and local resources and impart training and provide services in the following areas: Orientation and Mobility training, training in Activities of Daily Living, training in related Occupation, access to Facilities given by Government for the blind, Economic Rehabilitation when indicated, and Inclusive Education for the visually impaired children.

Pediatric Ophthalmology Learning and Training Center (POLTC): Some of the major hurdles in the elimination of avoidable childhood blindness are shortage of skilled human resources to address pediatric eye diseases, inadequate infrastructure and lack of good anesthesia and Para-ophthalmic support. To address these concerns in India and south-east Asia, ORBIS India partners has set up three Pediatric Ophthalmology Learning and Training Centers (POLTC) at Sankara Netralaya, Aravind, and LV Prasad Eye Institute, Hyderabad, in October 2006. The objectives of the POLTC program are: Training 5 pediatric eye care team; each team of 6 personnel (ophthalmologist, anesthetist, optometrist, nurse, counselor, and an outreach coordinator) will empower one institution in pediatric ophthalmology and further enhancing capacity.

A program to prevent diabetes was launched in Prakasam district (Andhra Pradesh) in May 2006 and is supported by the World Diabetes Foundation (2006-2011). It aims at developing a sustainable district level model to promote lifestyle changes in rural Andhra Pradesh using the child-to-family communication strategy. Diabetes being a major public health problem, with alarming increases in its prevalence, there is an urgent need for interventions in lifestyle to prevent an epidemic of diabetes, which is a major factor in causing many retinal eye diseases. It will adopt a multi-disciplinary approach (including modification in lifestyle, special diabetes oriented care of feet, eyes, etc.) and emphasize strong public and private partnerships (among LVPEI, district health administration and private practitioners) with effective community integration and participation within the district.

The World Diabetes Foundation is supporting another related project for a period of 5 years (2008 to 2013). This will focus on Capacity Development Program to Address Diabetes and Diabetic Retinopathy. This project aims at strengthening the existing infrastructure and building capacity to help better the quality of life of persons with diabetes in Prakasam district, Andhra Pradesh state.

From June 2006 to September 2008, 413 Villages were covered; 1,02,017 School children were trained and 7,043 teachers got trained. Training programs have also focused on 74 Primary Health Center doctors, 156 NGOs, 28,542 Self-help group representatives and 1029 Self-help groups.

Nimmagadda Foundation—LVPEI Children Eye Health Initiative addresses childhood blindness. Launched on July 7, 2007, the initiative aims at preventing childhood blindness so that "No child in Andhra Pradesh is needlessly blind or visually impaired by the year 2020". The Nimmagadda Foundation offers support in the areas of infrastructure development, screening and treatment including spectacles, awareness generation, development of information, education and communication (IEC) material, training and other community-based programs.

Community Linkage for Integration of Primary Health (CLIP)—CLIP project is an attempt to study how LVPEI plays a vital role in providing affordable, accessible and quality healthcare to the community in its service area.

LVPEI's Pyramidal Eye Care Model: The state of Andhra Pradesh provides excellent and equitable eye care to the community through permanent infrastructure and manpower. The eye care model is comprehensive in terms of controlling all the diseases that contribute to blindness; it has good geographical coverage and all the services are provided with appropriate delivery structures, relevant linkages and referrals. However, it was felt that with such a well-developed network of infrastructure and manpower, LVPEI could play an even greater role in providing linkages among various healthcare providers so as to provide quality healthcare at an affordable cost. LVPEI's eye care delivery structure and referral network can be a suitable vehicle for achieving comprehensive healthcare for all with community involvement, with each tier supporting and implementing each level of activity.

LVPEI will be a facilitator, linking all health services (public and private) and other welfare schemes, such as the Rajiv Aarogya Sri scheme, EMRI and HMRI services. The on-ground service delivery would be done through Village Health Volunteers (VHV)—a cadre of volunteers from the village, trained by LVPEI in preventive and promotive eye health care, awareness creation about early detection and referral of cases. These volunteers will ensure linkage between various healthcare providers and work closely with government machinery. They will help create awareness about community health rights, ensuring active community participation in all activities, thus creating long-term sustainability.

The LVPEI Pyramid of Eye care emphasizes the creation of sustainable permanent facilities within communities, staffed and managed by locally trained human resources, and linked effectively with successively higher levels of care.

The pyramid rests on a foundation of community involvement, in the form of VISION GUARDIANS, trained young people who, through door-to-door surveys and other informal means, keep an eye on the eye health of around 5000 people.

The second level has VISION CENTERS, which serve the primary eye health needs of the community. Each Vision Center caters to a cluster of villages with a target of around 50,000 people. The Vision Centers draw upon local talent;

they are staffed by persons from the local communities trained to address their eye care needs. The initial capital investment needed to set up such a center is around US $10,000 (20 cents per person).

The Vision Centers are networked with larger SECONDARY EYE CARE CENTERS that serve a population of 500,000 and provide ophthalmological care that can diagnose all diseases and offer high quality surgical care for cataract—the most common cause of blindness. These centers employ a team approach with almost all members of the team recruited from the local community and trained at the advanced tertiary center. The initial investment needed for such a center is US $100,000 (20 cents per person).

The secondary centers are linked to TERTIARY CARE HOSPITALS/TRAINING CENTERS in cities that provide a comprehensive range of services as well as training, each serving 5 million people. The establishment costs for such a center amount to US $1.0 million (again, 20 cents per person).

The tertiary Eye care centers are linked to a CENTER OF EXCELLENCE catering to a population of 50 million, which does service delivery for complex diseases, training of trainers of sub-specialties and rehabilitation, while also engaging in advocacy. The total cost of setting up a center of excellence is US $10 million (20 cents per person).

This model does not depend on external funding or expertise in the long-term, as the Vision Centers have the potential to grow into community hubs that address other health needs beyond ophthalmic needs. The cost of providing care, from base to apex, is just US $1 per person served.

LVPEI model evolved as a 'top down' model, has allowed it to leverage its existing linkages at the global and national level to bring the advantage of learning and influence to the grass roots. The development at all levels, but especially at the secondary and primary level, is based on community need, and is a tripartite arrangement among the community, LVPEI and an implementation agency, often an international NGO that supports the development with financial and material resources.

The Vision Centers have helped not only to bring services within the reach of villages that have been beyond of most health care services, but have also become important points of community health awareness and education programs that have a potential to change attitudes towards and service uptake of not only Eye Care programs, but also other social and health interventions in these areas.

(Information is based on LVPEI and Nimmagadda Foundation Internet resources)

The Government of India has adopted the 'Eye Care Pyramid Model' as an efficient model for Eye care service delivery in rural areas in its current five-year plan budget and the model will soon be rolled out in other states in a phased manner.

National Program for Control of Blindness (NPCB) Sponsored by Central Government was started in the year 1976 for reducing the prevalence of blindness in India. During 1994 to 2002, the World Bank assisted seven major States of India including Orissa. A large number of blind people in a country denote poor socio-economic development and an inefficient eye care service in the country.

In India, nearly 12 million people are blind, the major proportion of which remain in rural, remote and underserved areas. About 80 to 90 per cent of blindness is either curable or preventable. The *objectives* of the program are (i) to bring down the prevalence rate of cataract blindness from 1.49 percentage to 0.8 percentage by the year 2007; (ii) To expand coverage of eye care services to the underserved areas, and (iii) To develop institutional capacity for eye care services by providing support for equipment, material and training personnel.

The *strategies* of the program are: (i) Decentralized implementation of the scheme through District Blindness Control Societies. (ii) Involvement of voluntary organization in various eye care activities. (iii) Participation of community and Panchayati Raj institutions in organizing services in rural areas. (iv) Public awareness about prevention and timely treatment of eye ailments. (v) Gender inequity, it suggests "there should be a convergence with various ongoing schemes especially for the development of women and children". (vi) Development of eye care services and improvement in quality of eye care by training of personnel, supply of high tech equipment, strengthening follow-up and monitoring services.

Strategies to address gender inequity in cataract services may involve more tangential issues than simply finding out which women in a village would benefit from treatment. Transport to hospital may be a concern as some women may have little experience of travelling outside their environs and they may have a sense of fear or perceived danger. Appropriate counseling is another method that may be effectively used to address gender inequity. Men are more likely to express need, while women are more likely to hide their needs. Some women report feeling 'shame' in being blind. Counseling can be used to engage husbands, men, and children of widows to reach out to women, and to seek those who have visual loss. Active counseling also helps to establish or strengthen links between the community and eye care service providers. These strategies may increase the uptake of surgery by women, but in the long-term more innovative approaches are needed.

Addressing gender inequity in eye health involves more than enhancing the level of services, or increased effort by stakeholders. Eye health for women and girls must be seen within the context of comprehensive healthcare, and integrated with gender-responsive health care policies and programs. The gender gap also needs to be closed in other areas of development such as primary and secondary health education —in south India literacy was the most important predictor for females receiving cataract surgery.

Local NGOs and organizations often establish grass roots networks that may be of great value when linked to eye care efforts. For example, organizations related to child health may provide a platform for effective childhood cataract and refractive error screening. Partnering with industry may also be a possibility; for example if telecommunications companies can target rural outposts, could they not run eye health advocacy campaigns alongside?

Equal access to sight is attainable if eye health is integrated with general healthcare as well as the broader development agenda. Partnerships outside of eye care and public health may be required. As links develop and new partnerships are forged, the tools available for advocacy are also expanded, and these broader coalitions may ultimately improve the current status of gender inequity in eye health.

More trained pediatric ophthalmologists are needed. The handfuls of training programs with efforts from various quarters are not sufficient to meet the vast requirement across the country. NGOs point out that the government should take immediate steps to expand the curriculum for ophthalmology specialization to include pediatric ophthalmology. Further, the services of available ophthalmic surgeons in the country are not being adequately utilized. Many ophthalmologists are purely working in administrative jobs and are posted at peripheral units with no ophthalmic equipments.

Pediatric eye care services are not adequate in India. Only recently have institutions like Aravind Eye Care System, Sankara Netralaya and L.V. Prasad have forayed into it and are doing commendable work not only for city but for rural and unserved areas and the poor.

Two other eye care institutions Aravind and Shankra eye care institutions are doing equally commendable work as in serving the rural and unserved areas and the poor. There are many smaller Ophthalmology institutions that serve in the rural areas with their limited resources; and NGOs also contribute in these efforts.

Aravind Eye Care Hospital situated at Madurai in South India is the largest and most productive eye care facility. Taking its compassionate services to the doorstep of rural India, Aravind's stunningly effective strategies vaulted barriers of distance, poverty and ignorance to create a self-sustaining system. From April 2006 to March 2007, including the work done in the Managed Eye Hospitals, over 2.3 million out-patients were treated and over 270,444 surgeries were performed. In a 33-year quest to end blindness in India, Aravind has developed everything from cheaper intraocular lenses to a 20-minute cataract surgery that allows high volume at lower cost.

The network of not-for-profit hospitals and vision centers performs 300,000 eye surgeries each year—70% for free—using broadband connections to on-call doctors in city hospitals for instant diagnosis. Camps in rural areas screen thousands of patients weekly. "We are going from village to village to provide eye care to the unreached," says Aravind's chairman. Aravind won the 2008 Gates Award for Global Health.

Aravind Eye Care Hospital is an ophthalmological hospital with several locations in India. The hospital is named after Sri Aurobindo, one of the 20th century's most revered spiritual leaders.

Aravind is more than an eye hospital. It is a social organization committed to the goal of elimination of needless blindness through comprehensive eye care services. It is also an international training center for ophthalmic professionals and trainees who come from within India and around the world. It is an institute for research that contributes to the development of eye care and to train health-related and managerial personnel in the development and implementation of efficient and sustainable eye care programs. Aravind also is a manufacturer of world class ophthalmic products available at affordable costs.

Aravind partners with over a thousand community organizations and international NGOs such as the Lions Club International, Sight Savers International, Sewa Foundation, International Eye Foundation and ORBIS International. It is also linked with a number of prestigious medical schools and public health institutes. The World Health Organization has designated it as a Collaborating Center for the Prevention of Blindness. With funding from the Lions Club International, Aravind established the Lions Aravind Institute of Community Ophthalmology (LAICO) to help replicate the principles and practices that have worked well at Aravind. LAICO now works with more than 200 hospitals located all over India as well as in the developing world and has been helping them replicate the Aravind model in their own setting.

Aravind is experimenting with ICT use for eye care health; details are discussed in 'ICT: Rural Eye Health Care'.

Sankara Eye Care Institutions are dedicated to eradicating preventable and curable blindness in India through one of the largest rural outreach program in India. Their mission of "Vision 20/20 by the year 2020" aims to perform 1 million surgeries annually through 20 centers across India. Their three centers at Coimbatore and Krishnan Kovil in Tamil Nadu and Guntur in Andhra Pradesh already perform 75,000 surgeries annually. Sankara Tulsi National Institute of Community Ophthalmology is a post-graduate training center training eye surgeons, administrators to paramedical and field staff.

The super specialty eye center is equipped to provide the latest in diagnostic and therapeutic care and provide affordable specialty eye care in rural India. Sankara Eye Care Institutions are equipped with all modern equipments to provide comprehensive quality eye care of international standard to patients irrespective of their economic background. The Centers clinical faculty treats more than 200,000 patients each year and performs over 50,000 surgical procedures. Additionally, 24-hour emergency care and community-based ophthalmic care for the rural poor are provided. The Institute serves patients of all ages, from infants to senior citizens.

The out-patient department is equipped to provide specialty care in the fields of Cataract and comprehensive Eye Care, Cornea and External diseases, Glaucoma service, Low Vision service, Vitreoretinal diseases, Oculoplastic Surgery, Pediatric Ophthalmology, Uveitis and medical Retina, Contact Lens and an exclusive optical, and ESIRIS Excimer Laser System. (Excimer Laser is a form of ultraviolet laser which is commonly used in eye surgery and; ESIRIS is high technology Excimer Laser). It runs an eye bank launched in 2009. On 15th September 2009, Sankara Eye Care Institutions, India won the prestigious "FICCI Healthcare Excellence Award" in the category "Best Community Driven Healthcare Program".

ICT: Rural Eye Health Care

The objective is to improve and enhance the services offered by Primary Health Centers (PHCs) in the rural communities of India by applying novel solutions that take advantage of developments in harnessing solar power, computers, and information technology. Our strategy is to use technology to provide effective early medical intervention, deliver expert health care, and minimize the inconvenience caused to patients and health-workers from poor logistics and long travel time. An equally important role of PHCs is to provide health education emphasizing family planning, hygiene, sanitation, and prevention of communicable diseases. A final step in this process will happen through video consulting and examination, a technology we anticipate becoming available in rural areas by year 2010.

By the end of 2009, three quarters of India's population will be covered by a mobile network. Interestingly, many of these new "mobile citizens" live in poorer and more rural areas with scarce infrastructure and facilities, high illiteracy levels, low PC and internet penetration. The availability of low-cost mobile phones and the already broad coverage of GSM networks in India is a huge opportunity to provide services that would trigger development and improve people's lives.

Mobile Phone Health Monitoring System: A number of organizations have been working on various projects for enhancing the role of ICT in Healthcare. UK-based Loughborough University's engineers have entered upon a partnership with experts in India to develop a *unique mobile phone health monitoring system*. The system, which was first unveiled in 2005, uses a mobile phone to transmit a person's vital signs; presently the system can transfer the signals pertaining to the ECG, blood pressure, oxygen saturation and blood glucose level to a hospital or clinic anywhere in the world. Professor Bryan Woodward and Dr. Fadlee Rasid from the Department of Electronic and Electrical Engineering at the

Loughborough University have developed this mobile phone monitoring system.

UK-India Education and Research Initiative (UKIERI) has awarded Professor Woodward a grant to further develop this mobile phone monitoring system. They have tied up with the Indian Institute of Technology Delhi (IIT Delhi), All India Institute of Medical Sciences and Aligarh Muslim University and London's Kingston University, to further develop the system.

The research team is aiming to miniaturize the system, through designing sensors and mini-processors that are small enough to be carried by patients, and at the same time procure biomedical data. The network of sensors would be linked through a modem to mobile networks and the Internet, and to a hospital computer. Then, doctors can use this device to remotely monitor patients. The UK government will promote the device to improve the efficiency of healthcare delivery. In India, the project will link clinics and regional hospitals in remote areas to centers of excellence. The clinical trials of the system will take place in the UK and India in the next three years.

Sehat Saathi, a rural telemedicine system is being developed at Media Lab Asia research hub at IIT Kanpur. It can be used to extend medical care to patients in the remote parts of the country. The model provides for front-end contact through a suitably trained non-medical professional; back-end support from doctors, pathologists and other health professionals for diagnosis and treatment; use of digital technology to achieve objects; and dissemination of information on health and disease through digital means. ML Asia has also taken up a project with AIIMS for use of handheld computers (palm-tops) for healthcare data collection and planning.

In 2008, GE innovated an ECG machine, MAC 400 to serve the rural market. This ECG machine is portable. Rural clinics cannot afford expensive machines. The MAC 400 costs about Rs. 50,000 ($1,000), a fraction of the cost of the appliance-sized premium machines sold in the market. In 2009,

GE has brought an improved version of the portable ultra low-cost ECG machine into the US, which is sold as MAC 800. This low-priced ECG machine has created new applications in the US at accidents sites and in emergency rooms where portability and small size are huge advantages. For rural clinics, heart monitors and baby warmers are being produced at low cost.

Mobile-based PHC Management System: CDAC, Bangalore has initiated the development of Mobile based Primary Health Care Management System for deployment in the PHCs for betterment of management of Primary Health Care specifically in the rural and urban slums of India. The system will capture complete information related to an individual patient treated by a PHC. The Software components under development are—Patient Database management, Interaction between doctors and patients, capture of Medical data acquisition such as ECG, images of heart & lung, eye, etc. and Scheduling management.

The project involves development of the following: (i) A Web-based Information system for Management of Primary health care. (ii) SMS interface for integrating SMS messages from the patients using 2nd Generation mobile systems (GSM/CDMA) with the Information system. (iii) WAP Gateway for Web access Applications using WML for integrating GPRS/3G/4GMobile devices of Doctors and Nurses with the Web server and (iv) Development of Localization Support to National and other Indian languages in mobiles by providing interface for translation.

In this era of mobile access to majority of the villagers and the doctors, health officers and paramedic staff and computer facility at PHCs and district level CDC, we see future for Mobile-based Primary Health Care Management System. The Primary Health Care can be made transparent and easily accessible by the implementation of 'Mobile-based Primary Health Care Management System'.

The Primary Health Care strategy seems to be a right intervention in terms of basic preventive methods but it needs to be supported by other strategies as well to close the gaps.

Primary health care is presented as essential healthcare based on practical, scientifically sound and socially acceptable methods and technology, which is universally accessible to individuals, family and the community through their full participation and at the cost they can afford.

George Foundation Technology Use: Rural Health Care. It suggests the use of technology to make government PHC to be more effective. The long-term goal of the Indian government and international funding agencies has been to provide health care to rural communities through PHCs. The result of non-functioning PHCs has been that, in many cases, diseases are not diagnosed in their early stages nor treated. The rural population has to often travel to urban areas when they can no longer bear the suffering caused by the disease, thus increasing the load on hospitals in urban areas and ending up with serious complications that, in many cases, could have easily been treated at their early stages. The need to rectify this problem has become critical especially given the fact that over 650 million people live in rural areas across the country with poor awareness of health issues. This ignorance, coupled with the increased mobility between rural and urban areas, has led to an explosive increase in the spread of diseases like HIV/AIDS and Hepatitis B and C.

We envisage PHCs functioning as the first level in a hierarchical system of health care facilities. At this primary level, PHCs will play two equally important roles: First, diagnosis of diseases based on symptoms and simple laboratory tests, and their treatment either at the centers or through referral. Second, health education leading to family planning, better hygiene and sanitation, and prevention of communicable diseases, especially sexually transmitted diseases.

Initial screening of patients through computers in the PHC, computer will be critical tool for diagnosis by a software program called EDPS2000 (Early Detection and Prevention System, developed by The George Foundation). Screening through computer interview can be handled by a trained technician. Thus, uses of EDPS2000 will put in better health management system. Further, the diagnostic capability of

PHCs can be enhanced through video consultation wherein the patient (through the PHC) will access a physician (and even a specialist) via a two-way video camera and screen. Each PHC will be connected to its assigned doctor through wireless communications and a palm computer; as the social reality is there is dearth of doctors willing to practise in rural areas and their reluctance to travel to, let alone live in, remote areas.

Therefore, there is need to increase the effectiveness of doctors who are willing to work in rural areas. It can be accomplished by reducing the need for doctors in the initial screening of patients, and by allocating one physician for every five PHCs.

The central facility will be able to collect and update the data from all PHCs within its jurisdiction, and perform pattern detection and epidemiological analysis, thereby predicting epidemics and exposing widespread health problems in their early stages. Using the telephone link to the central facility, relevant training and educational material and specific health instructions will be periodically transmitted to the computers at all PHCs and the status of various educational programs need be monitored.

Either solar panels or diesel generators (depending on a cost-benefit analysis) can be connected to batteries for uninterrupted electric power for computers and laboratory equipment in PHCs.

George Foundation's rural health and eye health care institutions are using these technologies for effective delivery of services in rural and remote areas. The George Foundation co-managed a PHC in Tamil Nadu, with these technologies, and has set up its own Baldev Medical and Community Center in Hosur Taluk, Tamil Nadu, to demonstrate how healthcare, health education and many essential rural community services can be delivered in a cost-effective way within a 'private model' using technology. (Details in appendix 3B use of *EDPS2000*)

Aravind Eye Health Care: Technology Use

Enabling Eye Care in Rural India—Research at Intel: In 2006, a collaboration involving researchers from Intel and

UC Berkeley, with support from the National Science Foundation; together they are helping the Aravind Eye Care System, (a network of five hospitals in South India), to deliver affordable, quality eye care services to the rural poor.

Their contribution is a custom long distance, high-bandwidth, point to point Wi-Fi network that connects rural vision centers to Aravind hospitals. This experimental network will enable rural residents to have video consultations with doctors, eliminating the need for patients to travel to the hospital for routine eye care.

Long-distance (LD) Wi-Fi is a fixed point to point wireless technology, like microwave links, that enable organizations such as the Aravind Eye Hospital to develop their own wireless network in remote rural areas. These sparsely populated areas are low priority for wireless service providers and may not receive wireless coverage for many years. If wireless coverage eventually reaches these rural areas with bandwidth to support video conferencing, the long distance Wi-Fi fixed point to point networks can be migrated to wireless service provider networks with their added benefit of broader point-to-multipoint coverage.

In developing their custom networking technology, a key challenge for the researchers is that Wi-Fi is designed for short-distance communication. To make it work over the long distances between rural vision centers and Aravind hospitals, they modified the software specifically, the Wi-Fi Media Access Control (MAC) protocol. The result is a unique wireless network that can handle high-speed communications over distances as great as 40 miles.

Villagers had to walk as much as 12 miles and forego a day's wages to visit an Aravind hospital. As a result, many people who needed treatment didn't receive it. Aravind experimented with a few models of eye care delivery including mobile vans to determine which would best serve the many rural residents who needed access to eye care. First, Aravind launched mobile clinics, sending vans to rural areas. But the clinics were cumbersome to plan, requiring Aravind to find local sponsors to host them. In addition, the vans could only visit a given area infrequently, and without a permanent presence, it was hard to promote eye-care education, which is one key to the prevention of cataracts.

Aravind also experimented with two permanent clinics in Theni, installing technology to enable remote consultations with doctors in Aravind hospitals. But the technology had limited bandwidth and thus poor video quality. It also was expensive, and involved recurring costs to maintain the network. Even if the clinic concept were viable, it would be difficult to scale. Before Aravind could establish clinics in other areas of rural South India, it had to wait for third-party network carriers to provide coverage to those areas. These rural areas of Theni are sparsely populated and low priority for network carriers and service providers. It could take years before they provided adequate coverage.

To address these challenges, Aravind developed the *concept of rural vision centers—primary eye clinics in rural areas*, where patients can be remotely diagnosed by doctors via high speed wireless video-conferencing; get prescription glasses, eye drops and blood tests; be referred to an Aravind hospital if surgery is needed; and receive post-operative care.

Intel and UC Berkeley researchers are collaborating to build an experimental research proof of concept long distance, high-bandwidth, point to point Wi-Fi network to connect the vision centers to Aravind hospitals. That will enable rural residents to have video consultations with doctors, eliminating the need for patients to travel to the hospital for routine eye care.

The collaboration is part of the UC Berkeley TIER (Technology and Infrastructure for Emerging Regions) project, which is tackling the challenge of bringing the information technology revolution to the developing regions of the world. TIER is led by Eric Brewer, the Director of the Intel Research Berkeley lab. Sonesh Surana, a Ph.D. student and intern at the lab, is managing the field effort for the Aravind collaboration, focusing on the design of the system and most of the deployment, training, and sustainability aspects of the project.

UC Berkeley is funding the initial deployments of vision centers, through a grant from the National Science Foundation. Intel is contributing equipment and funding for the researchers, as well as project management by Brewer and Surana.

Establishing the Vision Centers: Intel and UC Berkeley researchers designed a point-to-point long-distance wireless infrastructure that combines a variation on IEEE 802.11 (Wi-Fi) technology with off-the-shelf video-conferencing software and tools that hospitals can use to maintain the network; this was used to connect the vision centers to Aravind hospitals. A key technical challenge the researchers faced was how to make Wi-Fi work over the roughly 10 miles between each vision center and the nearest hospital. The 802.11 networking standard, more commonly known as "Wi-Fi", is defined by a set of international standards that limit its range to about 200 feet.

Customizing the networking hardware (mainly inexpensive Wi-Fi cards) to achieve longer distances would be costly. So the researchers redesigned the software, modifying the Wi-Fi Media Access Control (MAC) protocol, which is designed for short-range communication. Specifically, they disabled some MAC features that weren't needed and implemented others that were, by creating a thin layer on top of the MAC.

By combining their modified Wi-Fi software with directional antennas and routers to send, receive and relay signals, the research team so far has been able to obtain network speeds of up to six megabytes per second (Mbps) at distances up to 40 miles (validated at another project in Ghana). These speeds are about 10 times faster than dial-up speeds and carry 100 times as far as standard Wi-Fi technology.

Results to Date: The prototype networking infrastructure was tested and validated at the first three vision centers deployed, at Bodinayakannur, Ambasamudram, and Chinnamanoor. At Bodinayakannur and Ambasamudram, the researchers replaced existing low bandwidth (33Kbps) wireless links with the new high-speed links. "We improved the quality of video-conferencing by roughly eight times," says Surana.

"And even with that improvement, the network is underutilized; there's more bandwidth available."

At Chinnamanoor, the new high-speed link enabled video-conferencing capability where it didn't exist before. "Previously we had no other option for network connectivity in Chinnamanoor, and so we were not able to start a vision center there, despite high demand for eye care services," says Dr. S. Aravind, Administrator of Aravind Eye Hospitals. Intel and UC Berkeley researchers installed the links at two of the clinics, but the Chinamanoor link was largely installed by local technologists. "The TIER team has trained our local providers as well as our hospital network administrators in order to ensure continuity," says Aravind. "Based on our training, we were able to install the Chinnamanoor network ourselves, with very little help from the TIER group."

In May 2006, local technologists installed two new links, at Periakulum and Aundipatti, with no help from the TIER researchers. The goal is to have all future installations done locally. "So many times people have come into an area to do a project and then, when they leave, everything falls apart," Surana said. "It's been a very important part of our research to make this a project that people can build on and manage all on their own."

Early results are encouraging. The first three vision centers established at Bodinayakannur, Ambasamudram, and Chinnamanoor screen about 1,500 patients each month. (Numbers are not yet available for the two other centers, which came online in May 2006.) Roughly 5-10% of patients that is nearly 100 people a month experience significant vision improvement as a result of treatment, usually via cataract surgery.

"Self-sustainability is a crucial aspect of the Aravind model, so we are greatly encouraged by all the indications that show these vision centers will break even sooner than we had anticipated. Based on our experience with the three initial centers, and the success of the cost-effective technology implemented by the TIER researchers, we are planning to penetrate new areas by scaling up to 50 vision centers in South India that will cover a population of 2.5 million.

"This is an exciting venture, and we believe it has the potential to effectively address the problem of eye care access in rural India. TIER's partnership has been invaluable in enabling this approach to get off the ground with such speed and success."

(Dr. S. Aravind Administrator, Aravind Eye Hospitals, Intel Corporation)

The Bodinayakannur and Ambasamudram deployments also validated that the vision centers can break even—a prerequisite for sustainability. Both clinics are projected to reach the breakeven point in less than three years, largely because the new networking infrastructure requires no annual subscription fees or ongoing maintenance costs.

The pilot project has proven so successful that the research effort will be expanded over the next two years to include five hospitals that will be linked to 50 clinics. These additional vision centers will be able to service half a million patients in rural South India—most of who have no access to eye care today.

These vision centers will positively impact the rural economy. A recent study by the Aravind Eye Care System showed that 85% of the men and 58% of the women who had lost their jobs due to sight impairment were reintegrated into the workforce following treatment. "This makes the role of the vision centers even more crucial," says Aravind.

The presence of rural vision centers that provide video access to doctors will encourage people to seek early treatment for vision problems—a pattern that's already emerging at the three initial centers. That could decrease the average time to first diagnosis and reduce the higher costs related to treating late-stage illnesses. In addition, low-cost network connectivity could enable each clinic to be monitored for key indicators, such as prevailing diseases and treatment results, which could aid in prevention efforts.

The clinics' networking infrastructure could be use in other ways as well—for instance, to deliver other kinds of medical services, to stream training videos to the vision center staff, or even to generate income by offering movies or other services to villages at times when the center is closed.

The experimental wireless networking infrastructure developed by Intel and UC Berkeley researchers could make it possible to deliver eye care services in other rural areas in the developing world. "Wherever there's a demand for eye care or other medical services, you can easily and inexpensively install one of our networks," says Brewer. "This could revolutionize the delivery of health care services and greatly improve the quality of life in the rural developing world" (Source Intel Corporation 2006). UC San Diego and IIT Khargpur are collaborating in healthcare initiative. The aim is to initiate technology leveraged education and research to provide holistic healthcare for the entire lifecycle at affordable cost to underprivileged poor and tribal population of the UP region (2009).

Challenges Ahead

Creating sound policies to achieve quality of life both through physical and psychological well-being for the rural strata is challenging. Education, employment and healthcare are necessary and important for people to achieve QOL. A healthy, educated and an empowered population contributes to improved productivity which, in turn sustains economic growth. Therefore, the challenge is "to invest in quality education, employability and employment". Rural Education Model needs to focus on easy accessibility, equity, quality of education and good performance.

Our efforts should be to deliver innovations in healthcare to majority of the people in rural areas, remote areas and the underserved and poor. Healthcare innovations come in medicines, the treatment, surgical procedures and the medical technology.

We may plan setting up the rural health delivery infrastructure but a number of challenging initiatives have to be taken to meet the acute shortage of human resources at various levels in the rural health sector—specialists, doctors, nurses and paramedics. The endeavor of all P4 participants should be to increase efficiency, improve quality, build better health plans, create healthier people and workforce and save more lives.

PPP approach is also one of the strategies for attaining improved service delivery of above development schemes to the targeted groups. Government, Private and Community initiatives have to work in tandem to deliver quality in rural education, employment and rural health care by filling the gap in performance and finances.

This approach is likely to improve the quality of government schools and capacity building of these institutions; also private and foreign investment is being encouraged for rural school education by government but so far there are few takers.

PPP models, ICTs and active community involvement would help in achieving success in special health segments in rural health care programs such as population control, eye care, and dental hygiene. Foreign investments both in funds, technology expertise and active involvement of foreign institutions with government, private and community is helping effective delivery of these special segments in rural healthcare.

The overall challenge ahead is to strengthen the bottom level of the rural society by developing QOL, their physical rural infrastructure and adopt PPP model and invite foreign funding; and these can drive rural economic growth.

5

Rural Infrastructure Development

Rural Infrastructure Development

Bharat Nirman is a time bound plan for building rural infrastructure. Bharat Nirman programs launched in 2005-2009 focus on six components for rural development: Drinking water and sanitation, rural electrification, rural housing, rural roads, irrigation potentials, and rural telephony. There has been all round progress in the implementation of this program. During 2005-2009, the allocation to this program has been increased by 261 per cent. An allocation of Rs. 40,900 crore for this program is made for the year 2009-10. We expect higher infrastructure fund allocation in a bid to contain the impact of the global economic slowdown. Among the likely focal points are the Bharat Nirman program (allocation of Rs. 312.8 bn. in FY09), and roads and power sector development.

Rural infrastructure development is a key focus area for the next five years which is fundamental enabler for economy. The role of community participation through village panchayats is given greater emphasis. Policy, procedural bottlenecks and delays have to be systematically removed for various sector programs. Tremendous growth is needed in rural areas which have not developed to a larger extent in the last 60 years by the government resources constraints. The partnerships of centre-state-local governments, private business sectors, NGOs and international agencies resources input are likely to be effective.

The Public-private partnership (PPP) projects a key element of the strategy and a large number of PPP projects in different areas currently waiting government approval would to be cleared expeditiously. Framework for PPPs has to be made more investment friendly. The efforts to build badly needed infrastructure will get a boost from the government who has strong mandate for reform, but the country needs sweeping changes in how it implements projects.

Physical infrastructure has a direct bearing on sustainability of growth and overall development. Creation of infrastructure, through its direct and indirect effects, has a significant impact on poverty reduction. In the Indian context, though there has been some improvement in infrastructure development in transport, communication and energy sectors and others in recent years, there are still significant gaps that need to be bridged.

The Rural Infrastructure Development Fund (RIDF)

The Rural Infrastructure Development Fund (RIDF) is the main instrument to channelize bank funds for financing rural infrastructure. It is popular among State Governments. The corpus of RIDF was increased from Rs. 5,500 crore in 2003-04 to Rs. 14 thousand crore for the year 2008-09 ensuring greater availability of funds for its activities. A separate window for rural roads was created under RIDF with a corpus of Rs. 4 thousand crore for each of the last three years.

In this chapter we focus our discussions on five above mentioned essential components of Bharat Nirman and the sixth component of rural telephony is discussed in Technology Growth chapter 6.

Water, Sanitation, and Environment

Safe drinking water and water supply for irrigation and other village enterprises, sanitation both household and village, agricultural nutrition, and clean physical environment, all of these have tremendous influence on rural health. Policymakers are motivated to create healthy environment through good practices. For eco-friendly good practices, we need healthy choices of people and supportive decisions of governance. For

India, the biggest challenge is to provide clean basic amenities like water, sanitation and garbage disposal both in urban and rural areas. We need water management schemes, public conveniences and toilets at homes; rural areas totally lack this amenity. Water in rivers, ponds, and lakes is polluted both by the humans by unhygienic practices and industries discharging pollutants in them.

Schemes have to be planned to control pollution created by humans even throwing indiscriminately polythene bags, and through industrial pollutants. Household garbage collection and recycling schemes in urban areas are not implemented well so it creates air pollution. In rural areas, no plans are set up for garbage disposal; the rural people must be made aware of the problem and guided how to handle it.

Rural Water Supply Program

Access to clean, safe and affordable water is basic human right but even in many countries people even do not get enough water to meet daily needs. Worldwide, the problem becomes twofold: one to get enough water for daily consumption, agriculture and manufacturing, and for other commercial needs; and two to get clean water. Today, the concern is billions of people worldwide do not have regular access to clean water for drinking, bathing, cooking or sanitation and nearly millions of children die because they do not have potable water and functional toilets and they suffer from gastrointestinal diseases.

UNDP report, 'Beyond scarcity: Power, poverty, and the global water crisis' in Human Development Report 2006 suggests many practical solutions. The remote towns or the expanding megacities in developing world all need major investments in water utilities, water-treatment facilities to get clean water. These investments can offset the health costs, low productivity and human lives, and build economic growth and quality of life. The UNDP report urges that every developing country have a national plan to accelerate water and sanitation spending at least 1 per cent of GDP. Currently, many developing countries spend much less than that.

Clean drinking water is a basic necessity of life. Supply of clean drinking water in the rural areas has always been one of the highest priorities of the government of India. A Technology Mission on drinking water *National Drinking Water Mission* (NDWM) was launched in 1986, which subsequently was rechristened as *Rajiv Gandhi National Drinking Water Mission* (RGNDWM) in 1991 with three key objectives: (i) Providing safe drinking water to all villages, (ii) Assisting local communities to maintain sources of safe drinking water in good condition, and (iii) Giving special attention for water supply to Scheduled Castes and Scheduled Tribes.

Accelerated Rural Water Supply Program (ARWSP) is being implemented to resolve the drinking water problem in rural habitations. The Central Government supplements the efforts of the states by providing financial and technical support. The Tenth Plan and subsequent Eleventh Plan emphasizes participatory approach where Panchayati Raj Institutions (PRIs) should be the key institutions for convergence of drinking water supply program at the ground level.

The strategies to achieve the objectives: (i) accelerate coverage of the remaining Not Covered and Partially Covered habitations with safe drinking water systems. (ii) To tackle problems of water quality in affected habitations and to institutionalize water quality monitoring and surveillance systems through a Catchment Area Approach. (iii) To promote sustainability, both of systems and sources, to ensure continued supply of safe drinking water in covered habitations.

Considerable success has been achieved in meeting the drinking water needs of the rural population through this scheme. There are more than 4 million hand pumps and 2 lakh piped water schemes in the rural areas. The ARWSP was launched during 1972-73. It is currently being implemented through the Rajiv Gandhi National Drinking Water Mission.

Drinking water supply is one of the six components of Bharat Nirman, which has been envisaged to build strong rural infrastructure in four years (2005-06 to 2008-09). The task ahead is to cover all the remaining uncovered habitations and also to cover the slipped back as well as the water quality affected ones. State and UT Governments will do Action Plans for achieving the goals of Bharat Nirman in a time-bound manner.

For ensuring sustainability of the systems, steps were initiated in 1999 to institutionalize community participation in the implementation of rural drinking water supply schemes. In 1990s, government made a major policy shift from its traditional supply-driven approach to demand-driven approach, as it was not financially or operationally sustainable. It piloted a new demand-driven approach with World Bank assistance. In 2003, this pilot was scaled up nationwide. The reform program promotes the active participation of beneficiaries in the design and implementation of RWSS projects. It decentralizes the delivery of services to local governance institutions, provides for institutional reform and capacity building of governments and communities, involves non-government organizations and alternative service providers, and promotes cost recovery.

Thus it focused on three basic principles: (i) Adoption of a demand-driven responsive and adaptable approach based on empowerment of villagers to ensure their full participation in the project through a decision-making role in the choice of scheme design, control of finances and management arrangements. (ii) Increasing role of government for empowering user groups and gram panchayats for sustainable management of drinking water assets and integrated water management and conservation. (iii) Partial capital cost sharing either in cash or kind or both and 100 per cent responsibility of operation and maintenance by end-users.

Sector Reforms Projects, based on the above principles were sanctioned in 67 districts on pilot basis. With the experience gained from these pilot projects, reform process has been scaled up in the entire country through *Swajaldhara* launched on 25 December 2002. A notable feature of *Swajaldhara* is involvement of Village Water and Sanitation Committee (VWSC), Panchayati Raj Institutions (PRIs) in planning, implementation, operation and maintenance. This would in turn ensure sustainability of the system. 10% contribution is made by the community and 90% funds are provided by the Central government. In case of SC and ST habitations, community contribution can be in the form of cash, kind, labor or land or a combination of these.

A Technology Mission on Drinking Water and Related Water Management has been constituted to cover the residual problem villages and provide potable water at 40 liter per capita per day, and 70 liters per capita per day in desert areas inclusive of 30 liters for cattle. The Mission is tackling the problem through 55 mini-missions in project districts and countrywide problem oriented sub-missions.

Rajiv Gandhi National Drinking Water Mission (RGNDWM) adopts an integrated approach so that conservation and augmentation of water sources as interrelated with rural water supply schemes to provide sustainable supply of safe drinking water to the rural population. The Mission seeks to provide supply of 40 liters of safe drinking water in rural areas.

An initiative has been taken by Government of India in February 2006 by launching the *National Rural Drinking Water Quality Monitoring and Surveillance Program* which envisages institutionalization of community participation for monitoring and surveillance of drinking water sources at the grass roots level by Gram Panchayats and Village Water and Sanitation Committees, followed by checking the positively tested samples at the district and State level laboratories. Another initiative taken by the Government from 2006-07 onwards is focused funding to tackle drinking water.

'Rajiv Gandhi Rural Drinking Water Mission' is envisaged to supply safe drinking water to uncovered habitations and slipped back habitations. An allocation of Rs. 7,400 crore for this programs for the year 2009-10 is made. Total Rural Sanitation Program is a continuous process. An allocation of Rs. 1,200 crore is made for this program for the year 2009-10 (Source: National Portal Content Management Team, Reviewed on: 31-03-2009).

India has one of the largest rural water supply and sanitation reform programs in the world. Over the years, the Government of India's investments in the sector have brought water supply infrastructure to more than 96 per cent of the country's rural habitations—some 720 million people. Sanitation coverage has also risen; 35 per cent of the population now has access to toilets in 2009. Though access to water supply and sanitation has increased, water and sanitation services for the people are not reliable, sustainable and affordable.

Most schemes are planned, implemented and managed by state engineering agencies and now a demand driven approach is followed. The various government departments in charge of the sector often have overlapping responsibilities. This increases the possibilities of schemes being inefficiently managed. New Strategies are being evolved based on the learning experiences of delivering water and sanitation programs in the villages in different parts of the country.

Earlier, *Strategies* 1: government—centralized—supply driven; it was changed to—*Strategies* 2: community—demand responsive—decentralized.

State strategies focus on Integrated approach to water sanitation and hygiene behavior for better health and environmental outcomes; focus on sustainability, and to achieve MDGs (millennium development goals) ahead of 2015.

Safe Water and More

The Tamil Nadu Agricultural Development Project started in 1991 is expected to be completed in 1998 was financed for government of Tamil Nadu by International Development Association (IDA), World Bank, and government of Tamil Nadu. It is a broad-based initiative to deliver agriculture development, safe water and more.

It aims at strengthening state-level institutions to provide more cost-effective rural-based services, thus raising agricultural production and rural incomes and enhancing the quality of life for the rural poor. The project supports selected investments in agricultural and rural development within the state's current programs, but in the process it is introducing a number of important innovations in technology, public administration, and policy. Besides improving the rural water supply, the project is encouraging more effective farmer extension services, seed production, integrated watershed management, livestock development, forestry, rural road infrastructure, and state-level agricultural planning. The US $133 million project is being supported with an International Development Association (IDA) credit equivalent to US $92.8 million and a World Bank loan of US $20 million to supplement financing from the government of Tamil Nadu and beneficiaries. The rural water supply component represents about 17 per cent of total costs. The project is a broadly based initiative—the first of its kind in India and aligns well with the Bank's goals of assisting India to accelerate agricultural growth, reduce rural poverty, and improve the health of its rural population.

The project is making possible the installation of 12,500 simple bore wells operated by hand pumps in rural areas of seven relatively arid districts of Tamil Nadu. In the past, state policy was to install one hand pump per cluster of 500 persons in rural areas, but this policy often proved arbitrary and missed many of the poorest persons in need. In the project, the clustering criterion has been relaxed, and now it is need-based on current access to a reliable supply of safe water is given more importance. As a result, scheduled castes and tribes have benefited particularly because they typically live in separate hamlets within village communities.

How the Rural Water Supply Component works under the project: a local panchayat is responsible for identifying those areas in its village that lack adequate year-round access to safe water. The district administration then consolidates this information from all panchayats under its jurisdiction and advises the state's Department of Rural Development. The department dispatches a survey team to a village to determine the likely soil depth at which water will be struck, the soil profile, and the likely water output. This team surveys common land around a household cluster to select the best location for the bore-well and to ensure access for all intended beneficiaries.

In the past, the government supplied all the necessary equipment to contractors. In the project, in contrast, contractors supply all needed equipment according to the department's specifications. Each contract includes installation of the bore-well pipe and hand-pump and construction of a simple concrete platform and soak pit. Newly introduced into Tamil Nadu's rural water supply program, soak pits prevent stagnation of spilled water, an extra health safeguard. The bore-well and hand-pump represent simple, easily maintained, internationally recognized technology available in India. Units can take from one day to three weeks to install, depending on whether they are located in relatively easy-to-work hard rock or more difficult mud, sand, or loose stone. Complete costs range from about US $1,000 for units in hard-rock areas to US $2,500 for those in sedimentary areas. Bore-wells averaging about 100 meters deep ensure year-round supply. After the unit is installed, the department tests its water for contaminants. So far, less than 3 per cent of the project's bore wells have yielded contaminated water. Once certified, the hand-pump is turned over to the local panchayat. Beneficiaries select a woman volunteer from their group to protect the pipe, clean the surrounding area, and do minor repairs and maintenance. For this, she receives training from the Department of Rural Development. For major repairs, a mechanic is dispatched from a regional panchayat union office.

The woman volunteer also organizes public health campaigns for pump beneficiaries. Health care workers from the panchayat union office come to these meetings and provide information to local residents on the safe use of water, the need to avoid water stagnation around the pump, and the importance of hygiene in its vicinity.

Outcome of this project: At the project's completion in 1998, 3.5 million persons are expected to be benefiting from project-financed hand-pumps, 30 per cent of whom will be from scheduled castes and tribes. The project is helping beneficiaries to get safe, dependable water close to their doorsteps, thereby reducing the drudgery of hauling water from open wells and rivers. Village women report that it takes them half the time formerly needed for getting daily water supplies for their households, providing more time for more productive activities such as day labour or childcare. Beneficiaries also tell of dramatic reduction in water-related diseases once the pumps go into operation. In addition, simple technology means that the pumps can be easily operated and maintained by local villagers.

Excessive fluoride in water is a major threat to human health in over 2800 villages. Excess nitrate in drinking water constitutes a threat to blue-baby disease. Near the coast, sea water intrusion as a result of excessive withdrawal of groundwater poses a perpetual threat. Dental and skeletal fluorosis, kidney and gall bladder stones, gastro-intestinal problems and skin disease are common ailments that afflict the young and old alike. Women of reproductive age and children are particularly vulnerable. Diarrhea is the most prevalent water-borne disease, responsible for a high percentage of deaths among children below five years of age. Infectious hepatitis, malaria, malnutrition and food poisoning are also common.

The Tamil Nadu Agricultural Development Project models were replicated in other parts of the country and another model need to be developed for handling excessive fluoride in water.

Gujarat Environmental Health Improvement Program looked to the community, once informed and organized, to take the lead in supporting water and sanitation infrastructure that ensures adequate village coverage; and practise water management and hygiene behavior that contributes to improved health and well-being, especially of women and children under the age of five. Physical interventions take place both at the individual and the community level. Toilets, bathrooms, soak pits, water connections and drainage connections are constructed for private homes. Cattle water troughs, extension of drainage and water distribution networks, construction of rain water harvesting structures are built by and for the community.

Poor sanitation and water supply services in parts of rural Gujarat have adversely affected the quality of the rural environment. The poor, particularly women, suffer the most. Girls, for example, are often forced to drop out of school for lack of toilet facilities, and instead, are burdened with the daily task of fetching water. Even at home, women rarely have access to sanitation facilities and travel long distances to fetch water for domestic use. The time taken in their search has adverse affects on their quality of life as it reduces their income generation capacity, affects their health and cuts into time they can spend with families.

One of the outcomes of sensitizing the community to potential benefits (health and non-health) of sanitation infrastructure was that women were quick to demand that interventions be introduced to their village. Surprisingly, reasons cited for installation of latrines and bathrooms had more to do with issues such as old age, menstruation and pregnancy that pertained to convenience and access rather than perceived and subsequent health benefits. Consequently, in addition to health benefits, non-health benefits of owning sanitation infrastructure are promoted as well. Some of these benefits are privacy, safety, convenience, status, and cost savings.

Addressing a two-day long National Rural Workshop on 'Water Supply and Sanitation in Rural India' at New Delhi, Union Minister for Rural Development emphasized upon the importance of the development of suitable technologies for drinking water supply; safe and potable drinking water to all citizens of the country, and sustainable sanitation options for achieving total sanitation by 2012, well before the timeframe of the MDGs.

Referring to the presence of arsenic in groundwater in Bihar, West Bengal and Assam; and fluoride content in Gujarat, Andhra Pradesh, Orissa and Karnataka; as well as salinity of water in the coastal areas of the country, the Minister emphasized on the training of local villagers in testing water quality and equipping them with newly developed test-kits. In order to ensure availability of safe drinking water, the Department of Drinking Water Supply is already running a 'Quality Surveillance under Bharat Nirman' program.

He also informed about the data management work done by the Department of Drinking Water Supply in carrying out survey of available water resources every year instead of the existing norm of survey once in five years (July 2009). Product 'Pur' by Proctor & Gamble for purifying water for drinking is safe, very inexpensive, can be done easily at home. Government should encourage its use

Sustainability of Water System is important and crucial in the drinking water sector. A number of dimensions and resources need to be converged for preparing a road map to sustainability. The most critical among these are technical know-how, human capital and financial resources. Technological resources for sustainability are changing from past practices to the modern technologies; human resources for sustainability focus on the role of various stakeholders: PRIs, CBOs and local communities; and financial resources for sustainability depends on the role of the state in these contexts.

S.M. Sehgal Foundation an NGO has been working as an implementing organization in District Mewat since 2002. Communities thrive where there is access to fresh water, thus it becomes important to nurture this precious resource and make sure it is not lost over generations. It is important to educate and plan for effective use of water resources in rural areas and make people realize the importance of this resource. The foundation efforts focus on reviving rural water resources in the rain scarce area of Mewat and Kurukshetra districts of Haryana, where the water table is depleting rapidly due to over exploitation of the limited water resources.

The Water Management program is an important component under the Integrated Sustainable Village Development (ISVD) model of the Foundation along with other programs on health, agriculture, life skills education and alternative energy. It is working on prevalence, consequences of saline ground water and is practising innovative solutions in order to revive rural water resources in Mewat and Kurukshetra districts of Haryana.

Besides various interventions in the area of water harvesting, it has also done successful projects in creating the sweet water pockets in the underground saline water areas, building check dams to increase the ground water table, community education programs on water conservation, especially for farmers on best agricultural practices like chiseling, drip irrigation, raised bed farming, etc. and to provide the safe drinking water through various filtration processes like bio-sand filters.

The Coca-Cola Foundation will award a total of US $1 million to support four innovative projects to improve water resources and sanitation in developing nations. The projects were selected by the Global Water Challenge (GWC) business coalition and Ashoka's Change-makers through "Tapping Local Innovation: Unclogging the Water and Sanitation Crisis", an online competition calling for groundbreaking solutions to some of the world's most pressing water and sanitation challenges. A total of 265 projects from social entrepreneurs in 54 countries around the world were submitted to the competition.

The project receiving funding in India is: Naandi Foundation project 'Clean drinking water for underserved populations in India'. It is working on Community-based Safe Drinking Water Systems.

Through a collaborative partnership between villages, technology partners and the states, the Naandi Foundation is facilitating the availability of safe drinking water to citizens in the Andhra Pradesh and Punjab states of India. The village panchayats support the development of water purification plants in the villages, and the partnership supplies water to villagers at a nominal user fee, which pays for the operations and maintenance that makes the plant sustainable. A public education program in the villages also creates an environment for greater understanding of health, hygiene and sanitation issues and the importance of safe and clean drinking water among local citizens.

Naandi Foundation has partnered with water health international (USA) and developed the Community Safe Water Systems (CSWS) model. It has also partnered with Tata Projects Limited—India, in developing a similar community based model to address fluoride contamination.

Water for Irrigation

Water is necessary for irrigation etc. which is organized by village community or government according to facilities available in the area; it may be canals, ponds, check-dams. In water scarce areas (e.g., dry lands and red groundwater areas with low and declining water levels), introduce free or low cost water entitlements for farmers using smart cards, vouchers or bank accounts and allow rest to be priced and traded. This will ensure efficient use of scarce water resources and payment by commercial users. Rain harvesting is also used for irrigation. The collection and storage of rain water for later productive use is defined as rainwater harvesting. Any rainwater harvesting system has three components: Catchment, Conveyance, and Storage.

There is need of artificial recharge of ground water and surface water harvesting along with awareness generation amongst the community so that all habitations in rural areas are covered with adequate and safe drinking water and there are no slipped back villages either in terms of quantity or quality of drinking water. Small-scale low cost environmentally sustainable water shed management projects like roof top rain-water harvesting should be taken up in villages particularly in schools to ensure sustainability of water sources.

Government is investing heavily in the Accelerated Irrigation Benefit Program (AIBP) and the Rainfed Area Development Program and in the management and augmentation of water resources. Under AIBP, 24 major and medium irrigation projects and 753 minor irrigation schemes will be completed in this financial year, creating additional irrigation potential of 500,000 hectare. The outlay for 2007-08 was Rs. 11,000 crore with a grant component of Rs. 3,580 crore. These are being increased in 2008-09, and the estimated outlay is Rs. 20,000 crore with a grant component of Rs. 5,550 crore.

The Rainfed Area Development Program has been finalised and will be implemented in 2008-09 with an allocation of Rs. 348 crore. Priority will be given to those areas that have not been the beneficiaries of watershed development schemes.

The centrally sponsored scheme on micro irrigation launched in January 2006 has brought an area of 548,000 hectare under drip and sprinkler irrigation within two years.

Agreements have been signed with the World Bank by the Governments of Tamil Nadu, Andhra Pradesh and Karnataka under the project to repair, renovate and restore water bodies. The three agreements are for a total sum of US $738 million that will benefit a command area of 900,000 hectare.

Irrigation and Water Resources Finance Corporation

While these ongoing programs will raise the level of investment in agriculture. Government is of the view that massive investments are required to be made in irrigation projects. Having regard to the magnitude of the challenge, Irrigation and Water Resources Finance Corporation (IWRFC) with an initial capital of Rs. 100 crore contributed by the Central Government. State Governments and other financial institutions will be invited to contribute to the equity. It is Government intention to mobilize very large resources that will be required to fund major and medium irrigation projects.

The Integrated Watershed Development Program (IWDP) is an important step in harvesting rainwater in rural India. It promotes groundwater recharge, checks soil erosion, improves soil texture and quality, vegetation, etc. Ultimately, it supports the livelihood of the people.

Another important step in rainwater harvesting is implementation of rooftop rainwater harvesting in all the schools. Karnataka is a pioneer in this project. Different water-harvesting structures like ponds, lakes, tanks, etc. were common in ancient times and also during the British period. Each village in Orissa has ponds. But presently, most of these structures are neglected and are on the verge of extinction due to siltation. Experiments have shown that removal of bottom clay from these tanks create ten-fold increase in recharge to groundwater.

Rural Sanitation in India

Though India has made significant progress in terms of the GDP growth and is at the forefront of developing countries in all areas of economic development, half of its people largely residing in rural areas still defecate in the open and live in unhealthy and unclean environment. The main reason for this is due to lack of awareness amongst people regarding maintaining clean and healthy environment and personal health and hygiene. This could have been a minor reason few years ago, the major reason now defecate in the open is lack of toilets and other sanitation facilities in the villages. That needs sanitation technology and finances which villagers could ill-afford on their own.

People particularly in rural areas pollute rivers and water bodies by taking bath, washing clothes and utensils, throwing garbage and even defecating and urinating near water sources. This leads to not only pollution of rivers but also threatens the safety of groundwater which often is the only source of drinking water in rural areas. This leads to many life threatening and preventable water and sanitation related diseases like Polio, Malaria, and Diarrhea which mostly affect women and children. 6000 die daily from diarrheal diseases, one billion affected with intestinal worms causing nutritional deficiencies and poor growth. Both are transmitted through human faeces in the environment.

The improper disposal of waste water, open drains, polluted water bodies, stagnation of water around hand pumps also ruins the condition of roads and becomes a breeding ground for all kinds of disease producing viruses. Therefore, along with provision of sanitary latrines to prevent open defecation, the problems of Solid and Liquid Waste Management in villages has to be addressed to prevent environmental pollution and diseases.

Keeping in view the critical importance of Solid and Liquid Waste Management, Government of India has included Solid and Liquid Wastes Management in its guidelines and Panchayats may utilize 15% of its funds for this purpose. Funds allocated under the Twelfth Finance Commission may be utilized by States for enhancing sanitation coverage and invest in Solid and Liquid Wastes Management in their areas.

It is now important to make all the government agencies aware and well informed, PRIs at State, District, Block and Panchayat levels and all the rural community about the importance of use of sanitary latrines and solid and liquid waste management. Awareness and participation of community through advertisements and door to door campaign is also very important for the program. ASHA and ICDS Workers, and village level motivators may be used for awareness generation and advocacy for construction and use of toilets and solid and liquid waste management.

Along with construction of toilets, sustainability of these systems is also crucial and there is a need for developing low-cost and environmentally sustainable, viable region specific sanitation technologies and systems. On one hand, the construction of two pit latrine which uses less water must be made compulsory in all rural areas and on the other hand, new and innovative technologies like ecosanitation, use of fecal matter for Biogas, etc. must be developed.

There is need to promote sustainable sanitation technologies that promote less use of water, treat and recycle the waste streams, keeping in view the geographical variations of water scarce, water logged, flood prone areas, hilly and rocky regions where often traditional sanitation systems fail. There are many case studies available in India and worldwide in developing and implementing these innovative re-use oriented sustainable systems and approaches which need to be highlighted and replicated wherever possible.

The workshop provided a forum for all researchers and practitioners to disseminate information to the implementing agencies and in turn to the village communities on new and innovative technologies. The workshop focused on talking about combining and upgrading the old and traditional sanitation systems and technologies being used by the people; and new and innovative modern technologies without compromising on health and hygiene aspects. Training of people in villages on these new technologies along with easy accessibility and availability of raw material and marketing facilities are crucial for sustainability of these systems. This also can lead to employment generation in village and funds can be accessed through the Gramin Rozgar Yojana (National Workshop on sustainable sanitation 19th-20th May 2008, New Delhi).

Community-led Total Sanitation (CLTS) Program: Rural sanitation is a State subject. The efforts of the states are supplemented by the Central Government through technical and financial assistance under the Central Rural Sanitation Program (CRSP). The community-led total sanitation (CLTS) program was launched in 1986 with the objectives of improving the quality of life of rural people and providing privacy and dignity to women through provision of household toilets.

Total Sanitation Campaign (TSC): Due to relatively poor performance and supply driven approach of the program, Government of India restructured the program with the launch of the TSC in 1999. The restructured program advocates a participatory and demand driven approach, taking a district as a unit with significant involvement of Gram Panchayats and local communities. It moves away from the infrastructure focused approach of the earlier programs and concentrates on promoting behavior change. Further, innovative approaches have been initiated to increase rural sanitation through CLTS program that emphasizes demand for services and community action instead of supply-driven programs of latrine construction by the government. It is based on grass roots movement of local community participation.

In addition to public health implications, lack of adequate sanitation forces households into the continued indignity of open defecation, which is an acute problem especially for women and young girls. On the other hand, access to safe sanitation in schools is linked to continued education enrolment of young girls and teenage women, particularly at puberty. School sanitation has been introduced as a major component to encourage wider acceptance of sanitation among rural masses.

TSC is community-led and people-centered campaign with focus on collective achievement of 'total sanitation'. The TSC approach emphasized awareness-building component and meets the demand through alternate delivery mechanism. It focuses on Information, Education and Communication (IEC) to mobilize and motivate communities towards safe sanitation; and motivating them for changes in personal hygiene habits and behavior. Self-help groups (SHGs) and Women folk can become a driving force to ensure people's participation, and developing local specific or community specific IEC models which have tremendous impact on the reach of the program.

In Tripura, SHGs consisting of tribal women are used as 'Tribal Social Capital' to convey the message of sanitation in tribal areas. The effective co-ordination between field level functionaries of nodal department and PRI members is crucial for successful implementation of TSC. SHG groups in Tamil Nadu through an intensive IEC campaign and community mobilization strategy could achieve the commendable target of construction of 300 Individual household Latrines in 3 days. They leveraged funds for this purpose not only from TSC but also as loans from the Bank and District Rural Development Agency (DRDA). The provision of sanitation facilities has also reduced diseases in the villages.

The TSC with its clear objective of sanitation in village is progressing well due to the simplicity of the sanitation system chosen. But there is a concern that especially in some areas such as high water table area, flood prone, rocky and cold desert, some of the implemented models may be unsustainable causing water pollution, wastage and loss of resources.

CLTS is being implemented at scale in 590 districts of 30 States and Union Territories (UTs). Against a target of 108.5 million individual household toilets, the toilets reported completed is about 57 million as of October 2008. In addition, about 0.68 million school toilets, 14,540 sanitary complexes for women, and 222,267 Anganwadi (pre-school) toilets have been constructed. After a slow progress in eighties and nineties, rural sanitation coverage received a rapid growth by implementing the TCS vigorously. With the result, IHHL (Individual household latrine) coverage grew more than double, from about 22 per cent in 2001 to 57 per cent in 2008. There appears an increasing growth rate in the CLTS program from 2001 onwards, growth spurt in 2005 and from 2001 to 2008, it has been rapid growth of toilet building.

Minister for rural development informed about the construction of nearly one crore toilets every year and hoped that by end of 2009 every rural school, Anganwadi center will have proper toilets (July 2009). Adequate financial resources have been allocated for the TCS programs in 2009. Different states are likely to achieve the CLTS targets differently according to the community efforts put. Statewise Sanitation coverage trends indicate that some of the states like Tamil Nadu, West Bengal, will achieve cent per cent coverage by 2011 and 2010 respectively while states like Bihar will be able to achieve this target only by 2069 if the current rate of progress is maintained.

In June 2003, Government initiated an incentive scheme for fully sanitized and open defecation free Gram Panchayats, Blocks, and Districts called the 'Nirmal Gram Puraskar'. The incentive pattern is based on population criteria. The incentive provision is for PRIs as well as individuals and organizations that are the driving force for full sanitation coverage.

The International Year of Sanitation 2008 is an attempt to focus intense and extensive attention on sanitation. The India Sanitation Portal is a collaborative effort towards highlighting issues and successes in sanitation and drawing more attention to sanitation. It was launched at SACOSAN 2008 (the Third South Asian Conference on Sanitation) in New Delhi in Dec. 08.

Salient Projects in Sanitation

Zero waste toilets were developed by IIT Kanpur in Feb. 2009. Soon it will be possible to have flush toilets with minimal wastage of water. Led by Prof. Vinod Tare, researchers from the environmental engineering department of IIT Kanpur have developed a toilet that will re-use the water that goes into flushing rather than discharging it along with the excreta. This will be possible by not allowing water and solid waste to mix. Indian Railways has approved the design and UNICEF will be involved in pilot project involving community toilets. A basic toilet should not cost more than Rs. 5,000.

Ecosystem and Ecotechnologies for Sanitation highlighted by participants on SACOSAN (the Third South Asian Conference on Sanitation in New Delhi in Dec. 2008) focused on ecosystem and ecotechnologies for sanitation. Re-use of sanitation products in agriculture is referred to as ecological sanitation. Various challenges that are being faced by India in the Sanitation sector are: uneven progress across states and within states, quality in construction, locally suitable technologies and design adapted to needs, effectiveness of current hygiene promotion initiatives, capacity of supply chain, trained human resources, Management of NGP, Monitoring of inputs and outputs, and Inclusive programming technologies. There is strong inter-connectivity between sanitation, and other factors such as water, health, nutrition, food security, access to basic education, sustainability, women's empowerment, combat HIV/AIDS, income generation, partnership for development and foremost poverty alleviation. Ecological sanitation plays a role in food security and climate change mitigation.

For sustainability, adequate and sustained allocation of financial, technical, and human resources is necessary and we should develop safe, affordable and socially acceptable sanitation systems that encourage usage. Challenges in scaling up sustainable sanitation include know-how, capacity, attitudes, demand, credit, financing policies, etc. Reforms of national and local governments are needed in these contexts. Demand should be used as driver for sanitation promotion.

Innovative changes are required for a paradigm shift in sustainable sanitation by diversion of grey water and re-use. There is improvement of health by minimizing the introduction of pathogens from human excrements into the water cycle; such as promotion of safe recovery and use of nutrients, organics, trace elements, water and energy, preservation of soil fertility and improvement of agricultural productivity. India can learn from some of ECOSAN projects in other countries like Peru, Syria, Jordan, China and Germany to upscale and upgrade its traditional sanitation systems.

National Workshop on Sustainable Sanitation in New Delhi in May 2008 which was participated by Minister for rural development, advisor Ministry of New and Renewable Energy (MNRE) and other policymakers, and NGO participants from Sulabh International, Center for Science and Environment (CSE) and Scope, National Health Systems Resource Center and others; deliberated, observed and recommended as follows:

Dr. Shukla, Advisor, Ministry of New and Renewable Energy (MNRE) India discussed the issue of Convergence of National Biogas and Manure Management Program of MNRE and total sanitation program. Sustainable sanitation cannot be achieved unless both energy and water are available. The energy needs of the rural areas are not met adequately. Biogas based electricity generation plants in rural areas are a viable option.

MNRE is using Sintex tanks and pre-fabricated HDPE based material for making Biogas Plants in rural areas. The biogas generated in the digester, if necessary can be stored in a suitable storage unit or membrane type storage balloon. Manure management is an integral part of a biogas based power generation system for arriving at an economically feasible operation level. Marketing strategy of the biogas slurry or the value added bio-manure is required to be defined. Any new efficient system for production of biogas, cleaning of the gas and conversion of the gas to electricity, etc. can also be used subject to prior approval of the Ministry. It can be used only for meeting the extra cost involved in raising the toilet level and its connection with a biogas plant. Biogas should be used from the plant attached with the toilet and the biogas plants should be completed in all aspects. He said that there is need to make installation of biogas plants mandatory.

Participants from Sulabh International emphasized the importance of Hygiene Education in WATSAN (water and sanitation) programs which is currently not being given a priority. Hygiene Education implies improved hygiene—keeping faecal matter away from hands and food and from water itself when it is stored in the home and that transforms health. Neglect of Hygiene Education in WATSAN programs explains that these programs have often not brought the health benefits commensurate with the investment made in the Water and Sanitation Sector. Promotion of hygiene can act as the means to create demand for sanitation and thereby increase coverage and more importantly, ensure sustainability of the same. Almost all water-borne, water based and water-washed diseases are spread through exposure of food and drinking water to human faeces. Therefore, hygiene behavior should be integrated with these programs.

He also raised the challenges facing the WATSAN sector like Capacity Building of PRIs and other grass roots level organizations for Primary Health Care, Environmental Health Surveillance and Hygiene promotion, development of Nationwide network on health and hygiene, developing effective coalition with Education, Environment, Nutrition and other allied Departments for Health promotion, Institutional Development and Capacity Building in health sector for Environmental and Water Quality Surveillance along with advocacy and awareness generation on Hygiene issues.

Participants from NGO SCOPE, highlighted that SCOPE is working with the vision to empower socially and economically weaker sections of society especially women by promoting sustainable Sanitation, adoption of locale specific technology, creation of multiple technological options and networking with like-minded Partners. SCOPE has constructed over 20,000 toilets from 1986 to 2005 in villages in Musiri and Perambalur Districts of Tamil Nadu. It initiated ECOSAN model in its

Thanneerpandal area and has set up a Training center there to promote *Ecosanitation* as a viable option for areas which have high water table. Women in coastal areas learn the benefit of ECOSAN.

Policy focus needs to be especially oriented towards relatively poorer states, which require substantial investments in terms of making the hardware available to poorer households free or at affordable cost. Community toilets, as often suggested, are not the practicable options to tackle the problems in rural areas due to poor management, availability of land and cost recovery. Cheaper hardware option and a more focused IEC efforts, particularly in remote areas might largely help.

Particpants from Sulabh International Academy of Environmental Sanitation highlighted recycling and re-use of effluent from 'public toilet linked biogas plants'. These complexes take care of effective treatment of excreta with sustainable technology, i.e. biogas with effluent treatment system. Biogas can be used for Cooking and Lighting purposes. Biogas plant effluent can be used as fertilizer.

UN-HABITAT is Piloting Slum Environment Sanitation Initiative (SESI) in 20,000 households (100,000 Population) in Bhopal, Gwalior, Indore and Jabalpur in a tripartite partnership model, bringing together resources and expertise from the UN-HABITAT, Water Aid India and local Municipal Corporations. The various activities under this program are construction of Demonstration toilets; construction of Community toilets; Roof top rain water harvesting in schools etc. 16 slums in MP have been made 'open defecation free'. Biogas units from Kitchen Waste have been developed. Policy makers should help in finding localized solutions towards attaining MDG targets of sanitation.

Participants from National Health Systems Resource Center suggested that formation, strengthening, and functioning of Village Health and Sanitation Committees (VHSC) in states to play key role in NGP efforts and to push for NGP to be NGP+ focused on health outcomes.

Constitution of Health, Water, and Sanitation Mission at State and District level is highlighted.

In contexts of deliberations, National Workshop on Sustainable Sanitation in 2008, further recommended as follows:

The overall objective of CLTS and TCS should be 100% coverage of sustainable sanitation in rural areas. By sustainable we mean systems that protect freshwater resources, minimize water use and recycle the nutrients in human excreta for energy, biomass and food production. This approach naturally must include sustainable water management. For its implementation, we would need appropriate and focused funding support schemes, and to streamline and dovetail the various existing schemes. Existing subsidy schemes are not leading to sustainable sanitation solutions.

The continued introduction of creative, (non-financial) incentives should be considered. Already, various successful examples of sustainable sanitation systems are available in various parts of the country. These systems are hygienically safe, use less water, do not pollute, recover nutrients and close the loop on (waste) resource streams. These sustainable systems need to be massively and urgently scaled up to cover especially the sensitive, critical areas and zones such as prone to flood, so that the benefits of the TSC reach all of rural India.

We need a massive effort to increase capacity and know-how in sustainability in the sanitation sector. It is essential for success and sustainability that there is a large component for training, follow-up, quality management, user support and reuse. In order to support the up-scaling processes, along with the implementation, comprehensive monitoring and research has to be carried out.

We should implement and teach sustainable sanitation and water management and nutrient re-use in all schools, colleges and universities to ensure these approaches are well understood and practised by the new generation. Inter-linkages between different professional groups and institutions of various disciplines should be sought to converge knowledge.

Along the lines of the National Water Policy, *it is most important that there is a National Policy on Sanitation* that addresses the needs, challenges and solutions in the sanitation sector and will accelerate, promote and fund sustainable sanitation in rural and urban areas.

Eco Sanitation: Necessary steps for effective management of Solid Waste are sorting out or segregation at household level, treatment and management of household level and community level waste, and waste through Windrow composting, Vermi composting and Biogas plant and the focus on collection and transportation of waste is also important.

Bio-Center is a biogas generating latrine block, managed by community groups, which can be situated anywhere in a slum as it treats human waste *in-situ* without requiring sewerage infrastructure. The Bio-Center can be built with locally available technology, local unskilled labor and requires minimal maintenance as it has no movable parts.

Grey Water Use: International efforts and programs to recycle toilet grey water in villages can help in agriculture, manure to safely fertilize the farmlands and replenish minerals and organic nutrient that our soils are lacking. This can be used for laundry, gardening, etc.

Social dynamics and behavioral patterns have a significant impact on the way communities deal with water supply and wastewater management issues, particularly with respect to grey water disposal. These behavioral patterns (and the drivers associated with them) must be taken into account when assessing specific grey water management options for individual settlements. This is particularly relevant when considering grey water use options in certain areas where potable water resources are limited.

The quality of grey water in non-sewered areas differs significantly to the grey water that is generated in higher-income sewered areas. There is a greater concentration of various hazardous pollutants. There is, therefore, significant risk involved with the on-site disposal of grey water in non-sewered areas. There are two central issues regarding the strategic management of grey water which allow for health improvement, water conservation, use (where possible) and environmental protection: (i) Challenge of turning grey water into a beneficial resource if it does not constitute a hazard. (ii) Response to crisis situations where grey water becomes a health hazard, e.g. in densely populated settlements. (iii) Health aspects—adequate controls must be in place to ensure that the risk of infection from any pathogenic organisms present in the grey water is negligible. (iv) Soil conditions should be suitable, or measures in place, to prevent damage to the soil resulting from the long-term application of grey water with high levels of salinity. The above issues imply that there is a need for strong institutional support and monitoring if the beneficial use of grey water is to be considered.

International Foundation for Science (IFS/SIDA) Sustainable Sanitation Initiative

This initiative aims at strengthening scientific capacity in the fields of sustainable sanitation and greywater re-use in developing countries. The overall purpose is to generate new knowledge relevant for a deepened understanding of crosscutting biological, chemical, technical and socio-economic factors that are necessary for development of technology for sustainable sanitation and grey water re-use. This will improve the livelihood of poor people also.

One major component of the global water crisis is the contamination of drinking water supplies with human waste. Some 2.4 billion individuals have no sanitation at all or are obliged to use a toilet that is totally unhygienic. The situation is unlikely to change soon if conventional approaches are continually promoted. With rapid urbanization, population growth, growing income disparities and increasing water scarcity, conventional approaches are becoming increasingly too costly, too complex, or just plain technically inappropriate. Still, the problem could be alleviated by refining and implementing existing technologies.

Beside all other pollutants, there is basic lack of good sewage system, lack of toilets for everyone in India. The poor defecate in the open. The amount of fecal matter and water is staggering and predictable result is raft of diseases and numerous viruses.

Environment

Narula (2008b) suggests that quality of life that people enjoy empowers them. Quality of life is affected not only by personal habits and choices, but it is also affected by the air that we breathe, the water we drink, the agricultural or dairy products we eat, the climatic changes that we enjoy or suffer, and the fuel energy we use for our daily needs, and the industries developing around us and the technologies. This suggests that environment factors are important variables for the quality of life. India is moving ahead by growing its economy by expanding the growth in various domains but it should not be at the cost of downgrading the quality of life and the clean basic amenities to its people.

India has to face the challenge of environmental issues particularly environmental pollution when transforming its economy through various industrial and other modes. These factors are controllable by individuals to some extent by keeping their environments clean and healthy, to a greater extent by governance by making efforts by good administrative practices to control the environment factors. Here, good governance and politics are important. But the environmental factors need greatest global control for better quality of life. The geo-politics play important role in this context. Therefore, it is imperative that awareness, information and knowledge about environmental issues be created locally, nationally and globally by government, people, environment activists and watch groups and by progressive environment policies both at national and global levels. Along with it, it is imperative that people, the leaders in various domains make efforts.

Villagers need to preserve their environment by preserving greenery around, not create pollution by dirty ponds, river or stream flowing nearby and other waterways to prevent mosquitoes menace, keeping the gutters, and dirt roads in the villages free of garbage and polluted and stagnant water to prevent flies, mosquitoes and other vermin/bacteria to grow and spread diseases. Even the fuel they use for cooking, such as firewood etc. is harmful for health. They must also find alternatives in the village itself like community created bio-gas etc. wherever possible.

Energy efficiency and conservation are most challenging in rural areas. World Bank "Human Development Report 2007-08—Fighting Climate Change: Human Solidarity in a Divided World," the global climate change threatens to undermine India's efforts to improve the well-being of its poorest people. The report, which focuses on the impact of climate change on the world's poor and vulnerable, highlights that the role of energy in human development is reflected in the record of CO_2. The report calls for greater efforts in developing countries to 'climate proof' infrastructure, deepen social protection for those who are most vulnerable, build community resilience and strengthen disaster response.

Major functions of the centre include collection, compilation, and dissemination of information related to environment and rural development to promote the participation of PRIs in environmental conservation. The climatic changes can affect the rainfalls, groundwater, seasonal temperatures in rural areas in India and these can affect the agriculture produce. The periodic IEC campaigns by government and NGOs creates awareness and to promote environmental consciousness among the rural masses, and motivate them to clean and preserve environment around them. Good environment means low diseases and better health. Gram Vikas model has been facilitating poor communities to come together to establish, operate, and manage their own water supply and sanitation systems through Rural Health and Environment Program (RHEP). Poor sanitation and water supply services in parts of rural areas have adversely affected the quality of the rural environment.

The current rural environmental health improvement program is led by rural communities. Community participation is important for better rural environment. It is a progress from 1982 village experience of learned dependency on government to clean the villages.

Rural Housing

According to the National Family Health Survey by the government in 2000, only 19 per cent of the rural population lives in pucca (brick) houses, while the remaining live in kaccha (mud, thatched) and semi-pucca houses with mud walls and thatched roofs. Eighty-seven per cent of the homes in the villages do not have toilet facilities. Cooking is usually done inside the house under inadequate ventilation with biomass such as dried cow-dung, fire-wood, dry weeds or crop residue, exasperating the risk of tuberculosis. The 2001 Indian Census estimated that 40 per cent of the rural houses do not have separate kitchens. When cooking is done inside the house, it is usually on the floor in the corner of a room, sometimes separated by a half-wall. Smoke fills the entire house during cooking, but occupants usually prefer to remain inside. Coughing and spitting are the resulting outcome, symptomatic of what finally leads to chronic illnesses.

When government builds homes for lower castes, it ensures this caste separation. In many instances, government sets up housing colonies exclusively for Scheduled Castes and Tribes, and hence, an entire new village might consist of families belonging to only those castes.

While the government is the main promoter of housing schemes, several NGOs and social entrepreneurship ventures have also entered the arena. For the most part, NGOs have to rely on donor funds that are hard to come by, and hence, their contribution has not been significant. Social entrepreneurs who expect a certain return on their investment are focusing on lower middle-class customers who are able to repay the mortgage or pay adequate rental; these investors have not found a suitable financial arrangement to offer housing to those who cannot pay interest.

Housing as Part of Community Development: In arriving at a new strategy for housing, planners must not lose sight of its other inter-related goals such as offering basic amenities, preventing diseases, and assuring social justice. Providing rural housing to people is imperative to improve the quality of their life. The programs have started in 1985 but had not made much headway for years. We need community, government and other multi-agencies efforts and coordination to make rural housing viable. The current efforts are on P4 model focusing on multi-stakeholders efforts.

According to George Abraham (2008), housing is interrelated with other aspects of life such as health and education. For example, children cannot study in a poorly lit house. Respiratory disorders among rural population in India are often the result of unfavorable housing and poor living conditions. Asthma and bronchitis are caused by pollen grains, dust mites, animal waste and several environmental factors are related to bad housing conditions. Poor sanitation and hygiene, inadequate ventilation and smoke inhalation are all associated aspects of poor housing that affects health and social development.

The Government is implementing *Indira Awaas Yojana* (IAY) since the year 1985-86 to provide financial assistance for construction and upgradation of dwelling units to the below poverty line (BPL) rural households belonging to the scheduled castes, scheduled tribes and freed bonded laborers categories. From the year 1993-94, the scope of the scheme was extended to cover non-Scheduled Castes and Scheduled Tribes rural BPL families, subject to the condition that the benefits to non-SC/ST would not be more than 40% of the total IAY allocation. The benefits of the scheme have also been extended to the families of ex-servicemen of the armed and paramilitary forces killed in action, 3% of the houses are reserved for the rural BPL, physically and mentally challenged persons. 2006-07 onward, funds and physical targets under IAY are also being earmarked for BPL minorities in each state.

***Financial Assistance for Construction and Upgradation*:** The ceiling on construction assistance under the IAY has been enhanced w.e.f. 1.4.2008, from Rs. 25,000/- to Rs. 35,000/- per unit in the plain areas and from Rs. 27,500/- to Rs. 38,500/- in hilly/difficult areas. For upgradation of kutcha house, the financial assistance has also been enhanced from Rs. 12,500/- to Rs. 15,000/- per unit. In addition, The Reserve Bank of India has been requested by the Ministry of Finance to include

IAY houses under the Differential Rate of Interest (DRI) scheme for lending up to Rs. 20,000/- per unit at an interest rate of 4%. Further, the dwelling units should invariably be allotted in the name of a female member of the beneficiary household. Alternatively, it can be allotted in the name of both husband and wife. Only in case there is no eligible female member in the family, the house can be allotted in the name of an eligible male member only.

Essentials: The Sanitary latrine and smokeless chullah (kitchen stove) and proper drainage are required for each IAY house. The construction of the houses is the sole responsibility of the beneficiary. Engagement of contractors is strictly prohibited. No specific type design has been stipulated for an IAY house. Choice of design, technology and materials for construction of an IAY house is the sole discretion of the beneficiaries.

Targets: About 181.51 lakh houses have been constructed under IAY since inception of the Scheme with an expenditure of Rs. 36,900.41 crore (up to 31/5/2008). During 2007-08, the Central allocation for Rural Housing was Rs. 40,322.70 crore. The target for construction and upgradation of IAY houses was 21.27 lakh. Against this target, 19.88 lakh houses were constructed and upgraded by incurring an amount of Rs. 5458.01 crore (including State share). The Central allocation for 2008-09 under the IAY is Rs. 5,645.77 crore for the target of constructing and upgrading 21.27 lakh IAY houses. Out of this, an amount of Rs. 1,694.48 crore has been released as part of first installment and 85,879 houses have been constructed so far (upto 31-5-2008). 60 lakh houses were to be constructed by 2008-09.

(*Source*: National Portal Content Management Team, Reviewed on: 31-03-2009)

To double target 12 million rural houses by 2014; government will introduce new housing scheme "Rajiv Awas Yojana" for slum-dwellers, urban poor Scheme on lines of existing Indira Awaas Yojana for rural poor. The PMGY envisages allocation of Additional Central Assistance (ACA) to the States and UTs for providing and improving the outlay of

Basic Minimum Services including "Rural Shelter" in the rural areas.

Schemes for affordable housing proposed via partnership Scheme for interest subsidy for urban housing is to be part of Rajiv Awas Yojana. States will get support for housing under JNNURM if they give property rights to slum dwellers.

Pradhan Mantri Adarsh Gram Yojana (PMAGY)

There are about 44,000 villages in which the population of Scheduled Castes is above 50 per cent. A new scheme called Pradhan Mantri Adarsh Gram Yojana (PMAGY) is being launched in 2009 on a pilot basis, for the integrated development of 1000 such villages. In the budget 2009-10, an allocation of Rs. 100 crore for this scheme is proposed. Each village would be able to avail gap funding of Rs. 10 lakh over and above the allocations under Rural Development and Poverty Alleviation Schemes. On successful implementation of the pilot phase, the Yojana would be extended in coming years.

The Action Plan for Rural Housing in 2009

It consists of the following components: (i) Provision for upgradation of unserviceable kutcha houses in Indira Awaas Yojana (IAY) in addition to new construction. (ii) Pradhan Mantri Gramodaya Yojana, Gramin Awaas, and Credit-cum-Subsidy Scheme for Rural Housing.

Credit-cum-Subsidy Scheme for Rural Housing: The Credit-cum-Subsidy Scheme for Rural Housing has been launched with effect from 1st April, 1999. The Scheme targets rural families having annual income up to Rs. 32,000. While subsidy is restricted to Rs. 10,000, the maximum loan amount that can be availed is Rs. 40,000. The subsidy portion is shared by the Centre and the State in 75:25 ratio. The loan portion is to be disbursed by the Commercial Banks, Regional Rural Banks, and Housing Finance Institutions. During the current financial year 2009, a provision of Rs. 82 crore has been kept under this scheme for the construction of 1.09 lakh houses.

Cheap finance for housing loans for villagers who do not qualify under specified brackets is a very important area where they probably need to strengthen National Housing Bank or they need to promote or encourage various micro finance agencies to work for providing credit to these consumers at the bottom of the pyramid.

Rural housing sector could get a big boost as the Budget 2009-10 has allocated Rs. 2,000 crore to the National Housing Bank's Fund dedicated to the sector. The allocation will help NHB dip into its Rural Housing Fund to refinance housing finance companies (HFCs) lending for rural housing. The HFCs will be able to get low-cost funds from NHB (Date: July 2009).

Innovative Stream for Rural Housing and Habitat Development: With a view to encourage innovative, cost effective and environment-friendly solutions in building and housing sectors in rural areas, this Scheme has been launched with effect from April 1999. During 1999-2000, Rs. 2.53 crore was released under this Scheme. During current financial year 2009-10, Rs. 10 crore is available under this Scheme. An amount of Rs. 3.95 crore has been released under the Scheme so far during 2009-2010. Rural Building Centers, Samagra Awaas Yojana and enhancement in equity contribution by Ministry of Rural Development to HUDCO is being set up.

Setting up Innovative Streams

Rural Building Centers: The objectives are: (a) Technology transfer and information dissemination, (b) Skill up-gradation through training, and (c) Production of cost-effective and environment-friendly materials and components. During the first year of the operation of the Scheme in 1999-2000, it was proposed to set up 2 Building Centers in each of the States. One was to be set up by a Governmental institution and the other by an NGO. The limit of these Building Centers per State has been increased to 4 during the current year. During 1999-2000, 9 project proposals for setting up of these Centers were approved and funds to the extent of Rs. 54 lakh released. During the current year 2009, 22 project proposals have already been approved and Rs. 1.32 crore released. The total allocation under this Scheme for the current year is Rs. 3.00 crores. For setting up a Building Center, a one-time grant of

Rs. 15 lakh is provided, which is released in 3 instalments in the ratio 40:40:20.

Samagra Awaas Yojana: It is a comprehensive housing scheme launched in 1999-2000, with a view to ensuring integrated provision of shelter, sanitation and drinking water. During the first phase of its implementation, it has been decided to take up Samagra Awaas Yojana in one block each of 25 districts of 24 States and one Union Territory which have been identified for implementing participatory approach under the Accelerated Rural Water Supply Program. The existing Schemes of housing, drinking water and sanitation follow the normal funding pattern. However, a special Central Assistance of Rs. 25 lakh is provided for each block for undertaking overall habitat development and for Information, Education and Communication (IEC) campaigns. Community contributes 10%.

So far, an amount of Rs. 351.90 lakh has been released for implementation of the Scheme in the States of Madhya Pradesh, Tamil Nadu, West Bengal, Karnataka, Himachal Pradesh, Kerala, Tripura, Gujarat, Rajasthan, Haryana, Punjab and Assam. Remaining States have also been encouraged to take up the implementation of the Scheme in their States. The coverage of the Scheme is proposed to be extended after assessing the impact of the Scheme in the States where it is already in operation.

Equity Support to HUDCO: To meet the requirement of Economically Weaker Section (EWS) and Lower Income Group (LIG) people in rural areas and to improve the outreach of housing finance in rural areas, it has been decided to increase the equity support to HUDCO. The resources raised by HUDCO as a consequence of increased equity share capital participation by the Ministry of Rural Development, is targeted to be used exclusively in the rural areas. Already, a separate dedicated Rural Housing Cell has been set up in HUDCO, which is the operational arm of the Ministry of Rural Development for the setting up of Rural Building Centers.

HUDCO through Human Settlement Management Institute (HSMI) also supports the training requirements of

Rural Housing sector professionals. Since 2000-01 onwards, it has been decided by the Ministry that State specific programs will be organized through Human Settlement & Management Institute (HSMI) with the objective of promoting State Specific technologies, materials, designs, etc. for cost-effective rural housing. In this context, HSMI conducts state-specific training meant for Project Directors, Executive Engineers, Assistant Engineers and NGOs.

National Mission for Rural Housing and Habitat: This Scheme is a part of the comprehensive Pradhan Mantri Gramodaya Yojana introduced during the current year 2009 to achieve the objective of sustainable human development at the village level. This has been set up by the Ministry of Rural Development to facilitate the induction of science and technology inputs on a continuous basis into the sector and providing convergence of technology, habitat and energy related issues with a goal to provide affordable shelter for all in rural areas within a specified time frame and through community participation. In this regard, an Executive Council under the Chairmanship of Minister of Rural Development and an Empowered Committee under the Chairmanship of the Secretary, Rural Development has been constituted. The PMGY envisages allocation of Additional Central Assistance (ACA) to the States and UTs for providing and improving the outlay of Basic Minimum Services including "Rural Shelter" in the rural areas in 2009.

Focus on Improving Rural Housing

Rural Houses: A traditional rural residence has important advantages—it is almost based on adaptations to the local environment, and is often built with the labor of the villagers themselves without the need for external mechanized inputs. The simplest way to build a house, in the past, was to look around for the materials needed for the structure, and begin building the structure yourself. For the construction of village homes, therefore, the challenge today is to acknowledge people's desire for long-lasting structures, and thereafter, ask what elements of functionality, value and aesthetics can be infused into the buildings.

M.N. Joglekar, a former Executive Director of HUDCO took up this challenge. An architect, he went beyond the standard knowledge of construction to study not just how these houses are constructed but how they are lived in. He set out to use rationalized traditional technologies, which are amply displayed at the Rural Building Center of National Institute of Rural Development (NIRD) in Hyderabad. Fourteen typologies of rural buildings—from those in the Himalayan region to the hilly North-East to the rain-battered coasts to arid Kutch and the Deccan Plateau, are displayed in the Rural Technology Park of NIRD campus. Recognizing the great potential in promoting local-material-based traditional technologies, HUDCO had initiated the Rural Building Center concept where building components can be manufactured by the rural people using locally available material and through skill up-gradation. Through this center, pre-cast components could be given to the rural people instead of cash, which is the typical form of assistance for home construction.

In 2008, HUDCO and Hari Om Ashram Trust—Nadiad, Gujarat have jointly sponsored the competition on 'Innovative Design & Construction of EWS (Rural) Houses in India' to encourage organizations who have designed and executed such projects, and have taken care to provide other developmental facilities like healthcare, education, community assets and income generating activities and other amenities in the houses. The sponsors planned not only to honor them for the exemplary work done by them, and would also like to disseminate their experiences so that more people come forward to improve the living conditions of the rural poor. The rural housing scheme is primarily aimed at ameliorating the housing problems of the economically weaker sections in villages throughout the country.

Rural Housing Survey (2008-09)

An analysis of the housing scene in the rural areas suggests continued poor quality of the rural housing stock in the country, though considerable improvements in quality have been indicated over the period. Also, while there has been continuous growth in the rural housing stock, its pace has been lower than urban housing. The rural areas in India are characterized by small and highly dispersed habitations, apart from a poor village or community level infrastructure. Also, as the principal occupation of most rural households is agriculture or its related activities, the space requirements of these households, apart from for residential uses, are for livestock and storage of grains and agricultural implements. It is only lately there has been an increase in non-agricultural employment.

Most of the poor households are reported to live in one- or two-room units. A dismal finding is the lack of access to basic amenities like drinking water, toilet and bathing facilities, and cooking space. The situation is particularly alarming in respect to toilet and bathing facilities. Access to electricity is somewhat better with over 60% households reporting electricity connections, especially for lighting purposes.

The survey also assessed the status of physical infrastructure and housing environment. Almost 50% of households have closed drainage systems, with hardly any inter-quintile variation. A little over half of the households are connected to paved roads, and about 10% are without any approach road. Our inquiry on the use of housing premises revealed that about 20% of the households had detached sheds for cattle and another 7% had sheds attached to the house. As to be expected, most households with detached sheds are relatively better-off. Also, a little over 10% of the households were reported to have separate sheds either for storage of output and or for keeping implements. In others, cattle would share the house at night, agriculture and other implements would also be stored.

The survey reveals that most households reported increases in income over the past decade with land-owning households showing about 25% increase. An analysis for this increase is an improvement in crop yields and better wages. While crop income and wages helped the bottom 60%, the top 40% benefitted from improved business activities and salaries. A positive feature is the widespread optimism among rural households with regard to their incomes over the next

10 years. This optimism is stronger among the richest 40% households.

In the context of housing, factors such as availability of land, skilled labor and building materials are critical. About 40% have their houses on agricultural land and an equal proportion on non-agricultural land. About 10% of houses are on Panchayat-government land. The houses on Panchayat land belong to the poor. Nearly one-fifth of the households felt that acquiring land is not easy. In case of building materials, most households were satisfied, save for the fact that materials are usually sourced from outside the village. It is the availability of skilled labor that seems to pose a problem.

In rural areas, tenants comprise about 2-3%, and most plan to build houses largely from savings aided by loans from cooperative societies. A small percentage is planning to tap bank finance and government help.

The rising average levels of income in rural India have led to increasing demand for all amenities, including housing. There is a strong impact of household income on housing development in terms of space, durability of construction or amenities. As income increases, demand for housing can be expected to rise. More innovative financial products would be needed to meet their requirements. As for expenditure priority on ownership of various assets, about 80% of households view buying a house important. Rural Infrastructure development is likely to influence householders' decisions on construction (Ministry of rural development/housing New Delhi).

Salient Private Partnership Efforts for Rural Housing

Holcim Initiative for Rural Housing: The world's leading cement manufacturer, the Switzerland-based Holcim Group, has mandated the National Council for Applied Economic Research (NCAER), New Delhi to conduct the first comprehensive study on rural housing in India in 2008.

The study 'Rural Housing in India' aims to review the current status of housing in rural India with a view to assess the prospects for its growth. The report will identify the regional barriers and drivers of growth in rural housing. The final report will also provide insights that would help develop customized solutions to address the problem of inadequate housing in rural India.

NCAER will review the existing policies and programs of the Union and State governments to consider the potential role for public-private partnerships in the area of rural housing.

While, housing for the rural poor has received considerable policy attention, the issues and constraints facing the rural population are relatively unexplored.

Holcim is also working towards developing a new business initiative for India that will cater specifically towards rural housing and infrastructure segment. Holcim's Indian group company ACC has already signed a formal MoU with a leading NGO. "Holcim has vast experiences in developing the housing consumer segment. We have successful models already operating in countries including Indonesia and Mexico. It is our responsibility to take a lead in developing sustainable and innovative solutions to serve the rural market."

Strong cement demand in early 2009 is result of rural demand. The demand was already there but it increased because of the free cash flow available in the rural sector. The government last year left a lot of money by loan waivers and rural employment schemes that have created enough economic gains there. Everything depends on gross domestic product (GDP) growth and how other sectors are doing. Cement is a core sector business, so demand depends on how the other sectors are doing.

SDC Initiatives and Rural Housing: The Swiss agency for Development and Cooperation (SDC) works in India with a central focus on poverty reduction. Geographically, its cooperation program has been concentrated on semi-arid regions of the Karnataka, Andhra Pradesh, Maharashtra; as well as on Kerala, Rajasthan, Orissa, Sikkim and Gujarat. SDC's programs have contributed to people's empowerment and poverty reduction by focusing on retention and sustainable use of water, rural energy and housing, rural finance and employment creation.

SDC in 2006 engaged into a new type of collaboration with India. The new program involves a shift from traditional and classical development cooperation, towards collaboration based on common interests and shared investments, with the ultimate aim of reducing poverty. A key feature of this program is the exchange of know-how and technologies between Switzerland and India.

The purpose of SDC's Global Environment Program (GEP) is to support developing countries in their efforts to implement the UN framework Conventions in the global environment domain. *Since 1992, the SDC India program has used Global Environment Program (GEP) framework to create options for disadvantaged sectors of the population, an opportunity to benefit from affordable and environmentally friendly technologies that make it possible to save energy, use renewable sources of energy, reduce pollution and facilitate the application of global environmental instruments that promote both local and global sustainability in the area of rural housing*, SDC concluded its involvement in June 2007.

Climate change constitutes the main focus area of the cooperation supported by SDC in India. It primarily includes innovative programs with a link to national, regional and global policy dialogue. The programs are designed to support efforts towards adaptation to the effects of a changing climate situation as well as towards mitigation of the causes of climate change by promoting renewable energy and energy efficiency measures. *SDC furthermore supports programs at the interface between climate change, food security, and disaster risk reduction.*

SDC partners are: Public sector entities in India such as government departments; academic and research institutions; Civil society organizations and advocacy groups; relevant private enterprises in the context of multi-stakeholder partnership; professional associations and other development actors.

An Assessment of Future Scenario

The study shows demand for housing stock for 2008 to 2025 under two alternative scenarios—business as usual (BAU) and higher growth (HG). The projected numbers of houses increase at an average annual rate of 1.48% and 1.56% under the BAU and HG scenarios respectively. The rate of increase in housing demand is related to the assumption of higher rate of income growth as compared to the BAU situation. During the 17-year period of 2008-2025, the rural housing stock is projected to rise by 42-44 million under both scenarios.

The projections draw attention to the need for continued expansion of rural housing. The projections presented here relate to the total housing stock and the distinction between kuccha and durable construction. The changes in terms of space, design, number of rooms and amenities in the house are of importance in improving the quality of housing. These changes may also be continuous in the nature of 'up-gradation of the house'.

Observations

An active housing sector in rural areas could indeed be both, a direct catalyst for promoting greater economic activity as it provides considerable employment at the local level and would also help in improving the health and productivity of rural inhabitants. Given the multiple dimensions of the rural housing challenges, a coordinated strategy needs to be evolved. Recognizing the fact that there are strong regional and local dimensions to rural housing requirements, local-level institutional arrangements to encourage rural housing construction are necessary. Policy initiatives for technical and financial assistance available in rural areas will stimulate rural housing. The trends suggest that there is considerable demand for improvement in rural housing conditions.

Rural Electrification

Key Issues in Rural Electrification

Electricity often profoundly affects village life. It can expand the productive and social hours in the day. Radios and television become accessible and provide affordable entertainment and education. Most important, electrification brings with it, expectations for progress and a better future.

Yet in many countries including India, where other infrastructure such as roads, drinking water, and sanitation is also needed, village electrification does not receive the priority allocations for subsidized funding that its advocates would wish for. The costs for rural electrification are higher than providing electricity in urban areas.

The difficulties in bringing electricity to rural areas are formidable. Low population densities result in high capital and operating costs. Consumers are often poor and their electricity consumption is low and cannot pay for use unless free or highly subsidized. Over and above, politicians interfere with the planning and operations of programs, insisting on favored constituents.

Many of the rural households in India do not have electricity and use kerosene for lighting lamps. Even for those rural areas, which are electrified, there is a tremendous shortage of power supply. Moreover, with any problems in the national grid, rural areas are affected the most, since the State Electricity Boards (SEB) provide urban areas with electricity on priority basis.

The Government of India recognizes the crucial connection of energy to the 'Millennium Development Goals' and to cut extreme poverty, disease and hunger by 2015. Despite of high costs, it is giving priority to rural electrification initiative which is expected to directly contribute to the development of rural areas by stimulating growth in education, healthcare, nutrition programs, and telecommunication, as well as businesses both, rural enterprises and others. Since access to electricity-energy is main supporting element for economic development to occur, the government is rightly setting ambitious targets to expand access to energy for 'empowering' the rural sector.

India's energy supply is inadequate to meet the demand arising from dynamic economic growth. Energy consumption is rising by 9 to 12 per cent per year. A stable, environmentally sound energy supply is a basic pre-condition for sustainable economic growth in India and for global climate protection. The important issues include energy efficiency, renewables, emissions trading, and the Clean Development Mechanism (CDM).

In rural electrification (RE) programs, improving efficiency in the generation, transmission and consumption of power is an important objective. The use of renewables (hydropower, wind energy, solar energy, and biomass) is seen as particularly important. Support is also accorded to programs that help reform the structures of the energy sector.

In a recent study of rural electrification (RE) in Asia, projects supported by the World Bank have had a satisfactory record, overall their economic returns have been considerably lower than projected and a wide range of expected indirect and external benefits have not materialized. In India, RE has had a crucial role to play in the spread of irrigated farming, in conjunction with other agriculture development programs. But experience in general shows that RE does not provide a primary stimulus for regional development through industrial growth. The study recommends more rigorous economic and financial analysis and improved tariff and demand management policies.

Experience suggests that the main reason is that most RE programs involved high costs but yielded fewer benefits than expected. The hard cost for consideration are investment cost, generation costs. Many of the benefits claimed for RE have not materialized, or have been much smaller than expected. One of the most persistent claims for RE is that, it can induce industrial growth in otherwise lagging low-income rural economies. The evidence from developing countries does not support this claim; RE has not, by itself, triggered industrial growth or regional development. In certain circumstances, however, it has supported growth led by a dynamic agricultural sector.

The study found that where other prerequisites of sustained development were absent, demand for electricity for productive uses did not grow. (An important exception is demand for electricity for water pumping to spread irrigated farming.) Without agricultural growth, the use of electricity in rural areas has remained low, and many of the expected economic benefits of electrification have not been realized.

Rural Electrification Programs

Government is using its own resources for RE programs. Since these resources are limited; there is innovative effort to meet the energy needs of rural Indians through *Public-Private and International partnerships*; these have been helping government's efforts for RE and to create the conditions necessary for more rural towns and villages to enter the economic mainstream.

USAID-GE India Projects: DRUM and Rural Electrification Partnership Project of USAID-GE India, India Government and India's Private Sector Malavalli Power Plant Private Limited are two major projects, cited for continuing RE efforts both by conventional and non-conventional energy sources. Government's own focused RE programs, Accelerated Rural Electrification Program (AREP), Rajiv Gandhi Grameen Vidyutikaran Yojana (RGGVY) and other smaller ones also highlights its efforts.

Accelerated Rural Electrification Program (AREP)

Indian government has directed Rs. 563.87 crore in the Tenth Plan under the Accelerated Rural Electrification Program (AREP), a scheme of 'Interest Subsidy' under the AREP for the electrification of non-electrified villages, hamlets, dalit bastis and tribal villages. This is increased in 11th plan and in budget 2009-10.

Interest subsidy under AREP Scheme is provided to State Governments and Power Utilities on loan availed by it from any financial institutions like Rural Electrification Corporation, Power Finance Corporation, Rural Infrastructure Development Fund, National Agricultural Bank and Rural Development for carrying out rural electrification programs which help to achieve national objectives of the Government for complete electrification of villages by 2007 and coverage of all households by 2012.

In addition, the government provides financial assistance to states under Pradhan Mantri Gramodaya Yojana (PMGY) and Minimum Needs Programs (MNP) for rural electrification. During the year 2002-03, an amount of Rs. 363 crore and Rs. 600 crore were released under PMGY and MNP respectively. In addition, Rs. 98.79 crore was released as grant to states under Kutir Jyoti Program during the year 2002-03. Under Kutir Jyoti Scheme, an allocation of Rs. 100 crore has been made for the year 2003-04.

Rajiv Gandhi Grameen Vidyutikaran Yojana (RGGVY)

Government of India, in April 2005, launched the scheme 'Rajiv Gandhi Grameen Vidyutikaran Yojana (RGGVY)—Scheme of Rural Electricity Infrastructure and Household Electrification' for NCMP, goal of providing access to electricity to all rural households in 5 years. The scheme is being implemented through REC. Under the scheme, 90% capital subsidy is being provided by Govt. of India for overall cost.

REC continues to play an active role in creating new infrastructure and improving the existing ones under the transmission and distribution network in the country. In line with the country's objective to provide power for all by the year 2012 and also reduce the AT&C losses, the Company has been financing schemes for expansion and strengthening of the transmission network and more importantly, modernizing of the distribution system.

Asian Development Bank (ADB) has approved in-principle, a line of credit amounting to US $225 million to REC on 27.11.08 to finance power transmission and distribution networks in the rural sector. The loan documentation is expected to be completed during 2009-10 and loan withdrawal is expected to commence during 2009-10.

Electrification of villages and BPL Households: Initial approval was for implementation of Phase I of the scheme for capital subsidy of Rs. 5,000 crore during Tenth-Plan period. 235 projects covering 1,80,699 villages (68,763 unelectrified and 1,11,936 electrified villages) with the total sanctioned project cost of Rs. 9733 crore was sanctioned by the Ministry of Power for implementation in Tenth-Plan period. Further approval has been accorded for capital subsidy of Rs. 28,000 crore for continuation of the scheme in Eleventh Plan for attaining the goal of providing access to electricity to villages. Definition of electrified village is where minimum 10% village households are electrified. During the 2008-09 year, 1,88,743 electric irrigation pump sets were reported energized under REC financed schemes.

Contribution of REC in promotion of Renewable and Decentralized Distributed Generation (DDG) Projects: So far, the REC has financed various Renewable Projects. Under the scheme, works have been completed in 48,533 villages (including 12,056 non-electrified and 36,477 electrified villages) and connections to 36.22 lakh rural households including 30.84 lakh BPL households have been provided during 2008-09.

RGGVY provides for DDG projects from conventional or renewable non-conventional sources such as biomass, biogas, mini hydro, and solar, etc. for villages where grid connectivity is either not feasible or not cost effective. DDG Systems are small power generation units near the load centers. 90% capital subsidy would be provided under RGGVY towards overall cost of the DDG projects under the scheme, excluding the amount of state or local taxes, which will be borne by the concerned State Utility. 10% of the project cost would be contributed by states through own resources or loan from financial institutions. A provision of Rs. 540 crore has been kept as subsidy for DDG projects under Eleventh Plan. The Guidelines for DDG projects under RGGVY have been issued by Ministry of Power on 12.1.2009.

Indian Energy Exchange (IEX): The country's first power exchange commenced operations in June 2008. REC is one of the co-promoters and holds equity to the extent of 4.68% in the venture. The core promoters of IEX are Financial Technologies India Ltd. (FTIL) and Power Trading Corporation of India Ltd. (PTC). Currently, it trades for the day ahead electricity market. IEX is India's first-ever, nationwide, automated, and online electricity trading platform. It is a demutualised exchange that enables efficient price discovery and price risk management.

REC is financing four projects under Clean Development Mechanism (CDM): Energy Efficiency Program-I has received government approval in January 2009 for availing carbon credits under offices and Training Center (CIRE) across the country. CIRE also conducted 11 programs on Distribution Reforms Upgrades and Management (DRUM) projects.

REC is emerging as a role model amongst the international agencies for foreign countries' seeking to promote and facilitate improved access to modern energy services in their rural areas. Recently, in 2009, many countries' delegations visited for consultations and also visited a RGGVY project having rural infrastructure.

Electrification of Remote Villages: Under the remote village electrification program, a target of electrifying 5000 remote villages has been set for in Tenth Plan against which, about 1944 remote villages and 594 remote hamlets have been electrified as on 31.03.05 since the inception of this program in 2001-02. A total of 403 remote villages/hamlets in 11 States have been electrified under this program during 2004-05 alone (Source Rural Electrification company annual report 2008-09).

New Initiatives for Creating Renewable Energy

Rural India does contribute to energy renewables—hydropower, wind energy, solar energy, and biomass to create energy efficiency for rural consumption.

Test Projects for creating 'Energy Security' in Villages: The Ministry formulated a concept of providing "energy security" in villages through biomass and other renewable energy sources. 24 test projects on Village Energy Security have been sanctioned during the year 2009-10. Employment opportunities for about 25 persons per village are expected in these projects. On the basis of the outcome of the test projects, a full-fledged program covering remote villages/hamlets may be formulated.

Major thrust is being given towards research, development, demonstration, commercialization and deployment of new and renewable energy systems/devices for transportation, portable and stationary applications for rural, urban, industrial and commercial areas.

Alternate Fuels for surface transportation including electric/hydrogen and hybrid vehicles. Bio-fuel is being developed for motive power for stationary and portable applications. A steering group, set up by the National Hydrogen Energy Board, under Shri Ratan Tata, is preparing final action plan for public-private partnership and the road map for hydrogen energy. A new component of cow dung-based power plants have been introduced in the biogas program.

Solar Electrification in Rural Areas: In India, one can already find LED solar lanterns from Tata BP Solar, which use high-power LEDs and work five hours every night on a single charge, which may be extended to run for a good 10 hours or even more by further research. Outdoor solar-powered lighting systems are also available in both LED and CFL versions. There are several pioneers in India who believe that the combination of solar and LEDs will provide a boon as far as rural electrification is concerned. LEDs lamps could also be used for rural electrification. Perhaps, lesser electricity poles would be required, if all of these poles were electrified by solar and used to light all of those LED lamps.

Copper Wiring Helps Rural Electrification: Support Rural electrification program of Government of India and Help make Rural Electrification successful. Copper India suggested Strategies of Wiring design & Specifications for "Below Poverty Line" (BPL) houses, and Training of village electricians and contractors in safe wiring practices and to support state utilities and central PSUs implement specifications.

REC agrees to the fact that copper is a better material in terms of safety, reliability, durability and maintenance and agrees to change the specification to only copper for BPL house wiring. But the subsidy by REC for BPL house wiring is not sufficient for meeting the standards and specifications. ICPCI is helping REC with wiring design for BPL houses and to arrive at a reasonable grant per BPL. REC recognizes the issue and subsidy amount is under scrutiny for upward revision.

The forward path taken is carrying 'Awareness campaign' amongst the electricians in villages for best wiring practices. The Special focus is on Uttar Pradesh, Bihar, Uttarakhand, Jharkhand, West Bengal, Orissa, Assam and Meghalaya States. Official launch of the project is October 2007 and Project completion is March 2009 (Source: India Copper Forum 2007).

Micro-utility Initiative for Rural Electrification

However, the recently enacted Electricity Act 2003, allows for the first time in India private utility companies to produce and distribute power. This provides a glimmer of hope not only for the country but more so for the rural areas. Hence, small rural private and cooperative power utilities can be empowered to supply electricity quickly and efficiently.

Nimbkar Agricultural Research Institute in Phaltan, Maharashtra. Study has shown that each Taluka in the country produces enough agricultural residues so that all its electricity demands can be met by using them in 10-20 MW biomass-based power plants. The NARI study also showed that besides providing power, the 'Taluka energy self-sufficiency' plan could also create 30,000 jobs per year. With the new Electricity Act, Taluka energy self-sufficiency can become a reality since the utility can produce and supply power to its customers without the need to go through SEBs. The Taluka utility company can also lease the existing transmission and distribution infrastructure of SEBs (state electricity boards) so that it need not invest in developing its own. This will also help the SEBs to get regular income from their infrastructure. NARI study also showed that Taluka energy program can produce Rs. 100 crores a year economic gain for its inhabitants in terms of biomass production and setting up of new electricity-based industries. With about 3500 talukas in the country, it is therefore possible to produce about Rs. 3,50,000 crore per year extra wealth through the Taluka program.

NARI has done pioneering work in developing sweet sorghum for ethanol production. Sweet sorghum can provide food, fuel and fodder from the same piece of land and requires much less water than sugarcane. Thus the Government of India should extensively fund the R&D program on biofuels.

Finally, for the rural electricity supply mission to succeed, it is necessary that a very close cooperation between corporate sector, government and NGOs is needed. The corporate sector can provide the necessary technological and managerial support, NGOs can create the necessary trust in such utilities and Government of India can help provide soft financing through its many rural development programs. Energy self-sufficient and rural India will prosper (Source: Nimbkar Agriculture Research Institute).

Rural Electricity Supply Technology (REST) Mission was set up in the Ministry of Power (MoP) in 2008. It is hoped through this mission to electrify all villages by 2010. According to MoP officials, funds of about Rs. 10,000-15,000 crore will be made available to the rural power utilities at 2-2.5% p.a. interest rate. With the new Electricity Act and this type of funding, it becomes very attractive for micro-utilities to come up in rural areas.

Thus, a small *rural power cooperative* can be set up to produce 200-500 KW of power and supply all the electricity demands of one or two villages. Again this utility can lease the existing SEB power line infrastructure for its purposes. The state government can also explore the possibility of allowing SEBs to lease these lines and provide standby power to rural micro-utility at substantially lower rates so that the state's social obligations to rural areas is also met. NARI has recently suggested this concept to Maharashtra Electricity Regulatory Commission (MERC). It is also envisaged that power cooperatives may function on the lines of TV cable operators in rural areas.

However, for small power packs of 500 KW and less to function smoothly in rural areas, it is necessary that they be powered by fuel from locally available resources. This will make these micro-utilities green and will create wealth in rural areas in producing value-added item. Thus there is a need to do sophisticated R&D in producing biofuels from renewable energy sources like agriculture residues and crops specifically grown for them. These biofuels can easily power the existing diesel gensets. Development of liquid fuels like ethanol and biodiesel from multipurpose crops should be done so that the issue of food and fuel from the same piece of land is taken care of.

DRUM Project: It seeks to introduce strategic planning, design and alternative financing concepts to advance electric power distribution reforms in India. One of the key interventions under DRUM Project would be to help development of alternative financing and lending mechanism to support broad distribution reforms in rural electrification. The experience of rural utility financing in the United States for cooperatively owned and operated entities both with and without public financing has important lessons for India. The Rural Utility Services of USA funded electric cooperatives with debt capital to cover 100% of the cost of building distribution systems and instituted and implemented a comprehensive system of financial and operating controls, governance, operating standards and oversight procedures to guide the operations of cooperatives.

The US experience demonstrates clearly that it is possible to develop credit worthy entities starting from relatively modest beginning. Therefore, for the purpose of developing a viable alternative financing and lending mechanism for rural electricity sector in India, assistance of Rural Utility Services (RUS) of the United States Department of Agriculture (USDA) is being obtained by Rural Electrification Corporation (REC).

The Ministry of Power has nominated PFC as the Principal Financial Intermediary for the DRUM project and the Rural Electrification Corporation as the Primary Beneficiary under the RUS Participatory Agency Agreement component of the DRUM project. The Ministry has also selected four states namely; Karnataka, Maharashtra, Gujarat and Delhi as DRUM partner states and four pilot projects respectively at Dodaballapur, Aurangabad, Umreth and Shakti Nagar have been proposed. A joint statement was signed by RUS of USDA and REC expressing their intention to cooperate under DRUM project in developing, testing and replicating models that would result in improved rural electrification in India.

REC-RUS cooperation activities started in January 2005 and continued upto Sept 2007 in accordance with a Work Plan developed jointly by REC and RUS.

Through DRUM project, U.S. government and private sector assisted the Indian government in successfully meeting its important goals for rural electrification. Based on the experience, an alternative model for rural electrification has been proposed.

USAID and GE Project: The current partnership between USAID and GE to promote commercially viable rural electrification systems will help translate the vision of our two nations' leaders into concrete, practical applications on the ground. It will provide an avenue for realizing some of the goals articulated in the U.S.-India Energy Dialogue and it will illuminate a brighter future for many Indians living in rural areas. Just as importantly, it will accomplish these objectives while protecting the environment, through the use of renewable energy resources.

This public-private partnership between USAID and GE will develop much-needed energy generation capacity in rural India. Renewable energy power systems using technologies supplied by GE will be installed and operated in four rural communities in India. USAID and partners like Winrock International India will work with the communities to develop user fees and ensure operations and maintenance of the hardware. It is hoped that the lessons learned from these models can be applied in other rural communities throughout India for replication and scale up.

Private sector partner (Malavalli Power Plant Private Limited) has joined GE and USAID in this important effort. MPPPL brings concrete rural electrification experience and solid experience in using renewable technologies in the rural context to the partnership.

By working in concert with the private sector, the government can expand and hasten its delivery of electricity to rural areas. In so doing, these public-private partnerships will create the conditions necessary for more rural towns and villages to enter the economic mainstream.

The U.S. Government has committed to work with the Government of India in helping to create conditions that are conducive to attracting additional private sector investment in India. The power sector offers an important arena for increased private sector participation. U.S. technologies and know-how, working in close coordination with Indian expertise, represents an attractive package. This important endeavor will help millions of people build better lives.

(USAID GE-MPPPL 2006).

Rural Roads

Building rural roads is one component of Bharat Nirman plan which is time bound. It started in 2000. A separate window for rural roads was created under RIDF with a corpus of Rs. 4 thousand crore for each of the last three years. The rapid construction of highways facilitates human and material movement across the country. Apart from improving connectivity, the development of secondary and tertiary roads can open up hitherto unconnected regions to trade and investment and step up access to goods, services and employment opportunities.

Rural roads are the tertiary road system which provides access to villages, interconnecting villages, to the main roads and various centers of activities. They pass through rural and agricultural areas. The traffic on these roads is relatively low, comprising of mixed modes of transport like bullock carts, bicycle and motorized modes of tractors, etc. Nearly, 55 per cent of the about 6 lakh rural habitations are provided all-weather road connectivity. In addition to these roads in rural areas, some villages also have cart tracts and footpaths connecting to the road system.

Rural Roads are a key component of rural development since they provide access to economic and social goods and services thereby generating increased agricultural income and productive employment. Transport investment links to the improved well-being of the poor. Transport was also identified as being highly relevant to the achievement of a number of the targets set under the Millennium Development Goals (MDG).

Two Approaches

Provision of quality infrastructure is a crucial prerequisite for sustainable growth. In the current Indian context, the program for infrastructure building is undertaken broadly through two routes: first, through planned execution of large infrastructure projects under the Central and State Government agencies and through private initiatives including PPPs, and second, through public works programs, which have the twin objectives of creating infrastructure and generating employment for the poor and mitigating urban migration of ruralites. As such, the expected impact of these two approaches to creation of infrastructure is different. While public works programs are concentrated in the rural areas with small, short duration projects, the bigger infrastructure projects have an urban-rural mix, which is different across sectors. Public work programs have been considerably scaled up in the recent years with the introduction of new nationwide schemes and the consolidation of existing schemes. Indisputably, both the approaches to creation of infrastructure would need to be invigorated. It is also equally important to ensure the coordination between these two approaches so as to promote balanced development of infrastructure throughout the length and breadth of the country.

Prime Minister Rural Roads Program

In 2000, India launched a highly ambitious national program (Prime Minister Rural Roads Program—PMGSY) with the aim of providing connectivity to all habitations having a population greater than 500 people, (250 persons in the hilly and desert areas) by good quality all-weather roads. The plan is to provide connectivity to 1,72,000 currently unconnected habitations that will require approximately 3,70,000 km of new rural road. To date, significant progress has been achieved with more than 57,000 habitations now connected as a result of providing in excess of 2,00,000 km of new rural roads at a cost of approximately US $88.2 billion.

Under Bharat Nirman, the target has to be achieved in a time-bound manner by 2009. The systematic upgradation of the existing rural road networks is also an integral component of the scheme. Accordingly, an Action Plan has been prepared for connecting 66,802 habitations with 1,46,185 km of all-weather roads. This Action Plan also envisages upgradation and renewal of 1,94,130 km of the existing rural road network. Subsequently, based on ground verification by States, 62,985 habitations were found eligible to be connected under the program, out of which 3421 habitations have been connected under other schemes. Thus, the revised target is to connect 59,564 habitations. It is estimated that an investment of about Rs. 48,000 crore would be required for achieving the targets under Bharat Nirman. The implementation strategy focuses on quality, cost management and 'on time' delivery.

Up to July, 2008, project proposals amounting to Rs. 81,717 crore have been approved against which a sum of Rs. 38,499 crore has been released for 86,146 roads covering a length of 3,31,736 km. Against these, 52,218 road works having road length of 1,75,629 km have been completed with a cumulative expenditure of Rs. 35,295 crore. Additionally, there are roads built by PWD and the Panchayati Raj institutions in the rural areas.

The National Rural Road Development Agency (NRRDA) under the Ministry of Rural Development (MORD) has been made responsible to monitor the program and oversee its implementation. The program is being implemented through the state level agencies by preparing the detailed district level rural road plans (DRRP) and the core network plans (CNP), which provide prioritized links for connectivity of habitations carved out of DRRP with quantifying population. Under this process, a huge database spatial and non-spatial, related to rural roads, is being generated all over the country (Source: National Portal Content Management Team, Reviewed on: 31-03-2009).

Improvement of Rural Roads, Bridges and Drainage Structures: There is significant progress in improving accessibility to the rural areas. At present, panchayats and panchayat unions are maintaining 52% of the total length of the roads in the state. But future management and maintenance of this expanded rural road network in a sustainable manner is an issue to plan for. Innovations with respect to involving local communities may be deliberated for routine maintenance and repair phase.

Rural Road Planning and Construction: Meanwhile, the working of the system at the local level is fairly effective. The standard of work achieved in rural and village roads is good. Community participation in the implementation of the construction program is effective. The villagers normally donate land for the road through their Panchayats. Sometimes, there is a labor contribution also. The villagers are always involved in the construction. They keep watch on the material used and the progress of work. Deficiencies are reported to the supervisory authorities and soon become an issue. There is a separate rural roads organization for back-up. Planning of works is on an annual basis and is transparent.

It is broadly estimated that from diverse sources—people's contributions, employment programs, contributions from local area development funds of members of the state legislature—from 20 to 25 kilometers of such roads are built annually. But there is no comprehensive plan for demand oriented road construction, in addition to the All India plan for rural connectivity.

Self-help Group Initiative: An instant in Gogalgaon group of five villages—Vitthalrao Vikhe Patil Cooperative Sugar Factory and many educational institutions provide employment opportunities with support of PIRENS Loni, an NGO. The villagers contribute 16 per cent of their daily wage earnings as their project contribution and 100 rupees per year per family as a maintenance fund. The entire project is being implemented with the help and cooperation of a village watershed committee which receives technical and managerial inputs from the project staff and takes the necessary decisions. Once in two months, all the villagers come together to review the progress of the project. They use this platform to discuss conditions, access to health care facilities and the need for a sports ground. The women of the villages have formed a self-help group. Discussions are ongoing about the economic activities they would like to start.

The first activity undertaken by the villagers, apart from the project work, was filling the craters on the approach road to the project site to facilitate the visits of people to see the progress of the project. They contributed the tractor time, stone and labor. As a goodwill gesture, the NGO met the fuel expenses to run the tractor. They covered the open drains at points where there was maximum seepage. A fairly good road which interconnects three villages and ultimately connects to the Mumbai-Nasik State Highway became the top agenda during village meetings. The road, as proposed by the villagers, would reduce by 10 kilometers the distance to stable markets for the fruits and flowers grown in the villages. It would improve access to the Indian Technology Institute and the arts, science and commerce college in Rahata. Sugarcane growers from Ashwi and nearby areas need to transport cane to the Pravaranagar sugar factory. For them, the distance would now be reduced. Students from Ashwi and nearby villages would have a shorter distance to travel to reach the schools and colleges, including technical, medical and dental colleges in Loni, if the new road is constructed. The specialty hospital in Loni would become more accessible to the villagers. The distance of the villages to Shirdi, a major pilgrim center, would also be reduced by 10 km. This pilgrimage center attracts thousands of pilgrims on major Hindu and Muslim festivals.

A technical team from the NGO visited the villages for a pre-feasibility study of the road project. Details about the ownership of the land that would be covered under the project were collected by the villagers themselves. There were village panchayat meetings and village level meetings where resolutions were passed to support this project. Representatives of the NGO participated in some of these meetings where the village leaders highlighted the existing road structure and the benefits of building the proposed road. Rough sketches of the project were prepared and benefits from it were worked out. Thus, instrumentalities for development planning at the local level is encouraging and can be productive.

Geographical Information System (GIS) for Planning and Management of Rural Roads

Tracking the build-up of rural infrastructure is marred by inadequate and lagged information base. The latest consolidated information available on the roads below the level of national highways is upto 2003-04. The generation of timely information is, of course, constrained by the multiplicity of implementing agencies and inadequate data management systems at the ground level. Nonetheless, there is an inescapable need to put in place mechanisms for obtaining updated, reliable information on infrastructure creation at all levels at regular frequency. Traditional methods are not only tedious and time-consuming, but it is difficult to sort and retrieve relevant information. To obviate these difficulties it is, therefore, considered necessary to develop all the spatial components and attribute data in digital format. Geographic Information System (GIS) is a computer-based tool which can handle the entire database and help in the management of the rural road systems.

GIS Potential Use for Rural Roads: The major components of rural roads are planning, project preparation, construction, monitoring and maintenance. Planning includes preparation of district rural road plans and core network plan (MORD 2001) which is helpful for identification of the links to be developed, and a broad estimation that is required for allocation of funds, since each selected link of rural roads is considered as a project. The detailed project report includes the survey information such as detailed design and drawings, cost estimates for various road works, etc. which are required for execution of the road works. The same information will be highly useful during construction monitoring, quality control and maintenance activities. Thus, the district rural road plan with the core network prepared in GIS platform can be extended as a road information system for each project by incorporating the detailed project report data and drawings. This in turn will be the basis for award of work, monitoring the progress of the work and quantity control in the field.

GIS Application in Planning: GIS technology is useful in network as well as geographic analysis in the field of rural road planning (Sikdar, 2002) and measurement of rural accessibility (Durai et al., 2003). To avoid any duplication in planning of rural roads, it is suggested that a master plan for rural roads at district level be prepared (NTPC, 1980; IRC, 1984, 2000).

Similarly, guidelines for preparation of District Rural Road Plan for implementation under PMGSY also suggest the master plan based prioritized rural road links for implementation. The master plan for rural roads prepared at Block level is convenient both from the point of map preparation and data collection and also for obtaining approval, under the Panchayati Raj System. All the block level information sets in a district can be combined easily to form a District Rural Road Plan. Normally, 1:50,000 scale is convenient and easy to handle at the Block level. Therefore, the base map for a Block is prepared at the 1:50,000 scale by referring to the Survey of India top sheets which have proper geo-referencing system.

In the first instance, if the base map for road network is being prepared in GIS environment, it will be easy for preparation of District Rural Road Plan (DRRP) and Core Network Plan (CNP). The relevant attribute data collected for preparation of the DRRP can also be incorporated easily in the GIS base map to generate the core network on population size criteria of habitations for connectivity as well as to do prioritization of the links for implementation. The network and the route analysis modules available in the various GIS software (Caliper Corp., 2001; ESRI, 2003) can be used to optimize the network by adopting the connectivity principles.

Construction and Execution: Some GIS software have modules that provide the facility to estimate quantity of cutting and filling, crust thickness design for various locations and estimation of cost for individual items. Thereafter, this information can be utilized, firstly, for award of the contract to the construction agency and then for monitoring the construction activities in terms of progress of the work in the particular link as a project of the core network. Road information system can be developed using dynamic segmentation module of the GIS tool. Dynamic segmentation involves the division or segregation of network links into segments that are homogeneous for the specified set of link attributes. The segmentation is dynamic because it is created in response to the current attributes of the network. If the attributes are changed, then "dynamic segmentation" will create a new set of segments (ESRI, 2002). It allows multiple sets of attributes to be associated with any portion of a linear feature such as roads to analyze the current condition and predict the future state and performance of the assets of the identified sections of a road. The information system of dynamic segmentation process of highway for monitoring/ management aspects is highly useful for monitoring the various works awarded along the road section.

Monitoring and delivery under PMGSY, the information can be monitored by the district administration as well as State Level Standing Committee and also at the Centre by the National Rural Road Development Agency or the Empowered Committee using on-line GIS enabled monitoring system. GIS maps can be web published using internet-GIS modules which can be enabled by various users and also stakeholders viz. administrative, business and public to view the information. The whole system of execution and monitoring of rural road projects will be transparent and will take less time for execution and will be useful in construction management of the project.

Maintenance Planning and Management: Most of the information required for maintenance planning aspects are already available in GIS environment in various formats such as base planning data from DRRP and Core Network Plans, DPR data including the design details of the road, traffic, materials used, etc. which can be used for maintenance planning activities. Further, by carrying out additional inventory surveys such as condition surveys at regular intervals, which can also be incorporated in the existing GIS database, the data can be used to assess the pavement improvement measures required for various sections. Based on the pavement damage data, it is possible to separate the medium and long-term maintenance measures required within the next 2-3 years for various periodic maintenance or rehabilitation measures. With the introduction of GIS technology, the basic philosophy of the planning and implementation of rural road network has changed (Source: Geo spatial portal, 2009).

Infrastructure Finance: To address these constraints, several initiatives have been taken by Government of India to create an enabling framework for PPPs. Progressively, more sectors have been opened to private and foreign investment, levy of user charges is being promoted, regulatory institutions are being set up and strengthened and fiscal incentives are given to infrastructure projects. Approval mechanism for PPPs in the Central sector has been streamlined through setting up of Public-Private Partnership Appraisal Committee (PPPAC). The inflow of foreign direct investments to the infrastructure sector increased by more than five times in 2007-08, but the pace of FDI inflows to infrastructure sectors was sustained during 2008-09.

About a third of the Planning Commission's estimate of Rs. 20,01,776 crore (at 2006-07 prices) required for infrastructure development during the Eleventh Five-Year Plan is expected to be met through private investment and public-private partnerships (PPPs). Besides supplementing limited public sector resources, PPPs bring in private sector expertise, cost reducing technologies and efficiencies in operation and maintenance. While encouraging PPPs, constraints have been identified in Policy and regulatory gaps, specially relating to specific sector policies and regulations.

The Economic Survey 2008-09, which also makes policy recommendations, however said finance availability was only one of the conditions for investment. The survey pointed out that project delays were also caused by land acquisition issues, lack of raw materials and other inputs. Once a project is financially closed, it is faced with issues like disputes in land acquisition, rehabilitation, contractual issues, shortage of raw materials, capital goods and fuel, environmental disputes and inadequate availability of skilled manpower. These problems result in delays in the completion of infrastructure projects. These problems have wide ramifications, yet, there is no option but to address them systematically, as timely implementation of projects is critical for ensuring their financial viability, as also for reaping the projected economic benefits.

Enablers for infrastructure finance companies to raise cheaper funds will be looked for too, industry watchers said. Angel Broking said it expected private non-banking financial companies (NBFCs) to tap funds from the India Infrastructure Finance Corp Ltd. which has been mandated to raise and lend to banks 400 billion rupees for infrastructure projects. "Also, some relaxation is expected in allowing NBFCs to borrow from abroad to finance the local projects," the brokerage said in a note to clients.

Indian infrastructure firms are looking to the government for increased spending in the sector and opening up routes to access cheaper long-term funds. India needs $500 billion of investment into its roads, railways, ports and airports in the period 2007-12. About $150 billion of that was to have come from the private sector. "Public initiatives are constrained by factors like inadequate shelf of bankable projects and shortage of long-term finance for projects," the government's Economic Survey for 2008-09 said.

Infrastructure Policy: The PPP model is an important development model if the government wants to meet the infrastructure needs of the country at a brisk pace. Government resources need to be backed by private sector resources—human, financial and knowledge. The PPP model of our country is a dynamic model; it has undergone several major changes and this process of change will continue. We will develop a system of continuous feedback from all stakeholders on all important issues and whatever changes are required for faster implementation of the projects, we will adopt them, government asserts.

The government has worked for equitable growth that involves sharing the fruits of growth with all sections of the society. So, it will be concentrating on an optimum mix of roads that serves economically advanced areas as well as backward areas. On one hand, the focus will be on projects like expressways and conversion to six-lanes while on the other hand, it will also be concentrating on two-lane roads connecting rural business centers in far-flung areas to the network of Golden Quadrilateral and the two corridors. Rail and road infrastructure have to complement and supplement each other. The two arms of the Golden Quadrilateral run parallel to the rail-freight corridor. Wherever required, spurs will be created in order to have a better integration.

Salient Rural Roads Sector Project

Country Partnership Strategy (CPS) currently under preparation is closely aligned with the priorities of India's Eleventh Five-Year Plan (FY2007; FY2011). The Plan continues to focus on infrastructure investment, social development, agriculture and rural development to make the growth process more inclusive. Accordingly, CPS reconfirms continuing ADB assistance for development of rural roads which are critical for rural development, as they provide access to markets, health, education, and administrative services. Specifically, the Country Operations Business Plan (COBP) for 2008-2010 includes PPTA preparing Rural Roads Sector III with indicative ADB financing amount of $1,000,000 and implementation of Rural Road Sector III (RRS-III) with indicative loan amount of $700 million. During the Country Programming Mission completed in November 2008, the assistance pipeline was reviewed and the amount of ensuing loan is now programmed for 2010 with an indicative amount of $450 million.

RRS-III provides a continuation to RRS-I and RRS-II currently under implementation. RRS-I (states of Madhya Pradesh and Chhattisgarh) and RRS-II (states of Assam, Orissa, and West Bengal) are assisting the Central government in its ambitious PMGSY program aimed at connecting all habitations with more than 500 people by all-weather roads.

RRS-III will focus on all above states: Assam, Chhattisgarh, Madhya Pradesh, Orissa, and West Bengal.

The impact of the project will be improved connectivity of rural communities in participating states to markets, district headquarters, and other centers of economic activity.

Outcome of RRS-III Investment Program will ensure cost effective and sustainable improvement in connectivity of rural communities. In implementation, (i) it will conduct road safety audits on the sample of DPRs and constructed roads and propose processes and measures to improve road safety to be implemented within RRS-III (by the end of month 11); (ii) Conduct feasibility study of the 500 km sample of roads proposed for RRS-III, 100 km from each participating state (by the end of month 12); (iii) Help achieve project readiness, including encouraging, assisting and monitoring the advance procurement (including safeguard compliance) and reviewing a sample of DPRs and Bid Documents for proposed RRS-III roads (throughout the assignment); (iv) Finalize Design and Monitoring Framework (DMF) for ensuing loan, develop a survey methodology and assist with a baseline survey (by the end of month 11); (v) Prepare Community Participation Plan (CPP) for 100 km of sample rural roads from each participating state in accordance with Community Participation Framework (CPF) (by the end of month 6); (vi) Provide all other necessary on-the-job training and knowledge transfer, including assisting and training of the PIU and PIC staff on safeguard procedures (throughout the assignment).

Rural Transport

Sustainability of the Road Transport System, Rural Roads Systems and Accessibility to Rural Areas: RT is concerned with transporting goods and people within the village, between villages and urban areas, linking village roads with district roads, state highways and national highways. Rural Transport System (RTS) consists of roads and vehicles of various types and capacities, ownership and investment patterns, maintenance of roads and vehicles, taxation and government regulations, etc. The efficiency of RTS will depend upon the perspectives and priorities given by the government. It has to be integrated into regional planning and state plans. Policies regarding state vs. private in laying roads and operation of vehicles have to be changed in order to make progress. Though bullock carts play a significant role in RTS for freight transport, long-term solution is FWR and AWR, which will enable motorized transport to penetrate into rural areas. Most state and private undertakings are using large size buses and they complain that load factor is low in rural transport. Smaller buses, with capacity of 12 to 25 are the solution. Planning of RTS has to be taken up for research, planning and resource allocation.

Challenges Ahead

The Eleventh Five-Year Plan (2007-12) has estimated an investment requirement of US $500 billion in infrastructure for broad-based and inclusive growth. The foregoing analysis indicates that achieving this is a challenging task. These are difficult issues but not insurmountable, given the resilience that the Indian economy and its financial system has demonstrated amidst adversities.

It is challenging to plan and implement effectively special infrastructure development strategies for rural India. The rural infrastructure of roads, telephony, irrigation, drinking water supply and sanitation, housing and electrification and connectivity through rural roads and transport need to function efficiently for economic growth; they are drivers for rural economic development.

The restructured programs for clean safe drinking water, sanitation and other infrastructure development advocate a community participatory and demand driven approach, involvement of Village Water and Sanitation Committee (VWSC), Panchayati Raj Institutions (PRIs) in decision-making about planning, implementation, operation and maintenance of these facilities. It is challenging to optimize achievement and sustainability by developing safe, affordable and socially acceptable sanitation systems; and promoting behavior change and hygiene education.

Rural roads are critical for rural development, as they provide access to markets, health, education, and administrative services. The impact of the road construction projects will improve connectivity of rural communities to centers of economic activity.

Administration of development programs in villages must be dynamic in order to adjust to changing contexts such as population growth, industrialization, economic reforms, globalization, education, employment, and other quality of life indexes and the effects of development activities themselves.

For 'empowering' the rural sector, government is setting ambitious targets to expand their access to these programs. Ruralites have received considerable support and implementation by government for water, energy, sanitation, rural roads & transport, environmental pollution control and housing. Still there are financial, expertise and technology constraints and private sector has to partner with government and lead in developing sustainable and innovative solutions. It is challenging to coordinate efficiently PPP with P4 model. These public-private partnerships will create the conditions necessary for more rural towns and villages to enter the economic mainstream.

6

Technology for Rural Growth

Telephone, Computer and Television are raising rural India's expectations. These transform the rural India of Today and Tomorrow

Technology for Rural Growth

When resources, national policies, needs and demands interact with one another, the outcomes may be many; such as changing patterns of the economy, occupation and employment, patterns of work, work ethics and organization practices, and infiltration of new values and ideas in the society. *India's rising expectations and achievements from Telephone, Computer and Television—these three together are transforming the rural India of Today and Tomorrow.*

Developing nations require the education, Internet connectivity and the access to the right technology to meet their unique needs. Intel, Microsoft, IBM and other technology companies are trying to bridge the digital divide among the rural and lower socio-economic population in developing countries through ambitious programs. *These are the next steps for developing Information Society among the poor and rural population by bridging the digital divide.* Overcoming the digital divide in conjunction with other socio-economic divides will remain one of the key development issues for decades to come.

Narula (2009) points that the have-nots are removed from the mainstream society by blockages of socio-economic benefits gap, knowledge-gap, communication-gap, and now IT gap. This is true of rural society also. The efforts of governance are to create equitable society by handling salient economic issues efficiently.

Narula (2009) further advocates that 'Connectivity' through these channels is important in this context. Urban India, with rising consumerism, technology and media explosion feels closer to the developed world. Rural India, many villages with no power, no schools, and little entertainment and poor communication are closer to being nowhere.

Digital opportunities could be built in rural India through ICTs. Impact of ICTs is defined in terms of opportunity, empowerment and security, and sustainability of ICTs for development activities. These technologies are embedded in social contexts, they can offer opportunity as well constrain human activity. The focus is on: (i) Social equity and public policy challenges of these transformative technologies for rural society. (ii) How social equity and human condition is affected by these emerging technologies? (iii) What mechanism and learning processes have been developed to assist governments and stakeholders engaged in the decision-making process associated with these technologies?

IT companies need to design technology that meets the requirement of rural India. They need it the most and it can also help stimulate growth. They should design technology in a holistic manner, that will make the product cost-efficient and the benefit can be passed on to the rural customer.

Next Generation Networks: In the next generation networks, multiple access networks can connect customers to a core network based on IP technology. These access networks include fiber optics or coaxial cable networks connected to fixed locations or customers connected through Wi-Fi as well as to 3G networks connected to mobile users. As a result, in the future, it would be impossible to identify whether the next generation network is a fixed or mobile network and the wireless access broadband would be used both for fixed and mobile services. It would then be futile to differentiate between fixed and mobile networks—both fixed and mobile users will access services through a single core network.

We premise that various media connectivity in rural areas and among ruralites can drive rural economic growth. We highlight this premise in our discussions.

Connectivity: Communication Technologies Bridges

Rural Telecommunication Policies aim at giving connectivity to ruralites through multi media channels of print, broadcasting and television, telecom—telephones both fixed line and cellular, and computerization. Policies need to be planned for giving access both, physical access through facilitating purchasing power and technology connection availability in the regions, and social access through community acceptance. The content planning and effectiveness of channels monitoring for rural usage for rural relevant content, social messaging and entertainment for all age groups and genders is important for connectivity.

These telecommunication infrastructure policies both at hardware and software have to be planned and implemented at three levels of Central, State and local governments. The effectiveness of these policies at all these three levels depends on the initiatives of the three government levels and people to create awareness, motivation, and physical and social access to use these technologies on one hand and on the other hand, how they will integrate and facilitate these in their life styles, occupational and employment benefits. Rural technology is necessary for telecommunication and other areas.

Meanwhile, the dramatic growth of the economy, the rapid rise in literacy especially in rural areas, and the improvements in transport and other infrastructure, as also the phenomenal growth in mobile telephony, and access to the Internet through a network of cybercafés and 'e-choupals' and the expansion of private commercial FM radio channels, are witness to the 'communication revolution' in India as well having impact on rural India.

Current perspective and progress in 2009 and historical perspectives of various media; TV, telephony, computer,

Internet and ICTs in general in rural areas is given to assess how much rural India has come ahead in connectivity through these media channels.

Current Broadcasting Scenario

Television in India

Current Television perspective: TV is in India since 1959 focusing on urban areas initially and expanding to rural areas. The discussion highlights how it has benefitted ruralites earlier and now; the current media policy for TV, and the physical and social constraints for ruralites in the process.

Despite the ongoing recession, financial year 2008-09 was boom year for television channels as over 111 satellite channels were approved by Central information and broadcasting ministry to begin operations. According to the annual report of the I&B ministry, the year 2008-09 counted for almost one-fourth of the total 394 TV channels that were granted license by the ministry till March 2009. The number of new TV channels has gained momentum due to liberalization and enhanced technologies.

The mushrooming of private cable and satellite channels in English and the Indian languages since the 90s has surprised the entertainment industry. This unprecedented growth has been given a new impetus with the state authorities offering uplink facilities to both domestic and foreign networks, and even permitting domestic networks to have their own earth-stations. But most importantly, the impetus has come from digital compression and the dramatic crash of satellite costs, in the opening up of the sector to foreign direct investment (FDI) and the new opportunity of media companies to go public for raising capital.

According to the latest FICCI-Price-Waterhouse Cooper Report (2007), The Indian mass media today comprises over 300 TV channels reaching 112 million households and around 300 radio stations. The Indian media and entertainment industry is worth over two hundred billion dollars and is projected to grow at the rate of 18-20% per annum.

There is also a growing selection of satellite transmission and cable services available such as Cable TV with CAS (Conditioned Access System), TV through DISH antennas and IPTV through Internet. The earliest transmission mode of rooftop antennas reflected by transmission towers has become totally obsolete in India. Most of the rural TV broadcast and to hilly and remote areas is through satellite transmission.

In India, only the government owned Doordarshan is allowed to broadcast terrestrial television signals. It initially had one major National channel (DD National) and a Metro channel in some of the larger cities (also known as DD Metro).

Satellite/Cable television took off during the first Gulf War with CNN. There are no regulations against ownership of satellite dish antennas, or operation of cable television systems, which led to an explosion of viewership and channels, led by the Star TV group and Zee TV. Initially, restricted to music and entertainment channels, viewership grew, giving rise to several channels in regional languages and many in the national language, Hindi. The main news channels available were CNN and BBC World. In the late 1990s, many current affairs and news channels sprouted, becoming immensely popular because of the alternative viewpoint they offered compared to Doordarshan.

Rural Television: Historical Perspective

Looking from historical perspective, rural India was media connected by transistors in 50s and then TV in 70s in big way. Media exposure to these two channels was tremendous. In 70s, rural people were exposed to TV through satellites, though many of the people could not buy them till 80s as they were expensive but government did put community TVs and radio in every village. Many villagers could buy transistor radio as they were inexpensive or many times they were distributed free by national and international agencies. In the sixth Five-Year Plan (1980-85), VHF sets were installed in five selected states for community viewing in rural areas. After 80s, electrified villages could access cable TV and later on many international TV channels.

Satellite INSAT 1B was a unique joint venture in 70s between department of space, television services (Doordarshan), and All India Radio services. Two extra powerful S-band channels could give direct telecast facilities to rural areas and remote and hilly areas where development programs needed mass media support. Doordarshan—the government TV center produces television software for rural communities besides other national target groups. INSAT television has two distinct features, direct telecast and nation-wide networking using terrestrial transmitters. The instructional objective of the INSAT television covered the areas of agricultural productivity, health, hygiene, family welfare, formal and informal education, and national integration.

The national television (Doordarshan) and radio (All India Radio, or Akashwani) networks are state-owned and managed by the Ministry of Information and Broadcasting. Their news reporting customarily presents the government's point of view. The personnel of the new broadcasting corporation are career civil servants to facilitate continued government control. In the early 90s, increasing competition from television broadcasts transmitted via satellite appeared the most effective manner of limiting the pro-government bias of the government-controlled electronic media.

Television programming beside political news was initially tightly controlled by the government. It focused on efforts to disseminate its development messages and also propagating Indian culture through soap opera, films, documentaries and even talks. In addition to the efforts at nation-building, the politicians of India's ruling party have not hesitated to use television to build political support. In fact, the political abuse of Indian television demanded increase in the autonomy of Doordarshan; these demands ultimately resulted in support for the Prasar Bharati Act.

Since the 1980s, India has experienced a rapid proliferation of television broadcasting that has helped shape popular culture and the course of politics. Although the first television program was broadcast in 1959, the expansion of television did not begin in earnest until the extremely popular telecast of the Ninth Asian Games, which were held in New Delhi in 1982. Realizing the popular appeal and consequent influence of television broadcasting, the government expanded it by 1990 and planned to provide television access to 90 per cent of the population; *though for many of the rural population, the TV sets were still not affordable and government provided community TV sets and these were giving the rural population much desired media exposure*. During this time, color TV sets were also initiated in the market.

90s brought a radical transformation of television in India. Transnational satellite broadcasting made its debut in January 1991, when owners of satellite dishes—initially mostly at major hotels began receiving Cable News Network (CNN) coverage of the Persian Gulf War. Three months later, Satellite broadcasting spread rapidly through India's cities as local entrepreneurs erected dishes to receive signals and transmitted them through local cable systems. After its October 1992 launch, Zee TV offered stiff competition to Star TV. However, the future of Star TV was bolstered by billionaire Rupert Murdock, who acquired the network in July 1993. CNN International, part of the Turner Broadcasting System, was slated to start broadcasting entertainment programs, including top Hollywood films, in 1995.

Competition from the satellite stations brought radical change to Doordarshan by cutting its audience and threatening its advertising revenues at a time when the government was pressuring it to pay for expenditures from internal revenues. In response, Doordarshan decided in 1993 to start five new channels in addition to its original National Channel. Programming was radically transformed and controversial news shows, soap operas, and coverage of high-fashion events proliferated. Of the new Doordarshan channels, however, only the Metro Channel, which carries MTV music videos and other popular shows, has survived in the face of the new trend for talk programs that engage in a potpourri of racy topics.

A study of India's public broadcaster, Doordarshan (DD) highlights how it has been struggling to respond to transformations in the media environment. Its past mandate of development broadcasting has come under severe pressure as DD competes with many new satellite and cable channels offering audiences ever more choices and more so, a new model of development broadcasting was ushering in a competitive and globalizing media world. There is both positive and negative impact of media globalization and commercialization on Indian society and culture over the last two decades.

Television and Public Policy

The significant changes that have come over the television industry over the last two decades, most notably a shift to deregulation in broadcast media, and the concern created about meaningful content available to the viewers. The political, economic, and technological factors have shaped the television sector in such a short span of time. Consequently, this sector has to be managed by issues of media policy and the regulatory framework. These could reflect the political, social and cultural role of television in Indian society more so its relevance and impact on Indian rural society.

Over the last 50 years, the impetus for India to venture into the cost-intensive development of television system was driven by the perceived importance of broadcasting to national development. India favored the development focus of the media and its role of IEC (information, education and communication) of messages that would improve agricultural production, health, education, national security and other vital areas based on the assumption that the mass media had very powerful, direct, and immediate effects on listeners and viewers.

Both media scholars in the West and media planners in the third world justified and theorized the significance of broadcasting in the development process. Communication scholars such as Daniel Lerner (1958), Wilbur Schramm (Lerner & Schramm, 1967), and Everett Rogers (1962) emphasized that developing countries needed broadcasting to establish a sense of national identity and to support modernization projects and campaigns.

Policy on broadcasting has been witness to major changes over the last two decades. Doordarshan, the national television network with 22 channels, and All India Radio, the national radio broadcaster, are now managed by an autonomous corporation known as PrasarBharati (Broadcasting Trust). It is an independent public service broadcasting service, less subject to state interference but still funded by the national exchequer. However, the PrasarBharati rarely asserts its autonomous status and continues to function as a unit of the Ministry of Information and Broadcasting.

The Cable Television Networks Rules (1994) and the Cable Television Networks (Regulation) Act (1995) were amended to Cable Television Networks (Amendment) Rules 2000. The new rules have made it mandatory for all cable operators—over 30,000 of them in the entire country to re-transmit at least two Doordarshan channels (the national and metro channels) and one regional language channel in the prime band. Most cable operators were giving little attention to these channels since they were free-to-air and did not fetch any revenue as the private satellite channels did. Further, cable operators were to be held responsible for programs that were offensive as well as for any advertisements of tobacco and alcoholic beverages. Clause vii (2) of the new Rules prohibits all advertisements which promote 'directly or indirectly, production, sale or consumption of cigarettes, tobacco products, wine, alcohol, liquor or other intoxicants'. Also banned are infant milk substitutes, feeding bottles or infant foods. But cable operators questioned the practicality of stopping overseas channels which carry such advertisements.

The amendment regulates or prohibits the transmission of any program or channel if it is necessary to do in the interest of the 'sovereignty or integrity of India or security of India or friendly relations of India with any foreign state or public order, decency or morality'. Central and State government authorities can seize equipment or prohibit any program or channel if it is not in conformity with prescribed program and advertising codes. The draft Broadcasting Bill (2007) revisits these codes.

The Bill proposes the setting up of a Broadcast Regulatory Authority of India (BRAI). However, the actual regulation of program content has been left to the broadcasters themselves.

Each broadcaster is required to categorize content on the basis of theme, subject-matter, treatment, language and audio-visual presentation. Content will be categorized into U (Unrestricted), U/A and A (Adult)—as is the case with content in cinema. Adult content will be scheduled only after 11.00 pm, and U/A content (for those above age 12) only after 8.00 p.m. The BRAI will oversee the work of content auditors appointed by each channel/network.

Political parties launched their own channels to propagate their own ideologies. By mid-2007, most major political parties in North and South India could boast of their own TV channels. Thus, the fundamentalist Hindu party, the BJP, the Marxists of Kerala, the DMK and AIDMK of Tamil Nadu, the Congress Party, and even the Catholic Church had their own TV channels.

Earlier, primary concern was government ownership and control over broadcasting, and the kind of effect this had on programming and policy. With the privatization of television, radio, computer and telecommunications technologies, the focus will need to be shifted to the media moghuls who have taken over international broadcasting, film production and distribution, telecommunication services, computer networks, and information databases. The convergence of the various media in recent years as well as their 'globalization' has changed the very dynamic of each medium.

The 'new' media has become problematic because of the global scale of access and reach. National governments would like to control and regulate them. but there are few international laws that assist them. The technology for blocking content on both the old and the new media is easily available.

However, as democratic gesture, India may not like to restrict the freedom of speech and expression of its citizens, even where the threat to national security and to law and order exists, as in the case of separatist movements in Kashmir and the North-East. But religious and political fundamentalist groups offer far greater threats to human rights and the freedom of the media.

Rural Telephony

Despite the positive benefits telephony can have for economic development, many people in developing nations are held back by a diverse set of factors—such as low connectivity in rural locations, duties and taxes imposed by governments, the costs of handsets and the cost of services. Once the hurdle of physical access to communication is overcome, people in developing nations still have to contend with the costs of services. Usage costs can play a large role in determining the purposes for which, and the frequency with which, people use their phones. It is often claimed that access to telecommunication facilities is a propeller of economic prosperity in developing countries. Mobile phones in particular are considered pivotal in encouraging growth.

There is a strong two-way co-relationship between economic development, literacy and general awakening of a region with its tele-density. Access to telecommunications has a strong and direct positive impact on the overall economic growth, development of the private sector, delivery of public services and integration of the rural and isolated areas with the rest of the country. The poor, specially the rural poor, have less access to telecom services than justified by their poverty levels and the emerging "digital divide" is widening. *It is an established fact that the income of the poor grows faster in telecom intensive economies and access to affordable telecom services is essential for any strategy for poverty reduction. In fact, IT can be an effective and potent weapon to eliminate poverty.*

Rural telecommunications can also help in improvement in ability of the people to participate in market economy and also improve productivity by saving time and transportation cost. It is, therefore, important to extend availability and access to affordable telecom services in rural and other vulnerable areas, whether on individual service basis or shared service basis in community kiosks.

Studies have indicated that there is a tremendous latent demand of telecom facilities in rural areas. This is expected to increase substantially with further improvement in *availability, accessibility and affordability*. This is a challenging opportunity for investment both by public and private investors.

It is also a prerequisite for delivery of social services like tele-education, tele-medicine, empowerment of masses and reaching them the benefits of e-governance, etc. Now when India is fast emerging as an IT super power on the global scene, it is imperative to bring the benefits of IT enabled services, tele-working, tele-trade and home-based work to the vast multitude of the rural masses. The telecom coverage of these areas would also open up huge untapped market for e-commerce.

Prahlad (2004), in *Fortune at the Bottom of the Pyramid asserts that defining change in the world's poorest economies will be led by access to* communications and not through the evolution of IT as was the case in the advanced *countries of the world*. Both government and private telephone operators 'One India initiative' enables people to talk from Kashmir to Kanyakumari at a very affordable tariff of Re. 1 per minute. Now in 2009, it has changed to charging by per second pulse for cell (one paise per second); this also promotes more cell usage by the poor. There is focus on lowering the cost of PC at below Rs. 10,000. This will increase PC penetration. The fact still remains that unless content is relevant, use of ICTs will always be constrained.

A study by the London Business School (Waverman et al. 2005) has also found that, in a typical developing country, an increase of 10 mobile phones per 100 people would boost GDP growth by 0.6 percentage points.

Rural Telephony: Current Perspective 2008-09

India's tele-density is low in rural areas. 670,000 route kilometers (419,000 miles) of optical fibers have been laid in by the major operators, even in remote areas and the process continues. BSNL alone has laid optical fiber to 30,000 Telephone Exchanges out of their 36 Exchanges. Keeping in mind the viability of providing services in rural areas, an attractive solution appears to be one which offers multiple service facility at low costs. A rural network based on the extensive optical fiber network, using Internet Protocol and offering a variety of services and the availability of open platforms for service development, viz. the Next Generation Network, appears to be an attractive proposition. Fiber network can be easily converted to Next Generation network and then used for delivering multiple services at cheap cost. There is Submarine cables Fiber-Optic Link Around the Globe (FLAG) with a landing site at Mumbai (2000).

By March 2002: Some of the achievements and gaps since April 1999 to 2002 for rural telephony in India are indicated below and the process is still going on. Rural tele-density has gone up to 0.68 per 100 rural population. As on 30.9.2000, out of total rural exchanges (22243), a total of 12410 rural exchanges have been provided with reliable media. Out of 6,07,491 villages in country, 3,80,148 villages have been covered by village public telephones (VPT). Out of total 326 SSAs in the country, 226 SSAs have been provided with Internet nodes and Internet access achieved in all the districts by dial-up access on local call basis. The total number of rural Direct Exchange Lines (DELs) is 4,827,280. About 72% of the total population have only 18% of the total telephones, i.e. 4.84 million out of 26.5 million DELs. More than 75% exchanges (21,669 out of 27,909 exchanges).

By March 2004: Out of the 6,07491 villages in the country, 5,22,347 villages have been provided with VPTs. Of this, 5,09,682 VPTs have been provided by BSNL. The number of rural DELs in the country has increased to 122.72 lakh. It is expected that a lot more would be done with the implementation of non-lapsable Universal Service Fund.

The year 2003-04 has witnessed a record growth of over 40% in the total number of phones, taking the total number to 765.40 lakh. The tele-density has increased from 5.11% in March 2003 to 7.02% in March 2004. Two important features of this growth are the increasing preference for mobile phones and the higher contribution of private sector in the incremental growth.

Cellular mobile phones contribute to about 34% of the total telephones and if the WLL mobile phones are included, the share is a significant 44%. The share of private sector in the total number of phones, that was just 20.96% on March 31, 2003, stands at 39.27% as on March 31, 2004. Several steps were taken to improve the tele-density in the country. Targets of additional DELs were enhanced. Intensive efforts are being made to cover more villages through Village Public Telephones (VPTs). Private sector is being encouraged to provide telecom facilities at a faster pace.

By 2008-2009: To achieve the targets of tele-density under National Telephone Policy (NTP) 99, the number of DELs (fixed and mobile) projected for the year 2005 and 2010 are 75.3 million and 174.3 million respectively. Similarly, to achieve the tele-density of 4% in rural areas, the number of telephone lines have to be increased from the current level of 4.8 million to 31.7 million. However, based on a review, the tele-density in rural areas may have to reach about 8% in 2010. Secondly, all the villages have to be provided with VPTs. Both would require provision of necessary additional funds and related subsidy. After the corporatization of the incumbent operator now, there would be need to provide the requisite resources to meet the net cost of uneconomic operations in rural areas.

There are 27,789 functional rural exchanges. Rural DELs are individual phone connections provided to the subscribers. These are different from VPTs in the sense that for Rural DELs, subscribers pay a fixed rental as against a VPT, which is a public payphone. The USO cost for Rural DELs comprise two elements, i.e. capital recovery and operational expenditure. Various cost models have been considered to work out NUSC for rural DELs.

With the special thrust given to rural telephony, the number of rural telephones went up from 12.3 million in March 2004 to 112.71 million in January 2009. The strategy for rural network expansion involves provision of phones through market mechanisms in the viable areas and through Universal Service Obligation Fund (USOF) in the non-viable areas. While village public telephones (VPTs) and rural community phones (RCPs) will enable public access, a scheme of RCPs has been launched under USOF to create the infrastructure in rural and remote areas. Out of more than 22.71 lakh public call offices (PCOs) functioning in the country, two lakh are in the rural areas. The Mobile Grameen Sanchar Sewak scheme providing telephone at the doorstep of villagers is in place in about 12,000 villages. These are all landline connections (July 09).

Bharti Airtel, speaking at a press conference stressed the importance of rural demand to sustain industry growth. The spokesperson said that while the total customer base crossed the 100 million mark in Q1, 60% of additional customers came from rural areas (23 July 09).

The changing communication practice in India is to provide cellular telephone connectivity as well increase tele-density in rural areas through cellular technology. It is cheaper and does not require rural electrification. The earlier efforts to give landline connections over the years have not shown desired progress.

Country's rural regions are also experiencing strong growth, with the number of mobile rural lines increasing from 12.3 million in March 2004 to 112.71 million in July 2009. Rural mobile tele-density reached 13.81 per cent over the same period. Tele-density is 81.3 per cent in urban areas in the same period. India's overall tele-density will be affected by Urban-Rural skewness. Would this eliminate digital divide? *The skewness of the rural urban divide will still be there.*

The low rural tele-density has prompted the Telecom Regulatory Authority of India (TRAI) to come out with a draft recommendation on the modalities for improving the phone penetration in the rural parts. TRAI has recommended revitalization of the Universal Service Obligation Fund (USOF) as a first step to improve rural phone. According to the Indian Government, at the pace with which the Indian telecom market is growing, the target of 500 million fixed and mobile phone connections by 2010 seems to be taking shape. India's Economic Survey for the year 2008-09, unveiled strong growth in the telecom sector with the country counting a total of 414 million fixed and mobile connections as of February 2009.

"We must replicate urban telephony conditions in rural areas to improve rural tele-density," TRAI says that the rural markets should now be viewed as an opportunity rather than an obligation, and private companies can only be attracted if the government also reduces charges for the license and the spectrum. That would mean a greater use of wireless technology, rather than wiring up rural India. "It is cheaper to take mobile technology rather than wires everywhere, that is why we want to take mobile technology to rural areas rather than fixed lines," he added. Earlier years, TRAI has been focusing on fixed landlines through rural exchanges which have not been a success. TRAI says that unless these recommendations are implemented at the earliest, tele-density in rural areas is likely to remain stuck at 3-4 per cent.

Cellular Technology: Rural

The changing communication practice in India should be to provide telephone connectivity as well as to increase tele-density in rural areas through cellular technology. It is cheaper and does not require rural electrification. Government is in the process of giving a final shape to a scheme for supporting infrastructure for roll-out of cellular mobile services in the rural areas. Keeping in mind the difficult conditions in these areas, it is proposed to provide financial support for land, tower, power and electronic equipment for transmitting, receiving and backhaul. A 'plug and play' scenario will be created for the telecom service providers. The emphasis will be on sharing the infrastructure so that capex costs can be kept down and on encouraging adoption of technology which can reduce power consumption and therefore operating costs. The infrastructure thus created will be used progressively for providing broadband connectivity and will be able to accommodate equipment of new and emerging technologies (July 09).

According to official data, other private companies making efforts for rural mobile telephony are: Around 30% of Bharti Airtel's wireless subscriber base resides in the rural parts of the country, for Vodafone, BSNL, Reliance Communications and Idea Cellular, the rural user base is around 31%, 34%, 19% and 30% of their respective wireless pie. Out of an all-India mobile subscriber base of 347 million as of 2008-end, the rural India contributed around 92 million, or 26%.

Government is putting its best foot forward in bringing village farmers closer to mobile phones. The objective being mobile connectivity and Internet accessibility would help farmers enhance farm production, and dictate a fair price for their produce from end consumers. State and privately owned communication companies will make cheap mobiles available for farmers for Rs. 500 for a piece. This will be done through digital technologies that help considerably cut mobile telephone costs.

A scheme has been launched by the Government to provide support for setting up and managing 7,871 infrastructure sites spread over 500 districts in 27 states for the provision of mobile services. The infrastructure so created shall be shared by three service providers for provision of mobile services.

Mobile services from these towers are likely to be launched in a phased manner. As on 28.02.2009, about 3,941 towers have been set up under this scheme. Mobile services from about 3,715 BTSs installed on many of these towers have started. About 10,128 towers are proposed to be installed under second phase of the scheme. Efforts are now being made to achieve the target of 600 million telephone subscribers by the end of Eleventh Five-Year Plan. It is also proposed to achieve rural tele-density of 25 per cent by means of 200 million rural connections at the end of the Eleventh Five-Year Plan.

State Wide Area Networks (SWANs) will be set up in rural areas over a period of five years. These SWANs will extend data connectivity of 2 Mega bits per second up to the block level in State or Union Territory in the country. The block level nodes in turn will have a provision to extend connectivity further to the village level using contemporary wireless technology (June 09).

While the wireless subscriber base grew at a compound annual growth rate (CAGR) of 75.9% per annum since 2003, the wire-line segment has been declining gradually.

USO Fund Activities continue to subsidize the developments in rural telecom sector through operation and maintenance of village public telephone (VPT). About 5,49,133 VPTs are currently eligible for financial support as on 28.2.2009. In line with the agreements signed with BSNL in November 2004 to provide subsidy support for provision of VPTs in 66,822 uncovered villages, 56,736 VPTs have been covered by BSNL as on 28.02.2009. The remaining will be covered in a phased manner by November, 2009.

In September 2004, under agreement, 40,705 rural community phones (RCP) are to be provided in villages with population of more than 2,000 and not having PCO facility; 40,616 RCPs have been provided till February, 2009. Multi-access radio relay (MARR)-based VPTs installed before April 2002 are being replaced under USO Fund. Out of a total of 1,86,872 MARR based VPTs, 1,83,756 have been replaced till February, 2009.

USO fund support is given for providing of rural direct exchange lines (RDELs) in all the 1,685 net cost positive short distance charging areas (SDCAs).

Rural Telephony in India: Historical Perspective

A Task Force was constituted in late 1970s to study the various aspects like policies and programs, technology choices, operation and maintenance, services and standards, etc. to provide telecom services in rural areas for development of its economy and people. In early 1980s, a Mini-mission of Rural Development was started and a Special Task Force was set up to open more and more small and medium sized telephone exchanges in the villages. Further, a time-bound program was undertaken to extend at least one public telephone in rural areas within easy reach of villagers. Several initiatives were taken, including Hexagon Policy; Long Distance Public

Telephone Program (LDPT) (in Period 1980-1991); Gram Panchayat Public Telephone Program (Period 1991-1994); Village Public Telephone (VPT) Program (1994 onwards).

In 1984, the latest world class indigenous switching equipments of Digital Electronic Exchanges and transmission systems suitable for Indian conditions, particularly for rural areas was being developed. The manufacturing of customer premises equipments like telephone instruments, drop-wire, etc. started in the private sector in 1984.

Telecom Mission Plans in 1986: Rural telephony was focused as priority area. India had taken indigenous production of rural automatic exchange (RAX) and experimented in 1987 in one village. The experiment showed that technology was effective but the cost of the services and receivers would prohibit individuals to have more than one telephone available in the village. RAX project aimed at proper connectivity to one billion rural people and 30 million phones against 3 million at that time in 1986. The solution for the government was either to have one telephone in the village and not to invest in RAX or make service inexpensive for ruralites to afford it. Less than 6% of 6,07,491 villages had public telephones in 2000. In 1990 to 2000 decade, the government focused on developing rural telephony but it did not take off. That was the time government was revitalizing landline telephony in urban areas, and mobile telephony was developing through private efforts. In 2000 decade, the mobile telephone receivers and the services have become inexpensive that rural people could afford it. Government also realized that cell phone is the answer for rural tele-connectivity rather than wiring the rural areas which was expensive.

In 1987, Mr. Sam Pitroda was asked by Rajiv Gandhi, Prime Minister, to help democratize access to tele-communications. The Indian Telephone revitalization was planned under Sam Pitroda. His response was to deploy instantly, telephone kiosks in every town and village. In the process, he helped to release the Indian telecom industry from state control and opened it up to dozens of private companies, paving the way for India's telecoms boom. Through World-

Tel, he now promotes similar policies in other parts of the developing world.

There has been a thrust on extending telecom services in rural areas in each successive Five-Year Plan. However, the process achieved a gradual momentum in 1980s and 1990s, and has got accelerated after new telephone policies—NTP 94 and NTP 99.

The specific objectives, targets and stipulations for rural areas of NTP 99 are: availability of affordable and effective communications for the citizens, provision of universal service to all uncovered areas, including the rural areas, and the provision of high-level services capable of meeting the needs of the country's economy; and to encourage development of telecommunication facilities in remote, hilly and tribal areas of the country; encourage development of telecom in rural areas making it more affordable by suitable tariff structure and making rural communications mandatory for all fixed line service providers.

Targets set up by the policy are: to increase rural tele-density from the current level of 0.4 to 4 by the year 2010. Telecom coverage of all villages in the country and provide reliable media to all exchanges by the year 2002. Areas of North East, Jammu & Kashmir and other hilly areas, tribal blocks, etc. are identified as special thrust areas for accelerated development of telecommunications.

Investments in Rural Telephony

The telecom services in rural areas have been unattractive due to the reasons of non-remunerative nature of operations in rural areas with relatively higher costs and lower returns. The availability of the suitable technologies and equipments as also maintenance aspects has also been another bottleneck for penetration and spread of telecom services in rural and remote parts of the country.

Private investment in rural telephony on sustained basis is necessary and is being encouraged through incentives. To contain the subsidy within reasonable limits, the need to upgrade the technology in rural areas along with an appropriate mix of technology with convergence of voice, data and video is necessary for improved usage and revenue generation on a sustained basis. It may be necessary to evolve certain measures to encourage investment in rural areas through a suitable mix of incentives like tax concessions, waiver of license fee for ICT and tele-centers operators in rural areas and interconnection charges, and to provide funds through USO Fund to the rural operators. The emphasis could be on time-bound achievement of rural coverage.

So far, the entire development in rural areas has been done by the incumbent operator through cross-subsidization. However, with tariff rebalancing, deregulation and corporatization of the incumbent operator, the situation has perceptibly changed to meet the rural telecom needs.

In order to keep the subsidy level at reasonable level for providing rural telecom services, clusters of contiguous villages may be organized, which could be served by private operators, including local bodies and cooperatives, in different scales of operations and with appropriate and cost-effective and most efficient technologies best suited to the region. Affordability by rural consumer is important in determining the size of market in rural areas. There is considerable latent demand in rural areas, which can surface with right conditions and stimulants making the rural operations profitable.

According to latest study on 'Emerging Rural Mobile Market in India' 2009, the mobile market in rural India has significant potential with number of subscribers anticipated to grow at a CAGR of around 32% during 2009 to 2012. The report thoroughly discusses about the factor which will drive the growth of rural mobile market over the forecasted period. This report highlights that the success mantra for rural mobile market in India lies in the operators' service pricing models coupled with the availability of low cost handsets that support affordable access for rural areas. It is forecasted that sales of mobile handsets in rural India will grow at CAGR of around 17% from 2009 to 2012. Availability of low-cost battery efficient handsets will drive the future sales in this segment. This research foresees immense opportunities for various industry players including mobile operators and handset manufacturers. Besides this, the report comprehensively analyzes rural mobile penetration in different states helping the clients to understand the mobile market trends and developments across the country. The study also evaluates various strategies that will boost the rural mobile market in India.

The provision of telecom facilities in rural areas can bring about significant changes in socio-economic conditions of these regions as also the integration with the rest of the market economy, bringing in considerable direct and indirect benefits to the economy. Some of the advantages are clearly seen: (i) Telecommunication facilities enhance the region's appeal as an attractive location for investment. (ii) Local producers and service sector get enriched through integration of market and provision of regional, national and international links, which can improve better price realization of goods and services. (iii) Diffusion of innovative technologies and information-based services is facilitated. (iv) The quality and efficiency of the government at the grass roots level can improve through e-governance. (v) Research and development in leading edge technologies can be stimulated. (vi) Two major barriers to rural economic growth i.e. the distance from the market place and lack of economies of scale can be broken by telecom facilities, particularly with broadband data communication facility. (vii) ICT centers in rural areas can be effectively used for providing information and delivery of public services on matters related to production, prices, health, education, animal husbandry, weather conditions and service sector (Tamil Nadu experience of M.S. Swaminathan Research Foundation and the Foundation of Occupational Development (FOOD), Tamil Nadu). (viii) Greater employment opportunities and other benefits through applications of information technology viz. e-commerce, e-governance, tele-medicine, distance learning, software development, e-business operation, etc. to the advantage of rural population.

Technology Issues for Rural Telephony

India's rural telecom network has undergone tremendous transformation with the induction of small and medium size electronic digital exchanges of C-DoT technology. About 22,243 telephone exchanges are working in the rural areas. Presently, about 18% telephones are working in rural areas. This means that out of 265.11 lakh DELs, 216.69 lakh lines are working in urban areas and 48.42 lakh in rural areas. Telecom technologies used for setting up telephone exchanges in India over time is given in appendix 4.

Telecom Technology: Appropriate technology in rural areas for rural telephony is provided in a cost-effective manner by taking advantages of the recent developments in access technologies. Of the total VPTs, about 56% are with MARR (Multi-access radio relay) technology and 43.9% are on overhead lines. The remaining is covered by wireless in local loop (WLL), INMARSAT and C-DOT-PMP technologies. The efficiency of existing systems at many places is not very satisfactory and a large number of VPTs do not function properly, due to inadequate maintenance, power and other problems. To provide satisfactory telecom services in the rural areas in the country, other technological options are being considered and Wireless in Local Loop 'WLL' for rural telecom with a range of about 25 Kms and GSM technologies are being inducted. Furthermore, 18,000 exchanges installed in rural areas out of total 22,032 are of C-DOT switching technology. These exchanges are very rugged and suitable for working without air-conditioning in extreme weather conditions of higher temperature and high humidity.

Existing MARR technology-based VPTs which are not functioning properly are being replaced; and other VPTs are also being upgraded for STD facility, and to serve as 'Public Tele-Information Centers and Information Dhabas (cafe)'. An ambitious scheme has been undertaken to set-up Community Communication Cafes (popularly known as Sanchar Dhabas) at village Panchayat levels. VPTs are also being provided in remote and far-flung areas on satellite. Considering the diverse terrain and geographical locations, specific cost-effective technological solutions have to be found for each of the clusters out of the various options.

Introduction of new services based on ISDN to the rural areas such as tele-education and tele-medicine have been planned. With the extension of Digital connectivity to the District headquarters and progressively to the sub-divisional level, it would be possible to provide latest telecommunication facilities to the rural areas.

In 2008-09, TRAI wants to take more and more of mobile technology to rural areas rather than fixed lines. Earlier years, TRAI has been focusing on fixed landlines through rural exchanges which have not been a success.

Reliable Media: Another important area of concern is the provision of reliable media in the rural areas. (Reliable media are voice boards which enable Main Telecom to offer call monitoring for customers who require the performance of their agents to be tracked.) As per the available information, of the total exchanges working in the rural areas, about 44% are without a reliable media. The severity of this problem is more in those States, which are relatively much large in area with difficult and varied geographical terrain. These include, in particular Maharashtra, Madhya Pradesh, Rajasthan, North East, Himachal Pradesh and Gujarat. This implies that a much bigger effort and investment would be needed in terms of providing additional equipment and OFC. As per the NTP 99, all the rural exchanges are to be provided with reliable media by 2010.

Viability of the rural telecom is to be guided more by the technological issues. These include the move towards provision of reliable media through adequate bandwidth, convergence of technology for voice, data and video to be utilized through ICT centers, adoption of appropriate technology mix, connectivity through OFC up to the last mile, wherever required. Finally, the emphasis should be on evaluation of available technologies rather than on evolution.

IDRC has been setting up tele-centers in the villages across the world for knowledge connectivity. Rural mobile telephony is being encouraged in developing countries as this is more cost effective than setting up landlines where lack of electricity is another issue.

Infrastructure to Accelerate Rural Telephony

The government's role in funding telecom infrastructure will be crucial to the growth and spread of mobile telephony in rural India. This is because operators will increasingly look for support from the USOF for setting up tens of thousands of telecom towers in rural India over the next three years, especially in areas where it would not be viable for them to invest in launching commercial telephony. Besides, subsidies from the USOF will also be vital if telecoms are to take broadband and Internet services to rural India. Telecom companies pay 5% of their adjusted gross revenues towards the USOF, which is used for funding telecom infrastructure in rural India. As per DoT, unutilized USOF has already crossed Rs. 10,000 crore.

DoT took the first step towards this earlier in 2006, when it invited bids from telecom operators and 22 standalone tower companies for setting up about 8,000 telecom towers across the country at an estimated cost of Rs. 2,500 crore. This project is estimated to help provide about 50 million mobile connections in rural India. More importantly, after finalizing the contracts for setting up for this, DoT will soon issue a subsequent tender for setting up additional 10,000 towers in rural India. With the tender rules mandating that a minimum of three operators share a tower, rural India will also have a choice of service providers.

In addition to sharing the towers, telecoms can also share the electronics located on the tower, which constitutes the active component and include antenna, feeder cable, node B, radio access network and transmission systems. Besides, they can also share their backhaul from Base Trans Receiver Station (BTS) to Base Station Controller (BSC), where such sharing will be permitted both on optical fiber as well as radio medium. "Non-availability of backhaul especially in rural areas has been a major concern. As the traffic in such areas is likely to be low in the initial stages, there is an obvious advantage of sharing of backhaul. Such backhaul sharing can also help to reduce the load of the backhaul antennae on the tower reducing the cost to set up such towers and increase the possibility of sharing same tower by more operators," TRAI had said in its recommendations. It may be necessary to synergize the existing infrastructure of various operators to optimize the resources and efforts in accelerating the telecom development in rural areas.

Apart from DoT and its corporations like BSNL, MTNL and VSNL, other agencies like Railways, Power Grid, State Electricity Boards and other Public Sector Undertakings like SAIL, BHEL, ONGC, etc. can all contribute to these efforts. The reach of rural telecommunication can be enhanced effectively by strategic alliances with these organizations and with minimum additional investment in infrastructure. The spread and coverage can be considerably multiplied by interconnectivity and usage of overall communication networks. Social sector projects, such as rural development, health, education, etc. may have infrastructure built in. For example, primary health centers can be interconnected with doctors in the civil hospital and tele-medicine project can be launched. Or, tele-education can be implemented through linking of schools (Rural telephone statistics, technology, infrastructure given are based on annual Telecommunication reports government of India).

Salient Current Rural Telephony Programs

Due to mobile telephony, there is social change in villages, people are more connected with others out of the village, they feel connected to the family and friends if they are out of the village and they feel going up the social ladder and occupational ladder also. A few rural telephony programs highlight the efforts being made in diverse directions and by diverse agencies to sustain and diffuse rural telephony.

Vihaan Networks Ltd. (VNL) India has set up a solar powered base station for mobile-communications networks to bring cell phone access to India's remote villages. Getting cell phone coverage to remote rural parts of India is hindered by high installation and high operating costs as well specialized knowledge needed to set up and run a cellular station. As a result, few operators have gone in these areas.

VNL is looking to overcome this obstacle with a low power cellular base station that requires little capital expense and almost no operating costs. The base station can be powered by a small solar panel in daylight, batteries provide backup for up to 72 hours. Another challenge was to make the device simple so that villagers can install it at low cost and operate it easily. The solution was inspired by Scandinavian retailer IKEA. The entire panel is delivered in six boxes, small enough to fit in an ox cart. Simple illustrated instructions show how to put the pieces together with color-coded cables; turning the station to the right microwave signal is easy—it emits a continuous beeping sound when the signal is strongest. Thus, the inexpensive base station can be assembled quickly and set up by unskilled villagers and can run entirely on solar power panels and batteries.

Transclick USA has set up real-time language translation of SMS, email and instant messaging in 16 languages to and from English on mobile phones and online.

"**Reliance** Communications has rolled out telephone connections to 40,000 villages hitherto devoid of any phones under this particular program. We are able to give impetus to the Government's rural initiative and fulfill our obligation by taking the telephone to far-flung areas. Our tariffs are made very attractive and affordable to benefit the rural people who have come to realize the necessity to stay connected with the rest of the world" (Press release). The company plans to boost its fiber optic, hybrid data network. Sources say the company may have ordered one million data cards from Huawei, ZTE. The data card investment may be worth Rs. 200 crore. It also plans to invest in vernacular content application development.

R-Comm's current fiber optic capacity is approximately 1.75000 km. Sources say it may add 15,000 km. more. They continue to invest in areas where there is an opportunity. In terms of the sachet pricing how much do they see possible increase in upticks especially from the rural areas for high speed Internet access? Today, when you look at the rural market and the suburban market there are about 4.8 million dialup users, the desktop penetration in the rural market is anywhere in the range of 1.5-4.5 million. So, when you put these two things together, we believe that there is a significant opportunity to go after the dialup market. The sources closer to the company said that some Rs. 1,000 crore would be invested in this entire initiative (August 09).

Unified Communications LifeLines India is bridging the Digital Divide in Rural India. It is a telephone-based information helpline, provides advice and guidance to improve the lives of rural farming communities. Unified communications is typically associated with improved business productivity, but in parts of the world it is also delivering a much more fundamental benefit; improving basic quality of life. In some of the most remote parts of rural India, an agriculture and animal husbandry information system powered by unified communications is providing small-scale rural Indian farmers with means of bridging the information gap. Access to the latest and often vital knowledge is helping them farm in a sustainable manner and ultimately improve the quality of life for their families and communities (March 09).

Google logs into rural India. It is also betting heavily on the mobile platform (as PC penetration is low) and plans to introduce services like Google Talk (instant chat application), and Google Maps through tie-ups with Indian mobile operators (July 09).

SMS Servers are replacing PCs in India. They ran an experiment replacing a PC-based system for helping a rural sugarcane cooperative with a mobile phone-based system. The new mobile system replicates almost all of the PC-based functionality. It is cheaper, adds additional functionality and is more popular. It is believed to be the first project of its kind in developing regions where an entire PC setup has been replaced with mobile phones (July 09).

TCS, Qualcomm woo Rural India: A system is under development which will use soil sensors to monitor moisture content and salinity. The data will be transferred to a central server via farmer on mobile phone and experts will advise the farmer on the kinds of crops that are ideally suited to his or her patch of land.

India tests biofuel for rural wireless: Biofuels are on trial as a fuel to power cellular networks in rural India. Local operator Idea Cellular, Ericsson and the GSM Association have set up a pilot project in Pune to power mobile base stations that are off the electricity grid (July 09).

SIDA is mobilizing Sweden's ICT resources to bridge the digital divide in the world. SPIDER, the Swedish Program for Information and Communication Technology in Developing Regions, aim at reinforcing the Swedish support activities in the field of information and communication technology (ICT) in developing countries. It is a national center that mobilizes Sweden's ICT resources, SPIDER is supported by SIDA and hosted by the Royal Institute of Technology, KTH, in Kista, Stockholm. Spider's main task is to pull together all ICT resources, related to sustainable development, in Sweden, and make them available to developing countries.

Nokia Corporation said the company aims to tap the fast-growing rural market with various new services. It would also look at lowering the affordability barrier for mobile phones by providing micro-financing facilities. "We estimate 500 million people will have the benefit of mobility by 2010 and the telecom sector would be the biggest contributor to GDP. We also believe that much of the growth will take place in the non-urban markets, where penetration is still low at 13 per cent," said Olli-Pekka Kallasvuo, President and CEO, Nokia Corp. He added that India is the second biggest market in terms of revenues for Nokia.

The company also announced the national roll-out of Nokia Life Tools services, which would eventually cover 17 States. Targeted at the rural customer, Nokia Life Tools provides useful information on weather conditions, farm inputs and market prices. Nokia also announced that it plans to offer a micro-financing facility for its phones across 12 States, for which it is currently in talks with few institutions. This facility would be aimed largely at women in rural areas. Mr Kallasvuo further said, "The Chennai factory, with an investment of

$250 million, is now Nokia's biggest factory worldwide. We're exporting more than half of our production from this plant to over 59 countries. He added that in retail, the company has around 1.9 lakh outlets across the country. The company plans to look more into local content as far as features such as music and games are concerned. The fine line between netbooks and smart phones is fast disappearing" (New Delhi, 19 Aug. 2009).

Changing Telecommunication Practices are empowering people in rural India. The changing communication practice in India and elsewhere in other developing countries is to provide telephone connectivity as well as increase tele-density in rural areas through cellular technology. It is cheaper and does not require rural electrification. Cheaper Cellular technology both hardware and software is creating wider and bigger markets even among the poor and bringing better connectivity and social change.

To sum up, India has achieved a high level of connectivity through telephones connecting both the urban and rural India through easy accessibility and affordability. Mobile telephone technology has been on the forefront bringing a leapfrog progress both in personal and enterprises connectivity, bringing social change by bridging the connectivity divide. The policy of allowing the private players to enter the telephones operations has created competition, better services, initiated new technologies, affordability for the customer and thus increasing the subscriber base and tele-density.

Computer

Computerization in Rural India

Two aspects are important for computer presence in rural India; computer literacy of the rural masses and use of computerization for village functionalities.

Computer Literacy Initiatives

Computer literacy in the villages is planned in two ways. Computer basics are taught to school kids and youth by NGOs hired teachers; community computers are also provided in the village so that it serve as cyber café as well self-taught by those who are learning. This initiative creates awareness and evokes interest for functionality uses and applications of computer technology among the villagers.

Computer literacy teaching will be picked up for younger school-going children and they would find it educative and informative and can even help the older generation in villages by researching for them the information that may need. But for the older generation and that too not literate, it may not be quick and easy but they can gain information and knowledge about functionalities at hubs, guided sites and forums.

Both government and the conglomerates are starting computer literacy and training efforts in their rural retail hubs. It will be easier to arouse computer interest and need for computer training among the rural shoppers who would visit these hubs. Seeking requisite information through Internet and online e-business even may actively interest them and encourage them for computer learning and applications. Government and the companies can through such ambitious programs multiply the effects of computers, Internet, education and marketing to accelerate the reach of technology benefits. They believe people in rural areas require the computer education, Internet connectivity and the access to the right technology to meet their unique needs; where consumers must cope with a lower income and limited access to credit. Villagers would benefit appropriately from these efforts.

Indian Institute of Technology, Kanpur in 2003 has set a computerization project creating a computer corridor, and provides free computer classes in six villages in Uttar Pradesh. It aims to use technology to improve education, health-care and access to agricultural information in India's villages. The project is funded by the central government.

Discover the PC Initiative

Intel through its community computer initiative in India is providing low cost PC in rural India. In March, 2006 it unveiled a prototype PC for use in India where dust, heat, and humidity can cause reliability problems. This PC can withstand these. Given the electricity problems in rural India, it can run on alternate power sources including a car battery. Another prototype of a full-featured computer notebook is expected to cost less than $400. It has started an initiative 'jagruti' (awakening) in coordination with this technology, with donation of community PCs to help bridge the digital divide. It could have the advantage of exposing children to technology at an early age. It opens up whole range of opportunities for the villagers. Intel sees potential in India and its talented pool of citizens. The low cost, fully-featured desktop PCs priced 20% lower than the current Intel configured ones were launched in 2006 and working with Indian manufacturers with HCL, Millennium, PCS, Wipro and Zenith Computers for 'Discover the PC initiative'.

As part of World Ahead Program (WAP), Intel plans to donate 100,000 PCs for use in classrooms in developing nations. The company has already been spending 100 million a year on educational programs. It has trained about three million teachers so far in the use of technology, and plans to train 10 million more over five years as part of the World Ahead Program. Chip maker Intel will boost its story in India with new initiatives planned to accelerate technology accessibility, Internet connectivity and effective education. The initiatives, coming under this program, include low-cost computers, pay-as-you-go PC purchasing models, small learning devices for education and extending WiMAX broadband connectivity in the country.

Intel in 2006 launched its Community PC, a flexible pay-as-you- go PC purchasing model in India. Another product set for introduction is an affordable, rugged learning device for students—code named Eduwise. The notebook to provide collaborative learning between teachers and students in developing countries was designed in Intel's Bangalore platform definition center. It was launched in the first half of '07. "PC penetration is immense and challenging. By multiplying the effects of computers, Internet and education, we intend to accelerate the reach of technology benefits in the country over the next five years". Intel will be investing $1 bn. in India in the next five years for R&D.

Indian Institute of Science (IISc), Bangalore has constituted a team of researchers to see how a fixed-line phone, with a five inch screen and broadband access can help take the benefits of computing to the masses. Both models, from IISc and Microsoft, have a simple interface that is easy to use and not intimidating for the target group-users in the villages, remote areas and the poor. What can good old fixed-line phones morph into if you have broadband and large screens? And if you have computers with audio and text user interface, or computers in classrooms that don't have just one mouse but multiple rodents, does it help anyone?

These are just three different ideas to meet one objective, i.e. bridge the digital divide. Such modified machines from IISc, Bangalore, and Microsoft Research India are helping domestic helps to find work in housing societies. Children in schools that have one computer to a class can use a device with multiple mice to help up to 10 students work on a single machine. *The computer with audio and text user interface is one of the ambitious projects of Microsoft Research that seeks to take computing to the underprivileged—much like an electronic voting machine enables even illiterates to vote.*

Websites will soon be accessible to the disabled, especially the visually-impaired, once the government makes it mandatory for all websites to go audible. For this, websites have to conform to the Web Content Accessibility Guidelines. This new standard, along with a screen reader, will make content audible through a headphone or a speaker. A visually-impaired person can use the keyboard to respond—the tab keys will take him or her through different links. "It will not only help blind people, but also aged and illiterate people". The policy would be extended to other hardware as well—like the ATM, television, washing machine and microwave. This will be the second phase of the project. This is going to help the rural illiterate even to participate in computerized rural functionalities (09).

Computerization for Village Functionalities

There are Internet sites and other sites which guide farmers on sowing suitable varieties of seeds of crops, demand, current trends and prevailing market prices in the neighbourhood, weather and rain forecasts. Information about different kinds of genetic seeds, irrigation facilities, machinery and implements with prices and functionalities are available through computers. Through these, villagers have access to land records, government village development efforts and the new schemes to benefit them. Thus, they can get direct information and it is not filtered. There are both government and private rural sites set up by NGOs, individual activists, and business enterprises.

MSSRF has linked twelve rural villages across Pondicherry in south India, providing them with computer and Internet access so that they will have update information to help them in their farming work. Through the Information Village Center, the farmers can check weather forecasts, bus timetables, crop prices as well as get advice on best practices when it comes to buying seed and growing their produce.

Computer Software applications are developed to help rural communities in India. Centre for Development of Advanced Computing (C-DAC), Bangalore, ITC Research and Training Center in India, have developed two software applications catering to the needs of people in rural areas, benefiting rural communities through appropriate computer software. The first, called Vyapar, is an online trading tool. The second, ECKO, provides a framework for building e-communities through collaboration and knowledge sharing. The software is being piloted with local organizations in India. Thus, computer can be used to increase productivity, efficiency, and participation in the local economies.

ITC company's e-Choupal program in India has contributed to overall programs of development. e-Choupal has helped increase the incomes and productivity of millions of farmers by giving them more direct access to markets, as well as pricing and product information, via village-based Internet kiosks. e-Choupal is now expanding its service to include education. It has opened 100 e-Choupals in Andhra Pradesh in 2006.

Rural e-Governance: The slow progress of e-governance in villages was due to low computer literacy, low accessibility of computers and low tele-density in rural areas. With improved tele-density by cellular phones and community computers, many e-governance projects and practices are targeting the rural areas for better governance.

Computer through Internet will not only make the benefits of the new "Information Society" accessible and meaningful for rural people, but in particular to raise public awareness and give deserved public recognition to the highest quality e-content produced all over the world. The following eight categories of content are focused: e-learning; e-culture; e-science; e-government; e-health; e-business; e-entertainment; and e-inclusion. Through this, the focus would be on a range of parameters which can be referred to as the 8 Cs of the digital economy: connectivity, content, community, commerce, capacity, culture, capital and cooperation. With wider access to computerization, the villagers would gain, though English language may be a constraint for some of the world sites. The availability of use of Hindi and some Indian regional languages have greatly facilitated the computer/Internet experiences.

Urban India has accepted the challenges of computerization and Internet as an important aspect of occupational and personal life of people and the significant role in people's daily routine. Now, government, businesses and rural community themselves aspire for the same and are ready to accept the social technology challenge of computerization by assimilating that as important aspect of their lifestyle. In rural India, this has to be integrated with education, vocational skill sets and tele-density and rural electrification to a greater extent. We presume this is likely to boost productivity in agriculture, and village trade. Marketing experiences through rural hubs and informed villagers, all put together are expected to boost the village economy.

Center for Digital Inclusion (CDI): CDI concept is using digital technology to empower the marginalized people. By partnering with grass roots organizations and cyber cafes, CDI creates centers in low-income communities, rural and indigenous communities and hospitals, etc. (i) These centers work with local marginalized people to help them identify the key challenges they face and it tackles their problems using technology, and (ii) for civic advocacy for their issues and cause, use presentations, blogs, videos as tools for social mobilizations and running e-mail campaigns. CDI can be used for villages in India.

Much like the private sectors, the social enterprise, NGO and hybrid sector need lawyers, doctors, managers, accountants, communications experts, etc. and those with a strong interest in entrepreneurship, strategy and innovation in the social sector. CDI identifies with institutional development, marketing, operations, finances and needs them all for various functionalities.

Computerization: Post Offices

The Department of Posts has launched "Project Arrow" to revitalize its core operations and to provide new technology enabled service to the common man in 2000. It has laid foundation for a vibrant delivery mechanism for many social sector schemes such as pension and NREGS and has focused its schemes to help the villagers.

By the end of 2008-09, a total of 9,674 post offices, including 1,233 rural post offices have been computerized and networked with the National Data Center. The strong IT-base has enabled a range of e-enabled services. The on-line domestic money transmission service, i-MO, launched in 2006, that enables customer to receive money in minutes from the post offices providing this service is functional at over 1,000 locations. Electronic Clearance Service (ECS) is offered at all 15 locations of RBI and 21 locations of the SBI for payment of monthly interest under Monthly Income Scheme. The electronic money order (eMO), launched in October, 2008, facilitates transmission of ordinary money orders through electronic media in the same tariff structure as the existing money order service. e-Payment under which different bills are paid by customers in post offices which are then electronically consolidated and paid to the service provider is now available in about 5,700 post offices and will soon be extended to all 9,693 computerized post offices.

Under e-Post service started in 2004 to bridge the digital divide physical messages are transmitted through electronic system as an e-mail and the message is printed and delivered anywhere in India as a letter.

Computerization facilitates post office functions for villagers such as i-Mo, e-Mo and e-Post service and ECS through banks for payment of monthly interest under Monthly Income Scheme of post offices.

The number of rural postal life insurance policies increased from 26.66 lakh in 2003-04 to 74 lakh in 2008-09. The payment of wages to NREGS beneficiaries is currently operational in 19 postal circles comprising of 21 states, through 90,000 post offices (including HOs/SOs/BOs). Nearly 2.92 crore NREGS accounts have been opened upto 31 March, 2009.

NABARD in collaboration with the Department of Posts is providing micro-credit to self-help groups (SHGs) through identified post offices. The corpus fund for implementing this project is given by NABARD. The pilot project is in operation in five districts. So far, 777 SHGs have been provided with a loan of Rs. 1.85 crore.

IT and Rural Economy: There are increasing opportunities for the IT industry in rural areas because of massive outlays on the rural employment scheme, and on health and education. IT industries are moving into rural areas and are setting up BPOs. The initiative started in 2008-09. This initiative will boost economy and create employment and skill development.

Rural BPOs operations head into rural communities. There is a big cost advantage to a company locating in rural areas because the infrastructure costs are low. It is estimated there are 80 to 90 million people that could be trained to take care of the back-office needs. These BPOs are emulating the original 'India model' in which work is broken up into small tasks, appropriate ones outsourced for execution in India. This is then sent back and reintegrated. The very same approach is being followed for work being done in a large facility in urban areas i.e. break it into manageable pieces, ship appropriate ones to the rural BPO, have it executed securely and well, ship back and reintegrate.

Now going to remote rural areas could be the next big shift to offer everything from native language capabilities to data entry type services. It is the same as moving jobs from USA to India—to cash in on cheaper talent and office space. "Tying up with rural service providers will keep our gross margins from domestic business similar to those from international business (22-24%)."

The average billing rate for domestic clients is just $3-4 per hour for every employee, compared with $8-12 offered by global clients. This makes offering services to domestic clients from metros to big cities unviable; hence the move to rural areas is 60% cheaper. For instance, in a tier-I city, a fresher gets about Rs. 8,000, while in a tier-III city, it is around Rs. 3,500, and even less in villages. These centers are likely to do routine tasks like data entry, processing of utility bills, native language help desk and e-mail response.

The emergence of large deals from the Indian market in recent years has evoked interest from large players such as Infosys, Wipro and TCS which are seeing a slower growth in their traditional markets—USA and Europe, where customers are delaying their technology spends. The company would be aggressively using the technology platforms to service the Indian markets.

Indian tech majors—Infosys technologies and Wipro are set to enter the booming domestic back-office service market, multiplying by more than one-third every year, and join a tech revolution happening in rural India. At present, there are about a dozen rural BPO players including RuralShores, DesiCrew HOV Services, Sai BPO and DesiCrew in India, accounting for just a fraction of the domestic industry. RuralShores, a year old startup gets technical support from WIPRO. Byrraju's unique Gram IT initiative has established the viability and success of outsourcing work to the village level. There are large number of rural BPOs and the fact that, despite many difficulties, they are all doing well. An example is Vintes, with 100 seats in three pilot projects in rural Kerala, which is emulating and adapting a model it developed for decentralized rural manufacturing.

Firstsource Solutions, which services both international and domestic clients, agree that, it makes sense to have a distributed capability to access talent and cut costs. "We are also looking at leveraging rural areas or very small towns for delivering services," RuralShores—which has a 160-people center in Bagepalli village, three hours from Bangalore, and another one at Ratnagiri in Vellore district of Tamil Nadu—is planning to open 500 village centers across the country over the next seven years with 20-30 seats.

Tie-ups with the likes of Infosys and Wipro will help these small startups attract big clients in mobile phone and banking industries that are making major inroads into rural markets. "It makes sense for rural BPOs to look at tie-ups as they may not be able to bag large contracts on their own."

Infosys BPO. The $316-million back-office service arm of Infosys, plans to tie up with service providers with shops in rural areas and small towns for its domestic operations, company officials said. The revenue-share model will see Infosys getting the customers and the rural operators doing the service. A couple of village-based players around Bhubaneshwar and Udaipur were likely partners.

As part of its concerted bid to tap the rapidly growing domestic market, Infosys BPO proposes to tie-up with the rural BPOs, besides setting up a separate delivery team of 500 employees by the year-end to service the local market. "We are in talks with the rural BPOs and have evaluated a couple of them," said CEO, Infosys BPO, stating that the "company would engage them on a need basis to service specific contracts". Such an engagement with rural BPOs, which are located outside of large cities, is also expected to help Infosys bring in the multilingual capabilities and also service such portion of contracts, such as document scanning, that require basic skills.

Infosys will factor in the cost benefits of Rural BPO model in its pricing to the client, and will own the engagement and entire delivery (including that of Rural BPO). The pricing and revenue sharing will be worked on case-to-case basis. Further, the kind of work that will be outsourced from the rural BPO would be of low to medium complexity, entailing low or no interaction with the client such as data processing work. It has drawn up a broad strategy to address the Indian market and has identified about three to four areas to enhance its presence. As part of the strategy, the BPO outfit plans to work closely with the Systems Integration division of Infosys' India Business Unit to pursue the IT-BPO deals. Besides, the BPO outfit would also be targeting the existing customers of Finacle, which commands a huge market share in India. "We plan to have a team of some 500 people by the year-end to be located in Jaipur to service the domestic market." The company also plans to target the large Indian corporate and multinationals with its specific shared services offerings, such as payroll processing, procurement among others. "Lot of Indian companies would be willing to work with us, considering our brand equity," adding that Infosys BPO was seeing lot of interest for its offerings from companies in the manufacturing, telecom and banking verticals. Infosys BPO expects revenues from the Indian market to flow next year. Currently, the BPO outfit does not derive any revenues from the Indian market, which accounts for 1.3 per cent of the Infosys' overall revenues. "Tie-ups with small startups; besides revenue share, we will also train people in villages and tier-II, III towns." These centers will do routine tasks like data entry, processing of utility bills, native language help desk and e-mail response.

Wipro BPO. The $395-million, BPO will enter the domestic market soon. It already provides technology and other supports to a few rural service providers and may also explore service delivery tie-ups with them. Wipro BPO is eyeing business from top 100 customers in India. So, as the business spreads to the smaller cities and villages, your call to fix the desktop or buy a new mobile phone plan may well be answered from a village back office.

Rural BPOs are, however, not expected to scale up dramatically as while the manpower is cheap, its availability is extremely limited. There are other limitations also such as lack of skilled manpower, poor broadband connectivity and frequent power blackouts. "Rural areas will be good for some niche tasks. These can work well as a hub-and-spoke model, with tier-II and in the domestic space."

Rural BPOs will create new opportunities for rural development. If such rural BPOs can help to retain even a small proportion of educated youth in villages, it can transform the face of rural India. Appropriate government policies can help kick-start such a process. There are some of the essential steps through which Government and industry, working in tandem, can bring IT to rural India such as tax incentives, similar to exports; rural employment zones, with the same fiscal sops as SEZs, schemes to train educated rural youth, and high-quality broadband connectivity in rural areas. IT operations in rural India will certainly boost the rural economy. ICTs can be used to assist small and medium-sized enterprises to increase productivity, efficiency, and participation in the local and global economies.

Internet

Internet Access: The aim is to reduce the digital divide by providing Internet access and IT enabled services to the community at large and to facilitate citizen interface with the government by establishing 100,000 web enabled Citizen Service Centers or CSCs in rural areas, which will serve not only as the front end for most government services, but also as a means to connect the citizens of rural India to the World Wide Web. CSCs would extend the reach of electronic services, both government and private to the village level. It is these advances in ICT technologies, which have enabled the government to take concrete steps towards turning citizens' dream of "Government at your doorstep" into a reality.

Internet Promotion: National Internet Exchange of India (NIXI) has been set up to improve the quality of service and help in efficient routing of the domestic traffic within the country. Four Internet Exchange Nodes have been set up and made operational at Noida (U.P.), Mumbai, Chennai and Kolkata, and as many as 40 ISPs have been connected with these nodes. Government has installed three mirror Internet root servers at Delhi, Mumbai and Chennai. The root servers form a critical part of the global Internet infrastructure.

Internet Content: Most of the Internet content is in English. Language is, therefore, an important barrier. There is increased focus on Indian languages and making packaged software available in local languages. To enable wide proliferation of ICTs in Indian languages, government has taken a major initiative to make available tools and fonts in various Indian Languages freely to the general public. It has released in the public domain, various Tamil language fonts, e-mail client, Optical Character Recognition (OCR) software, spell checker and dictionary in April 2005. Similarly, the Hindi and Telugu software tools and fonts were released in June 2005 and October 2005, respectively. Software tools and fonts in Punjabi and Urdu are released. All Indian languages are expected to be covered soon. Software tools and fonts in different languages would promote rural Internet also and give better connectivity. Cyber café in villages would be able to work through regional languages.

Internet Cost: Government is making efforts to make Internet and telephones affordable to all. As a first step towards making long distance tariffs more affordable, government in May 2005 made telephone calls within States equivalent to local calls. The second step was taken in November 2005 where the government significantly reduced the entry barrier for acquiring national and international long distance licenses. On 1st January 2006, government allowed Access Service Provider to provide Internet telephony, Internet services and Broadband services. From 2006 to 2009, there is greater reduction in Internet tariffs and telephone calls because of increased competition among telephone operators, wider facilities and reach of new technologies and equally important is the role of greater consumer usage.

Rural Broadband

The era of mobile broadband has commenced wireless as access network technology, for broadband is the main technology for remote and rural areas. Fixed wireless access in UHF and higher frequency bands is becoming popular solution for rural communication and as point-to-point corporate access. But no clear standards have emerged in this area. 3G evolving with HSDPA (High Speed Downlink Packet Access) is going to soon become wireless broadband standard and will find its extensive use in rural areas due to cost advantage as the incremental cost of extending networks to cover more and more villages will work out less.

In 2008, DoT has also initiated discussions with both private and state-owned telecom operators to utilize the USOF for broadband roll-out in rural India through a bidding process. DoT's plans include providing broadband connections within a 10 km. radius of all block headquarters in the country. It envisages a minimum speed of 512 kbps, where the network connects community centers, primary schools, banks, health centers, panchayats and police stations located close to all block headquarters.

The project also proposes that users are charged only annual rentals with the subscriptions being provided free of cost. In a bid to ensure that the broadband infrastructure created with USOF support is utilized fully, DoT has decided to rope in various other government agencies such as Panchayats, health, agriculture and education to jointly evolve a strategy for it.

Broadband connectivity from urban homes and small and medium businesses is extending to villages for e-services to improve the quality of living of vast majority of Indians living in rural areas. Trials for WiMAX technology are going on in number of Indian states to develop a low cost business model for rural applications. Five years back, Wireless Broadband Alliance was created to drive the state-owned telecom operators to utilize the USOF for broadband roll-out in rural India through a bidding process.

Recognizing the importance of increasing broadband connectivity for the growth of knowledge-based society, several steps have been taken to promote broadband. As a result, the broadband subscribers grew from a meager 0.18 million as on March 2005 to about 5.69 million by February, 2009. There is potential of Broadband service in growth of GDP and enhancement in quality of life through societal applications including tele-education, tele-medicine, e-governance, entertainment as well as employment generation by way of high speed access to information and web-based communication, government has come out with a Broadband Policy to provide affordable services to the public.

Broadband Policy

An agreement has been signed with BSNL in January 2009 to provide wire-line broadband connectivity to rural and remote areas by leveraging the existing 27,789 rural exchanges and copper wire line network and by facilitating the service providers in creating broadband infrastructure. Under this, BSNL would provide 8,61,459 wire-line broadband connections from rural telephone exchanges with subsidy from USOF. The speed of each of the broadband connections shall be at least 512 kbps always on, with the capability to deliver data, voice and video services in the fixed mode.

The rural broadband connectivity will cover Government, institutional users, gram panchayats, higher secondary schools, public health centers and individual users. Subsidy would also be provided for setting up one kiosk from each rural exchange for providing public access to broadband services. A proposal is being considered to provide broadband connectivity in rural and remote areas in a phased manner, under which 5,000 blocks would be connected by wireless broadband and villages coming within a radius of 10 kms of the taluka, block headquarters would be covered. Guidelines have been issued for broadband wireless access (BWA) services. BWA services will increase broadband penetration. It is also envisaged that Internet and broadband subscribers will increase to 40 million and 20 million respectively, by 2010.

In a bid to improve governance at the grass roots level, the government has decided to extend broadband connectivity to all villages by 2012. Out of about 2.5 lakh village panchayats across the country, 30,000 have been provided with broadband connectivity. It has been planned to provide broadband connectivity to all village panchayats in a progressive manner by the end of 2012.

USOF has planned to provide broadband connectivity to about 5,00,000 villages in a phased manner. This fund being raised through a 5 per cent levy imposed on telecom operators' revenues, is utilized for supporting telecom services in rural areas. It has also signed an agreement with BSNL for subsidy disbursement for providing 9,00,000 wire line broadband connections including customer premises equipment and computer or computing devices in rural and remote areas. Out of the 21,389 villages in Andhra Pradesh, 6,871 are broadband-enabled (Minister of State for Communications and IT July 10, 09).

Bharat Sanchar Nigam Ltd. will finalize bids from equipment vendors for rolling out WiMax-enabled broadband services in the rural areas. The State-owned company plans to buy 7,000 WiMax base stations to set up Common Service Centers (CSC) across the country. The project is estimated to be around Rs. 1,500 crore. Global WiMax vendor majors, including Huawei, Samsung, Alvarion and Harris Stratex, may bid for the project. Chinese vendor Huawei and local equipment maker Gemini had bagged the contract in the first round of this project, which envisaged about 1,000 base stations.

The PSU plans to roll out WiMax in three phases. Phase-I will set up broadband infrastructure in the rural areas for which the bids will be opened on 25 August, 2009. In the second phase, BSNL plans to roll out broadband infrastructure in the urban areas. For this, Huawei has been selected for rolling out services in Punjab and Harris Sratex has got the contract for Kerala. Tenders for other urban areas will be floated later. The third phase is based on the franchisee model which has hit rough weather after BSNL scrapped the tender twice.

Investment in Rural Broadband

The phrase "cyber-bridge to nowhere", which has assumed some prominence in discussions about stimulus investments in rural broadband, has cast doubts as to whether any investments outside metropolitan centers and their suburbs would yield an acceptable return. It is unfortunate that this has fed into a broader rhetoric that divides urban from rural rather than recognizing the extraordinarily important contributions that rural India will be called upon to play in the 21st century. Rural India will be at the very heart of innovation and development in food production and processing, village enterprises, alternative energy, natural resources, BPO initiatives, and re-creative activities. Its people will need to be educated and skill trained and it is imperative they have access to update information and its networks. High-speed Internet access is a critical component of progressive future.

Over 70 per cent of urban Indians access and use the Internet at work, home, or by mobile hand-held devices, and consumers are increasingly replacing dial-up services with broadband wherever it is available because of its advantages in speed and capacity. Broadband is nearly ubiquitous in Indian cities and consumers have many choices among technologies and providers in suburban and urban communities.

Unfortunately, while telecommunications providers expanded the national broadband market five-fold between 2001 and 2006, they have been less eager to tackle broadband deployment in rural communities. One estimate is that roughly one-third of households in rural India cannot subscribe to broadband Internet services at any price. A recent study showed that per capita income had no statistically significant influence on availability of broadband but that the key determinants were size and concentration of population along with terrain, distance and population density.

Broadband facilitates economic well-being of rural areas because it represents the very means for counteracting these challenges of low population density, long distance, and difficult terrain. It is critical for the economic development of rural areas as it allows entrepreneurs and businesses to participate in the global economy wherever they happen to be located. In health care, broadband technologies enable the use of tele-medicine networks to supplement rural and long-distance health services and to achieve significant cost savings in health care costs. In rural school systems, broadband access has proven to be essential to expanding educational opportunity. In the areas of government services and public safety, there is potential to increase transparency, improve customer service, update and streamline bureaucracy, and cut costs—all essential objectives for hard-pressed local governments across rural India. These will enable rural communities to remain viable and sustainable.

Broadband is a critical part of rural development infrastructure. Investments made to stimulate broadband infrastructure in rural would have undoubtedly substantial and positive impact. But this investment has to continue as demand increases and new technologies evolve. For rural, this investment is as important as other infrastructure investments such as roads, electricity, or water. Programs to encourage investments and demands will vary from community to community.

Rural poor can connect with wireless broadband through cyber cafés in the villages. They can send e-mail, and soon would be able to make cheap voice calls through VOIP. In India, another huge growth market WI-Lan a Canadian firm has supplied US $500,000 worth of broadband equipment to Gujarat state government. That network provides voice, video and data links between key agencies within one township such as community hospitals.

ICTs Initiatives in Rural India

By multiplying the effects of computers, Internet and education, we intend to accelerate the reach of technology benefits in the country over the next decade. The target group—users in remote areas, and the poor. Rural segments in general will be empowered more in economy and development through ICTs accessibility. Overcoming the digital divide in conjunction with other socio-economic divides will remain one of the key development issues for decades to come.

Over time, there is greater realization about the widening digital divide between urban and rural segments, and between men and women which is hampering the development process in India. There are both national government and private partnership efforts; there are also international efforts to bridge this digital divide. It is assumed ICTs will empower women particularly in rural areas; and rural segments in general will be empowered more in economy and development through ICTs accessibility. The increased focus is on tele-density, cellular phones, Internet connectivity through broadband access and wireless access, computer literacy and computer accessibility and affordability of these information technologies. Both national and local efforts, government and private are made to bridge the digital divide to certain extent.

But, despite the reported rapid adoption of ICT into administration, education and several sectors of the economy, the greatest challenge still remains; how can ICTs be demystified to appeal to the majority of the rural population. In whatever human trait you view ICTs, most people have widely accepted that it plays a key role in shaping the socio-economic development of any society. But the technical nature and the complexities involved in understanding ICTs tools have created the digital divide between rural and urban segments and between the have and have-nots in the society.

The key to unlocking ICTs for development involves a focus on a range of parameters which can be referred to as the eight Cs of the digital economy: connectivity, content, community, commerce, capacity, culture, capital and cooperation (Rao, 2002). In other words, it is important to have affordable and widespread access to ICTs, locally relevant content in local languages, offline and online forums for discussing ICT applications, e-commerce services, and human resource capacity, a culture which embraces innovation, investment capital, and cooperation between multiple stakeholders. These are relevant for application of ICTs in rural areas in India.

The digital economy of India during 2003-04 was marked by an explosion in the cellular phone market, a boom in outsourcing, steady Internet growth, media convergence, growth in rural ICT initiatives. ICTs scenario in India presents lop-sided scenario, paradoxically; India still has a long way to go in making ICT widely available to its population especially in rural areas where most of India's population lives. ICT use can be broadened by connecting secondary schools and distance schooling through broadband in rural areas.

India is making efforts to provide IT and IT enabled services to the lower socio-economic groups and in rural areas. This is changing the way computers are being used and these devices are changing the information processing and knowledge gain in many sectors relevant to their life and occupations. The role of new communication media in the development process through which a country moves from being an agriculture-based economy towards becoming an information society is commendable.

Human resource development is necessary for ability to use ICTs in rural areas. Education is the fundamental enabler of the knowledge economy. Government, business enterprises, NGOs and educational institutes are focusing on education and training in the area of IT to make available skilled people in specific IT domain. Simple applications of ICTs in rural communities are helping to reap even the basic benefits of life by adapting these technologies to local environments. Affordability, accessibility, learning, and practical applications give them information and knowledge gain for better living.

Microsoft Saksham Project

Microsoft "Saksham" is a public-private Initiative to energize the rural economy through ICT in India. Saksham Initiative assumes that imbalance in socio-economic development and urban-rural divide can only be stopped if the infrastructure in rural areas is made sustainable, qualitative and growth-oriented and a business environment is created. However, in developing countries, especially in India, ICT interventions are still on a concept stage. Rural-urban divide should be reduced with a clear vision to increase rural wealth.

The task can only be completed by aligning and putting thrust on all levers, crucial for providing solutions to existing challenges of desirability, affordability, accessibility and acceptability among the rural masses.

Since 2005, India efforts focused on using IT for upgrading rural communities through one of Microsoft innovative efforts —'Project Saksham'. This project through its four levers of innovative business models, public-private partnership, localized content and affordable solutions will address the issues that have so far affected the uptake of IT in the rural segment—be it the lack of infrastructure or of affordable and relevant IT services and solutions. The initiative also effectively addresses concerns regarding the economic viability of existing kiosk models.

'Saksham' has been developed in close consultation with industry partners and imbibes the principles of public-private partnership to create a sustainable economic model and a strong rural IT ecosystem. It will not only provide local entrepreneurs with the opportunity to set up and manage these kiosks for content and services, but also provide the local ISV (Independent Software Vendor) community with the opportunity to develop rural content and applications. The rural portal which is under development currently, will bring all of these services together in a comprehensive manner at the front end, and provide a seamless experience to the end user.

Launched by Microsoft in 2005, it is one such project that will energize the rural economy in India by creating an environment for inducing a convergent approach between all the stakeholders with the broader objective to increase the Rural GDP through IT interventions. This will be implemented through creation of a network that will provide a platform for various stakeholders to interact, jointly drive programs to reach out to the rural markets, cross leverage business models and work towards a common goal of ensuring growth of rural economy.

"Microsoft is committed to technology enabled socio-economic development to provide affordable access to rural markets with main objective to enable the rural ecosystem through public private partnerships to accelerate government efforts. Microsoft is keen to work with corporate, government and other organizations to create an ecosystem where ICT-led socio-economic development can flourish and lead to rural employment generation and wealth creation. We look forward to working with the government, banks and FIs, technology companies, NGOs and any other organization present in rural areas to provide services, applications, financing, infrastructure and support to make these kiosks a viable and scalable village micro-enterprise."

The focus is on: Public and Private Partnerships, Rural Credit Delivery System and Kiosk Financing, Content and Services—(online and offline), Service Delivery Infrastructure, Innovative Business Models, and providing other multiple services progressively.

Public and Private Partnerships focus on partnering with government for convergence of various government and non-government projects; leverage resources, funds and grants available through various rural development schemes; cross leverage network and infrastructure leading to optimum use of resources and increase accessibility to rural India; innovate delivery and business models to ensure network sustainability through increase kiosk usage; providing and orchestrating a model for making the kiosk a self-sustaining microenterprise.

Rural Credit Delivery System and Kiosk Financing (For Banks & FIs): To provide rural microcredit for setting up the kiosk network; extend banking related services through the network; leverage kiosk as a delivery mechanism for rural credit for setting up micro enterprises.

Content & Services—Online and offline Content through ISVs & rural portal. Co-share content and digital information to maximize usage of kiosk across various levels; build, localize and integrate technology applications relevant to rural communities through ISV's at the district level. Develop and extend online and offline services and applications that address critical needs of the rural population and to develop capacity building through on-ground IT training for rural communities.

Service Delivery Infrastructure—Service Providers & Nodal Agencies. Identify, nurture and build capacity in organizations willing to run chain of kiosks in rural areas. System Integrators willing to run the kiosk operations as a business.

Innovative Business Models—NGOs , ISGs, Academia, and Research. Policy and IPR will critically examine various interventions and provide future directions and interventions. Socio-economic development and capacity building will provide multiple services progressively with revenue generation potential that can be delivered through kiosks in addition to e-government services:

(Saksham—Enabling Rural Ecosystem Project by Microsoft 2009).

National Alliance Mission 2007, chaired by M.S. Swaminathan, is an initiative to promote the use of ICTs in villages in India, by providing knowledge connectivity to the rural citizens. The Jamshedji Tata National Virtual Academy for Rural Prosperity (NVA), India, is seeking rural men and women from developing countries to be appointed as Foreign Fellows of the NVA. The main aim of the NVA is to bring Indian and foreign experts together with grass-roots level communities in a two-way communication to facilitate the objective of knowledge in Rural Development and Agriculture reaching 'every home and hut' in rural communities. Indian and Foreign Fellows who are selected will have demonstrative leadership qualities and social commitment to their communities, and are strong role models in promoting the use of ICTs for rural development in those communities.

Pratham has over the past few years started its IT educational initiative—"From illiteracy to e-literacy"—in slums and rural areas. The IT education program is already operational in seven states throughout India, with Uttar Pradesh being the latest state targeted. The program aims to reach almost 37,500 students through a direct and catalytic methodology. The catalytic method being implemented for the first time in the program, aims at reaching schools around the direct schools with computer labs which already have the necessary hardware through government grants and other charitable initiatives but are effectively obsolete due to lack of operational knowledge, pedagogical methodologies, or sheer ignorance and apathy in some cases. The computer curriculum is updated. The teachers are trained in educational software and better pedagogical methods. The students are tested throughout the program to gauge improvements in their learning levels. It is effective, efficient and a sustainable and cost-effective model.

NIIT, the hole in the wall project to expose the uninitiated children and youth to create computer awareness and motivation for e-literacy. It started in slums but this model can be replicated in rural areas also.

Technology Innovations for Everyday Use: The latest four innovations are making the rural life more comfortable. These are Pureit, Pur Chotu Kool and Oorja Stove for rural kitchen and Portable ultrasound machines and ECG machines for rural clinics. For the village family struggling to get clean water to avoid being sick, there is water purification product 'Pureit' by Hindustan Uniliver for Rs. 2,000. Earlier 'Pur' a sachet costing few paise to purify water is also marketed for rural markets by Procter and Gamble. For the villager, who wants to have cold water and lassi, there is Godrej 'Chotu Kool.' It runs on cooling chip and fan similar to cool computers. It uses high-end insulation to stay cool for hours without power. The cost is Rs. 3,000, affordable for even middle class ruralites. It has the option to run on batteries though when run on electricity, the consumption is very low. It is portable and has handles. It is easy for migrant worker to carry to the fields.

Oorja Stove by First Energy Company is a boon to the rural women. It uses gasifier technology generally used in power plants to burn it efficiently, uses small fan to deliver air to the burning pellets, and burns three times more efficiently than a regular wood fire and with very little smoke. Engineers from Indian Science Institute, Bangalore designed a stove with perforated chamber that uses a small fan to get just the right amount of air to keep it burning at a high temperature with less smoke and quicker cooking. Gasifier technology and fuel pellets are innovated by First Energy Company engineers. Dry pellets are made of agricultural waste like corn and peanut shells. It costs only Rs. 1,000. This is life changing for rural women and family, less smoky environment, ease and efficiency of burning, and collecting wood fuel time is saved for women. Thus, it is environmentally friendly also. It has reached 4,00,000 households in short-time.

Now, to make cooking easier for rural housewives and smoke-free kitchens, government in Oct. 2009 launched an ambitious scheme to expand coverage of domestic cooking gas to rural areas, and plans to give poor people LPG stoves free of cost to bring at least three-fourth of the population under the LPG coverage. The Rajiv Gandhi Gramin LPG Vitrak scheme aims at setting up small size LPG distribution agencies in areas, which till now were not considered as economically viable, Petroleum Minister Murli Deora told reporters after launching the scheme. The scheme would, however, require the consumers to buy LPG cylinders from the agencies and transport themselves as against the present model of distributors doing a home delivery. Small LPG distributorship would be set up in rural areas with a potential of selling 600 refills a month as against the present convention that requires an agency in place with no less than 3,000 cylinder sales.

The scheme is initially being launched in eight states of Madhya Pradesh, Uttar Pradesh, Rajasthan, West Bengal, Bihar, Jharkhand, Chhattisgarh and Orissa, covering over 1,200 locations where the reach of LPG is very low. "Home delivery of the cylinders will add to the cost of the distributor and will make the whole scheme economically unviable given the low sales," IOC Chairman S. Behuria said. Minister of State for Petroleum and Natural Gas said, "It is proposed that oil firms utilize 15 per cent of their CSR funds to give free LPG stoves to BPL families".

Let us look at the healthcare needs of rural India. There are nearly 6,00,000 villages in India where 65% of the Indians live. This is a huge market, but it cannot be served by Western style products. Hospital infrastructure is either inadequate or absent in rural India. Therefore, rural patients cannot go to the hospital, the hospital has to come to the patient. So, portability is critical. Portable ultrasound machines and ECG machines produced by GE in 2008, 2009 at low cost can equip the rural clinics as well being portable can be used for rural critical patients on sites.

In India, we have the engineers who have brainpower and bandwidth to deliver these types of products. Indian engineers are reinventing products to cut costs and reach the billions who live on less than Rs. 20 a day. Instead of distributing through traditional supply chains, these companies are using Self-help groups and microlenders that are already plugged into villages.

Bridge Digital Divide: 2000 Decades

During 2000 decades, national government and private partnership efforts and international efforts are being made to bridge the digital divide. The increased focus is on tele-density, cellular phones, Internet connectivity through broadband access and wireless access, computer literacy and computer accessibility and affordability of these information technologies. It is assumed that rural segments in general will be empowered more in economy and development through ICTs accessibility. Many Indian villages are poorly wired making wireless technology the most reliable web connection. It is cheaper to take mobile technology rather than wires everywhere that is why we want to take mobile technology to rural areas rather than fixed lines. Earlier years, TRAI has been focusing on fixed landlines through rural exchanges which have not been a success. Intel's through its community computer initiative in India is providing low cost PC in rural India and community PCs customized for public access.

In 2000 decades, ruralites feel highly connected by cell phone, television exposes them to news and images of world around them and education makes them understand the world and themselves as a component in that. They are equally motivated that computer and Internet will connect them to the world around them and make them understand it as television does. These are pointer to the fact that there have been integrated efforts for rural communities to grow. Ruralites accept the integrated challenge and push themselves to achieve it and be on the road to growth as urbanites are.

In 2000 decades, releasing the Indian telecom industry from state control and opening it up to dozens of private companies, paved the way for India's telecoms boom. The competition and more forwarding approach with latest affordable technologies from private operators boosted TV channels and its multifarious content, mobile telephony, computer functionality and Internet in rural areas apart from its ever growing widespread in urban areas in its globalization connectivity.

Earlier discussions are pointer to the fact that there have been integrated efforts towards this for rural communities—education, telephone connectivity through mobile telephones, computer accessibility and affordability through low cost and broadband Internet accessible and affordable through low cost; and television has become the ubiquitous part of their lifestyle through the same process of accessibility and affordability. Government and businesses pool financial resources and subsidies.

At one point of time, government set up community radio, television, and video, in the villages, to familiarize the villagers with the technology and its utility and advantages. By and by, they were accepted in the lifestyle. Lately, cell phone is accepted as important connectivity technology. Now it is the turn of community computer and Internet Kiosk to be set-up in the villages or nearby cluster of villages to facilitate further connectivity. Rural retail is accessing to purchase and microfinance is increasing their purchasing capacity.

Communication revolution in rural India is likely to be a great booster to drive the rural economy, efficiencies of its people and improved quality of life for the ruralites. Growth in applications of ICTs in rural settings may drive the rural economy. Tele-density and computerization would be the major booster; therefore, government must focus resources on developing these in the villages. Information technology can develop rural markets and business, and create employment for villagers in the village itself by setting BPOs. In the process, these BPOs would train people in computer applications and motivation for education and computer literacy. Saksham project of Microsoft is an excellent integrated ICT approach to boost rural economy. TV has been a good disseminator of news and impacting the change of life styles.

It is an established fact that the income of the poor grows faster in telecom intensive economies and access to affordable telecom services is essential for any strategy for poverty reduction. In fact, IT can be an effective and potent weapon to eliminate poverty.

7

Business Markets for Village Economy

Development of Rural Markets

Rural markets development may focus on shelter, healthy and enough food, durables and non-durables on one hand and on the other hand, spending on education, health, employment boosting, and entertainment such as media, telecom, computerization and tourism; and to localize marketing strategies and offer products fine-tuned to meet their tastes. The rural markets will be more complicated than the urban markets. Therefore, it may be strongly suggested that marketers select and employ educated unemployed from villages and venture into wider areas and create awareness and information about the products and its diverse uses. Models that are going to work in bottom-of-pyramid markets need not only to be economically viable but also need to address for social and environmental performance.

Rural India is set to witness an economic boom, with development of rural markets. "Overall there is a huge market which is waiting to be served, ready to splurge, willing to explore new products and services, and retailers can tap on their wallets," said the national industry director (consumer markets), KPMG India. In rural markets, consumers are practical and price sensitive. Even though consumers at the bottom of the pyramid do not seem to have predictable income (affects purchasing dynamics), the rural market proved to be surprisingly loyal. So if companies get it right, they could really reap the rewards, experts added.

This is particularly true as changes in the rural economy such as people moving from agriculture into manufacturing, which pays better, are likely to lead to economic boom. In order to earn brand loyalty in the rural market, product design will need to go beyond ideas like smaller sizes (such as single use sachets) to create genuinely new products that appeal to this segment. This requires a deep understanding of the market and an appetite for innovation, posing a challenge for both consumer products companies and retailers as there is still lack of shared understanding about the ever-changing rural Indian market and types of consumers that make it (E&Y India).

There is increasing exposure of ruralites to the life styles of various Indian regions, cities and additionally to the global lifestyles and variety of products and services through increased media exposure specifically, TV both national and international channels. Vertical integration of the food market from farm to firm to fork becomes the best way to achieve efficiency and serve the interest of every stakeholder in the chain—the farmer, the processor, the retailer and the consumer. As their disposable incomes grow, so does their propensity to spend on houses, financial services, entertainment and consumer durables leading to a cumulative growth of various sectors of the economy.

Even in the last quarter of 2008, consumer spending and retail sales in India did not witness a significant decline. Much of the prosperity in India has been starkly visible in the top 20 cities of India. A look at the earnings structure across India's top 20 cities reveals that the average graduate earns Rs. 1.8 lakh per year compared to just Rs. 91,000 in rural areas. When translated into spending patterns, nearly 68% of households in the top 20 Indian cities have color televisions compared to 47% in other cities and 17% in rural areas. Clearly then, if India expects to grow its economy at 8% per annum and now in 2009-10 may be even 6.4% per annum, decline being due to various factors. There has to be more spending on rural infrastructure and tier 2 and tier 3 cities to bring them at par with the growth of the top-20 cities.

Rural Market Segments

Low-end Markets

Business practices are changing in the developing countries to focus on low-end market of poor in the urban and rural areas. These practices have to focus on (a) market capacity, (b) different types of consumers, (c) different types of products and services fitting to poor people's needs, (d) products and services fitted into affordable price band and a huge segment of market, and (e) developing easy, efficient credit line for these consumers needs for different products and services, and in different price band which is affordable. The quality cannot be compromised, price must be affordable. These market demands can meet cost effectively by changing business practices. Secondly, creating awareness through cost-effective modes of advertising and marketing through cost-effective channels of distribution and retail sale, and delivery of products and services in cost-effective packaging can be done. Thirdly, the focus is on microfinance to let them buy these goods and services.

Business Models for Rural Markets

Currently 75% of population lives in rural India. Ruralites have low connectivity with inadequate physical infrastructures such as roads, public transport, etc. They have low density of telephones and only some of them are exposed to electricity and TV, etc. It is only recently that businesses understand the importance of rural markets since these have been so far ignored. Now new Rural Business models are being developed.

There are three kinds of rural markets to focus: the rich middle-class ruralites which is negligible in number and its consumer characteristics remain the same but for purchasing capacity; lower-middle-class who have low purchasing capacity but same consumer characteristics; and poor consumers with negligible purchasing capacity and limited consumption patterns for essentials only such as food. These markets have huge potential when commodities are available at affordable prices to all the three types of consumers and when the purchasing capacity of the consumers is augmented. *These new markets require partnerships not only with other companies but also with local communities, non-profit organizations. Corporations have to deal with them to create a much more inclusive and interesting business model.*

There are Basic Rural Business Model, Co-Creation Business Model, and business models focusing on different segments, such as agro products and services and farm accessories, village enterprises and crafts, for personal life styles—food, toiletries, other durables and non-durables like TV, Cell phones, computer, etc.; clothes, footwear, jewelry, furniture and decorations, kitchen essentials, construction materials such as bricks, sand, etc. Some of these may be produced in the villages and others procured from outside—neighboring villages, city markets, factory outlets, etc. The business models should be P4 model (public-private-Panchayat-people partnership).

Basic Rural Business Model

This model focuses on four characteristics of rural markets and consumers and four phase market strategies: (i) purchasing capability, (ii) durable and non-durable consumer needs according to rural lifestyles. For example, they would need a different kind of food, different kind of soaps and detergents. Quite likely, there may not be any market for toilet tissue and paper napkins, (iii) sachet economy will be the priority for durable consumer goods and for non-durable consumer goods, they must be hardy and not needing complex repairs and service should be available at doorstep or close by, (iv) businesses need to tap the market for farm implements, accessories and farm goods and provide doorstep delivery system.

The first phase of market strategies is to sell products according to ruralite's needs and specifications and purchasing power. The second phase of market strategies is delivery system. It is the most crucial part of the marketing strategies since villagers have low mobility, less knowledge and familiarity with the urban markets for purchasing and price negotiations. In the third phase of their marketing strategies, the focus should be to enhance their purchasing power by providing microcredit, and through micro-credit, businesses also capture some share of market for regular products and services in course of time and thus increasing their total market share.

Fourth phase of market strategies but running parallel is to understand the fast changing consumer patterns. The peculiarity of the rural market will be the fast changing consumer scenarios due to their exposure to media channels of TV where they are exposed to life styles of various Indian regions and additionally, to the global lifestyles and consumer goods. Therefore, the businesses need to consider this factor also. Building rural consumer base is important and is the fifth marketing strategy. Rural consumerism could be the dynamic for rural economy. Businesses must have first hand knowledge of consumer patterns for goods and services to understand the consumer dynamics for (their) consumer products and services. Business teams may need to live with them for a while to get that kind of understanding.

Co-Creation Business Model

This model focuses on doing business with poor consumers with low purchasing capabilities. How to create markets for the poor who are at the bottom-of-the-Pyramid and who may be earning even less than few rupees/a few cents a day? We need the Co-Creation Business Model. They are the masses but they do need the basics and necessities of life and can buy according to, 'as and when and as much' they can spend for their needs. It is a mass market. As such, the poor consumers' major demand is 'sachet economy'. The main strategies of this business model are: tap this mass market, and do marketing of products according to their lifestyles without encouraging materialistic consumerism, produce according to their low purchasing power, mobility and accessibility. Thus, there are three essential dimensions of Co-Creation Business Model: (i) produce products and services for the poor, low income masses matching their purchasing power and capabilities, (ii) enhance their purchasing power by providing micro-credit,

(iii) through micro-credit, businesses also capture some share of market for regular products and services in course of time and thus, increasing their total market share.

Prahlad (2004d) talks about the 'Invisible Market'. We need a new world economic order in which there is an invisible market constituency of these 5 billion poor people. In developing countries like India, China, Brazil, Mexico, Indonesia, Turkey, Russia, South Africa—they represent 70-75 per cent of the world population of poor. If the poor, due to its limited purchasing power can buy small sachet of shampoo or small packets of food for a couple of servings such as quarter size or half-size bread loaves—then businesses should produce them, market them to this mass market. The demand is there and it will continue in the same proportion but in different time-scale since the poor can spend limited amount on a specific consumer product at a point of time. If a business can sell cheaper the same product without packaging frills, then produce and market the same to this segment of market. In short, this segment of market has demand for the product but it has to be marketed differently. The poor want value for their money; and businesses can deliver that by marketing differently and in turn, they have the business of 70-80 per cent consumers segments to make profits.

Needs Assessment Business Model

Prahlad (2004c) talks about how to connect with the invisible market of consumers (both rural and poor). As a practice in recent years, Hindustan Lever in India has made it compulsory for a person who joins the company in regular job to live in villages for three months at a stretch before starting work in the company. It does not matter who you are and at what level you join. You have to develop a project in that village, so that you are working closely with the local people. Why? The company wants you to understand your consumers and be in close interaction with the villagers to assess their needs, tastes, preferences, and affordability. So that it can co-create product accordingly for this segment, which is a huge market. Further, to connect with the poor consumers, every year for one day, everyone from chairman to down, have to get out of the office and visit a poor-family consumer. Then, after the visit, when they come back, they write a report about what they have learned and how it will impact upon management and product development practices.

Generally, top management and employees are disconnected with the poor and rural consumers. And there is a huge disconnect with all managers and not just senior managers, in multinational companies and five billion potential consumers in low-income and poor. Because we do not interact with poor, we do not know how they live. Other big companies are also following the example. Most of them are even encouraging their senior managers to visit their targeted villages to have face-to-face and hand-on experience of the feasibility and marketability of their products. They work on the presumptions that sitting in air-conditioned offices in the cities far from the villages cannot give them reality check on the rural markets and low-end markets.

How do we sell to the poor? Create capacity to buy through easy loan and hire-purchase system. Earlier, the poor could take loans from the moneylenders but in the process, they suffered the exploitation from the moneylenders paying exorbitant rates of 500 per cent interest. But now the banks can give them microloans at 10 per cent and develop their capacity to buying, saving and consuming simultaneously. The corporates can let them buy their products on hire-purchase system. They are paying in easy instalments and consuming simultaneously.

Both Co-Creation Business Model, and Needs Assessment Business Model, are corollaries of Basic Rural Business Model.

Government Rural Business Models

Government business models for ruralites is through subsidies for seeds, fertilizers, electricity power and petroleum or kerosene oil for running agro machines, water for irrigation and at times through loan waivers. These are procured and supplied to the farmers through government agencies at subsidized rates. Government totally funds building such rural infrastructure as small dams, irrigation canals, and digging tubewells and handpumps for drinking water in the villages, and sanitation facilities and products. Both Central and State governments are responsible for these. Government also funds R&D for agriculture and related areas such as milk procurement and management of its products in its agricultural institutes and universities to develop new methods, seeds and technology and other ways of marketing them efficiently. Government also totally funds the training programs—agriculture extension programs for ruralites.

A huge potential exists in the country for economic development in rural areas through employment and income generation by promoting handicrafts through village enterprises. However, some of the fundamental challenges faced by this sector include product diversification, technology upgradation, standardization of raw materials, quality of product, product packaging, continuity in supply, etc.

Government sponsored Rural Business Hubs (RBH) provides intervention to address some of these issues. The RBH is aimed to allow people living in communities to use their skills in manufacturing products while the government and the private sector render assistance on developing the products and exploring the markets in order to create jobs, income and strengthening the communities. It operates in two fronts; on the one hand, it would be concerned with how to enlarge the market share of the best products from different villages and on the other, it provides technical know-how, innovative design, product packaging, adapting and using new materials and craft styles, etc. to make the products acceptable internationally. These RBHs are different from the RBHs run by MNCs around the villages. These two are discussed in detail in later sections.

Government is also currently focusing as new practice to encourage Public-private partnership or even on BOT basis so that more funds are available to provide these facilities for more villages. The P4 model (public-private-Panchyat-people) is being encouraged and currently experimented for many small infrastructure projects.

Rural Markets and Consumerism

Building Consumer Base

Co-Creation theory advocates that consumer is supreme and pivotal for product demands and the market is co-created through consumer demands and expectations whether consumer is elite or down the pyramid. There are elite and informed consumers, and then there are poor and not so informed consumers who are at the bottom-of-the-pyramid. There are urban (both elite and poor) consumers, and consumers in rural areas. All these four categories have different levels of exposure to information channels. All are important for the business to develop product and market segments for the same.

London Ted (2005) points that when MNCs go overseas, they typically look for customers that are the most familiar. As a result, in the developing world, they tend to target the wealthy. But now there has been increasing interest in reaching into the second tier of the pyramid that you could call the middle class, maybe 1.5 billion people. These are people that are beginning to get some wealth but are still in the middle class in these developing countries.

What they have not targeted is the 5 billion plus people in the base of the socio-economic pyramid. The focus is on what it takes for an organization to profitably, or in a self-sustaining way, serve this market in a manner that is environmentally sensitive and culturally appropriate. This latter component is crucial, as we really believe the models that are going to work in BOP (bottom-of-pyramid) markets need to be economically viable but also need to address for social and environmental performance. They tend to charge a premium for services that are offered to people in the same general geographic location who are wealthier.

Rural consumerism could be the dynamic for rural economy just as urban consumerism has pushed the urban economy and national economy in the last two decades. The essential are people having purchasing power and existing markets caters to ruralite's needs, demands, tastes and affordability.

Purchasing power comes from employment and economic gain from occupational pursuits, and further by credit availability. Employability generation both in farm and non-farm sectors is necessary. Ruralites will follow urban economy development model through healthy consumerism as per their traditional values till they are ready for change in their lifestyle values and then demand for a different pattern of consumer goods and services will evolve.

Rural markets development may focus on shelter, healthy and enough food, durables and non-durables on one hand, and on the other hand, spending on education, health, employment boosting, and entertainment such as media, telecom and tourism. On the occupational front, the rural markets are developed to focus on agriculture development through technology and modern techniques; that way, it not only procures more economic gains but also generates more employment in not only people tending to farms and food crops but jobs related to the technology of food production from tractor running to tending irrigation canals, technology for food distribution and supply chain and storage facilities, etc.

The changing practices in businesses are that a 'Big Corporation Think Small'. The marketing products to rural markets and poor who are bigger consumer markets are the changing trends by bigger companies through sachet economy. Newer business practices are being explored to fit in this market and get the best consumer response and profits. Prof. Christensen (2006) commenting on this trend said, "There are three ways of doing this: One, by making a complicated product affordable; two, by creating low-end disruption through low-cost products; and three, by executing new disruption by penetrating frontier markets where no corporation had ventured before." Elaborating this he said, "Intel had developed the Celeron chip to storm the low-end market with a complicated yet affordable product. In doing this, it had addressed over-served customers with a lower cost business model instead of bringing a better product in an established market. Likewise, Canon unleashed low-end disruption through low-cost products by introducing small, smart copiers with better scanning." He further commented that companies could also grow big by penetrating unexplored frontier markets as had been done by a Chinese manufacturer of microwave ovens at a low-price point of $39, in the process, bringing in 160 million new customers. It is not low-cost labor, but consumption that creates a market for big volumes and success. Corporations seeking to figure out their capabilities and inadequacies in accomplishing success need to focus on resources, processes and profit models. To do this, the top management needs to clearly articulate its priorities.

Rural Markets and Rural Consumption in India: Emerging Practices

Many Indian businesses are going rural. In a bid to expand their market base, companies are now exploring the rural hinterland. Hindustan Lever (HLL) for one has been continuously strengthening its marketing network in the villages and is producing goods to suit the needs and budgets of rural consumers. ITC Company, one of India's foremost private sector companies, which has a diversified presence in tobacco, hotels, paperboards, specialty papers, packaging, agri-business, branded apparel, packaged foods and other fast moving consumer goods, initiated e-Choupal in 2000. This program has contributed to overall programs of development. It has helped increase the incomes and productivity of millions of farmers by giving them more direct access to markets, as well as pricing and product information, via village-based Internet kiosks. It placed computers with Internet access in rural farming villages. The e-Choupals serve as both a social gathering place for exchange of information (Choupal means gathering place in Hindi) and an e-commerce hub. This is its business model. It is now expanding its services to include education. It has opened 100 e-Choupals in Andhra Pradesh in 2006 and is in the process of opening more in other parts of India.

Otherwise, farmers have only an approximate idea of price trends and have to accept the price offered to them at auctions on the day that they bring their grain to the mandi. As a result, traders are well positioned to exploit both farmers and buyers through practices that sustain system-wide inefficiencies.

e-Choupal has also established a low-cost fulfillment system focused on the needs of rural India that has helped in mitigating rural isolation, create more transparency for farmers, and improve their productivity and incomes. It is seen as a medium of delivering critical market information independent of the mandi, thus allowing the farmer, an empowered choice of where and when to sell his crop. The second benefit is to facilitate collaboration between the many parties required to fulfill the spectrum of farmer's needs. As a communication mechanism, this goal is related to the commitment to address the whole system, not just a part of the system.

It is noteworthy that ITC did not hesitate to install expensive IT infrastructure in places where most people would be wary of visiting overnight. It is a manifestation of the integrity of rural value systems that not a single case of theft, misappropriation, or misuse has been reported among the thousands of e-Choupals.

Along with soaps, detergents and toothpaste, ITC's Sagar sells almost everything—TVs, DVD players, pressure cookers, room heaters, watches, sewing machines and grinders. Farmers can also buy motorbikes, or even tractors. ITC has launched its own rural range of clothing and shoes too—tailored for the village folk. ITC officials claim that the RBH is doing brisk business. Other companies are Pepsi Foods, Tata Kisan Sansar, EID Parry—the list is expanding everyday. They are all taking the rural route to expand their market base, as well as to procure raw materials for their agro ventures. Many companies are setting up contract farming in the villages. This business plan benefits the company as well as the farmers. One, farmers learn new and improved ways of growing food. Secondly, sale of their produce is assured. These companies are using the RBH for promoting these products and services.

A larger number of Indians live in villages but what is significant is that villages have undergone drastic changes in the post-reform era. While the trickling-down effect of higher GDP growth and a low inflation rate have improved the economic conditions of the villagers, the exposure to new products through media especially broadcasting channels has changed their consumption patterns also. The delivery of those goods through the efforts of the businesses in various areas, and in different ways further facilitates those consumption patterns.

Indian villages have become more health conscious and are now spending more on medicines—share of medical expenses in monthly consumption expenditure has increased from 5.7 per cent in 1997 to 6.8 per cent in 2002. Despite the fact, government highly subsidizes or provides free delivery of health and medicines to the rural consumers. They are spending higher amount on clothing also. Their conventional food consumption patterns have also changed from home-made lassi to Pepsi and other soft drinks. Higher expenditure on healthcare will keep them fit, but Indian households are no longer prepared to ignore the worldly comforts either. The most dramatic change has been witnessed in the non-durable consumer goods sector. They would like to buy TV, VCR, DVD, washing machines and refrigerators for personal comforts. They would be equally interested to buy tractors and other agriculture machinery to enhance their agriculture productivity.

It may be the demonstration effect caused by the opening up of the economy to the global market. But the fact remains that their expenditure on consumer goods, services and consumer durables and non-durables has increased sharply during the period. The business model of co-creation and marketing strategies targeted to this segment vide the above mentioned three-tier efforts would increase markets for the businesses. Businesses are built on developing the capacity of the poor. There are 300 million cell phones in China or 40 million cell phones in India and they are adding 1.5 million subscribers per month. They are not all in the hands of the rich. In fact, in India, the poor skilled or unskilled in business, plumber, electrician, carpenter or vegetable vendor are utilizing it for connectivity for their business. Now, more and more cell phones are ubiquitous in rural areas also. Diffusion of cell phones is creating business connectivity beside social change. The cell phone businesses are (being) built around the consumer demand and experience of the poor people. In these countries, they have the growth opportunity.

Rural Retailing: Next Phase in Retailing

Organized retailing may have not set its foot firmly in metros and other major cities yet, but Corporate India is already firming up concrete plans to tap the 100 billion dollar rural retail market with innovative schemes and human resource policies. There may be a slowdown in urban retail, but the next phase of growth is expected to come from rural markets with rural India accounting for almost half of the domestic retail market, valued over $300 billion.

What has prompted India Inc. to turn its energies to rural retailing are a slew of facts that rural markets are growing at double the rate of urban markets, 75% per cent of the country's 1.12 billion population live in rural areas and 87 per cent of rural markets do not have access to any sort of organized marketing and distribution. Meanwhile, India's $200 billion rural economy is also poised for sharp growth due to greater efficiencies in food supply chain driven by the growth of an organized retail sector. While a number of products on the rural retail shelf are agro-based. Companies are eager to make available products varying from cricket bat to customized credits in association with banks in rural areas, following the expansion and entry of new players into this emerging sector.

The retail market strategies are changing. Rural consumers are far less homogeneous than their urban counterparts and differ from region to region. The Indian rural market consists of about 70-80 per cent of the population of the country, but it does differ in its various regions. Apparently, in terms of the number of people, the Indian rural market is large, but scattered and diverse. It exhibits linguistic, regional and cultural diversities and economic disparities, and hence, it can easily be considered as being more complex than the market of a continent as a whole. The prices of rural marketing pose many problems due to the vastness of the country and a high potential for providing an effective marketing system. Another myth is that their purchasing power is low.

Christensen (2008) remarked that at 15.6 million 'middle class' households, the rural areas compared well with 16.4 million in urban India. Companies have begun offering urban-like shopping experience at venues where rural business transactions are undertaken. But rural consumers are more value-conscious than the urban consumer and market watchers are wondering whether marketers can retain the interest once the novelty runs out. As a long-term measure, these initiatives will bear fruit, but experts say there's no concerted effort by other companies to make in-roads. Companies need to step up investments in wider distribution systems. "The question is what attempts are being made to localize marketing strategies and offer products fine-tuned to meet their tastes. The rural markets will be more complicated than the urban markets. But the number of people who will go to the malls to buy big-ticket items, where deliberation is usually done will be fewer in volume terms."

He further argued that the problems stem from the underdeveloped markets. The awareness of rural consumers about products is obviously lesser than the urban markets and therefore, more purchasing power is not enough. Also, urban and semi-urban-based salesmen are not able to tap the full potential in the villages. We have strongly suggested that marketers select and employ educated unemployed from villages and venture into wider areas. Another changing practice in India for rural markets is setting of rural business hubs for village arts and crafts, and rural retail business hubs.

Rural Business Hubs

The major challenge for India today is to 'include' the rural economy into its present robust economic growth and bridge the widening urban-rural divide. Rural Business Hubs (RBH) is a big stride in this direction. The government has identified

846 products for which the business community could have a partnership with Panchayat for establishing rural business hubs based on Chinese model. Two types of rural business hubs are being set up which focus on different objectives.

The first type is the ***rural business hubs (of village arts and craft)*** scheme, launched in 2004, to be set up in partnership with CII (Confederation of Indian Industries) would upgrade and up value the skills and the products made by the villagers. This is a new experiment based on P4 model (public-private-Panchayat-partnership). With the high-level involvement of CII and different wings of governments and Panchayat, the image of rural India may be transformed through products produced and marketed through these hubs. The initiative will facilitate direct business linkage between industry and the rural community. This would promote bottom-up economic integration and a good driver for rural economy by generating employability and employment.

Second type is ***rural retail business hubs*** which are being set up by businesses focusing on variety of products and services and developing rural markets for them. These are being set up closer to cluster of villages. This is a new experiment based on PPP model (public-private-partnership) also and so far 72 companies have shown interest in setting up such business hubs.

Rural Retail Business Hubs

These are set up by businesses focusing on marketing of variety of products and services. 'Rural Retail: The Next Phase in Retailing', a report by CII-Yes Bank (Sept. 2007) has estimated India's rural retail market to grow by 29% to Rs. 1.8 trillion by 2010 driven by rising rural incomes and changing consumption patterns. Rural retail includes fast-moving consumer goods, durables, agricultural inputs and autos like tractors. Rural per capita income is estimated to double to Rs. 14,000 by 2012 as more rural families would switch over to commercial from subsistence farming. Village households are expected to rise to 153 million in 2009-10 from 135 million in 2001-02, probably making rural India the market with the largest potential in the world.

According to the report's findings, poor infrastructure, supply chain inefficiency, unorganized marketing and product pricing can be the major bottlenecks for the growth of rural retail. There exists no organized marketing and distribution in 87% of India's villages, wherein 50% of the rural population resides. Corporates are promoting rural markets as drivers of future growth. Such enterprises need to view rural retail development as a long-term commitment, and must be continuously innovative as rural consumers are often more worried for price than quality conscious, observed the report. The development of organized rural retail in rural India will create jobs, check rural migration, generate more tax, and improve agricultural efficiencies.

Once the rural retail grows, there would be a number of positive implications like boost in employment, infrastructure, increased revenue and tax generation and check rural migration. However, poor infrastructure, seasonality of demand, heterogeneous population, complex buying behavior and price sensitivity are the main challenges that need to be overcome by the companies planning to enter the rural retails. Further, according to report's findings, an estimated India's rural retail market will grow 29% to Rs. 1.8 trillion by 2010 driven by rising rural incomes and changing consumption patterns.

Though one of the key features of RBH retail is to provide a mechanism for industry to procure agro produce directly from the farmers, it has been conceptualized as a model for overall development of the rural sector. The industry provides interventions in terms of technology and know-how, good farming practices, agriculture inputs, standardization and quality enhancement measures, value addition, branding and marketing, training and skill development and elimination of non-value adding activities. Farmers gain in terms of higher incomes through increased yields, improved quality, and transfer of know-how, entrepreneurship development and reduced transaction cost. On the other hand, Industry saves procurement costs and most importantly, obtains standardized and quality produce. The second important feature of the RBH retail is that it can leverage with on-going developmental schemes of the government at the local level to ensure an overall development of the rural sector, including setting up of required infrastructure, accessing soft loans and procurement of needed technology inputs.

So far, 72 companies have shown interest, and 31 MOU have been signed towards the RBH retail project involving Reliance, Tata, Coca-Cola, ITC, Mahindra & Mahindra and Microsoft among others (2009).

Bharti-Wal-Mart joint venture, for example, plans to invest substantially in the next 3-4 years for establishing supply chain network in rural India. Reliance Retail's Rural Hubs (procuring-cum- processing hub and one-stop farmer shop) has plans for Punjab, Maharashtra, West Bengal, Andhra Pradesh and Gujarat. Pantaloons also plans a similar procuring-cum-processing hub for setting up farm input malls in rural areas. A few others are already set up; DCM Shriram launched its Hariyali Kisan Bazar in 2002 in Punjab, Haryana, Rajasthan, Madhya Pradesh, Uttar Pradesh and Uttarakhand. It has more than 70 stores with an average store area of 9000-10000 sq. ft. and a catchment's radius of 25 km. "Our focused expansion is into Northern and Central India and eventually into Southern states. We plan to add another 200-250 stores in the next 12-15 months," said DCM Shriram Consolidated President. "Our stores are one-stop shop for farmers with agricultural consultancy as an add-on service by sales executives who are agronomists. They also have 'produce' buyback arrangements."

Even public sector companies entered the fray. Indian Oil Corporation's (IOC) rural retail initiative was launched in 2006 in Uttar Pradesh, Madhya Pradesh, Punjab, Tamil Nadu, Karnataka and Bihar with more than 1,400 stores and an average store area of 4,400 sq. ft. covering a radius of 10-15 km. "Ours is a low-cost and de-risk model and leverages on IOC network for fuel and non-fuel retail. Our thrust is mainly agricultural inputs and FMCG products. We have plans to add 3,000 stores in the next 4-5 years," said IOC General Manager.

Tata Chemicals (TCL) too launched its Tata Kisan Sansar (TKS) three years ago in Punjab, Haryana, Uttar Pradesh, Bihar, West Bengal and has already more than 800 TKS franchisees with an average store area of 300 sq. ft. and cover 10 km. "The thrust of TKS is a link to states where TCL has a majority market share in fertilizer business. Our success is due to factors like strong relationships and brand awareness among farming community, focused approach on agricultural inputs and consultancy, produce buyback and farmer credit arrangements," said Tata Chemicals CEO (Agro-business). The corporates are taking special efforts to ensure the quality of products and services offered to rural customers.

Free training courses are offered at the RBH retail by the companies for the products that the consumers buy, this is an added incentive for the consumer as well the company to build market share. These companies create market awareness, and persuade customers by teams' expertise and experience in the product line; give consultancy to create further demands for the products and services. Rural consumers gain market awareness and product confidence about the brands. They may not stick to a brand but would give feedback to the companies for demand, need for improvements and innovations according to their needs. This attitude and action of the rural consumers and their sustained dialogue with the companies will help companies to produce and market appropriate products and services for the rural markets. Redefining markets in terms of consumers' feedback, actions and outcomes would create market growth. There may be ways of applying technologies or products to the problems, when management observes people think about new products in their daily life. The expert teams may suggest logics of their problems and solutions, risks and gaps to make better market decisions.

Such dialogue will also create 'trust' for the companies' products and services, an essential factor for building brand loyalty and consumer base. The 'trust' factor has been highlighted to the companies' employees in rural retail. Unlike urban retail customers, in rural retail there are fix set of customers. The area that would be addressed is within

25-30 km range. And again, unlike urban retailing, customers come from far-flung areas and are visitors from other states. "The relationship factor is stronger in rural and smaller towns. They just keep coming to you or stop if they are not convinced about the quality, price or service."

While the trickling-down effect of higher GDP growth and a low inflation rate have improved the economic conditions of the villagers, the exposure to new products has changed their consumption patterns also. The delivery of those goods through the efforts of the businesses in various areas, and in different ways further facilitates those consumption patterns. It may be the demonstration effect caused by the opening up of the economy to the global market. But the fact remains that ruralites expenditure on consumer goods, services and consumer durables and non-durables has increased sharply. The significant point in this context is to focus on increasing the purchasing capability of this segment through varied microfinance practices.

Many retail products are being produced for rural markets specifically. For instance, in a bid to combat under-nutrition, PepsiCo India expects to test-market its products to fight anemia among rural women sometime in 2010. The soft-drinks major is working on low-cost prototypes of both beverages and snacks that can deliver the benefit. Chairman, PepsiCo India, in an interview to Business Line, said, "The price of the product has to be affordable to the bottom-of-pyramid; we are looking at a consumer price of between Rs. 1 and Rs. 2 per serve. This is a global project, he said, with India being the lead country. The product is being developed through close teamwork between our local R&D teams and our global experts. The team is making rapid progress. We tried some very exciting prototypes in the past month. The next major step will be trials to ensure that the product delivers in the Indian environment. As per the National Family Health Survey 2005-06, 50 per cent of young Indian women, irrespective of income, suffer from iron deficiency.

PepsiCo is setting up partnerships in line with the Government's priorities and it is looking to leverage the right expertise among different partners, NGOs included. The company is also exploring sustainable business models and commitment to reducing hunger and malnutrition among the poor (News 2008). There are many more such products in the line being developed for rural markets only by other companies also.

Rural Business Hubs (of village arts, craft & village industries) Scheme

The MoPR (Ministry of Panchayati Raj)—CII Rural Business Hubs initiative will provide an opportunity to introduce quality Indian products to the national and international markets; products which embody India's centuries-old local talent, skills, art and culture. This is the inspiration and motivation behind this initiative. The project will encourage rural people in every block panchayats, to unite and create a product that represents the talent, skills, art and culture of their localities in order to generate extra income during their free time. Since there are about 6,097 blocks and intermediate panchayats all over the country, the MoPR—CII—RHB Council will select only the products that are export-ready and of outstanding quality to promote at the national and international levels.

RBH has been conceptualized to synergistically link rural products, skills with the marketing and professional skills of the industry. It is a unique concept of P4 model partnership to involve industry to improve and refine locally available resources and produce goods of international quality and standards and to address this lacuna in the market structure.

These indicate a group of entrepreneurs including farmers and artisans working together under the aegis of a block panchayat to enhance value of their products with private sector participation for greater market access and prosperity. It encourages people living in communities to use their skills in developing and manufacturing products through government and the private sector assistance. It is an open concept and since the basic philosophy is to establish the direct linkages between industry and local community, many permutation and combinations can be formed. The concept is based on the successful Thai experience of One-Tambon-One-Product (OTOP) model with suitable modifications.

RBH scheme is a Central Sector scheme to extend part funding to viable business activities in rural areas. These are required to be based on local resources and skills; presence of a business partner willing to provide market linkages to the products and involvement of Panchayats. Assistance under the Scheme is available for engaging professional facilitators who will help in identifying viable business activity and willing business partner, prepare project documents acceptable to the stakeholders and also help in implementation of the project. Scheme also extends part funding for training and skill building of artisans, setting up of common facilities, and for minor equipment etc.

It does not restrict to just agro-produce, it covers a broad spectrum of activities, including handicraft and handloom products, hand-woven, embroidery works, rug making, Jaisalmeri Pattu, wood carvings, bamboo products, madhubani paintings and other folk arts, etc. Village industries range to poultry farming, aquaculture produce, food processing, medicinal plants, bio-fuels, bio-mass based power plants, Jatropa cultivation, etc. Agro-product processing, Distillation units, Areca Nut leaf Plate Manufacturing, Tamarind leaf collecting, processing and marketing, Honey Bee farming, Organic manure production, Vermi & Dairy Compost production, Compressed Bricks manufacturing, etc. The produce range would include food and drinks, herbal products, clothing, handicrafts, handloom, furniture and other items indigenous to the selected rural areas.

RBH State Councils have been established in order to bring about the all around development of the RBH of the states. The Minister for Panchayati Raj or the Secretary of the Rural Department generally heads the state Rural Business Hub Councils. They are co-chaired by the chairman of the CII State Council.

CII supports its engagement in RBH. The chairman put forth that "nearly sixty years after Independence, most of us in the industry are yet to unlock the true potential of this massive production and consumption hinterland. Rural India has stayed off our radar screens partly because of inadequate knowledge, but mostly because our products and processes have become urban-centric. It's time to come out of our comfort zones and widen our sphere of influence. It's time to facilitate business projects in regions that—over the next couple of decades—are likely to emerge as India's biggest growth markets. With this in mind, we at CII have forged a unique partnership with the Ministry of Panchayati Raj, Government of India, to promote Rural Business Hubs (RBHs) of village arts, craft & village industries across the country."

Each hub will provide members of Indian industry, a unique opportunity to participate, learn and profit from sustainable rural ventures. Each RBH venture will seek to improve the quality of local produce and products in handpicked rural business hubs (approximately the size of a village block) by using modern training and production processes. The objective is to improve market access and ensure profitability across the value chain.

Under the proposed RBH business plan, industry—both large and small—will come together with farmers or local artisans to enhance the market value of a selected product. The local panchayat of the village/block will act as a facilitator, knowledge repository and a troubleshooter. The idea is to combine the inherent skills of people living in local communities and combine them with production capabilities of CII member companies. Once the products are found to be commercially viable, CII members, and various government departments will assist in providing market access.

The RBH venture is not a social exercise; members would not be expected to take up projects unless they are commercially viable or can be modified to become viable. At the same time, the effort would be to develop a business model where every stakeholder in the project benefits, especially the rural population. Moreover, member companies' venturing into this initiative will get whole-hearted support in terms of policies and procedures from the Ministry of Panchayati Raj and State Governments (CII 2009).

CII believes that, since creation of RBH will bring economic prosperity to the Rural India, the government must consider allocation of certain funds for RHBs in their financial planning. If funds allocated to several government schemes for rural development through various ministries such as Agriculture, Agro and Rural Industries, Food Processing, Small-Scale Industries, Department of Industrial Promotion and Policy, etc. as well as various departments of the State Governments; are made available through appropriate official notifications for development of Rural Business Hubs, this initiative could be set in motion at the shortest possible time; since the objectives of the two overlap (News 2009).

State RBH Councils

State Rural Business Hub Councils look after the well-being of many sectors that function in the rural areas of the states. The various rural sectors are: Food processing, Horticulture, Animal husbandry, Biofuel production, Handicraft and handloom, Dairy farming, Fisheries, and Rural tourism.

The objectives of State RBH Councils are to work along with the state governments in order to bring about an all-round development of the rural areas of the states. Further, these are responsible for bringing in industries to improve the quality of the products that are available locally and to manufacture products that will be both internationally and nationally acceptable. It also includes setting up of a mechanism through which the industries can procure directly, agricultural products from the rural people. This would benefit the rural people and the industry; for the rural people would get the right amount for their products due to the absence of the middlemen. The industry will also benefit, as they would get high standard and quality products with low procurement costs.

State RBH councils have encouraged many companies to set up their industries in the rural areas of the states. This has generated a lot of employment opportunities for the rural people, which in its turn have given a major boost to their economic condition. Further, it has developed the infrastructure of the rural areas of the state by setting up R&D centers, cold storage facilities, model farms, soil testing units, tissue testing laboratories, and bio-control laboratories. The industries that have been set up in the various states due to state RBH councils efforts have brought with them in the rural areas; the latest technology, agricultural inputs, skill and training development, good agricultural practices, marketing and branding, value addition, and standard and quality increasing measures. All this has helped the rural people of the states; for their incomes have increased due to better quality, entrepreneurship development, less transaction costs, and increased production.

Few examples: Size of the processed food market has a potential to grow to $300 billion by 2015, due to constraints such as long and segmented supply chain, resulting in high cost of products and poor products quality, the sector is not growing at a desirable level. The concept of RBH is a viable option to address this issue. Food processing industry provides technical know-how to farmers to improve the quality of their produce. In return, they get better and standardized produce at a reasonable competitive cost.

In 2009, the size of the processed food market in India is estimated to be $102 billion that includes $62 billion market in the primary processed food (packed fruits and vegetables, packed milk, unbranded edible oil, milled rice, flour, tea, coffee, sugar, pulses, species and salt), and 40 billion dollar market in the value-added foods (processed fruits and vegetables, juices, jams, pickles, squashes, concentrate, processed dairy products such as ghee, paneer, butter, branded edible oil, biscuits, snack foods, pasta based foods, processed meat, poultry and marine products, confectionary and chocolate, alcoholic beverages, etc. The food processing industry is highly fragmented with 70% of the total capacity in the hands of small and medium size players from unorganized sector. However, fruits and vegetable processing segment is equally divided, with organized sector contributing 48% of the total capacity ('Vision, Strategy and Action' Plan Report of the

Ministry of Food Processing Industries, Government of India, 2009).

The other area where there is a substantial scope for RBH is ancillaries for companies having factories in the rural areas. Corporates having factories in hinterland require host of products in their factories. Many of these small items do not require a very high technology and can be made by community outside the factories. The demand for these items is year round. This serves three purposes: cultivating goodwill with the community living around the factories, entrepreneurship development and employment generation, and for factories saving cost on transportation and inventory as many of these items can be procured closer to the factories.

The various states where RBH Councils have been set up are: Punjab, Assam, Andhra Pradesh, Haryana, West Bengal, Jammu and Kashmir, Chhattisgarh, Kerala, Maharashtra, Goa, Uttar Pradesh, Bihar, Himachal Pradesh, Madhya Pradesh and Uttarakhand.

RBH is taking roots in Andhra Pradesh with at least five companies, including two large agro-processing companies, showing interest in joining the hub, two more expressions of interest were received in the bio-diesel sector establishing water purification systems and mobile medical systems in rural areas (Nov 08). The Southern India Chamber of Commerce and Industry (SICCI) welcomed the State government's decision to set up 10 rural business hubs on P4 model. There is need for formation of professional teams for setting up the hubs while ensuring adequate and timely funding to primary producers and rural entrepreneurs, the statement added (22nd June 09).

CII and the Khadi and Village Industries Commission (KVIC) under the Ministry of Micro, Small and Medium Enterprises are converging their efforts under the RBH initiative. The collaboration is aimed at *generating rural employment and higher and sustained income for rural producers by better marketing of products through convergence of schemes and efforts of KVIC and Panchayats.*

The Process: After identifying the product, the Council sets up a Task Force with participation of key stakeholders and resource personnel as envisaged for development of the RBH. The Task Force ensures development of the RBH in a set time frame and the Chairman of the Task Force will be a member of the State RBH Council and report to the Co-chairman of National Rural Business Hubs Council. This would enable the Task Force to ensure necessary support and assistance from the Government agencies to implement its activities gainfully.

Stage III is Evaluation of the Product, Process and Gap Analysis by the Task Force. The Task Force will meet with the entrepreneurs, PRI leaders and State Government Officials of the identified RBH in the State. At this meeting, the product sample of the entrepreneurs will be evaluated. Stage IV: Providing technical support for product development, training on quality management, packaging, etc.; establishing market linkages, establishing e-trading site, and developing database for sourcing information (More details on the Process of establishing RBH in Appendix 2).

A one-stop information center, in which those looking to source the products within RBH project, should be established. To make this initiative a success, the system must evolve a mechanism to maintain consistency and on time delivery by rural entrepreneurs; and it is established as a self-sustainable system.

Training facilitators involved for programs such as CII cluster development program and skill development trainers are: mentors of Bharatiya Yuva Shakti Trust, rural facing NGOs (Dastkar, SEWA etc.), training bodies (Institute of Engineers, NID, NIFT, NPC, NSIC, etc.), large corporate entities operating in the rural areas (such as Titan, Parry's, HLL, Dabur, Hero Group, Himalaya Drugs, ICICI, ITC, etc.), ICT providers (such as Microsoft, Wipro, Cisco, IBM, Intel, HCL, etc.), and International trade promoters such as JETRO. Foundations formed by corporates such as Thermax, Tata, Wipro, Usha Matrin, etc. and Rural facing banks (Yes bank, Rabobank, ICICI, HDFC) and Global agencies such as World Bank, IFC, DFID, KFW, UNIDO, etc.

RBH state councils have taken several measures in order to bring about an all round development of the rural areas of the states. RBH state councils must continue with its efforts so that the condition of the rural people in the various states improves even more. By July 2009, over 32000 villagers from 15 states have been benefitted under the RBH scheme. Since 2007-08, the scheme has an annual allocation of Rs. 2 crore. Under the scheme till 31.03.2009, financial assistance has been sanctioned to 42 projects across 15 states. The scheme is operational in all the districts of the North Eastern States and in all the districts covered under Backward Regions Grant Fund Scheme. The Minister also clarified that there is no proposal to extend the Scheme to all parts of the country in view of the limited availability of funds.

Special Segments Markets

Commodity Exchanges: However, with the ongoing economic liberalization and globalization processes, not only the need to provide better prices to the farmers but also providing the participants with a platform for risk transfer was felt by the government, thus leading to the advent of commodity exchanges in 2003. The move definitely augments the potential of the market places to help the rural areas unlock values in their economy and help spread benefits of economic growth. Smart way to unlock value in India's rural economy is through setting commodity exchanges. Indian producers and traders have remained "price takers" despite our significant share in global supply.

It is imperative to have efficient markets for an economy to compete globally in a cost-efficient way so that ecosystem participants and consumers benefit. To enhance the competitiveness of our domestic commodity exchanges, there is an urgent need to allow capital infusion to help them put up a robust market infrastructure.

Consumer Markets: Other segmented markets are specific consumer markets focusing on agro related products such as for village field fresh produce, milk collection, and farm implements and fertilizers; even marketing of bio-gas if the village is producing it or for any alternative fuel products. The markets are also organized for arts and crafts produced in the villages. Mostly, such markets would be focusing on cities in different regions and in festivals and craft melas organized both for national and international audiences. Even there is scope for online markets also for village arts and crafts. When village enterprises on arts and crafts, and small-scale village industries are encouraged; these kinds of consumer markets would create economic gains and boost rural economy.

Consumer-led Growth Key to India's Recovery: Finance Minister's budget (2009, 2010) reflects the philosophy that consumption-led growth is the way out for the Indian economy. He stated that domestic consumption is the key since the global economy hasn't recovered enough. "There are lots of steps in the budget to boost demand whether it is the focus on rural sector, whether it is social sector etc. or even benefit for the urban person through reduction in surcharge on Income Tax, retention on duty rates, etc. It [the budget] will stimulate demand and consumption and that will lead to investment demand as well because after all companies will go in for capacity creation." Execution will be the key for going forward. The budget is a plan. The main challenge is to convert this into reality and therefore, execution is going to be the key. The Finance Minister seems to have pushed for consumption-led growth, by the larger outlays allotted to both the rural sector as well as many social schemes. He seems to be betting on the fact that there will be a slower global economic recovery and hence in the interim, he needs to boost the domestic market—especially rural markets. Indian story has always been primarily driven by domestic demand and consumption. It is a consumption-led growth economy in the last several years.

Rural Financials

Rural Financial Institutions in India

Rural financial system is classified along five channels: policy financial institutions, commercial banks, niche market financial institutions, co-operatives, and the informal sector. We have had an extensive network of regional rural banks for decades, while non-bank finance companies and NGO MFIs have, in recent years, become a significant part of the rural financial system. Measures concentrate on the financial sector. The focus is on programs to support micro credit, the reform of rural cooperative banks, the development of financial and other promotional instruments for small and medium-sized enterprises, and the development of social security for the poor. The priority is to find systems and solutions that can be applied on a broad basis. It is particularly important that measures should reach poor, disadvantaged groups such as untouchables. Low-cost rural banking ATM with biometric sensor—Gramteller has been developed for use in India in 2008. Establishing the identity of a rural depositor through biometrics makes it possible for illiterate or barely literate folks to become part of the banking user community.

Microfinance: Microfinancing or giving tiny loans were/are considered an essential tool to lift the poor entrepreneur. The year 1970 was the start of Grameen (rural) Bank in Bangladesh by UNDP for microfinance rural women. Government of India started rural bank (NABARD) for giving agriculture loans to farmers but the default rate is much higher and has not been a successful experiment. The Emerging Practices are micro-finance by profit microlenders, national and private banks and through private-public partnerships. Some of the profit micro-lenders companies may be even foreign companies operating for developing countries.

Promoters of microfinance are those who help in the formation of groups, invest in building the capacities of customers, and link them to a financial institution. Providers are those who involve themselves in direct financial transactions with clients.

Microfinance Practices are Changing: The awareness of poor, low-income and rural people for a comfortable lifestyle, and use of technology for agro-production and other small-scale industries, and entertainment is sufficiently aroused by media and interpersonal advertisements and campaigns. The awareness thus created demands the products and services. Businesses must make efforts to increase markets among this segment of consumers by focusing on increasing the purchasing capability of this segment without being exploited. Microfinance is the solution for it. Earlier, this segment was exploited by the village money-lenders whenever they needed loans. Historically, these people only took loans for dire emergency or for agriculture machinery for tilling the land and women were even denied that also.

Earlier, microfinancing was done by charitable institutions and at one point of time international development aid agencies and national governments made some efforts in developing countries.

Microfinance may be a social safety net when no other social safety nets exist, which is the case in the vast majority of the ruralites in India. Microfinance is the solution for it. Microfinance is considered an essential tool to lift the poor entrepreneur.

Emerging Microfinance Practices: Four such practices have been significant in helping the poor, low-income, rural, and women in this segment; and have been helpful in reducing the poverty and their economic helplessness to some extent. The practice of microfinance has now changed for profit making by making the working model efficient and at the same time, financing and helping the poor ruralites for more diverse products without any gender differentiation. This practice created more scope. The second significant practice that has emerged is that it is not only available for the products for starting enterprises and buying technology and machinery for livelihood; but for the consumer goods also—both durable and non-durable for comforts of life and to improve their lifestyle. The third practice is the combined effect of these two and beneficial for businesses. The first two emerging practices created markets and increased the business volume for products and services targeted at them. The fourth practice that emerged as consequence of these was of utmost significance as this consumer segment is recognized as deserving the goods and services and right to comforts and improved lifestyles. They could buy TV, DVD for entertainment or could take loans to start or increase efficiency of an enterprise.

Emerging Microfinancing Practices in India: In India, microfinance enterprises, businesses, banks and rural banks have played key role in emerging microfinance practices. Self-help groups of companies like ICICI bank, the ITC e-Choupal, the adult literacy program by TCS, and Shakti Initiative of HLL have realized the need to work their supply chain backward; starting with the consumer expectations and experiences and to develop their capacity to purchase. Earlier, the bottom-of-the-pyramid persons have to depend on moneylenders and take loans at exorbitant interest rates. Rather than developing their capacity to purchase over time, it rather lowered their future capacity as they could never repay even their interest. The loans were mainly taken for agriculture and personal emergencies and so it was not conducive to improving their enterprises or lifestyle even.

ICICI and other banks saw these people as critical to its future. But how to convert them into customers in cost effective way? Initially, ICICI bank organized village self-help groups. These groups of 20 women are taught about saving, borrowing, investing and so on. Each woman contributes to the joint saving account with the other members of the group. Based on the self-help group's track record, the bank lends money to the group, which in turn lends money to the individual members. ICICI is working with local communities and NGOs to expand its reach.

For instance, MYRADA set up an MFO called Sanghamitra Rural Financial Services (SRFS), while SEWA set up the SEWA Cooperative Bank. At the next level, we find NGOs helping the poor in economic activities. Their purpose is developmental. They see microfinance as an activity that feeds into economic activities. For instance, the South Indian Federation of Fishermen's Societies (SIFFS) started as a support organization for fishermen, providing technical and marketing support. The latest practice in microlending or microfinance is by profit microlenders. In India, three such companies are operating, SKS microfinance, Share Microfin Ltd., Bhartiya Samrudhi Finance and many more are coming on the scene as social entrepreneurship is developing. They give tiny loans to the poor entrepreneurs in villages that help them to lift themselves up from the poverty rung. But this approach is being criticized as of not much help.

Rather, there are upcoming suggestions that tiny loans will not create much entrepreneurship benefits for poor, rather, it should be given to cluster of poor people who can put together to set up a group enterprise on a cooperative basis with these loans. Individually they are responsible for their personal loans but success would be more in the combined efforts.

SKS has changed the earlier standard model which was not efficient, had more overhead expenses and not making money. This model has its limits; poorly managed and unscalable. Now it follows the business model of McDonald or Starbucks using technology and standardized systems to bring efficiency. It made the model efficient. First, by streamlining the loan process system to deal with the borrowers; by organizing them to meet together in groups at appointed time and at one appointed place, to get the payments in pre-sorted denominations to save counting of soiled currency notes.

Second plan was to attract capital from big banking institutions. Now Citigroup, ABN AMRO, HSBC Holdings, ICICI banks are giving millions of dollars to SKS to lend out in India, since India has the potentialities. Once SKS has more than 100,000 borrowers with default rate 2 per cent, they will be willing to invest. SKS put forth the argument, pay SKS to find borrowers and manage loans for you and you will get backdoor access to Indian consumer market.

In India, International Venture Funds foraying into microfinance will not have to grapple with conflicting rules of operation. The government has passed a bill to regulate the sector, which is expected to grow to Rs. 35,000 crore, by 2010. The big funds that are planning to make a foray into the sector include, the Maharashtra government promoted VC Fund-Urjankur, UK-based CDC, Unitus Private Equity and Delhi-based Lok Capital. Even IFC has set up a fund with the Andhra Pradesh Industrial Development Corporation (APIDC) for the purpose.

The Microfinancial Sector (Development and Regulation) Bill, 2007 in India seeks to promote the sector and regulate microfinancial organizations (MFO). The legislation provides a legal framework for entities engaged in microfinance and facilitate flow of financial services to the un-banked population of the country.

National Bank for Agriculture and Rural Development (NABARD) shall regulate the microfinancial sector. Every MFO that accepts deposits needs to be registered with NABARD. Conditions for registration include (a) net owned funds of at least Rs. 5 lakh; and (b) at least, three years in existence as an MFO. All MFOs, whether registered or not, shall submit annual financial statements to NABARD. Every MFO that accepts deposits has to create a reserve fund by transferring a minimum of 15% of its net profit realized out of its thrift and microfinance services every year.

The central government establishes a Microfinance Development Council to advise NABARD on formulation of policies related to the microfinancial sector. NABARD shall constitute a Microfinance Development and Equity Fund to be utilized for the development of the sector. The Fund would include (a) all grants received from the government and other sources; (b) any income received from investments made in equity of an MFO; and (c) the balance outstanding in the Fund maintained by NABARD before the commencement of the Act. The Fund would be managed by the Board of Directors of NABARD and would be used to provide any financial assistance to an MFO, invest in equity of an MFO, and meet any other expenses for the promotion of the micro finance sector.

There are different mechanisms through which the delivery of microcredit loans takes place. First, banks may lend directly to customers. Second, NABARD sponsors the Self Help Group-Bank Lending Program (SBLP). Under SBLP, self help groups (SHGs) need to save regularly for a minimum of six months and maintain prescribed records and accounts in order to become eligible to be linked to local banks. This program provides credit to 22.38 lakh SHGs. Third, commercial banks or apex institutions lend to MFOs for further lending to groups or individuals.

MFOs lend to SHGs and joint liability groups (JLGs), which are also known as Grameen groups. The number of

MFOs in India involved in lending activities is estimated to be around 800. These MFOs vary significantly in size, outreach and credit delivery methodologies. Presently, the lending activities of MFOs are not regulated except for those registered as NBFCs. This would provide a regulator for the banking needs of more than 400 million Indians, who are currently out of the banking system.

The emphasis will be given on development and nurturing of the microfinance movement in the country. The formal and informal channels should club synergies, to push growth and yet be development oriented. The prevalence of somewhat higher interest rates in the sector is being justified, saying it was not possible to keep the transaction costs low for the system to be sustainable. The government was, therefore, against putting a cap on the interest rates, as it would create artificial scarcity. Microfinance is seen as an extremely profitable venture, with low levels of non-performing assets. Another variation in microfinance in 2006, a Philanthropic fund is set up to help the small entrepreneur in developing countries.

Another emerging practice upcoming in microfinance in India in Nov. 2006 is to set customers overdraft facilities as opposed to conventional loan. Banks in India have now announced some rather unique ways in microfinancing to get them to deposit savings. Citibank has launched the Pragati saving account for its microfinance customers. This account is similar to a no frills account and does not require any minimum balance. The bank will provide services through a biometric ATM that will also speak to customers in Hindi, Marathi, Tamil, Telugu languages. "As the customers start saving, there will be ability to sweep this money into deposits so that they earn better interest than the conventional saving account. As we start getting imprints of customers in terms of deposit behavior we may be able to set them overdraft facilities as opposed to convention loan," says Business Manager of Global Consumer. What's unusual about the Citi bank India product is that it is offering microsavings, while most banks offer microloans. Other banks like Andhra Bank and Bank of

India, ICICI Bank also offer biometric ATM facility to their microfinance customers. In fact, banks see this untapped segment not as philanthropy but as sound business, at a time when cheap deposits are hard to come by (Nov. 2006).

Big insurance companies are validating microfinance insurance loans for the impoverished. American International Group Inc. (AIG) and Allianz are pursuing the idea of micro-insurance—tiny policies targeting the same market. In its simplest form, micro-insurance is like life and disability coverage for low-income people in emerging markets. It is paired with microfinance loans. The insurer makes good on the debt if a fledgling entrepreneur gets a loan and is disabled or dies, or the sewing machine or motor cycle that he bought with the loan is lost or broken. Such business may be tiny but it has the potential to become sizable. AIG has a strategic goal of building a base of future clients. Bajaj Allianz, a joint venture in India, offered its first Micro-insurance product in 2003. The aim is to design and sell a product that would cover the outstanding balance of a loan in the event the person who took the loan dies. The policy would also pay the loan taker's family double the amount of the loan.

Potentially, it is a huge market. One challenge is building a business large enough to be economically worthwhile. A related problem is logistical difficulty in reaching potential clients in isolated rural areas. There is a shortage of historical data on policies and claims on which the underwriters typically rely to set the policy prices. Nonetheless, Bill & Melinda Gates Foundation, Aga Khan Foundation USA, The Munich Re Foundation, ACCION International are pushing micro-insurance. They see this as complement to microfinance loans, something that can increase financial sophistication in far-flung areas, while protecting people vulnerable from ruin when breadwinner gets sick or dies.

Bandhan, one of the country's leading microfinance institutions (MFI) in Kolkatta, received Rs. 250 crore credit line from the Small Industries Development Bank of India (SIDBI). This will help the seven-year-old MFI grow its lending portfolio and cover five lakh additional borrowers this fiscal.

Its chairman confirmed "We will receive the term loan in several tranches by March 2010. We will be able to offer micro loans to five lakh additional borrowers with this fresh support from SIDBI." The MFI has nearly 19 lakh existing borrowers.

SIDBI supports the country's endeavor towards micro-credit expansion via the SIDBI Foundation for Microcredit (SFMC). It offers loans to MFIs with a view to support micro enterprises and non-farm income-generating activities. SIDBI general manager asserted, "West Bengal is an under-served state as far as microfinancing goes. We are planning to lend Rs. 300-400 crore to MFIs in the state this fiscal."

To smooth creases in the microfinance practices what was needed were; to attract capital from big banking institutions, regulate it through legislation and efficient management of loans through simple loan management software that reduces the accounting time from hours to minutes. The software also helped to diversify the risks from giving loans for buffalo purchase, tractor repair, setting up tea shops, or tire retreading, for durable and non-durable FMCG, and for insurance.

Now SKS is hopeful about this model's efficiency and utility. It plans to bring health and crop insurance to the poor. It hopes to use Visa card technology to make microloans as simple as getting cash from an ATM. Thus, entrepreneurs get big banks to back small loan. ICICI bank in India plans microfinance and sell insurance also to them. India's Central Bank is so optimistic about this model that recently it changed its regulations to allow small rural organizations to act as agents for banks.

The efforts would be needed for training and setting facilities for microfinance at the village level through enterprises, banks, cooperatives and social entrepreneurs; and training and setting facilities for macrofinance from urban level banks. These policies are framed focusing at local, State, Central government levels. These facilities are likely to generate employment at village level also.

Unique Rural Banking Services

Large state-owned banks like Canara Bank, State Bank of India, Punjab National Bank and others are required to maintain thousands of branches in rural areas, and remote areas; earlier, they were considered burdensome but now they prosper on financial aid for farmers. Loan demands through banks remains strong and largely unaffected by the global turmoil that has hit the Indian urban middle classes putting a drag on bank performance. Government policies that create jobs, build infrastructure and support prices of staple crops like wheat and rice have spurred deposit growth in rural areas. In 2008, total bank deposit climbed 20% from 12% in 2007 whereas urban rates slowed from 28% to 19% (RBI source). Government-funded programs are raising incomes and expanding opportunities and farmers can take loan to avail of them.

Fresh view on rural banking services might foster entrepreneurship and lift people from poverty. Encouraging more savings and borrowing in rural areas will generate economic growth in the rural areas. State bank of India rural deposit grew 30% to 2.16 trillion rupees ($45 billion), advanced loans of 1.21 trillion rupees ($25 billions) up to 18%, loan default rate is 0.5% for fiscal year ending 31st March 2009.

In 2008, Banks made efforts to educate farmers about banking and encouraging them to open accounts. Canara Bank dispatched a fleet of jeep to drive from village to village, Punjab National Bank New Delhi has lifted borrowing limits on its credit card for farmers to as much as $40,000. IngVysya bank expanded its rural branch Network to 10% and trained its loan officers about growing chili, grapes and rice to better understand the customer. Foreign banks' operations are modest so far, Standard Chartered Bank PLC and HSBC Holdings PLC are also getting into rural banking. Each of them reported 40% rise in Indian rural lending in 2008. In addition to low default rates on rural loans, Indian banks endorse that government subsidizes payments by covering as much as 3% points of interest due. Individual loans tend to be small and lending rates are capped and offered for less interest rate than the microfinance companies and money lenders.

RBI sets targets that require State banks to open accounts and extend loans in the rural areas. In 2008 for its operations, it hired 5000 employees; added 1050 branches to its 7500 locations and would add 1000 in 2009. It has also been outsourcing basic services to rural areas giving it a presence in additional 50000 villages in 2007-08.

The State Bank branch is now functioning with a smart phone and finger prints—it is called Zero system. The smart phone uses to keep data on accounts, depositors, fingerprints, photo and voices. The zero system is helping a construction worker in city to open bank accounts and send home money in the village. Zero system is developed by Anurag Gupta.

The State Bank uses zero system for unique outsourcing services through a freelance SBI agent. There is no SBI branch or ATM in the area. Agent honors withdrawal requests through a cell phone, finger print scanner and cash. Customers prove their ID by providing account number and finger scan, which pulls up customer photo on agents' cell phone. Such operations from freelance SBI agents have added more than 20 million rural accounts in 2007-08 reaching 28 million while expanding deposit by 65% and the loan portfolio by 50% (July 09 head of rural business SBI).

Banks annual performance is monitored with special reference to lending to key areas like agriculture, micro, small and medium enterprises, housing and education. Ministry officials have been collecting information from banks relating to lending to these key areas.

An ATM dispenser in a remote village that helps users withdraw money from their savings account with voice guidance in the local language is reality now. An integrated cash dispenser is the next generations of Integra Microsystems' financial applications secure terminal—iMFAST Branchless Solution, introduced in the market four years ago. Integra Microsystems, a Bangalore-based software development company, has designed and developed the cash dispenser.

Country Head—Sales, Integra Microsystems, says that all features required for a rural ATM have been incorporated in the system. Some of the other features include voice guidance, fingerprint sensor with live fingerprint detection system, contact-less and contact-based smart card, magnetic swipe card, in-built GPRS and CDMA-based communication for online and offline data uploads, in-built global positioning system (GPS) to capture co-ordinates, impact printer and full keyboard. According to him, banks are keen to use the integrated system in urban centers too for disbursing pension funds.

How It Works: The cash dispenser can be placed in the business correspondent's (BC) location. The BC could be anyone such as a grocery shopkeeper, PCO owner. "The cash dispenser is operable only when the BC (operator) logs in using his smartcard and authenticates himself with his fingerprint. A customer can perform operations such as balance enquiry, withdrawal, printing mini-statement," he adds. The cash dispenser currently supports two denominations—Rs. 50 and Rs. 10, and the currency notes could be old ones too. At a time, the cash dispenser can be loaded with 2,000 notes of each currency denomination. The model could be expanded to support more denominations. The BC can replenish the cash.

"iMFAST Branchless Solution, is a technology-enabled banking platform built to bank the country's unbanked population and thus facilitates financial inclusion. It makes possible the concept of branchless banking and takes banks to the doorsteps of the rural customers with minimal cost". While the terminal, which would include the portal and application, is available at about Rs. 30,000, the whole solution—terminal and cash dispenser—would be priced at about Rs. 1 lakh.

The BC or agent-assisted portable financial transaction terminal acts as a front-end point-of-service device and associated software at the back-end for identifying, authenticating the users of the system and interfacing with the bank's existing database for online and offline transactions. About 1,300 terminals have already been deployed. The clients for the terminal include Bank of Baroda, Bank of India, Canara

Bank, Central Bank of India, Corporation Bank, Indian Bank, Indian Overseas Bank, Pragati Grameen Bank, Punjab National Bank, State Bank of Mysore, Syndicate Bank and Vijaya Bank.

iMFAST can also be detached from the cash dispenser, so that the BC can carry the iMFAST mobile terminal to do mobile or door-to-door transactions. In this case, the cash will be handled by the BC manually.

The Reserve Bank of India (RBI) is set to rope in more entities, such as owners of grocery stores, medical shops, petrol pumps, as business correspondents and also ramp up the range of services to be offered by them. The services will include allowing business correspondents to authenticate the unique identification number (UID) of a customer and function like a micro-ATM. The move will help provide over 41% of India's unbanked population access to banking facilities. A formal announcement is likely to be made in the quarterly-review of monetary and credit policy and an indication to this effect was given by deputy governor, RBI.

Business correspondents are allowed to do banking business as agents. "Even an owner of a grocery store could be a business correspondent equipped with a phone, a fingerprint reader, a software that functions as an ATM and allows a person to withdraw, say, cash in remote villages that do not have bank branches. The fingerprint reader will authenticate the beneficiary and allow him to undertake a financial transaction."

It is reckoned that the float-funds in accounts, especially of beneficiaries of government-sponsored schemes, such as the NREG Scheme, will rise as many of them may withdraw only in tranches. There will be a huge opportunity for banks, given that the allocation under the NREGA alone is around Rs. 39,000 crore. The UID will be a powerful catalyst for financial inclusion.

Currently, over 90% of the retail payments are cash-based and once they become electronic-based, it would help prune transaction costs and make banking business more viable. Cash transactions account for over 2.5% of the country's GDP and even a 50 bps drop will be significant. The cost of equipping the business correspondent with the required infrastructure is estimated at around Rs. 5,000. The average value of transaction through this channel will be around Rs. 50, far lower than the average value of a transaction done on an ATM. The UIDAI is also in talks with banks, Life Insurance Corporation of India, other insurers, state-owned oil companies, among others, to become registrars or points for enrollment. It intends to provide on-line authentication of residents.

Disaster Loan Funds (DLFs) for Ruralites

These are financial reserves and usually derived from the initial donor grant to the microcredit lender. Don't give free cash to the poor. The experience is when aid is free, poor get the least of it and they inflate their needs. While some handouts are necessary in times of disasters but giving micro-loans helps. This keeps costs down and rebuilds the fund for the next disaster. Microlenders help people restructure their loans or give new loans on favorable terms. Microfinance has helped millions reach a better life through their own initiative. It has also given them valuable skills as well as crucial financial back-up in case they ever face a natural disaster like floods, draughts, etc. Giving someone a hand-up does not require a handout. The most important point is that people get back to work while letting them hold on to their self-respect through micro-loans.

Industrial Initiatives

People Empowerment through Industrial Initiatives: When developing industries around villages by acquiring land; industrialists develop the villagers also not only through finances but by giving training for jobs and employment and providing healthcare facilities and schools. Tata group of industries optimism is well founded. It selected 29 tribal youths whose families were displaced by industrial projects, gave them technical training and jobs. And more such youth will be selected. Although some tribal leaders see Tatas' initiative as a move to break their agitation, the youth see an opportunity.

"We know that any how some day, the government will take our land for the steel plant. So why not cooperate with them and get benefited from it," said a beneficiary. Further, a youth employment program aimed at helping the underprivileged sections of the society was launched by Tata Group's community development branch in partnership with Dr. Reddy's Labs. Neev Foundation—the initiative of Tata Companies, and LABS (Livelihood Advancement Business School) would collaboratively work towards enhancing the employability skills and improve employment opportunities for the youth (2008).

South Korean steelmaker Posco is also working with the people. In Paradeep, Posco plans to set up a 12-million ton steel plant, costing Rs. 52,000 crore. Posco got its Korean staff to learn Oriya and offered Orissa students scholarships also. It flew in doctors to treat cleft-lip patients at free medical camps. Now it will offer vocational training. It will need 4,000 acres on which it wants to start building in April next year. And it's confident of winning the people's support (2008).

Many other big companies such as Mittal steel, Reliance, Birlas, Mahindra and Mahindra are all taking initiatives to provide financial compensation and loans, training for employment to the villagers where they are setting up their industries. Companies improve social and environmental conditions' sustainability. They take initiatives to help local communities in education, healthcare, environment protection and agriculture development consultancy. But many times, these industry initiatives get misfired, as political activists with vested interests mislead the village beneficiaries and they regress back rather than getting developmental assistance. In 2009, the recent cases have been of Tata's Nano Car Project in West Bengal, Reliance retail in UP, and Mittal steel and Posco stagnating in Orissa.

Government Efforts

The business models that government is adopting to help in rural financials is through subsidies for seeds, fertilizers, electricity power and petroleum or kerosene oil for running agro machines, water for irrigation and at times, through loan waivers. These are procured and supplied to the farmers through government agencies. At one point in the past, government had set up rural banks to provide loans and credit to the farmers only for buying farming tools. But that scheme has failed as many times, farmers either intentionally, or unintentionally do not have the means to repay the loans. Rate of return has been poor; many times government has to waiver such loans.

In its major efforts for development of agriculture and totally subsidized, government builds such rural infrastructure, small dams, irrigation canals, check dams (to regulate water flow) on the irrigation canals to regulate water supply to all the farmers and digging tubewells and hand pumps for drinking in the villages. Both central and state governments are responsible for these. Government also funds R&D for agriculture and related areas such as milk procurement and management of its products in its agricultural institutes and universities to develop new techniques, seeds and technology and other ways of producing and marketing them efficiently. Government also totally funds the training programs—called agriculture extension programs for ruralites.

Government is also encouraging national and international organizations to foray into these areas. DuPont has developed genetic seeds and supply them free to the farmers. Pepsi and other companies have got into 'contract farming' with farmers. This way they focus on improving the crops quality and supply good seeds and fertilizers freely plus train farmers in improved and modern ways of farming, harvesting, storing, etc.

The private enterprises like Amul, Nanak, Paras, Milkmaid, and Mother dairy have in a big way organized the procurement of milk through a good supply chain from villages; processing and pasteurizing milk and preparing other milk products through modern technologies in clean and healthy way and organizing sound distribution system to reach the consumers fresh, clean and at affordable prices. With this, government has stopped its earlier efforts to procure and distribute milk to consumers through its milk schemes. These private efforts have reduced the milk and its product shortages and so also the bread shortage so ubiquitous in 90s. Upcoming is Danon One for fruit yogurt, others for tonic water, canned coconut water and vitamin water, etc. Government wants more of domestic and international enterprises to enter these forays. These create economic gains as rural produce, milk, etc. are used.

From time to time, government waives the farmers' loans to ease their difficult situations in times of natural disaster, low monsoon rains, drought, and floods, etc. which spoil their crops. It is a way of subsidizing the farmers. There are positive and negative impacts of OTS scheme of farmers' loan waiver 2009. A large number of farmers have already thronged bank branches to get the benefits of either the loan waiver or the OTS offer barely 24 hours after the FM's sensational jumbo farm loan waiver proposal. Four crore small and marginal farmers will get the benefit of the FM's proposed loan-waiver scheme. That means, each small/marginal farmer will enjoy an average loan waiver of Rs. 12,500. Other farmers would get a cumulative loan waiver of Rs. 10,000 crore if they repay 75% of their outstanding loans upfront through the OTS scheme (2009).

"The quality of life, in general, will doubtless improve in the rural belt as these farmers are likely to spend more on consumer durables and create assets as they would be cleared off their dues," a senior banker said. The OTS scheme, particularly, will generate cash surplus in the hands of farmers. They are expected to step up consumption levels. The consumption demand, if it happens, in turn, would have a positive impact on the economy. A higher consumption demand is also anticipated from many small and marginal farmers eligible for availing of the loan waiver scheme. All these farmers will also be eligible for fresh farm loans with a clean slate. This would, in turn, lead to a higher spending on farm inputs like pesticides and fertilizers. However, this loan waiver scheme may impact banks in a negative way in terms of recovery of loans. Farmers to be benefited from the scheme may generate a tendency to delay their repayment anticipating further sops in the future," a top banker said.

Mobile Wallet: m-payments

Empowerment of the bottom-of-the-pyramid never looked so feasible. A revolution is silently but forcefully sweeping the developing countries, that could soon equip every single person with a mobile wallet and provide them with not just digital payment facilities but huge savings as well. The trend in mobile wallet usage has shown such vigor in countries like the Philippines, Malaysia, Thailand and Pakistan, not to mention Asian leaders in that domain, Japan and South Korea, that it could give a complex to consumers in western economies.

Speaking at a seminar ('Sustaining Growth: In a Downturn through Technology' Mumbai May 09) Justin Ho, co-CEO of Singapore-based Utiba, a company that is a global supplier of mobile commerce platforms for mobile operators and financial institutions, the spread of mobile payment systems promises to lift the economic status of a significant number of people across the world.

Interestingly, the entire concept of m-payment is based on the fact that each mobile phone number in the world is unique to the user of that number. Says Mr. Ho: "All one needs to know while sending money to someone else through m-payment is the other person's mobile number. That makes m-payment instantaneous and far less cumbersome than a telegraphic money transfer, for instance." He says the number of m-payment users is on the rise as more mobile owners realize the pleasure of getting cash into their mobile wallet to enable them to make m-payments. "In many Asian countries including the Philippines, there are significant number of people who get their salary into mobile wallets", says Mr. Ho.

According to him, the benefits of m-payment are most for the have-nots. "In the Philippines, for instance, there are farmers who have to commute hours to their banks to pay interest on their loans, and the commuting costs sometimes exceed the interest. M-payment would provide huge savings for them in both time and money," he says.

According to Mr. Ho, Indian farmers who sell cereals are learnt to be benefiting only to the extent of 53% of the final sale price while the middlemen make as much as 31%, and that the situation is even more distorted in the case of fruit and vegetable farmers. He says the availability of price quotes on the mobile and the facility for farmers to receive money on their mobiles from the co-operatives would give them substantially higher earnings.

Five million m-payment users in the Philippines and over 6 million in Kenya point to the strong patronage for the tech edge among the masses. Utiba has associated with Western Union for m-payment services, and is expecting Bangladesh to be the next economy to wake up to the possibility of empowering its masses with the m-payment edge. He added, financial inclusion failed to take off due to lack of technology and business model (among banks), poor delivery mechanism, and also because rich do not have compassion for the poor. The Utiba honcho says that a lower m-payment culture in the West could be owed to the existence of other digital payment options there; pointing out that in the USA for instance the high mobile penetration was not matched by a high m-payment culture.

In India, the RBI is yet to take a final call on the formalities of the m-commerce domain. Speaking at the same seminar, C. Rangarajan, former governor of RBI said, "What is required now is not creating new institutions for extending their outreach, but finding ways and means to effect improvements within the existing formal credit delivery mechanism and evolve new models for extending the outreach."

Mobile phone payments in villages are implemented in a unique way in India. (i) It is done by banks through zero system. (ii) Money is transferred through cell phones in villages, when a person outside sends message to a cell phone kiosk in the village to transfer that amount to the village person. He/she deposits that much amount to the cell phone account. (iii) Mobile payments are done through post office computerization; international money order (i-MO) launched in 2006, enables a village customer to receive money in minutes from the local post offices. The electronic money orders (e-MO), launched in October 2008, facilitate transmission of ordinary money orders through electronic media instantaneously. (iv) Farmers use mobile services to pay interest on their bank or microfinance loans.

Village mobile phone Kiosk is the important link for all such payments. All such messages for payments and otherwise are sent on mobile phone in the Kiosk which is run commercially by the village agents who are paid commission by the government or sponsoring industries or NGOs for such services, though the villager is not charged for such services.

Observations

Development of rural markets for rural consumer base can drive the rural economy. Rural consumerism could be the dynamic for rural economy. Right kind of initiatives can be taken by businesses and industries and they are waking up to the bottom-of-the-pyramid market opportunities which can boost both rural economy and their business economy. The significant point is ruralites are ready for it. Redefining markets in terms of ruralites consumers' feedback, actions and outcomes would create further market growth and economic gains. Corporates are promoting rural markets as drivers of future growth. It is imperative to have efficient rural markets for an economy to compete with mainstream national economy and globally in cost efficient ways so that ecosystem participants and consumers benefit.

Rural business hubs with value added services are promoting entrepreneurship development and generating rural employment; and higher and sustained income for rural producers through convergence of schemes. Efforts are also made through these hubs to provide latest technology, skill and training development through P4 model. Opportunities thus created for the rural people would give a major boost to their economy.

Ruralites need to have purchasing capacity and that can be built, and even rural entrepreneurship can be built up by microfinance. Ruralites with little or no access to traditional financial institutions can be empowered by microfinance. The microfinance loans, microcredit, microsavings, microfinance insurance are the emerging practices in India promoted by

Businesses, Banks, through Industrial initiatives and government efforts. Micro-legislation 2007 will further regulate these; so villagers are not exploited by entities providing microfinance. Unique banking services through technology-enabled banking platform is being provided to rural unbanked population and thus facilitating financial inclusion through programs like Gramteller, Zero system, M-wallet, and iMFAST Branchless Solution.

8

Rural Policies

Rural Policy Frames

India has planned development. In India, the basic socio-economic policies are planned through periodic Five-Year Plan which sets the targets and modalities and funding allocations for various programs under several heads. Currently, we are running Eleventh Five-Year Plan (2007-2012).

These basic policy frames undergo changes through yearly Economic surveys done by government and other agencies and mid-term appraisals of the Plan. There are exigencies like draught, low monsoons, price rise and inflation rate, scarcity of commodities, oil price rise and even the global melt down which can impact these policy frames.

Policies are planned for Central, State and Local levels for urban and rural population and their development. There has to be active involvement of all these levels to make the policies workable. The focus of all the policy frames is socio-economic well-being of 'people' in its various facets. Therefore, people must be actively engaged with these policy frames—to plan, demand, implement and give feedback.

Rural policy frame in India are to enhance institutional capacity, local governance, health care delivery, educational opportunity, upgrading human capital at all levels; increasing availability of appropriate financial capital, rebuilding and improving physical infrastructure, building institutional capacity among planning and service delivery organizations in rural regions, Rural tourism and preservation of cultural heritage and Information technology (ICTs). Healthcare, education, occupational and vocational education and training, employment, and teleconnectivity will create economic gains for ruralites and hence create healthy physical environments conducive to quality of life both through physical and psychological well-being. Hence we need to create sound policies to achieve these for the rural strata. Right on, we need special rural policies in these areas to bring them at par with urban and national mainstream economy as there is wide lag in it.

IEC programs are planned to create awareness, change of attitude and behavior, education and motivation to engage in participation of these policy frames. Therefore, we need sound communication polices focusing on Mass Media—both traditional and new media, interpersonal and ICTs to make IEC programs effective. We have discussed the progress at length from rural perspective of these policy frames in earlier chapters.

Rural Policy Development

India's economy can be boosted by majority of its people enjoying quality of life. Quality of life (QOL) and other drivers—personal and occupational are both peripheral and central to boosting economy. 75% of India's population living in rural India needs to be focused to enjoy quality of life. Our introductory chapter does highlight how government has focused on these people since independence through various social development plans but the results have not been encouraging. The majority of rural population is at the bottom of the pyramid, and they need to be boosted up to be at par with the urban peripherals at the bottom. Though overall objective of the rural policies should aim for inclusive economic growth for bottom of the pyramid both at rural and urban level. That should be the real economic growth parameters and GDP. It is assumed that, urban lower levels do get the trickle-down effect of urban development but not so the ruralites.

Our next moot question is who is to be blamed if ruralites are at the bottom of pyramid even after 60 years of exclusive rural development plans? *There are three pointers: People themselves are to be blamed first, local government is second and the central government too since it focused exclusively on social development and then economic growth. Its varied programs were too ideal for people threshold, lacked people participation though they were planned as people's programs and most of all implemented sporadically.*

Indian Prime Minister said (June 2009), India could not only sustain its high growth momentum but also push it to 10% with the right policies and dedication. "Our economy has demonstrated resilience in meeting the challenges posed by globalization. In the last two decades, our industry—both large and small—has restructured and become globally competitive. Pointing out that too many people in the country lacked access to basic services like health and education, the Prime Minister added, we need a growth process that will achieve a rapid reduction in poverty, accelerate the pace of both industrialization and employment-generation, reduce the rural-urban divide, and bring measurable benefits to SCs/STs, minorities and other excluded groups. Development is a process that should not divide but should unite," the Prime Minister said, stressing that the Centre and States should work with a new sense of direction and focus. *Attributing the rural-urban divide to poor performance in the agriculture sector*, he said: "We are faced with a peculiar puzzle whereby on the one side, the growth rate is accelerated to more than 9%, but on the other side, the share of agriculture in our GDP has dropped to below 20% without any appreciable shift in the proportion of population dependent on agriculture." Singh emphasized that *it was essential to improve basic facilities and infrastructure in rural areas to mitigate impoverishment and prevent large-scale migration.*

The Prime Minister also asked for several taskforces within the plan panel, in areas like irrigation, agriculture, hill states, and quick clearances for industrial and infrastructure projects. While the emphasis in agriculture is on ensuring food security and a district-specific agricultural plan, in the case of infrastructure, the emphasis is on public-private partnerships. The Planning Commission estimates that the country will need investments of up to $500 billion during the plan period to meet its infrastructure deficit.

There is need for constant policy review and attention because a country like India will have constant policy problems. "A country like India cannot have simply one orgy of decision-making annually. Once in a year, you announce policy platforms and for the rest of the year, we don't do anything. India is too large and too diverse a country and too varied in its economy to lend itself to this kind of process. There is a third reality, which is special reality in all democratic countries and when we talk of economies, we are not talking pure economics. We are talking of political economy. And in a democratically elected government, we always have to live within the realm of what is democratically possible, achievable and not touchable."

Prime Minister Manmohan Singh commenting on the Governance policy advocated the need that bureaucrats must do more to address public dissatisfaction and instill confidence in people. In the interaction with his officials, the Prime Minister discussed the agenda of the government and ways of improving the delivery system. He told his audience that in sectors like education, health and employment generation, the challenge was one of effective and equitable delivery of public services (June 09).

India needs a positive movement on rural social sector reforms because it is the progress on social sector and the promise it holds out for greater inclusion which creates a social consensus for modernization and driver for rural economy to grow. There would be a significant flow of private investments in roads and power sectors etc. The focus should be on effective and equitable delivery of public services through such *PPP* investments. *PPP policies* for rural development in many fields are focused: Public-Private Partnership (PPP) not only creates more efficiency in the way projects are implemented, but it leverages whatever resources government has by bringing in more resources from the outside. Not only Central Government but many of the State Governments have in fact made significant progress in implementing projects in roads and other rural infrastructure projects in the PPP modes. Telecom probably is ahead of target in PPP mode.

Rural Economic Policy

India's average ruralites in the 2000 decades have very low spending power and almost negligible savings. Economically, they have been in both personal and occupational denial mode so far. To strengthen the economy as well as their economic choices, it is necessary to promote consumerism through creating special products and services for the rural consumers; and to strengthen spending power through gainful employment, microfinance institutions and hire-purchase system.

Since there are no savings for all the three levels of society—middle, lower middle and poor, and there are no government or non-government social security schemes, so, social security net has to be created through such policies like, rural insurance schemes for life and agro crops, unemployment insurance and pension schemes, and microfinance to dispel no saving anxiety. Fiscal discipline among ruralites could be developed through spending, savings, loan availability and no anxiety for the future financial security in old age and in disability, and the aim is to provide a comfortable life.

Three types of Rural economic policies are planned (i) long-term which will be planned and implemented by Central government, (ii) short-term which are planned and implemented by State governments, (iii) local policies which people plan for themselves in the villages. All the three policies implementation will be successful and will speed growth by people participation and active involvement both at planning and implementation stage. Dialogue strategies, public discourses are the best strategies to achieve such participation both at planning and implementation levels.

We need to develop stronger and more equitable rural policies through public discourses and dialogue strategies on the issues involved. We need to understand impact of urban policies on ruralites. We face the critical challenges in rural domestic policy and critical role of rural healthcare, education and employment policies in these contexts. We need policies on the occupational front: (a) for vocational education and training for selling and marketing of their produce, (b) training and setting facilities for microfinance at the village level through people and social entrepreneurs, (c) training and setting facilities for macrofinance from urban level banks. These policies have to be set up at local, State, and Central Government levels.

After many decades, it is being realized that the philosophy for driving rural growth is bottom-up, rather than depending on the 'trickle-down effect'. We are focusing on moving with the majority, rather than focusing on the affluent minority. Thus, current budget is a clear shift in terms of its ambitious vision for driving economic growth. It would need innovative thinking and a clear plan for ensuring that the ambitious spending plan of the government delivers growth. It has to take into account behavioral economics on how rural spending by the government can be productively used by rural consumers to enhance their quality of life.

The government's focus should shift from expenditure to effectiveness of expenditure. Across the last decade, we have heard about government spending to boost employment, to boost the economy, and give fiscal stimulus. "The public has given a great mandate to the government in 2009 and now it should shift action to delivery and implementation. There are three questions that need to be asked. One, are we going to have ministers who will provide effective governance and carefully look after implementation? Two, will the Finance Ministry on a quarterly basis carefully look at schemes and programs where expenditure is being made from taxpayers' money? Three, are the benefits actually going to the intended end-users?"

The government should regularly conduct an audit to check deliverance on the ground and effectiveness of expenditure. This should be a strict mandate with strict operational control and review certainly on a monthly or quarterly basis to see that taxpayers' money is properly spent and not increasing government expenditure into plans and programs where money is siphoned through corruption. So we should look forward to new mechanisms of control of projects and delivery, monitoring and implementation, and all done in effective mode.

In the recent years, five strategies have made implementation of rural polices more effective and further evolvement of those planned polices to create effective implementation and achieving planned targets and results: (i) restructuring Panchayat—the local level of village government since 1989 (we have discussed in later section the restructuring process and format and how it can empower the villagers); (ii) since 2000, government had made implementation of policies and programs demand driven rather than earlier supply driven approach; (iii) this paves the way for Action Oriented Community Participation; (iv) operating P4 model—public, private, people and NGOs coordinating to implement; (v) periodic monitoring and appraisals of the ongoing programs whether those are achieving the intended results for the intended audience without corrupt practices and the need for continuing the same, or changing the non-effective dimensions. People's feedback is built in this process. In earlier chapters, we have discussed the applications of these five strategies in contexts of ongoing and planned programs.

Further, these programs discussed in earlier chapters envisages need for rural policy contexts in such areas (a) Rural healthcare, education and employment, (b) Income generating occupations both farm and non-farm. In this context, policies related to farm economy, farm practices and management, and policies focusing on development of village enterprises, rural entrepreneurship and setting BPO, (c) Rural infrastructure, (d) Social security policies, and (e) Rural tourism policies.

Current Rural Policies in Operation

Rural infrastructure development policies are crucial for development of rural economy. (i) These policy initiatives need to focus on rural electrification, development of roads; rural connecting road system is shoddy, needs improvement to carry produce to the markets. They need to be connected within the village itself, with the surrounding villages, and with highways and expressways going to urban areas, (ii) food and crop storage facilities which need to be improved drastically, (iii) better irrigation policies are needed either it is dependent on monsoon rains or deep aquifers are over-extracting water from the soil, (iv) training in improved farming practices and technology are needed, (v) infrastructure for rural industrial base, rural markets and hubs development, and infrastructure for capital flows to rural areas both national and international and creating infrastructure for rural tourism development, (vi) rural policies, system and development schemes in healthcare, sanitation, water, irrigation, education and employment, (vii) policies and schemes for rural telecommunication infrastructure to give connectivity to ruralites and that is driven for economic and social growth of ruralites in various areas, (viii) providing shelter to people is basic necessity of life, we need rural housing policies, (ix) preserving rural environment is also important for health of ruralites and we need sound policies to preserve these by efficient fuel policies, disposal of garbage and toxic waste in the villages.

We have highlighted the need, shortcomings and change overs, successes and disappointments in these areas over a period of time in the earlier chapters.

Panchayati Raj Policies for Local Rural Government

Panchayati Raj infrastructure in rural areas was initiated in 50s to give local government and village autonomy to villages. The earlier format of Panchayati Raj System: single tier Panchayat system, block is the unit of implementation of development programs, block development officer is the head of the Panchayat samiti and responsible for and supervision of development programs. Block extension staff consists of Panchayat inspectors for various development programs, the Panchayat secretaries and the village level workers (VLW). VLWs are assigned 2 or 3 villages depending on the size of the villages and the Panchayat secretaries are assigned 3 or 4 villages according to the work load produced by the villages. The village Pradhan is the member of the Panchayat Samiti and is the elected leader of the villagers, heads the local

Panchayat. It was too idealist for the people at that time or its effectiveness was lost because not having effectual checks and monitoring; and also because of government's paternalistic attitudes interfering the villagers' autonomy.

Our observations in the context of rural economy development policies suggest that local contribution is crucial for planning, implementing and effectiveness of these rural policies. There has to be collaborative efforts of Central and State governments and local government in the villages. Therefore, in recent decade, currently both Central and State governments are keen to revive the Panchayati Raj and monitor its effectiveness in giving autonomy to the villagers.

In 1989, Panchayat format was restructured by a constitutional amendment. Panchayat is the democratic local government in villages, it is elected and its two-third members must be women, scheduled castes and other minority groups in the village areas.

***Rural Judicial Reforms and Power of Panchayat*:** Gram Nyayalaya is launched through an Act of 2008, which will be operationalized from October 2, 2009. Gram Nyayalaya will be located at the intermediate level of the Panchayats. The idea of these Nyayalayas will be to complete the cases in six months of registration. Junior magistrates, through a summary of proceedings, will decide the cases. Once the Gram Nyayalaya will be operationalized, 50% of the 2.75 lakh cases pending in courts will be solved.

Rural Housing Policies

If the focus is on addressing the issue of affordable housing and affordability of housing, then the strategy would be different. One very important thrust area for the government should be in trying to provide access to cheap finance as a housing loan because many of these people are unable to access housing loans from any bank at whatever rate of interest. There is no organized funding for these consumers. Hence, that is a very important area where they probably need to strengthen National Housing Bank or they need to promote or encourage various microfinance agencies to work for providing credit to these consumers at the bottom of the pyramid.

The research study shows demand for housing stock for 2008 to 2025 under two alternative scenarios—business as usual (BAU) and higher growth (HG). The projected numbers of houses increase at an average annual rate of 1.48% and 1.56% under the BAU and HG scenarios respectively. The rate of increase in housing demand is related to the assumption of higher rate of income growth as compared to the BAU situation. During the 17-year period of 2008-2025, the rural housing stock is projected to rise by 42-44 million under both scenarios.

Overview of Housing Policies and Outlook: Economic growth has offered opportunities to individual households, who have been able to benefit from such growth, for improving their housing conditions. However, rural households do not have the same financial capacity as their urban counterparts to undertake improvements. An active housing sector in rural areas could indeed be both a direct catalyst for promoting greater economic activity as it provides considerable employment at the local level and would also help in improving the health and productivity of rural inhabitants.

The government's policy initiatives have attempted to stimulate rural housing. Given the general handicaps of the rural areas and more specifically, the weaknesses of different segments of rural population, the policies have also been evolving. Given the multiple dimensions of the rural housing challenges, a coordinated strategy needs to be evolved. Recognizing the fact that there are strong regional and local dimensions to rural housing requirements, local-level institutional arrangements to encourage rural housing construction are necessary.

The policy initiatives require both financial commitment and design of delivery systems to make technical and financial assistance available in rural areas. Increasingly, involvement of NGOs and the private sector is becoming important in both providing and delivering this assistance. While the Panchayats are playing a greater role in identifying beneficiaries for subsidies, they should also take up the responsibility for the overall development of rural housing in terms of streamlining land records for housing, enforcing standards of building construction and providing a facilitating environment for housing development so that the finance agencies, construction industry and non-government sector can be more effective in their functions.

The trends suggest that there is considerable demand for improvement in rural housing conditions. The assessment of the future scenario points to the rise in housing stock and more importantly, construction of more durable housing stock. However, the quality of a significant proportion of rural housing stock would continue to be poor; demand for upgrading it could be as important or significant as the demand for new housing.

Components that would need attention now and in future are: land availability, cost of construction, appropriate building materials and technology, building design not only for just one house but for the village habitat as a whole, skilled labor for construction so that housing construction is of reasonable good quality and construction process utilizes resources efficiently and access to affordable housing finance, not only for construction of new houses but also for continued up-gradation of existing housing.

Moreover, village-level community infrastructure that would improve the quality of living in the villages could be constructed. A coordinated approach to rural housing development that brings together building materials industry, housing finance, public policy and civil society organizations is necessary.

The government has set an ambitious target to construct as many as 12 million houses for rural poor during the next five years—nearly double of those built between 2005 and 2009. Under the first phase of the Prime Minister's Bharat Nirman program, 6 million houses were to be constructed from 2005-06 to 2008-09 but the target was surpassed and over 7.1 million dwellings were built. "It has now been proposed to double the target to construct 12 million houses during the next five-year period of phase two of Bharat Nirman starting from the current financial year," Rural Development Minister told reporters (Sept. 09).

Farm Economy—Farm Practices and Management Policies

Farming of land, good seeds, fertilizers and training in latest farming practices and technology is required for optimum results and produce and good quality. It is necessary to create good supply chain of produce and to get the reasonable good price.

Agriculture and extension training without caste and gender differentiation; and use of ICTs for agriculture and sustainable agriculture practices as discussed in earlier chapters needs sound evolving polices with the changeover agriculture scenario, peoples' expectations and farm technology and ICTs development in these contexts.

We do not want the people now involved in farming to migrate to cities and towns where they will work as laborers or other menial workers and create urban slum living conditions. Therefore, farm related as well non-farm related sound rural policies would help in mitigating these problems.

Rural Tourism Policy

Government tourist policies focus on mainly urban tourism though interestingly many of the heritage sites, or religious Ashrams and old temples are close to villages but so far, polices have never focused on villages around these sites. Urban and rural tourism is interdependent. So far, India has focused on developing urban and historic—cultural-religious sites, tourism and government tourist policies focus on developing infrastructure related to these. Now there is new interest in developing rural tourism in its various facets.

A new component of the current tourist polices is being developed focusing exclusively on 'Rural Tourism'. Those who travel to India in 2010 will be offered special packages such as Rural Tourism, Ecotourism, Adventure Tourism and Wellness Tourism. A lot depends on the workability of such campaigns and easing of the global economic situation. But government is consistently focusing on developing rural tourism as it will bring both revenue and employment as well help in developing the village's special areas and their environments. This is likely to encourage people in new ways of looking at things and life when they meet tourists from different regions and who may expose them to new ideas and experiences. Thus, it is necessary and important to develop rural tourism from different angles.

Rural tourism policy development will envisage three approaches: (i) rural tourism focus, (ii) development of physical infrastructure—both rural and urban, and (iii) investments in organizing and developing the tourism focus areas, and tertiary physical infrastructure in the villages as main urban and rural physical infrastructure will be taken care of under other policy heads. In fact, as we will observe, rural tourism policy has to be an integrated policy and will be inter-coordinated with other policies and agencies and their programs. Archeological policies, policies for water, sanitation, environment, healthcare, village enterprises and RBH can all work towards this end.

Rural tourism can be efficiently developed through P4 model—government, private enterprises, NGOs and community, all participating actively. Government will plan policy, regulations, guidelines and consultations for interagency coordination, tourist security, and provide land for tourist spots wherever needed. Tourist security from thefts, murders, and exploitation and damaging and pilfering the tourist facility; both for the community and by the community is of utmost importance.

Interagency coordination such as RBH and culture ministry for artisans spots, culture ministry for folk and cultural festivals and living experiences, religious melas, Ashrams, important temples like Amarnath, Badrinath, Kedarnath, Yamnotri, Gangotri, Budh Gaya, etc. in North; health agencies for nature cure, Yoga, herbal and other medical tourism. Agriculture ministry, institutes and universities can coordinate agro festivals such as Baisakhi, about herbal-medicine plants, and even ways of doing agriculture work in fields, milking cows, making Gur, etc. Village living experience offered can be both contemporary and anthropological. Sports ministry and agencies can associate with adventure tourism and other local sports related attractions for the tourists. Government will also develop and invest in tertiary infrastructure connectivity with the villages. Private enterprises and NGOs selectively develop and invest in tourist focus areas according to their expertise. Government makes it mandatory for them that they must spend certain percentage of revenue on community betterment; though they may be spending some on their own also to create better image of their facility. It will also be mandatory to give employment to the community as well train them for it such as if it is a tourist guide selected from the village, they must train him/her with background factual information about the facility and its importance. These will be licensed guides. If art, craft and artisans spots are organized, then RBH can help in marketing, pricing, packaging and mailing for the tourists. They will orient the village community for cleanliness of the surroundings, hygiene, courtesy, non-exploitation, honesty and integrity and also Panchayat leaders for their leadership roles, so that tourists are attracted and find safe to visit the facility again as well recommend others to visit. It will be good word of mouth advertisement. The orientation programs have to be ongoing.

Community and village Panchayat gets engaged in allowing and planning the focus area in their village and in their life styles; they also get actively involved in running and maintaining these facilities through employment. There is more active community involvement when the focus area is village festivals, village living experience or artisans showcasing their arts and crafts.

It is important that Tourism Ministry through its agencies orient, guide, consult with all P4 stake holders in developing safe and responsible rural tourism. It is important for all P4 stake holders to develop a specific tourist village-hub and make it show case from all angles.

Rural tourism is gaining popularity. India plans to strengthen its rural tourism projects so as to expose the country's unique rural way of life to domestic as well as foreign visitors. Innovative rural tourism projects positions India's rural way of life as a unique visitor experience.

Packaged programs will provide insights to rural art and craft imparted by skilled artisans and artists, together with accommodation created using local material, local style and local skill or in home-stays providing local cuisine. For entertainment purpose, you have the village entertainment groups who disclose history and culture, natural and oral treasures. "Such tourism is the perfect way of integrating the locals with tourism creating a situation where both move forward together."

Craft persons representing four of 36 'responsible tourism' sites Hodka (Gujarat), Banavasi (Karnataka), Nepura (Bihar) and Raghurajpur (Orissa) had been selected to participate in the India@60 event organized under the Incredible India banner at Singapore in the first week of April 09.

According to latest Tourism Satellite Accounting (TSA) research released by the World Travel and Tourism Council, India Travel and Tourism is expected to generate approximately Rs. 4 trillion ($100 billion) in 2008, rising to Rs. 15 trillion ($275.5 billion) by 2018 over the next ten years. The report also says that while travel and tourism is expected to contribute 6.1 per cent to India's national GDP, with no increase in the coming decade, the anticipated growth will create 30.5 million jobs in 2008, 6.4 per cent of total employment, rising to 40 million jobs, 7.2 per cent of total employment by 2018. Plans are to organize rural tourism to share part of this flux in organized way.

Conservationists in the recent years view local peoples' support for protected areas management as an important element of biodiversity conservation. This is often linked to the direct benefits, which local communities get from the protected areas. These benefits could be in the form of biomass resources, park funds diverted to local villages by state agencies and revenue from wildlife tourism. There are a very few studies which have attempted to study the direct relationship between benefits from wildlife tourism and local support for conservation. In India, wildlife tourism is restricted, and mostly controlled by state and private agencies. Wildlife conservation policy does not view tourism in protected areas as a source of revenue for the local communities. Some of these sites are Sariska Tiger Reserve, Jim Corbett Park and Bandipur wildlife sanctuary.

Meanwhile, the tourism ministry is also looking at the possibility of involving state governments and professional organizations such as IL&FS and IDFC to make a concerted plan for beautification of villages near hill stations and also resorting hill stations for recreation and vacations. Most of the hill stations are transforming into concrete jungles due to haphazard construction and commercialization. They have lost the quaint charm.

Overseas offices of the tourism ministry would soon be asked to undertake road shows so that more and more foreign tourists can explore the possibility of visiting India's hillside. The ministry is already investing heavily in promoting rural tourism at hill sites such as Nagar in Himachal Pradesh. The ministry has also launched several promotional offers such as free-air passage to the companion of a foreign tourist to win back foreign visitors.

Responsible Tourism

Responsible Tourism is about developing tourism around preserving ecological balance. It is not synonymous with rural tourism but close to it since most of it is developed around rural open sites; therefore, it becomes imperative that when developing responsible tourism, rural environs are taken care of.

Some examples

Ecotourism: Director of Kerala Tourism points out that for responsible rural tourism, "We have already begun implementing the concept in Kumarakam and Kovalam where stakeholders—village panchayat, self-help groups, traders, property holders, and even tour operators are sensitized about the gist of responsible tourism." Speedboats, which would "mob through" country boats or houseboats in backwaters disturbing their movement and that of the ecosystem, for instance, have been slow ever since this was brought to their notice.

On World Environment Day on June 5, 2008, majority hotels asked their guests to go easy on water, food and electricity as part of the 'Responsible Tourism' as a policy. Although responsible tourism is in its nascent stage, there has been a growing realization among policymakers that until stakeholders are made accountable in the process, tourism would not survive for long.

In Siliguri, West Bengal, 'Help Tourism', a social enterprise by locals, has given a boost to tourism. "We have experimented with responsible tourism across 32 sites of all north-eastern states. In Manas Tiger Reserve, Assam, for instance, we have created an army of 1,000 volunteers (once branded terrorists and poachers) from neighboring villages who check poaching and act as tourist guides." The exercise has brought the local community out of isolation and made them value their culture and their natural resources. 'Help Tourism' shells out 80% of its earnings through tourism to promote responsible tourism in the region. "The hand-holding needs about seven years; by then one generation would have completely understood the concept to pass it on to the next generation."

In remote locales of Himachal Pradesh, the 'Muse Creative Initiatives for Sustainable Development', have made six Himalayan villages embrace responsible tourism. "We realized that not everyone in the village was benefiting from home stay of tourists and unless all of them are made stakeholders of tourism, not everyone could be made accountable for the developments happening in the region," says Muse co-founder.

Adventure Tourism: Some of the land-based adventure sports such as mountaineering and trekking are fast becoming popular in the country; air-based sports, Para-sailing and Paragliding, are also becoming popular.

Adventure tourism cannot take off in the country if companies are not allowed to import adventure equipment freely. There are just too many restrictions, tourism secretary said. The ministry is also looking into the issue of opening more mountain peaks for foreign tourists for trekking. It has asked ATOAI to give a list of peaks which are open for trekking. Following this, it would ask home and defence ministries to open up more peaks. It will also ask home and external affairs ministries to liberalize the process of issuing visas for mountaineering. Mountaineers should also be allowed to enjoy easy visa approval facility like medical tourists, an official said.

Rural Tourism Infrastructure Development

It is necessary to develop rural tourism infrastructure and it is interdependent on urban tourism infrastructure. The primary component is development of roads, ports, airports and urban amenities and the secondary development is of these physical infrastructures connecting to the rural sites through tertiary infrastructure and various means of transport so that destinations are reachable.

Government tourist promotion policies are both centre and state concern. Tourism ministry at centre has taken steps to provide funds, although meager, for rural destination and circuits, and special tourist focus development but the capacity of the state tourism departments to spend the money is woefully inadequate to develop both urban as well rural tourism. There are inadequate institutional capacities of tourism departments in the states in planning and coordination in tourism infrastructure development, partnering with other line departments, and the private sector and local communities. This is also reflected in the negligible effort to attract private investment in infrastructure projects and absence of single window clearances for private sector investment in infrastructure projects. The same concerns will be reflected in development of rural tourism policies.

Rural tourism infrastructure can boost economies as it creates more revenue and employment. Tourism is the fastest growing industry in the world in terms of employment and revenue. On an average, 7 million people travel internationally and 70 million domestically every day. Now India should focus on sharing it with rural tourism; which is still underdeveloped. Rural tourist can be attracted through developed urban tourism; therefore that should also get the major focus. The concept of community-based tourism infrastructure is unknown.

Infrastructure Investment: All tourism program components should be financed and implemented by private investment and management (including FDI). Public infrastructure and infrastructure services that have the potential for commercial viability should be financed and managed through PPPs and all those components not amenable to private investment, such as link infrastructure, should be financed and implemented by the public sector. Tourism master-plans should be developed including all three modes of investment to ensure proper synergies (News July 09).

This would also require putting in place cost recovery strategies. These include user charges and fees such as airport terminal fees, tolls, advertising revenue, lease of land along right-of-way, etc. for municipal water and sanitation infrastructure, and parking and entry fees and concessionaire income in the case of public area tourism infrastructure.

Rural Tourism Constraints for becoming globally competitive tourism destination are: inadequate tourism infrastructure and weak institutional support frameworks. Even though the tourism ministry has taken several key initiatives to improve tourism infrastructure such as increasing the capacity of tourist superstructure facilities, especially hotels and convention facilities, public infrastructure continues to be largely poor. Quality and capacity of air, road, rail and water access and connectivity infrastructure is substandard and services unreliable; urban environmental infrastructure at tourist destinations is poor; tourist infrastructure such as toilets, parking, lighting, directional signage and interpretation at major cultural heritage sites is largely absent, and site conservation practices are non-existent. These constraints are compounded by institutional and regulatory constraints. Tourism as a subject is treated more in terms of promotion and event management while the more difficult part, the development and management of infrastructure remains the responsibility of other agencies.

There is also very little regulation of the tourism infrastructure and services (barring the hotels). Current level of conservation, protection and management of cultural and natural heritage assets is inadequate. Comprehensive tourism laws are non-existent and the regulation of private sector—licensing, insurance, standards, compliance and handling of consumer complaints is asymmetrical and not institutionalized.

Rural Tourism has yet not been recognized for its potential to contribute towards more inclusive development, revenue and employment creation. No focused effort has been made for local community participation and public-private partnerships (PPP).

Very little effort has gone into using PPP model in organizing tourism focus and managing tourism infrastructure. Marketing and promotion support mechanisms also need to be strengthened. Rural tourism marketing in its various facets—priority circuits or as single destinations is essential to make investment in tourism infrastructure and superstructure commercially viable.

Whereas, many of these revenue streams have already been tapped, tourism sector which generates significant portion of these revenues is starved for resources. A focused and well coordinated program for tourism infrastructure development can give significant returns and create sustainable livelihood in the rural areas. However, to achieve this, (a) there is a need to include rural areas in major tourism circuits in the country by restoring the existing and creating new tourist attractions in the villages and semi-urban centers that lie in the circuit route; (b) public financing and private financing of tourism infrastructure should be complimentary.

Rural Entrepreneurship Policies

Rural Entrepreneurship can be both business and social. Business Entrepreneurship can focus on making rural base for developing industries, and secondly create rural markets for their industries situated in hinterland rural areas and thirdly create market hubs for consumer and non-consumer goods and village arts, crafts and cottage industries in the rural areas.

The focus of Social Entrepreneurship is on creating capital flow—the macrofinance to develop industries and markets in the rural areas through facilitating businesses' efforts by providing them baseline of ruralites needs, demands and purchasing power. On the other hand, to create capital flow for the people to have purchasing power through microfinance schemes and through rural banks. Third important role that social entrepreneurs can play is to coordinate corporate social responsibility schemes (CSR) viz. rural consumers.

Rural Entrepreneurship policies are being planned and implemented by corporate, social entrepreneurs, three levels of government—central, state and local levels, and rural consumers. The government policies focus on creating regulations and laws for entrepreneur development, focus areas and modes of rural entrepreneurship, capital flows both domestic and international and creating right ambiance for both kind of entrepreneurs. They abide by these for their development, and demand and dialogue with government for further facilitations in these contexts which help in improving or further development of rural entrepreneurship policies.

Social Security Rural Policies

Government since 2000 has made concerted efforts to provide social security to ruralites through insurance policies in rural areas to provide life cover—health and farm-related. In 2007-08, Insurance sold over 5 crore insurance policies of which over 1.1 crore policies were sold in rural areas. Not the so-called rural areas which are industrial hubs, but the real rural areas—the interiors and in the backward areas. These are life insurance and varied farm related insurance. It is done through both LIC and Postal Insurance Policies—both organizations run by government. Some of the salient schemes are listed:

Rural Group Life Insurance Scheme of LIC to provide social security cover to rural families since 1995; any person insured under this scheme would be eligible for a life cover of Rs. 5000/-. There are two types of policies available under this scheme. General scheme is available to all people in rural areas. The premium for this policy is fully payable by the applicant.

Subsidized Scheme is applicable only to households below poverty line and is restricted to only one policy per household. Premium is subsidized by 50% to be shared equally by state and central government. Scheme is implemented through Gram Panchayats and Taluk Panchayats.

Aam Admi Bima Yojana (AABY): Under this scheme, launched on October 2, 2007, insurance to the head of the family of rural landless households in the country will be provided against natural death as well as accidental death and partial or permanent disability. Up to December 31, 2008, the scheme has covered 60.32 lakh lives. *Aam Aadmi Bima Yojana* is for the welfare of rural landless families, where one earning member is aged between 18 and 59 years. The scheme will be administered by the Life Insurance Corporation of India. The scheme is a social security plan, which would cover the head of the family or one earning member in the rural family. The scheme provides an insurance cover of Rs. 30,000 to the members and in case of death or permanent total disability due to accident, it will provide a cover of Rs. 75,000. The scheme also offers a cover of Rs. 37,500 for partial permanent disability due to accident. A special feature of this scheme is that it provides scholarship of Rs. 100 per month, payable half-yearly on July 1 and January 1 each year, to a maximum of two children studying between classes ninth and twelfth. The premium paid under the scheme would be Rs. 200, of which 50 per cent will be subsidized by the Centre and remaining 50 per cent would be contributed by the Administration (News June 09).

Rashtriya Swasthya Bima Yojana (details given in Appendix 3.)

Raj Rajeshwari Mahila Kalyan Bima Yojana: This new scheme is being introduced to cover all cross-sections of women in the age group of 10 to 75 years irrespective of their income, occupation or vocation. The scheme would benefit housewives, students, domestic labor, skilled or unskilled labor and other women engaged themselves in similar or other types of activities in rural, semi-urban areas. Since this is a low cost insurance cover, it is hoped that the State Governments would come forward and extend all support for its implementation.

Bhagyashree Child Welfare Policy is a novel scheme for girls and provides insurance cover to one orphaned girl child in a family who loses either the father or the mother due to accident. The scheme provides for an orphaned girl child below 6.

Kisan Package Policy provides for 15 items from farm to durables like TV. This provides indemnity to damages to personal accidents, against fire and allied perils for items as the stock of farm produce, Pedal cycle/Cycle rickshaw, insurance of artisans in village/cottage industry, and tiny sectors including biogas. Kisan Agricultural Pumpset, animal driven carts, Medical hospitalization expenses excluding domiciliary hospitalization. Insurance for Agricultural Tractor, Plantation, Horticulture, Aquaculture (Shrimps and Prawns), Bio-Gas Plant (Gobar Gas), and Khalihan Insurance package policy which provides cover to unprocessed grains kept in Khalihan awaiting processing, animal driven cart without animals and thrasher operator.

Kisan Credit Card—PAIS is a Personal Accident Insurance Master Policy covering all the Kisan Credit Card holders. This will include the holders of KCC issued by the District Central Coop. Banks, RRBs and commercial banks throughout India. This scheme will cover all the KCC holders against Death or Permanent disability resulting from accidents caused by external, violent and visible means and occurring within the geographical jurisdiction of India.

National Agriculture Insurance Scheme (NAIS) is central sector farm-related Insurance scheme since 2000 (i) to provide insurance coverage and financial support to the farmers in the event of failure of any of the notified crop as a result of natural calamities, pests and diseases, (ii) to encourage the farmers to adopt progressive farming practices, high value in-puts and higher technology in agriculture, (iii) to help stabilize farm incomes, particularly in disaster years.

This scheme is available to all farmers—loanee and non-loanee both irrespective of the size of their holdings. It is compulsory for loanee farmers and optional for non-loanee farmers. Sum insured may extend to the value of threshold yield of the area insured; coverage of all food crops (cereals, millets and pulses), oilseeds and annual commercial and horticultural crops in respect of which past yield data is available for adequate number of years since 2000. (Source Oriental insurance.nic.in/rural insurance).

Rural Postal Life Insurance (RPLI) Endowment Scheme under the brand name of Gram Santosh (2009) by India Postal Services. In a move to make post office financial schemes more attractive, India Post has enhanced bonus for the endowment program of its rural PLI schemes from Rs. 50 to Rs. 55 for every Rs. 1,000 of sum assured, if the policy term exceeds 10 years. The applicable bonus would be Rs. 52 per thousand if the policy term is less than 10 years. This enhancement of bonus makes RPLI more attractive option as compared to traditional insurers who cover the life risk of individuals under endowment assurance scheme. The premium of RPLI is collected through counters of post offices, thus keeping the operational cost low as compared to other insurance companies. "Rural PLI passes on the benefits of low cost of operation to the customers in the form of higher bonus rates and lower premium rates," an official in the department of posts (DoP) said, "customers of the scheme can get a benefit of upto Rs. 1,000 per year over the existing benefits as the maximum limit under the scheme is Rs. 2 lakh. A new rural postal life insurance scheme from Feb. 2009 is being offered. The new policy will be of Rs. 100,000 of sum assured in which a person has to contribute only Rs. 1.25 per month or Rs. 15 per year as premium."

The Unorganized Workers' Social Security Act 2008 and 2009. The salient features of the Act are: Section 2 provides for the definitions, including those relating to unorganized worker, self-employed and wage worker provides for formulation of schemes by the Central Government for different sections of unorganized workers on matters relating to (a) life and disability cover; (b) health and maternity benefits; (c) old age protection; and (d) any other benefit as may be determined by the Central Government. Section 3(4) provide formulation of schemes relating to provident fund, employment injury benefits, housing, educational schemes for children, skill upgradation, funeral assistance and old-age homes by the State Government.

Welfare of Workers in the Unorganized Sector: The unorganized or informal sector of our economy accounts for 92% of the employment and absorbs bulk of the annual increase in our labor force. The Unorganized Workers Social Security Bill, 2007 ensures social security schemes for occupations like weavers, fishermen and women, toddy tappers, leather and handicraft workers, plantation labor, construction labor, mine workers, bidi workers, and rikshaw pullers. Action has already initiated and will be implemented at the earliest. Necessary financial allocations will be made for these schemes (July 09).

Community-based Health Insurance scheme in rural India can potentially protect people from healthcare costs and ensure equitable pooling of risk between rich and poor, and sick and healthy. One such effort is by SEWA—a self help group. There is also *Swasthya Bima Policy for members of SHGs and Credit Linked Groups, Universal Health Insurance Scheme for BPL Families.* Oriental Insurance Company has been nominated by Govt. of India to provide Universal Health Insurance Scheme to the people who are below poverty line in the States of Delhi, Haryana, Himachal Pradesh, J&K, Punjab, Rajasthan, U.P., Uttarakhand and Chandigarh (UT). This policy provides medical reimbursement of hospitalization expenses upto Rs. 30,000/- to an individual or family with sub-limits (Maximum per illness Rs. 15,000).

PREM—an NGO initiated in 2002, an innovative health insurance targeting the poor tribal population spread over two districts. It is a comprehensive program which covers preventive and promotive healthcare along with curative treatment while insuring. This in-house scheme is one of the few using public health facilities to deliver health care service covered under the insurance plan. With support of PLAN-International, the scheme also innovated in setting up some 500 Village Medicine Depots run by trained volunteers aiming at ensuring doorsteps availability of essential medicines at affordable prices. This unique experience in India is seen as a major factor explaining the scheme's success in enrolling the local population with high renewal rates observed over the years. According to a study recently released by WHO, medicine costs amount to some 45% of the entire health care expenditures borne by poor households in India. The availability of essential medicines through a network of village depots may thus be seen as an essential component of any community-based health insurance scheme to be promoted among the poor.

Bank also introduced deposit schemes viz. Village Balika Savings Bank Account and Village Balika Term Savings Account for a minimum of 100 new farmers per rural and semi-urban branch.

Apart from the primary risk policies like Credit Risk, Market Risk policies, government in 2009 has initiated Integrated Risk Management policies.

Integrating Rural Economy with National Economy through Rural Centric Policies: The country has by and large developed a consensus around accelerated inclusion of the rural economy in the wider growth process. We expect added thrust on two critical components of the rural economy: strengthening of irrigation infrastructure and a larger role for the private sector to improve agricultural productivity and rural income. The government needs to attract more private companies towards agricultural R&D through appropriate tax and financial incentives.

In the service sector, facilities and subsidies given to telecom sector (as discussed in chapter 6) would help operators penetrate further into the rural hinterland and enable telecom to play a key role in the integration of the rural to the national economy.

On the whole, Corporate India supporting government resources would not only drive economic growth in rural areas but ushers in the key instruments for equitable growth.

Rural-Urban Integrated Policies

To bridge the rural-urban divide and ensure the 'aam aadmi' is at the center of the development process and its programs and schemes, budgetary allocation for all rural-focused schemes have increased by 45-144% in budget 2009-2010. Government has set aside a reasonable amount of resources for schemes that would ensure inclusive growth in India. In the current budget it allocates higher resources for those schemes to ensure inclusive growth. All rural spending schemes will have direct impact on urban growth. Thus, the focus of these polices is Rural-urban integration.

This suggests a major rise in government spending for schemes such as NREGS, Bharat Nirman, Rajiv Gandhi Grameen Vidyutikaran Yojana and Indira Awaas Yojana. All this is to further stimulate demand in rural India, which has also been responsible for the perking up of many industrial sectors.

NREGS has got top priority with its allocation increasing to Rs. 39,100 crore which marks an increase of 144% over 2008-09 Budget Estimates. Finance minister said that to increase productivity of assets and resources under NREGS, convergence with other schemes is being initiated. In the first stage, a total of 115 pilot districts have been selected for such convergence with other schemes relating to agriculture, forests, water resources, land resources and rural roads. There is a clear emphasis on infrastructure building. Higher income in the hands of the rural population through NREGS, etc., should help industry indirectly.

The budget has also proposed to boost low-cost housing and speed up the spread of rural housing by raising the allocation for Indira Awas Yojana by 63% to Rs. 8,800 crore; a Rs. 2,000 crore rural housing fund has also been created in the National Housing Bank (NHB). A direct beneficiary of these measures would be infrastructure companies in steel and cement sectors.

"If the government opts for a public-private partnership (PPP) model for the rural housing as well as for providing 1 lakh houses to paramilitary personnel, this could give a boost to the realty players," said DLF group executive director. Finance minister also announced the launch of a new scheme—*Pradhan Mantri Adarsh Gram Yojana*—for integrated development of villages where the population of Scheduled Caste is above 50%. Allocations for Bharat Nirman and RGGVY have also been increased substantially to address other infrastructural needs of rural India. Moreover, the Swarna Jayanti Gram Swarozgar Yojana has been restructured as the *National Rural Livelihood Mission* to make it universal in application, and achieve a time-bound poverty eradication target by 2014-15.

Two flagship schemes—*National Rural Health Mission* (NRHM) and *Rajiv Gandhi Drinking Water Mission*—have also been provided higher plan allocations, and work on the *National Food Security Act* (NFSA) has begun, which will directly benefit families living below poverty line in both rural and urban areas. The scheme will ensure that every family living below the poverty line in rural or urban areas will be entitled by law to 25 kilos of rice or wheat per month at Rs. 3 a kilo.

Bharat Nirman with its six schemes is an important initiative for bridging the gap between the rural and urban areas and improving the quality of life of people, particularly the poor, in the rural areas. The allocation for this scheme has been stepped by 45 per cent in 2009-10 over the budget estimate of 2008-09. The Pradhan Mantri Gram Sadak Yojana (PMGSY) is one of the most successful programs under Bharat Nirman. The allocation for this program is stepped by 59% over to Rs. 12,000 crore. The allocation for the Rajiv Gandhi Grameen Viduytikaran Yojana (RGGVY) has been increased to Rs. 7000 crore which represents a 27 per cent increase over 2008-09 budget estimates.

The allocation for the Indira Awaas Yojana (IAY) is proposed to be increased by 63 per cent to Rs. 8,800 crore in Budget Estimates 2009-10. To broaden the pace of rural housing, the budget has allocated, from the shortfall in the priority sector lending of commercial banks, a sum of Rs. 2,000 crore for Rural Housing Fund in the National Housing Bank (NHB). This will boost the resource base of NHB for their refinance operations in rural housing sector.

Pradhan Mantri Adarsh Gram Yojana (PMAGY). There are about 44,000 villages in which the population of Scheduled castes is above 50 per cent. A new scheme called Pradhan Mantri Adarsh Gram Yojana (PMAGY) is being launched this year on a pilot basis, for the integrated development of 1000 such villages. The budget has allocated Rs. 100 crore for this scheme. Each village would be able to avail gap funding of Rs. 10 lakh over and above the allocations under Rural Development and Poverty Alleviation Schemes. On successful implementation of the pilot phase, the Yojana would be extended in coming years.

Empowerment of Weaker Sections: The Swarna Jayanti Gram Swarozgar Yojna (SGSY) is being restructured as the National Rural Livelihood Mission to make it universal in application, focused in approach and time bound for poverty eradication by 2014-15. Emphasis will be laid on the formation of women Self Help Groups (SHGs). Apart from providing capital subsidy at an enhanced rate, it is also proposed to provide interest subsidy to poor households for loans up to Rs. one lakh from banks. The Women's Self Help Group movement is bringing about a profound transformation in rural areas. There are today over 22 lakh such groups linked with banks. Our objective is to enroll at least 50% of all rural women in India as members of SHGs over the next five years and link these SHGs to banks.

The *Rashtriya Mahila Kosh* has been working towards the facilitation of credit support or microfinance to poor women and has developed a number of innovative schemes for their benefit. In recognition of its role as an instrument of socio-economic change and development, the corpus of the Kosh, which at present is Rs. 100 crore, would be raised to Rs. 500 crore, over the next few years.

Female literacy: The low level of female literacy continues to be a matter of grave concern. It has, therefore, been decided to launch a National Mission for Female Literacy, with focus on minorities, SC, ST and other marginalized groups. The aim will be to reduce by half, the current level of female illiteracy, in three years.

Integrated Child Development Services: Government is committed to universalization of the Integrated Child Development Services (ICDS) Scheme in the country. By March 2012, all services under ICDS would be extended, with quality, to every child under the age of six.

Student Loans to Weaker Sections: To enable students from economically weaker sections to access higher education, it is proposed to introduce a scheme to provide them full interest subsidy during the period of moratorium. It will cover loans taken by such students from scheduled banks to pursue any of the approved courses of study, in technical and professional streams, from recognized institutions in India. It is estimated that over 5 lakh students would avail of this benefit.

Welfare of Minorities: The Plan outlay of Ministry of Minority Affairs has been enhanced from Rs. 1,000 crore in budget estimate 2008-09 to Rs. 1,740 crore in 2009-10, registering an increase of 74%. This includes Rs. 990 crore for Multi-Sectoral Development Program for minorities in selected minority concentration districts, grants-in-aid, and scholarships for minorities.

Peri-Urban Policies: Purushottaman & Shukla (08) advocate that investment in rural-urban integrated policies is crucial for development. Execution of infrastructure investment and manufacturing incentives in urban and peri-urban areas (rural-urban fringe areas) could strengthen rural-urban linkages. If urban development is not placed squarely alongside rural priorities, we risk policy errors that will impact severely the country's development.

Peri-urban areas typically grow faster than traditional cities and many face a rapid transition away from agriculture. It is time to move beyond the basic rural and urban split and allow for a transitional category. Addressing peri-urban centers, with many clustered around manufacturing activity, is pivotal now.

Incentivizing the manufacturing industry across these fringe areas in particular and the peri-urban and rural non-farm sector in general, will further provide a long-term outlet for the country's semi-skilled employment crisis.

Urban demand could be one important, and largely overlooked, engine helping to drive the shift from farm to non-farm employment in rural India. It is well known that urban growth is a key driver for food production, but even more generally we see signs that urban consumption appears to translate into a boost for rural non-farm employment and household incomes. We need to expand innovative linkages running both ways between urban and rural growth.

We are in a position to prepare for oncoming demographic change. Urbanization is low, only roughly 30% of the population is urban. Our best guess is that 45% of India's population will be urban by 2050. Even on these numbers, 379 million people will be added to urban spaces over the next 40 years.

Is rural-urban migration causing cities to swell? Contrary to most of the images we see, natural increase (the excess of births over deaths) is the major factor in India's urban growth —not rural migrants rushing to the cities. In India, 60% of growth in urbanization is due to natural increase, 18% is due to reclassification, and only 22% is due to migration. In fact, roughly 60-70% of migration in India is composed of rural to rural movements.

Mumbai has the highest number of migrants by far, followed by Delhi, Kolkata, Pune and Surat. As a share of total population, Surat has the highest composition of migrants, with 31.1% of total population made up of migrants who have moved within the past ten years. This is followed by Chandigarh, Pune and Faridabad.

Rural-urban flows are typically lower in the southern cities. Chennai's share of rural migrants is just 35.4%. Just over half (52.8%) of all migration takes place within state. Southern cities (with the exception of Bangalore) have a much higher share of in-state migration that is 91.7%.

In contrast, about half of migration in Mumbai and Surat is within state. One in every two out-of-state migrants is from UP or Bihar. 38.3% of migrants from UP and 40.8% of migrants from Bihar move to Delhi. Another large share of UP migrants goes to Mumbai (34.8%), while migrants from Bihar are split between Kolkata and Mumbai. Migrants from Bihar make up 57.6% of Kolkata's out-of-state migrants. South-South linkages are high, with many out-of-state migrants from southern states moving to neighboring southern cities.

Despite our present low levels of urbanization, there seems to be a desire to 'slow it down', with the assumption that rural-urban migration is causing cities to swell. Strangely, while the scale of urbanization tends to be exaggerated, the practical function of urban centers is virtually ignored. Total urban spending in India as a share of GDP has remained stagnant for the past 15 years. Against comparable countries, India's spending on cities reflects its grim fiscal position with severely constrained administrative capacity at the local level. Part of the larger problem is the lack of integrated rural-urban policy which has to do clearly with perceptions of need. Absolute poverty measures (standards like below $1 a day, $2 a day, etc.) make it hard to ignore the difference in urban-rural poverty rates. Using standard poverty thresholds, rural poverty soars relative to urban poverty.

Investment in rural India is crucial, and we have to view urban India as part of the solution. Execution of infrastructure investment and manufacturing incentives in urban and peri-urban areas could strengthen rural-urban linkages. Also, given that the entire shortfall from priority sector lending is not being channeled into agriculture and RIDF (Rural Infrastructure Development Fund), RIDF money could further be considered for low-cost housing and infrastructure development in small towns and cities.

Monitoring Rural Policies & Programs

As we stated earlier, monitoring periodic appraisals of rural programs and policies and economic surveys help in effectiveness of policies and programs and effective expenditures. In this context, rural policy research, Eleventh Five-Year Plan Mid-term appraisal on blueprint of what needs consolidation and change over; and yearly economic surveys help to assess which programs are useful, needs more fund allocation and in what mode; to be extended to which areas and people and in what mode or to be dropped from current programs.

Rural policy research programs should be set up to assess the rural economy needs and demands, factors accelerating or decelerating, i.e. driving forces for its economic growth, and adapt to rapidly changing economic circumstances. Agricultural universities such as at Delhi and Pantnagar, MNC DuPont efforts at BT cotton and generic seeds, Reliance for better breed of Jatropa for producing fuel, sugar companies research in sugarcane for producing ethanol, rice research institute, Swaminathan agriculture research institute, and Pepsi's better variety of potatoes and oranges based on research are contributing to such efforts.

The key players who are associated with India's economic growth—those in governments at the Centre and in States, in the political establishment, business community, economists and other professionals, mass media, and others should evolve a common approach towards how to achieve accelerated growth with the primary objective of poverty eradication, productive employment generation, equitable development of all sections of rural society. *They can do better through rural policy research efforts.* India needs effective rural policies, and able policymakers and good administrators depending on periodic rural policy researches.

Eleventh Five Year Plan: Mid-term appraisal on blueprint of what needs consolidation: There are two separate issues; one is convergence of the different schemes so that schemes that roughly seems to be in the same area; resources that go into these different schemes can be devoted in a re-consolidated way to achieve a developmental plan objective.

The most commonly thought about is the NREGA. The present guidelines say that one of the priority areas for the NREGA should be related to water; water conservation, water management. There are other programs in the field which deals with water conservation and management. At the moment, the two are not dovetailed together, so if there is some way through appropriate district planning where the projects can be taken as a holistic group, some parts of it gets funded under one program, some part of it gets funded under the NREGA. There would be a way of bringing these two resources together. There is also a lot of overlap. There are many small programs that have historically evolved which actually suggest their merger into a single programme.

As part of the mid-term appraisal, we should look at whether the external environment which we now face is a temporary event; whether it implies a significantly different external environment for the rest of the Plan period and if so, what modifications if any are needed in the Plan that is very much what the mid-term review of the Plan should produce and that should be fed into the next Budget 2010-2011.

Government is giving a big focus on to rural areas and the Eleventh Plan which began two years ago, really did emphasize that focus. So, to a large extent, it amounts to strengthening the effectiveness of these schemes and trying to see whether in the light of experience gained, we should modify their guidelines in some way.

It's normal in the course of plan period, that during the plan, some new schemes may come up. The existing plan includes a very substantial focus on the prosperity in rural areas both farm and non-farm and building of infrastructure in rural areas. 'Bharat Nirman', the first phase is more or less complete and now we need the second phase and we are quite encouraged by the success that has been achieved and would therefore assume that in the second phase of the 'Bharat Nirman', we may set ourselves some ambitious targets (Monetek Singh 2009).

Eleventh Five-Year Plan (2007-2012) planned policies. India's Eleventh Five-Year Plan approved, thrust on agriculture, education and infrastructure all areas that remain a concern in a rapidly growing economy. 'Towards Faster and More Inclusive Growth' is the central theme of the plan that seeks to lower poverty by 10%, generate 70 million new jobs, and reduce unemployment to less than 5%. It promises to accelerate economic growth and make it more inclusive. As many as 27 detailed national targets have been set in the plan, ranging from enhancing incomes and reducing poverty, to education, literacy, health, infant mortality, maternal mortality and child development.

It is focusing on healthcare systems and policies at national, state and local levels; sanitation policies—system and development schemes; water and its management policies and schemes: potable water procurement; irrigation policies—system and development schemes; energy policies viz. rural energy development schemes; education policies—system facilities, and development schemes; employment policies—system, employability generation development schemes; and occupational and vocational training policies—system and development schemes both at urban and rural levels.

There is greater focus on rural development programs encompassing these policies.

Economic Survey 2009

Economic survey focus on assessing the effectiveness of ongoing economic development programs, gaps and shortfalls, more funds and other resources needed and modalities of such efforts, both in rural and urban development in multiple sectors. These yearly surveys done by government, industry and non-government groups in collaboration provide effective and constructive feedback for policies and programs.

"The development of rural India is imperative for inclusive and equitable growth and to unlock the potential of the population. It would be an effective exercise also to generate demand when conditions elsewhere in the country remain sluggish, said an official with the Planning Commission. Bharat Nirman is the main focus of rural growth in Eleventh Plan."

The survey suggests the need for increased allocation for other flagship programs such as the Integrated Child Development Services, National Rural Health Mission, Rajiv Gandhi Drinking Water Mission and Total sanitation campaign, NREGS and Bharat Nirman, aim at improving rural infrastructure and providing investment opportunities to both the private and public sectors, is expected to appeal to the 'aam aadmi' (common folks). These programs are also important to the government's efforts to bring rural India to the forefront of the initiatives to counter the economic slowdown. Economic survey also suggested convergence as well upgradation of certain rural programs and schemes for integrated rural development and quality of life for people.

Economic Survey 2010/Budget 2010-11 Allocations

The first challenge before us is to quickly revert to the high GDP growth path of 9 per cent and then find the means to cross the 'double digit growth barrier'.

Growth is only as important as what it enables us to do and be. Therefore, the second challenge is to harness economic growth to consolidate the recent gains in making development more inclusive. The thrust imparted to the development of infrastructure in rural areas has to be pursued to achieve the desired objectives within a fixed time frame. We have to strengthen food security, improve education opportunities and provide health facilities at the level of households, both in rural and urban areas. These are issues that require significant resources, and we have to find those resources.

The third challenge relates to the weaknesses in government systems, structures and institutions at different levels of governance. Indeed, in the coming years, if there is one factor that can hold us back in realizing our potential as a modern nation, it is the bottleneck of our public delivery mechanisms. There have been many initiatives in this regard, in different sectors, at different points of time. Some of them have been effective in reforming the way the Government works in those areas. But we have a long way to go before we can rest on this count.

With development and economic reforms, the focus of economic activity has shifted towards the non-governmental actors, bringing into sharper focus the role of Government as an enabler. An enabling Government does not try to deliver directly to the citizens everything that they need. Instead it creates an enabling ethos so that individual enterprise and creativity can flourish. Government concentrates on supporting and delivering services to the disadvantaged sections of the society.

(Finance Minister Speech Union Budget 2010-11 on February 26, 2010)

Economic survey 2010 and budget allocations 2010-11 highlight further financial, administrative and technological impetus given to rural development through upgrading the existing schemes and programs and setting up new programs for further facilitation. Rs. 66,100 crore for Rural Development is allocated.

Health: The Economic Survey presented in the parliament observed, "India needs over 6,800 more hospitals in rural areas to provide basic health facilities to people, there is still a shortage of 4,477 primary healthcare centers and 2,337 community healthcare centers as per the 2001 population norms. This means the requirement for hospitals will be much more if the population figure in 2010 is taken into account. The survey also said that through the NRHM mission, the government aimed at improving the health infrastructure vis-à-vis population, but the ratio of population to health centers remain low with the targeted number of new health centers not being established. There are several glitches in the flagship NRHM mission, it is trying to address all these problems that need to be ironed out soon to improve health infrastructure. Almost 29 per cent of the existing health infrastructure is in rented buildings. Poor upkeep and maintenance, and high absenteeism of manpower in the rural areas are the main problems in the health delivery system."

It is proposed by government that an Annual Health Survey to prepare the District Health Profile of all Districts shall be conducted in 2010-11. The findings of the Survey should be of immense benefit to major public health initiatives particularly the National Rural Health Mission, which has successfully addressed the gaps in the delivery of critical health services in rural areas.

Mahatma Gandhi National Rural Employment Guarantee Scheme has completed four years of implementation during which it has been extended to all districts covering more than 4.5 crore households. The allocation for NREGA has been stepped up to Rs. 40,100 crore in 2010-11. Bharat Nirman has made a substantial contribution to the upgradation of rural infrastructure through its various programs. For the year 2010-2011, an amount of Rs. 48,000 crore is allocated for these programs.

Skill development: Prime Minister's Council on National Skill Development has laid down the core governing principles for operating strategies for skill development. The Council has a mission of creating 50 crore skilled people by 2022. Of these, the target for the National Skill Development Corporation, which has started functioning from October, 2009, is 15 crore. It has completed a comprehensive skill gap study of 21 high growth sectors and approved three projects worth about Rs. 45 crore to create 10 lakh skilled manpower at the rate of one lakh per annum. Other projects are in advance stages of consideration.

Women Welfare: The plan outlay for Women and Child Development by almost 50 per cent. Several new initiatives that were launched in 2009-10 are now ready for implementation. A mission for empowerment of women is being set up. The ICDS platform is being expanded for effective implementation of the Rajiv Gandhi Scheme for Adolescent Girls. To further improve female literacy rate, the Government has recast the earlier National Literacy Mission as a new program "Saakshar Bharat". It was launched in September, 2009 with a target of 7 crore non-literate adults which includes 6 crore women. A Mahila Kisan Sashaktikaran

Pariyojana to meet the specific needs of women farmers is being launched. Rs.100 crore is provided for this initiative as a sub-component of the National Rural Livelihood Mission.

Housing : Under phase-I of the rural housing component of Bharat Nirman, 60 lakh houses were envisaged through the Indira Awaas Yojana all over the country during the four years from 2005-06 to 2008-09. Against this target, 71.76 lakh houses were constructed with an expenditure of Rs. 21,720.39 crore (Rs. 217.2 billion), it was now "proposed to double this target and to construct 120 lakh houses during the next five-year period starting from the current year 2009-10", the survey said. Cost under this scheme per unit is raised to Rs. 45,000 in the plain areas and to Rs. 48,500 in the hilly areas because of the increase in the cost of construction. For the year 2010-11, the allocation for this scheme is being increased to Rs. 10,000 crore.

Rural water: "Under Bharat Nirman for rural water supply, in 2009-10, a budgetary provision of Rs. 8,000 crore has been made out of which Rs. 5,669.88 crore has been utilized." The survey observed, India's rural drinking water policy is a classic case of policy gone wrong because it focused too much on infrastructure creation and too little on outcomes from infrastructure. Consequently, significant sums of money have been pumped into asset creation. India's experience with delivering safe drinking water in rural areas is a mix of good and bad. The good news is that the infrastructure is in place. Estimates from 2008-09 government data indicate that 93% of rural habitations have access to drinking water facilities. The bad news is that access has not translated into supply of safe water. According to the World Bank's Water and Sanitation Program projections, less than 40% of rural India is likely to be drinking safe water in the next 10 years.

Rural Roads: It further said that up to December 2009, a total length of about 250,554 km of roads has been completed under the Prime Minister's Grameen Sadak Yojana (PMGSY) at a cumulative expenditure of Rs. 59,800 crore.

Fertilizers: A Nutrient Based Subsidy policy for the fertilizer sector has since been approved by the Government and will become effective from April 1, 2010. This policy is expected to promote balanced fertilization through new fortified products and focus on extension services by the fertilizer industry. This will lead to an increase in agricultural productivity and consequently better returns for the farmers. Over time, the policy is expected to reduce volatility in the demand for fertilizer subsidy in addition to containing the subsidy bill. Government will ensure that nutrient based fertilizer prices for transition year 2010-11, will remain around MRPs currently prevailing. The new system will move towards direct transfer of subsidies to the farmers.

Economic survey has observed the problems of *Food inflation*: Larger issue is high growth and rising incomes (NREGA) leading to more demand for food items while supplies languish. More recently, supply shortages on account of drought/floods, continuous increase in MSPs, delayed response with regard to imports, poor PDS management and speculation have aggravated inflation. Rabi output and recent administrative measures of government will help in cooling prices. Government will enact the National Food Security Act to provide 25 kg of rice or wheat at Rs. three a kg per month to families below the poverty line. This legislation will also be used to bring about broader systemic reforms in the public distribution system.

Banking: Regional Rural Banks (RRBs) play an important role in providing credit to rural economy. The capital of these banks is shared by the Central Government, sponsor banks and State Governments. The banks were last capitalized in 2006-07. It is proposed to provide further Recapitalization to strengthen the RRBs so that they have adequate capital base to support increased lending to the rural economy.

Financial Inclusion Fund (FIF) and the Financial Inclusion Technology Fund: In 2007-08 the Government had set up a Financial Inclusion Fund and a Financial Inclusion Technology Fund in NABARD, to reach banking services to the unbanked areas. To give momentum to the pace of financial inclusion, an augmentation of Rs. 100 crore for each of these funds is proposed, which shall be contributed by Government of India, RBI and NABARD.

To provide appropriate Banking facilities to habitations having population in excess of 2000 by March, 2012; it is also proposed to extend insurance and other services to the targeted beneficiaries. These services will be provided using the Business Correspondent and other models with appropriate technology back up. By this arrangement, it is proposed to cover 60,000 habitations.

Micro Finance: The program for linking Self Help Groups (SHGs) with the banking system has emerged as the major micro-finance initiative in the country. It was re-designated as the 'Micro-Finance Development and Equity Fund' in 2005-06 with a corpus of Rs. 200 crore. The fund corpus is being doubled to Rs. 400 crore in 2010-11.

As a part of the strategy to bridge the infrastructure gap in backward districts of the country, the Backward Region Grant Fund has proved to be an effective instrument. Allocation to this fund is enhanced by 26 per cent from Rs. 5,800 crore in 2009-10 to Rs. 7,300 crore in 2010-11.

A loan agreement for US $150 million has been signed between the Government of India and the Asian Development Bank on 22nd December, 2009 for implementing the comprehensive Khadi Reforms Program. This program will cover 300 selected Khadi institutions.

National Social Security Fund for unorganized sector workers: As a follow up to the unorganized Sector Workers Social Security Act, 2008, it has been decided to set up a National Social Security Fund for unorganized sector workers with an initial allocation of Rs. 1,000 crore. This fund will support schemes for weavers, toddy tappers, rickshaw pullers, bidi workers etc.

The Government had launched Rashtriya Swasthya Bima Yojana on October 1, 2007 to provide health insurance cover to below poverty line workers and their families. It became operational on April 1, 2008 and so far more than 1 crore smart cards have been issued under this scheme. In view of the success of the scheme, it is now proposed to extend its benefits to all such Mahatma Gandhi NREGA beneficiaries who have worked for more than 15 days during the preceding financial year. Budget has allowed 100% foreign equity to be allowed in insurance firms of rural areas.

To encourage the people from the unorganized sector to voluntarily save for their retirement and to lower the cost of operations of the New Pension Scheme (NPS) for such subscribers, Government will contribute Rs. 1,000 per year to each NPS account opened in the year 2010-11. This initiative, "Swavalamban" will be available for persons who join NPS, with a minimum contribution of Rs. 1, 000 and a maximum contribution of Rs. 12,000 per annum during the financial year 2010-11. The scheme will be available for another three years. Accordingly, an allocation of Rs. 100 crore for the year 2010-11 is made. It will benefit about 10 lakh NPS subscribers of the unorganized sector. The scheme will be managed by the interim Pension Fund Regulatory and Development Authority.

Agriculture: The section on Agriculture and Food Management of the 2010 Economic survey concludes with the following statement: "We need to address the challenges of the agriculture sector through comprehensive and coordinated efforts. Renewed attention needs to be paid to improving farm production and productivity, better utilization of agricultural inputs, proper marketing infrastructure and support, stepping up of investment with the emphasis on environmental concerns and efficient food management." The anxiety on the food front arises from the steep fall in agricultural GDP (–0.2 per cent) during 2009-10, reduced water availability in 81 major reservoirs, fall in agriculture's contribution to GDP (15.7 per cent), inadequate growth in on-farm employment resulting in 52 per cent of the workforce still dependant on agriculture for their daily bread and the prevailing food inflation. The production of pulses and oilseeds, which are the important crops of rainfed areas, is stagnating. Allocation for agriculture in state budgets has been only 5.84 per cent during 2008-09, in spite of the fact that this sector is the backbone of the rural livelihood security system. Growth in irrigated area is slow and groundwater is being over-exploited. Large numbers of farmers (over 40%) want to quit farming, if there is another option. The redeeming feature of the agricultural scenario is the availability of nearly 47.5 metric tons of rice and wheat with government in January, 2010.

It is in the above context that the approach adopted and allocations made in the Union Budget for 2010-11 assume importance. Finance Ministry, for the first time in recent years, has laid out a road map for agricultural recovery and progress based on integrated attention to the conservation of the ecological foundations essential for sustainable agriculture, cultivation based on the principles of conservation and climate-resilient farming, consumption with attention to food safety and quality, and farmer-centric commerce. The Finance Minister has also mentioned that a draft food security bill be placed in the public domain soon.

Agriculture Growth: The agriculture sector occupies centre-stage in government resolve to promote inclusive growth, enhance rural incomes and sustain food security. To spur the growth in this sector, the Government intends to follow a four-pronged strategy covering (a) agricultural production; (b) reduction in wastage of produce; (c) credit support to farmers; and (d) a thrust to the food processing sector.

The first element of the strategy is to extend the green revolution to the eastern region of the country comprising Bihar, Chattisgarh, Jharkhand, Eastern U.P., West Bengal and Orissa, with the active involvement of Gram Sabhas and the farming families. For the year 2010-11, it is proposed to provide Rs. 400 crore for this initiative.

In the 60th year of the Republic, it is proposed to organize 60,000 "pulses and oil seed villages" in rain-fed areas during 2010-11 and provide an integrated intervention for water harvesting, watershed management and soil health, to enhance the productivity of the dry land farming areas. Rs. 300 crore is proposed for this purpose. This initiative will be an integral part of the Rashtriya Krishi Vikas Yojana.

The gains already made in the green revolution areas have to be sustained through conservation farming, which involves concurrent attention to soil health, water conservation and preservation of biodiversity. An allocation of Rs. 200 crore for launching this climate resilient agriculture initiative is proposed.

The second element of the strategy relates to reduction of significant wastages in storage as well as in the operations of the existing food supply chains in the country. This needs to be addressed. As the Prime Minister has said recently, "We need greater competition and therefore need to take a firm view on opening up of the retail trade. It will help in bringing down the considerable difference between the farm gate prices, wholesale prices and retail prices."

There is wastage of grain procured for buffer stocks and public distribution system due to acute shortage of storage capacity in the Food Corporation of India. This deficit in the storage capacity is met through an ongoing scheme for private sector participation where the FCI has been hiring godowns from private parties for a guaranteed period of 5 years. This period is now being extended to 7 years.

The third element of the strategy relates to improving the availability of credit to farmers. Banks have been consistently meeting the targets set for agriculture credit flow in the past few years. For the year 2010-11, the target has been raised to Rs. 3,75,000 crore from Rs. 3,25,000 crore in the current year. The Debt Waiver and Debt Relief Scheme for Farmers was a major initiative of the UPA Government. In view of the recent drought in some States and the severe floods in some other parts of the country, the period for repayment of the loan amount by farmers is extended by six months from December 31, 2009 to June 30, 2010. Subvention for timely repayment of crop loans from one per cent to two per cent for 2010-11 is made. Thus, the effective rate of interest for such farmers will now be five per cent per annum.

The fourth element of the strategy aims at lending a further impetus to the development of food processing sector by providing state-of-the-art infrastructure. In addition to the ten mega food park projects already being set up, the Government has decided to set up five more such parks. As a part of the farm to market initiative, External Commercial Borrowings will henceforth be available for cold storage or cold room facility, including for farm level pre-cooling, for preservation or storage of agricultural and allied produce, marine products and meat.

Agriculture & Related Sectors: In supporting the strategy outlined for development of agriculture, a few key areas that call for focused attention are: (i) A strong supply chain for perishable farm produce to reach consumption and processing centers promptly; (ii) Infrastructure and technology to convert such produce into value-added products; and (iii) Infusion of technology to augment agricultural production. Similar attention needs to be paid to related sectors such as apiary (for bee honey), horticulture, dairy, poultry, meat, marine and aquaculture.

For achieving these objectives, import status and concessional duties are provided for setting up of mechanized handling systems and pallet racking systems in 'mandis' or warehouses for food grains and sugar as well as full exemption from service tax for the installation and commissioning of such equipment; and for initial setting up and expansion of cold storage, cold room including farm pre-coolers for preservation or storage of agriculture and related sectors produce; and processing units for such produce. Full exemption from customs duty to refrigeration units required for the manufacture of refrigerated vans or trucks.

Concessional customs duty for specified agricultural machinery not manufactured in India; central excise exemption to specified equipment for preservation, storage and processing of agriculture and related sectors and exemption from service tax to the storage and warehousing of their produce; and full exemption from excise duty to trailers and semi-trailers used in agriculture is proposed. Concessional import duty earlier provided to specified machinery for use in the plantation sector is extended to March 31, 2011 along with a CVD exemption.

One of the prerequisites for agricultural productivity is access to good quality and disease-resistant seeds. It is proposed to exempt the testing and certification of agricultural seeds from service tax. Transportation by road and rail of cereals and pulses will be exempted from service tax.

M.S. Swaminathan, Rajya Sabha member (2010) commenting on the Finance Minister's recipe for agricultural renewal involving convergence and synergy among numerous ongoing programs observe and comments:

While a road map for agricultural renaissance has been indicated in the budget, the achievement of the goals of above steps will be possible within the very small amounts provided in the budget only if State governments can introduce a "deliver as one" approach with reference to the implementation of different projects. For example, substantial outlays are available under several ongoing programs like the Rashtriya Krishi Vikas Yojana, National Horticulture Mission, National Food Security Mission, Mahatma Gandhi National Rural Employment Guarantee Scheme and National Rural Livelihood Mission. If such an approach involving appropriate changes both in attitude and action is not adopted, the small amount of money allotted for the above mentioned purposes will not yield the anticipated results.

Another issue which needs careful consideration is the policy regarding the opening up of the retail trade. Mini-retail and small holder farming are the largest self employment enterprises in our country. Creating jobs is the greatest challenge facing us now. Therefore, the opening up of retail trade to large companies, whether national or multinational, needs to be taken up only on the basis of an employment impact analysis. Another issue which needs to be considered in its totality is the impact of the rise in the price of diesel and petrol. This will have serious implications for all sectors of the economy and particularly for the farm sector. During 2009, which was a severe drought year, Punjab-Haryana farmers increased rice production to a level higher than the previous year by resorting to ground water irrigation. This involved a large investment by farmers in the purchase of diesel for pumping water. It is because of this effort that we have now a comfortable reserve in rice. Unfortunately, irrigation which is the most important input for agriculture does not find special mention in the budget speech, although provision would have been made under Bharat Nirman.

Finally, it is high time that the sentiments expressed by the Finance Minister in relation to post-harvest technology and particularly grain storage are converted into action without delay. In April-May 2010, the Food Corporation of India and other agencies may have to buy over 20 million tons of wheat in Northwest India. Even the existing stocks of wheat and rice are not stored properly. It will be sad if during a period of hardship as a result of food inflation, we should allow wastage of precious grains. It will be useful if the Prime Minister and the National Development Council initiate as soon as possible the steps needed for such a reform in governance.

Monitoring: The Government had announced the setting-up of an Independent Evaluation Office (IEO) to undertake impartial and objective assessments of the various public programs and improve the effectiveness of the public interventions. IEO would evaluate the impact of flagship programs and place the findings in the public domain. It has been decided that it would be an independent entity under a Governing board chaired by the Deputy Chairman, Planning Commission. It would be funded by the Planning Commission.

Observations

After many decades, it is being realized that the philosophy for driving rural growth is bottom-up, rather than depending on the 'trickle-down effect'. Our observations in the context of rural economy development policies suggest that local contribution is crucial for planning, implementing and effectiveness of these rural policies. There has to be collaborative efforts of Central and State governments and local government in the villages.

The policy initiatives require both financial commitment and design of delivery systems to make technical and financial assistance available in rural areas. On the whole, Corporate

India supporting government resources would not only drive economic growth in rural areas but ushers in the key instruments for equitable growth.

Bharat Nirman with its six schemes is an important initiative for bridging the gap between the rural and urban areas and improving the quality of life of people, particularly the poor, in the rural areas. Government since 2000 has made concerted efforts to provide social security to ruralites.

Investment in rural India is crucial, and we have to view urban India as part of the solution. Execution of infrastructure investment and manufacturing incentives in urban and peri-urban areas could strengthen rural-urban linkages through insurance policies in rural areas to provide life cover, health and farm related. All rural spending schemes will have direct impact on urban growth. Thus the focus of rural polices should be Rural-urban integration.

For the success of rural polices it is important that these policies are also endorsed and supported by other opposition political parties. Such inclusion creates a social consensus for modernization and drivers for rural economy to grow. Thus political economy is an important factor.

9

Rural Integrated Transformation

> *Whatever the drawbacks, barriers, and problems, people not only get by but also frequently manage to improve their lives and of those around them and that happens because of the innateness of Indian society—something that comes from tolerance, diversity, problem solving skills, argumentativeness, democracy and commitment to family and community growth.*

What is significant is *what* and *who* will drive the rural economy or how it will move towards growth, and what is transforming rural economy. The discussion-analysis of rural development historic and contemporary scenarios highlights the transformation.

We discussed and analyzed and did a historical perspective about what had been ailing rural economy, why a greater incidence of poverty and hunger and low quality of life since the last sixty plus years. Who is to be blamed if ruralites are at the bottom of pyramid even after 60 years of exclusive rural development plans? There are three pointers: People themselves are to be blamed first, local government is second and the Central Government too since it focused exclusively on social development and then economic growth. Its varied programs were too ideal for people threshold, lacked people participation though they were planned as people's programs and most of all implemented sporadically.

We discussed-analyzed the policy initiatives, schemes and programs focusing on technology and finances for occupational planning and choices and personal life style. A contemporary analysis is done of issues, challenges and opportunities for rural economy and ruralites. The contemporary analysis highlighted why and how the rural economy is growing and ruralites are progressing for better quality of life. We concluded that since 2000 decade, three paradigm shifts, PPP and P4 and development of rural infrastructure are human dimensions that have been the drivers of current rural economic growth.

Dynamics for current growth of rural economy are discontentment, demand, motivation and participation of rural communities on one hand; and on the other hand, their co-operation, co-ordination and consumption involving other stakeholders. Success stories can provide all the ingredients—teach, inspire, and motivate people but to succeed the efforts must come from them.

Observations

Our discussions and retracing the history of socio-economic development in villages since the last six decades highlights what are the next and current drivers to boost rural economy for growth to bring it up to mainstream economy. Interestingly, *mainly 'technology' will be the rural economic growth driver*; and ruralites are low on it. Over the years, low efforts have been made for technology initiatives in rural areas. Since 2000, the technology efforts and resources inputs are raised by government, business and technology related enterprises both national and international and NGOs. Thus, since 2000, there is spurt in technology initiatives both from national and international resources. Tele-density through mobile telephones and rural computerization both for functionalities and computer literacy are the major technology initiatives significantly needed to let rural economy grow fast and efforts are currently being highly focused on these. In order to develop fast these areas, it would need active, consistent and fast support of financial and technical resources of government, businesses and NGOs, and social technology of people to absorb these in their lifestyles.

But significantly important is social technology perspective of people by active participation as individuals and community in these technology initiatives and accepting and incorporating in their lifestyles. The good point is that, people are keen to learn, utilize these technologies to better their socio-economic growth whether it is telephone, computer, drinking water, sanitation or agriculture, etc.

Second significant growth impetus is the three ***'Paradigm Shift'*** in planning and delivery of socio-eco development in the villages since 2000. Demand driven, community participation and PPP & P4 models and governance transformation are the nodes in paradigm shifts which are driving the rural economy to grow.

First 'Paradigm Shift' is about community participation and individual villager and community initiative in development programs in the villages. Villagers are fast realizing that they will have better quality of life if they participate and collaborate in development efforts of other policy administration stakeholders and build powerful stakeholder relationships based on trust, interest and involvement. After many decades, it is being realized that the trigger for driving rural growth is bottom-up, rather than depending on the 'trickle-down effect'.

Earlier, there were IEC campaigns by the government and NGOs to inform, educate and motivate them to achieve quality of life in various areas. But it was not effective, achievement was poor, because the government initiative was taken for granted and as we have mentioned earlier, there was 'learned dependency' on government and there was no individual initiative to maintain or boost the services or products provided.

Since 50s, government had paternalistic attitude towards the ruralites and provided them well through developmental efforts and spent more resources than on the urbanite low income group. Even provided them with democratic local government—Panchayat Raj. But people did not bother to benefit from those amenities provided, boost or maintain them, and share them collectively; rather they squabble more on caste and creed differences and there was no self-reliance. Village level workers and other village officials were corrupt and irresponsible to their duties. People did not gain, rather they remained underdeveloped as well complaining.

Government did put the community radio since 50s and TV since 60s for the benefit of the whole community but due to the narrow perspectives of people regarding caste and creed and gender, they were not able to enjoy the entertainment or the social messages that government beamed for the benefit of all through organized media forums. In 1982-1986, government spent resources to provide sanitation and water facilities in the villages but there were no community initiatives to maintain those facilities. Thus, these were all supply driven facilities provided. There was discontentment; government and other agencies were discontented as their efforts did not commensurate with the resources spent, and rural communities were discontented as the facilities were getting unusable quickly and in shambles as they were not being maintained and they blamed government for this sorry state.

The significant changeover came over in 2000. Government gave up all rural socio-eco supply driven development efforts and made it demand driven. *Their message to people was, 'you demand, we will provide, you must cooperate, and put your efforts to achieve it and maintain it thereof. We are ready to give you technical knowhow and finances but we need your participation'*. This was in context to such programs as education, employment and employability skills, water, sanitation, housing, electricity, rural connecting roads, rural business hubs and village enterprises, farming techniques programs and even with village Panchayat system which the government in its present democratic restructuring had made it inclusive of all communities in the village; even the lower caste or woman can head the Panchayat.

The communities who came forward gained and there were success stories. Other communities soon realized if they want to enjoy quality of life and all other facilities, and the economic gain, they will be able to achieve it only through their own participation and demands. They will gain more visibility and accessibility to comforts and necessities of life—even the basic minimum needs (BMN) through their own collaborative efforts.

Thus, there is more progress in these programs and schemes since 2000 when government initiative and spending as well as community initiative has become demand driven as well community participatory.

Narula (1983) based on her researches of rural communities has highlighted the model that discontentment, demand, motivation and participation is necessary for development of rural communities. In current scenario in 2000 decades, these dimensions are not sufficient; now ***added dimensions of co-operation, co-ordination and consumption have become necessary conditions. All these six dimensions have become dynamic for growth of rural economy.***

Ruralites realization that QOL will come through their own efforts and participation, and so will be the economic gains. This realization and change of attitude is a significant driver for growth of rural economy. There will be more visibility for and more accessibility to necessities of life—definitely BMN and comforts if they are willing to slog through, cooperate and coordinate with other agencies to achieve these goals.

Let rural economy be community demand driven to let it grow and transform itself. Rural People participation is the major driving force for rural economy to grow and so is their growing demand for inclusion in the mainstream economy.

Second 'Paradigm Shift' is about public-private-partnership (PPP) and public-private-NGO-community partnership (P4). These two models have been crucial in rural economic growth since 2000 decades and are immensely driving the economy growth since then.

We presume the future rural economic growth will depend on the political leaders' visions and planning for growth of rural economy, entrepreneurs' efforts to develop market forces to set impetus for such growth and ruralites consumer confidence and consumerism to boost it. An inclusive pattern of growth will focus on social and physical infrastructure, and several initiatives to integrate the rural economy with the mainstream national economy by various flagship schemes and programs. PPP model will be the driver for rural economy.

The policy initiatives require both financial commitment and design of delivery systems to make technical and financial assistance available in rural areas. On the whole, Corporate India supporting government resources would not only drive economic growth in rural areas but ushers in the key instruments for equitable growth.

Government message now is, "we will take policy initiatives for various segments of development in rural sectors, but we have limited financial resources, manpower resources; we want business enterprises, financial sectors to collaborate with us with their expertise and financial resources in delivering those programs speedily and efficiently to the rural masses. In turn, this will create growth of business for them speedily and efficiently". Earlier, government will say, "We have ideal visions and planned policies for your progress in life; it is solely our responsibility to deliver them but not all visions and policies can be reality and implemented as we have resource constraints".

PPP initiatives has been of tremendous help in development of world class physical infrastructure like roads, expressways, railways, airports, ports, oil refineries, etc. For any segments of rural health care such as eye care, dental care, population care or even general health care PPP model become necessary for its success, and lots of community awareness as well involvement is necessary for its implementation and important for its success. This model is facilitating in creating employment and employability and raising standards and levels of general and IT education in rural areas. By such initiatives both government and private enterprises are the gainers and of course the targeted community.

P4 model suggests Public-Private-NGO-Community partnership is necessary for rural time bound socio-economic growth. Government realizes it cannot take total onus for such growth; it needs partnership in these efforts. Village Panchayat tiers cannot say, "We need spoon-feeding from government development bureaucracy to implement flagship programs". Village Panchayat has to take leadership role and guide (demand) from government, business enterprises, NGOs what they want for community and village development and how that should be implemented and with active involvement of the village community. Panchayat will assess local priority programs in collaboration with community through dialogue strategies.

Panchayat has to shed biases against lower castes and women; though now mandatory by law, it must come from within. Panchayat Raj has to be democratic local rule, planned and executed by the village people and for their own good. Village community supports Panchayat by their active involvement. Community will demand and get both Central and State Governments' continuous interest in providing policy initiatives, technical, financial and manpower resources for economic programs based on their demands and priority assessment.

Private sector cannot work in isolation, whether it is industries in rural hinterland, BPO in the village, rural retail, RBHs or tourist spots in the villages; or sanitation and water management schemes in the village. They would need collaboration and coordination with other stakeholders for effective success.

Business enterprises will develop business model for bottom of the pyramid in rural population. This model will focus on consumerism through accessibility, availability and affordability. It will focus on providing technical know-how, creating employability and employment, education through ICTs. Business enterprises will create rural markets by investing their own funds, through venture collaborations and FDI. Through corporate social responsibility programs businesses will contribute to rural socio-economic programs also.

NGOs domestic or international, and social entrepreneurs adopt specific village and program according to their expertise such as technology, medical, social, and financial capacity.

They provide action oriented plans, IEC programs and campaigns supporting those plans or only IEC campaigns, and financing them in big or small way; for community betterment and encouraging its participation and total involvement. Thus they push forward both people and programs through their social activist and business models.

We say that again Community Initiative, i.e. community discontent, demand, participation and involvement, co-operation, co-ordination and consumption are of utmost importance.

Resources of all four stakeholders are collaborated, coordinated though they are all independent and self-reliant; given the enormity and complexity of rural development in modern times; a single stakeholder can no longer say, "I can do it alone. Rather, I will be in 'Interdependency loop' with other three stakeholders to succeed".

(The 'Loop Model' and Interconnected Interaction for interdependence loop details in Appendix 5).

After many decades, it is being realized that the trigger for driving rural growth is bottom-up, rather than depending on the 'trickle-down effect'. Our observations in the context of rural economy development policies suggest that local contribution is crucial for planning, implementing and effectiveness of these rural policies. There has to be collaborative efforts of Central and State Governments and local government in the villages along with private sector entrepreneurs and NGOs.

In nutshell, policies succeed and outcomes are good when people participate and these policies get demand driven because of people's participation. Since resources are limited, let them grab the opportunities to develop. Business enterprises are realizing that their focus on developing 'bottom-of-the-pyramid' low-end markets help them in expanding their business markets beside discharging social responsibility in P4 model.

ICTs for agro innovation will require more knowledge and information input from research and extension services which will have to respond to specific farmer requests for information in demand-driven, location-specific, customized and tailor-made technologies and services to serve different categories of farmers. Economic liberalization and globalization, is radically changing the spectrum of service providers to the rural community. Effective linkages are being forged among research, extension and farmers. These and other ICTs efforts in various rural domains are likely to facilitate growth in the rural economy.

Ongoing rural programs focusing on socio-eco initiatives in P4 model can be driven for growth of its economy.

Third 'Paradigm Shift' about transformation in governance has significant beneficial consequences through e-governance and institutionalizing accountability and transparency. This could be effected through various steps: (i) an ongoing, independent evaluation and public reporting of progress in implementing government schemes; (ii) big strides in e-governance; (iii) decentralization and empowerment of Panchayat and NGOs to implement and monitor government schemes; (iv) breaking barriers between departments and schemes to achieve synergy, integration and better utilization of existing resources; (v) innovative regulation of health, education and provision of public services; (vi) liberal use of technology in welfare transfers and achieving public awareness; and (vii) institutionalization of the government's basic commitments by requiring all to specify how their proposals would enhance the goals of equity or inclusion, innovation and public accountability.

Transparency is important to provide for the legitimacy and credibility of the outcome approach and of information and reports. Many ways are being used to make information transparent. We need strong commitment from the top, be it top level of bureaucracy, or at a political level. But at the same time, we need commitment from the lower levels as well, down to those who are really delivering the services to the public.

The emphasis is also on institutionalizing accountability. A model Public Services Law would be legislated, in consultation with the states, to hold functionaries in health, education and rural development accountable. District level monitoring committees and ombudsmen should attend to grievance redress that would strengthen flagship schemes like NRGS, TCLC, drinking water mission, and NRHM. It will be challenging to set up better systems for food, supply chain, water, medicine, education, roads, etc. in rural areas. Smarter and improved systems will make meaningful difference to the prosperity of rural economy. Internet based public accountability (PAIS) system will help in monitoring transparency and accountability.

Challenges and Opportunities

We get opportunities to grow but we do face challenges to achieve the optimum benefits when rural economy is progressing. There are challenges in the socio-eco sector to see that rural India, which is going to be the backbone of economic growth, has enough stimuli and moves on. A constraint to India's economic strength at this point in 2008-09 are domestic imbalances between the rural and urban sector as well as the fact that in India the level of per capita income is still quite low.

Inclusive growth is imperative, growth has to benefit all sections of people. They have to face challenges and opportunities in education, employment, quality of life, energy and climate change, public health, and physical infrastructure and digital infrastructure. Initiatives have to be taken to integrate the rural economy with the national economy by political leaders, governance and business enterprises.

In these contexts, we face challenges. There will be Social equity and public policy challenges

Saul (2006) suggests that India grows when there is inclusive growth "Historically, the rich states of today set off on a path of economic growth only when they began to invest in infrastructure and education for all. Only when wealth is fairly well spread out does the wealth of a nation solidify to form a strong base for further growth. "A healthy, well educated, well-to-do population is the best wealth-creating tool a country can have".

Ongoing Challenging Issues

There are biggest challenges for the coming years to boost rural economy in India: (i) To educate villagers through revitalized education system in village schools and create skilled workforce both farm or non-farm related. (ii) To create high level computer literacy and computerization in most of the villages; and the generation of non-farm employment, as well as creating more farm ancillary jobs such as food processing or cold storage industries around the villages. (iii) Thus, education, skills, employment and creating employability are the targets to develop rural economy and it needs more resources and sustained efforts of both government and private sector than necessary for urban sector.

Since rural sector has long been away from the mainstream; the next decade must put efforts to bring rural economy at par with urban economy—the mainstream economy.

Dynamics can be worked out from the focus of challenges of business expansions, infrastructure development, developing human capital—through skilled workforce, technology and connectivity challenges, and the challenges of creating resources through indigenous efforts and foreign capital flow.

India's economy is growing, it has to focus to eliminate poverty and ensure substantial improvement in living standards of people across all the sections of the society. The benefits of economic growth, education, employment, and healthcare and technology development should reach all. Rural base needs special focus to be brought closer to the main stream.

The Indian government has set itself ambitious development goals in its current Five-Year Plan (2007–2012). They are geared to the Millennium Development Goals. The slogan of the plan is "faster and more inclusive growth". The aim is to achieve annual growth in GDP of more than ten per cent by 2012. The agricultural sector is set to grow by an average of four per cent per year, thereby increasing its contribution to economic growth. In addition, new jobs are to be created reducing regional disparities in income, and universal access to education and medical care is to be promoted.

Finance Minister in Budget speech (2009-10) emphasized that the government recognizes the challenges that this task entails, particularly at a time when the world is still struggling with an unprecedented financial crisis and an economic slowdown that has also affected India to some extent.

Challenges that Government Faces in 2009-2010

The first challenge is to lead the economy back to the high GDP growth rate at the earliest. Growth of income is important in itself, but it is as important for the resources that it brings in. These resources provide us with the means to bridge the critical gaps that remain in our development efforts, particularly with regard to the welfare of the vulnerable segments of our population.

The second challenge is to deepen and broaden the agenda for inclusive development, and to ensure that no individual, community or region is denied the opportunity to participate in and benefit from the inclusive development process.

The third challenge is to re-energize government and improve delivery mechanisms. Our institutions must provide high quality public services, security and the rule of law to all citizens with transparency and accountability.

Salient Challenges: Ongoing Rural Programs

The flagship programs are progressing well, achieving their targets and more and more resources and new dimensions are being added on these programs to make them effective and successful, but they pose challenges to be addressed.

Water and Sanitation Challenges: Sustainable sanitation cannot be achieved unless both energy and water are available. The energy needs of the rural areas are not met adequately, biogas based electricity generation plants in rural areas are a viable option. Domestic sewage is the major source of pollution in India in surface water which contributes pathogens, and is the main source of water borne diseases along with depletion of oxygen in water bodies.

The challenge is how to make ecological sanitation and treated grey-water safe in relation to drinking water and crop production. Development of other sustainable sanitation methods than ecological sanitation is reuse of grey-water for irrigation, monitoring on improved availability of water for agriculture due to reuse of grey-water.

Capacity building challenge in Health Sector for villages along with advocacy and awareness generation on hygiene issues is important for sanitation. Equally important is capacity building of Panchayat Raj Institutions (PRIs) and other grass roots level organizations for Primary Health Care for action and advocacy and awareness generation for sanitation. It will be equally challenging to create nationwide network on health and hygiene, environmental health surveillance and hygiene promotion. A convergence of TSC initiatives and Department of Health will be more productive.

A Capacity Building Scheme for end-user is equally challenging. It envisions an institutional framework for state level strategic decision-making including setting up of State e-Governance Mission Team (SeMTs), at an outlay of Rs. 313 crore, was approved in January 2008. A Capacity Building Management Cell (CBMC) has been set up in DIT (Department of Information Technology) for its overall coordination and implementation.

Water: Scientists have estimated that the amount of water consumed by agricultural evapo-transpiration would increase by an enormous amount given current trends. The possibility of identifying sources of this extra water is low and so the alternative, higher productivity ('more crops per drop'), together with reducing the amount of water wasted in irrigation will more likely plug the future (and present) food gap. Scientific, social and economic factors must all be considered in the research context.

The challenge is how we encourage farmers to make long-term investments in the well-being of soil and land management to prevent soil degradation and deterioration which cancel out savings in water usage and agricultural productivity. Notwithstanding the difficult and complex challenges, there is need for a new generation of water professionals who are able to rise to this challenge.

To get 'Safe Drinking Water' in rural areas is challenging. Drinking water scenario in India, both rural and urban highlights that water purification and treatment needs urgent attention on war footing basis to let people not suffer the adverse health effects. Managing water through water purification and treatment practices by using update technologies, and managing the groundwater resources and aquifers is important and necessary. Even the water that flows out of the taps in Delhi or many Indian cities is a cocktail of carcinogenic substances. Future of Water matters most to us. It is ultimate renewable resource.

Water supply schemes, eventually generating large amounts of waste water in consumer areas, are normally designed and built, especially in developing countries, without the required matching drainage networks and waste water treatment facilities. Quantity is generally managed separately from quality, as is water science and water policy. This fragmentation approach also impedes coherent hydrological analyses at regional, continental and global scales. We need 'blue revolution' before underground water is exhausted by careless overuse.

In India, the green revolution was supported by water access for irrigation through dams and canals. But that water was not enough as rivers did not have enough water. The farmers in their enthusiasm hired drilling rigs and bought electric pumps to mine water that lie beneath their land. Farmers are tapping their own groundwater and have been using it efficiently for the last two decades. But how long there will be underground water. There is no regulation to control to pump water and to put bore wells which are sunk deeper and deeper to get water. As the water table falls, farmers use heavily subsidized electricity to bring water to the surface. The electricity grids cannot take the strain and there are widespread blackouts.

The dairy industry is one of the major reasons for water crisis in Gujarat in the recent past. The dairy farmer understands that and worries about the water disappearance. But he has to make his living by getting enough water.

We need new ethos on water based on technical fixes and managing the water cycle for maximum social benefits. The new ethos will harness modern methods and ideas for high tech irrigation, while taking care of water realities of finite resources inside river basins. It will explore new ways to combine different parts of water cycle. Why build huge dams when you have natural resources beneath your feet. Proposals for large scale of monsoon flood waters of the rivers into the aquifer beneath its plain could make sense. Also, we may revert to modern versions of Qanats to maintain water table levels and reducing pumping.

We need to practice the following water management strategies: (i) recycle the water such as recycling sewage water for irrigation; (ii) water treatment to deliver safe and potable water to people; (iii) to maintain water table levels and reducing pumping; (iv) treating industrial effluent before they are open in the waterways. Otherwise effluents polluted water irrigating the soil will dry the soil and create toxicity in the crops and thus make them unfit for human consumption or if consumed would spread many diseases; and (v) rainwater harvesting.

Hunger, malnutrition and poverty handling in context of ruralites is challenging. The notion of hunger, malnutrition and poverty in rural areas though related are distinct in nature, both conceptually and in terms of policies required to address them.

Poverty in rural areas happens when there are no family earnings. This is more crucial for non-farm hands that do not have farms or any other village enterprise to make money. Result is hunger—inadequacy of basic food, or even families may go without food for days when they have no money to buy food. Therefore, employment is necessary to redress both poverty and hunger.

Poor experience being left out, looked down upon, pushed aside, and ignored by those more powerful at all levels. This affects their access to resources and opportunities and their ability to influence decisions that shape their lives. They are often deprived of information about jobs, economic opportunities, and credit services, as well as from information on government services and their own rights as citizens. It is challenging to narrow these gaps and let poor have a basic quality of life and not just survival strategy.

Poverty also perpetuates itself through self-defeating habits and behavior such as not acquiring marketable job skills, having more children without means to support them, even indulge in criminal acts such as drug dealing, violence etc. and even social isolation and economic stress may even turn them into social rebels and terrorists. Poor people are caught in the web of multiple and interlocking deprivations, limited resources, and poor leverage.

The challenge for policy and practice is not only to enhance their earning capabilities but provide them ongoing work on stipulated wages; but it is challenging to build upon poor people's initiatives, hard work, and resilience in the face of insurmountable problems of accessing market opportunities, government services and civil society resources. There is ongoing government program of NREGA guarantees work and wages for minimum 100 days a year per person to minimize incidence of hunger.

There are development policies currently planned to increase poor men and women's access to opportunities and resources and their freedom of choice and action and be heard and represented in decision-making that affects their lives at the local and national levels; thus to empower the powerless in their struggles to find a place of dignity and respect in society.

But the challenge is to implement planned policies of giving access to opportunities and resources, freedom of choice and action in practice.

Since in the absence of education and job skills, people cannot earn enough and government financial resources cannot create enough of infrastructure to support them. Poverty cannot be tamed with a single solution. It needs solutions focusing on education, healthcare, housing, access to basic services, and access to capital through microfinance.

The new search for solutions focuses on empowering the poor through their active participation and involvement with other stakeholders in directly attacking the root cause of poverty, i.e. low education and lack of job skills, low health—poor nutrition and diseases, and unemployment with low or no incomes.

Long-term poverty reduction in Indian rural society can happen with sustained economic growth which requires a strong and responsible business sector and educated, skilled and employable work force.

Malnutrition refers to an imbalance of both macro and micro-nutrients, which could be because of inadequate or inappropriate intake and/or inefficient biological utilization due to physiological or environmental factors or lack of knowledge. Malnutrition, as measured is estimated at 45.9 per cent as per National Family Health Survey 2005-06. Most of them are not aware of malnutrition in their daily food or its relationship with diseases. Even poor have no choice where nutrition is concerned they eat what they get.

Ruralites children and young women of reproductive age; older people suffer from very specific diseases because of imbalance of nutrition in food; and most of the people suffer from malnutrition related diseases, even eye diseases.

Ruralites grow their own food and as preventive healthcare measures; IEC programs through media and interpersonal channels regarding food nutrition can help them. There are ICDS and midday-meal programs in schools to take care of food nutrition need of children. But people must take their own impetus to include this in their daily life style. For this, all but especially women have to be educated and trained about healthy and nutritious food intake for the family. They need to be informed and educated about the environmental hazards of unsafe drinking water supply, water storage, latrines, open drains, cooking stoves with wood or kerosene fuel, ventilation in houses, and also need for behavioral change, e.g. hygiene practices and hand washing. Environmental health can be cost-effective means to improve health of the ruralites. Such programs for rural women, men and children should be planned periodically.

Flagship housing schemes for the ruralites in general and poor are being pursued actively currently and adding onto the targeted housing plans. Policy initiatives for technical and financial assistance available in rural areas are stimulating rural housing. Even government is fully subsidizing housing for poor and scheduled castes and easy financing for others. So far there has been no initiative from private sector to build or finance rural housing. People themselves are low on the economic scale to build houses on their own. Except for one or two affluent villagers who could afford brick houses, all of them have been living in thatched or mud-houses since long time. They aspire living in brick houses and government wants to fulfill this dream for majority against odds of land availability and finances. Ultimately, government must tap PPP or P4 models for success of these schemes.

An active housing sector in rural areas could be both a direct catalyst for promoting greater economic activity as it provides considerable employment at the local level and would also help in improving the health and productivity of rural inhabitants. Given the multiple dimensions of the rural housing challenges, a coordinated strategy needs to be evolved. Recognizing the fact that there are strong regional and local dimensions to rural housing requirements, local-level institutional arrangements to encourage rural housing construction are necessary. The trends suggest that there is considerable demand for improvement in rural housing conditions.

Creating Rural Markets Hubs both by public and private sectors would drive economy. Rural Retail Business Hubs (RBH) are set up by private sector businesses focusing on marketing of variety of products and services. Poor infrastructure, supply chain inefficiency, unorganized marketing and product pricing can be the major bottlenecks for the growth of rural retail. There exists no organized marketing and distribution in 87% of India's villages, wherein

50% of the rural population resides. Free training courses are offered at the RBH retail by the companies for the products that the consumers buy, this is an added incentive for the consumer as well the company to build market share. These companies create market awareness, persuade customers by teams expert and experienced in the product line, give consultancy to create further demands for the products and services. Rural consumers gain market awareness and product confidence about the brands.

While the trickling-down effect of higher GDP growth and a low inflation rate have improved the economic conditions of the villagers, the exposure to new products has changed their consumption patterns also. The delivery of those goods through the efforts of the businesses in various areas, and in different ways further facilitates those consumption patterns.

Second RBH scheme of village arts and craft, industries in villages will provide an opportunity to introduce quality Indian products to the national and international markets; and will bring economic prosperity to the Rural India.

Corporates and government through both the RBH schemes are promoting rural markets as drivers of future growth. Further, the development of organized rural retail, and village arts and craft, industries in rural India will create jobs, check rural migration, increase tax generation and improve agricultural efficiencies.

Education and Employment: Employability generation for rural workforce who could be dividend for the economy; a sound education system with skill development focus in farm and non-farm areas is important and all stakeholders—public-private partnership is actively involved in this endeavor. Technology education by technology partners both domestic and international initiatives are also encouraging rural youth, women, even functional literate to access technology education, training and functionality use in different areas and that is also empowering them for employment in technology through BPOs, and even use of technology set ups in villages for agriculture, water, sanitation, medical, etc.

Since the awareness and demand for higher education and skills is created among the ruralites, it must be supported by good work ethics of teachers and other village education administrators. We cannot overlook the immense reservoir of human talent and potential in rural population. Education has the greatest potential to move society forward. A sustained investment in education brings economic prosperity, enhance QOL and village democracy. Impetus for change should come from people. The power of human energy is to use its energy efficiently, wisely and find solutions for such usage.

Rural Healthcare: A review of the National Rural Health Mission points to the acute shortage of human resources at various levels in the health sector—specialists, doctors, nurses and paramedics. There is actual human resource shortage as well humanly created shortage by unwilling medics to work in rural areas or to be absent for work in rural clinics. A self-enforced good work ethics can help meet the challenge but how do we promote that? Rural health programs in general must focus on PPP models from funding, expertise and better human resource control point of view, and active community involvement in enforcing the work ethics as well following the health and hygiene practices themselves. Such preventive approach will cut down on healthcare expenses in the long-run. Both PPP and P4 models can meet the rural health challenge.

Today's healthcare environment is challenging, the endeavor of all P4 participants is to increase efficiency, improve quality, build better health plans, create healthier people and workforce and save more lives.

Monitoring, Evaluating, and Reporting on Outcomes of currently operating, ongoing rural policies, schemes and programs to benefit the rural masses is important as well as challenging. Such stance is necessary when we are initiating new schemes and programs to benefit the ruralites and allocating substantial resources both financial and technical to attain successful outcomes.

Narula (2008b) highlights the multiple stances necessary for success of outcome approach for various schemes and programs. Countries have found that being able to document what actually happens is absolutely critical to an outcome orientation. Without good information on what has happened, a focus on results is impossible. And for good information, one requires monitoring or tracking of progress in accordance with objectives and indicators, along with evaluation that can look at broader considerations. Much of the current activity is at the monitoring level, and the need for more attention to evaluation is identified.

Evaluation is required to assess the continuing relevance and appropriateness of strategies and programs, and to provide information about all types of impacts, including unintended or unexpected consequences. Evaluation also can identify the continued appropriateness of objectives and of indicators used for monitoring. It is needed to demonstrate causality or attribution, to determine if the program intervention was responsible for any documented results. ***Perhaps, most importantly, evaluation can help to make informed decisions on future actions.***

The outcome focus needs to take into account the entire results chain. Given that major outcomes depend upon numerous factors working together and are usually sometime in the future, there is also a need to pay particular attention to intermediate level outcomes and even to output. The priority should be given to results that matter to people.

An outcome focus is an essential component of a learning approach that can identify how policies and program approaches may need to be adjusted, improved, or replaced with alternatives. It is essential not only to demonstrate that outcomes have occurred, but that the interventions in question have contributed to these in some way. Result-oriented management clearly is both good economics and good politics.

Transparency is important to provide for the legitimacy and credibility of the outcome approach and of information and reports. Many ways are being used to make information transparent. We need strong commitment from the top, be it top level of bureaucracy, or at a political level. But at the same time, we need commitment from the lower levels as well, down to those who are really delivering the services to the public.

Civil society is identified as being able to play three important roles in the development and sustainability of an outcome approach: (i) To provide legitimacy to the government's goals and strategies, (ii) Adding support and pressure for results demanding that government focus on results that matter to citizens and document what is actually being delivered, (iii) Providing validation and credibility to the results information.

Outcome Approach: Narula (2008b) further suggests that moving toward an outcome approach is important. It is basic to the appropriate and effective management of government and the delivery of public services. An outcome focus potentially can provide a framework for an integrated "whole of government" approach involving the coordination of different policy and program areas that are all expected to contribute in some way to the same outcome, such as employment creation, economic development, or the improved health of the population.

An outcome focus has been used by the political leadership in many different countries as a means of demonstrating how they are addressing the needs and concerns of their citizens. In this way, it can represent a powerful tool to increase the credibility of political institutions, with corresponding political gains in some jurisdictions.

Implementing an outcome focus represents a fundamental shift in the nature of thinking, acting, and managing within the public sector, away from a focus on *process* and on what one needs to do, to a focus on *benefits*. This in turn has implications for many other aspects of management—for example, to existing accountability and reward mechanisms, as well as the manner in which government relates to its citizens.

Both a top-down and a bottom-up approach are needed. Strong support from the top political or administrative levels is essential to provide legitimacy and priority to an outcome orientation and to make sure that it actually will happen. But unless there is also support throughout the system, and particularly at the middle management levels, an outcome focus runs the risk of becoming a mere administrative exercise rather than representing an actual change in thinking or managing.

Lack of sufficient capacity and expertise in result-oriented thinking and managing, can be a hurdle in more specialized tasks. For example, monitoring and evaluation, which provides an opportunity to identify what is and is not working well.

Managing change in society should come under Public Administration and it must be their responsibility to manage changes effectively for people to prevent disparity and social tensions. Public administration must be monitored by regular surveys of feedback given by people expecting services from general administration departments. These continuous monitoring will bring the much needed sense of process and discipline in the administrative departments. The key to the whole thing is to manage everything efficiently, while maintaining low key.

Governance implies the capacity of the country's institutions, through both formal and informal mechanisms to implement and enforce policies in a coordinated manner. Effective governance works on the basis of key principles like accountability, participation, predictability and transparency.

Monitoring the Program Projects: With a view to improve transparency in distribution of funds and prevent leakages, an Internet based public accountability (PAIS) system should be set up to provide information to the targeted population about (i) the expenditure allocated and spent, the receivers of the expenditure, (ii) the major programs inputs purchased (sources, amounts), the people hired and their actual attendance record (e.g. teachers), (iii) the output of the program and its quality. The target beneficiaries (users) should be allowed to put up their own evaluation of the program alongside the government provided data and information. This would empower them.

PAIS system should be designed for the police and courts and introduced on an experimental basis in Delhi and other

Union Territories. PAIS systems could also be designed for local roads, sewage and sanitation, drinking water supply and tested in the Union Territories. In states, PAIS would be a geographically multi-level, multi-layered system in which higher levels would present data after aggregation and integration from lower levels and layers.

There is also a need to strengthen the project monitoring and evaluation system for public programs and linking the performance and feedback with subsequent allocations of resources and continuation of programs. PAIS system for rural programs would help better action and intended benefits for the beneficiaries of the programs. This would block the corruption practices.

Vision is to strengthen the existing right to information into 'duty to publish' on the part of the government. Except for matters of strategic importance, the rest of government decision-making should be made available in the public domain, without anyone specifically asking for it, so that members of the public can act on the information and hold the government accountable.

Significant e-governance expansion is envisaged; Bharat Nirman common service kiosks would deliver a variety of government services in villages and make information available to the public. Scholarships and welfare transfers would be made initially to post office accounts and eventually to smart cards. NGOs would be funded through a portal, in a transparent manner, to help implement key schemes.

The emphasis is on institutionalizing accountability. A model Public Services Law would be legislated, in consultation with the states, to hold functionaries in health, education and rural development accountable. District level monitoring committees and ombudsmen should attend to grievance redress that would strengthen flagship schemes like NRGS, TCLC, drinking water mission, and NRHM. It will be challenging to set up better systems for food, supply chain, water, medicine, education, roads, etc. in rural areas. Smarter and improved systems will make meaningful difference to the prosperity of rural economy (News items 2009).

Unique Identity Scheme

Unique Identity (UID) scheme is initiated to create a central database and generate UID for residents primarily for *effective reach of social sector benefits to the ruralites and poor*. A UID Authority has been set up under aegis of the Planning Commission. Since its objective is to help the poor in particular to access the benefits of various government schemes with greater ease, the aim is to develop a system whereby the identity of a person could be established through just a call from a mobile phone.

"If any agency wants to confirm the identity of a person, it would have to just take the fingerprint of the person on a cell phone and send it across to a central database and receive authentication within seconds." Instead of a card, the UIDA would only provide a number to every citizen linked to a person's demographic and biometric information.

The database would be developed in partnership with the government and private agencies, such as mobile service providers, cooking gas outlets, passport offices, NREGA and PDS authorities.

The aim of the project is providing a robust system to eliminate duplicate and fake identities, apart from verification and authentication of the identity in an easy manner. The system would be developed in such a way that whenever a partner agency sends the data of an individual for registration, the central database would perform a search on key demographic and biometric attributes so that there is no duplication. Noting that the present situation of multiple databases has given individuals "an incentive" to provide different personal information to different agencies, since the mechanism for de-duplication in the UID system would ensure that the residents would have only one chance to be in the database, the individuals would provide accurate data. "The incentives for giving correct information would become especially powerful as benefits and entitlements would be linked to UID."

Rural People Empowerment

Managing changes in society effectively can prevent disparity and social tensions. The outcome approach in public administration, linking outcomes to citizens' needs and strategies will be effective to empower rural people. People empowerment develops through creating political consciousness at younger age. When people are exposed to political and social conflicts in their societies through media and interpersonal communication channels at a younger age; their minds are ready to understand the logistics of those conflicts and focus on strategies and solutions. Through such an approach, rural people will be able to choose better their political and social leaders/activists and not exploited by them.

Changing practices communicated in the right perspective would empower rural people. Technology and higher education initiatives can empower them. They together with government, NGOs, and global forces can envision and invent better future for rural India.

Narula (2008b) advocates that the empowerment of people will not occur in vacuum; we suggest the essential and important stakeholders would be governance, bureaucracy and public administration, politicians and political will. It can be strived for in conjunction with all the stakeholders. The practices have to focus on people having power to deal with the local and national issues. It highlights the primary empowerment loop for people; it is the 'Interdependent Loop' with interactions. Governance, public administration and bureaucracy of countries which empower its own people (as well as people globally) when they handle the problems effectively, and when they are transparent and accountable.

The Indian rural economy is being predicted to go stronger in future, it has become absolutely essential for the governance; public administration, bureaucracy and people themselves to be effective, transparent and accountable.

Rural people need not be silent voices any more. Narula (1984) advocates that on one hand, the dynamics of development model are awareness, knowledge, information and motivation, and these push for development. On the other hand, the discontents, demands serve the dual purpose of both pulling you away as well as pushing you for development. And much depends on how participatory communication of people and governance facilitate both these positives and negatives.

Rural people need not be the silent voices any longer. They must speak out and be heard. Awareness, Knowledge and Practice (AKP) are the keys to be heard effectively. Awareness and knowledge about political consciousness, current issues and issues needing action are best created and heard through public discourses.

Narula (2008b) suggests action should be taken according to the consensus. *Therefore, consensus building is important.* If we do not participate in this democratic process, then we are the losers and we need not complain about it. *We must vote to project our special concerns. Public discourses help in choosing the right leaders.* Thus, in rural community participation contexts people must raise the issues that impact their daily lives through public discourses. They must react and participate in the issues raised. These issues must be participated by all to take action for and against. In the restructured Panchayat all are given voice including the lowly, and without any caste and creed, and gender differentiations.

Indian development analysts have always felt that a strong informal village opinion leadership structure is necessary for development communication and now for *consensus building.* As stated in prologue, 82-83 research studies reflect its negative aspects. How this can be restructured to be of value in present context?

An informal village opinion leader differs in its role now than in earlier times. People should choose a leader who is aware of their lifestyle issues such as civic, health, education, employment, etc. of the area and their impact on people's lives in short- and long-term and well-versed with the policies pertaining to them. Such a leader must have the initiative to encourage people participation and public debates on the issues. He can only supplement the earlier information role because now new channels of communication both media and interpersonal provide information.

Horizontal links of peer group are limited in effectiveness because they contain relatively little information, authority and specific solutions. But with education, information and mass media exposure these can be improved. People can effectively share their experiences and information when communicating with others when participating in discourses and consensus building.

Participatory Communication is necessary and important in the above contexts. Narula (2006) highlights that development economists concentrate on the quality of the development process. More important is how economic growth is used to improve human capabilities and their utilization. Politics and economics are intertwined. From this perspective, a planned change of values, attitudes, and behaviors of individuals in developing countries becomes necessary. *The emphasis is on the development of human manpower to fit modernity roles*. Further, the local social structure is not just an obstacle to overcome for modernization but a context from which development activities derive their meaning and significance.

The communication practices are changing for Participatory Development and Good Governance (PDGG) model. The focus is discourses, dialogues with communities in multiple contexts. A productive, just and humane, participatory society is aimed at through democratic way of discourses and dialogues. Community voices are heard, their concerns are addressed, and solutions are found and implemented through discourses and dialogues. The chosen options and its consequences are addressed through discourses and negotiated through dialogues and multilogues of various stakeholders involved. This is the positive approach to participatory communication.

The changing communication practices that are emerging are the three participation approaches: dialogue strategies, discourse techniques, and consequential approach. These will facilitate in organizing the content. People's voices based on their experiences provide the content, active participation of silent majority of people, and their efforts to choose the right leader further facilitate the participation.

Currently, in 2000 decades, more and more ruralites are experiencing the urgent need to take positive approach to participatory communication as government is making all development demand driven and facilitating its delivery on P4 model. Private and Public sector and NGOs, the three components of the P4 model are implementing 'Participatory Development and Good Governance (PDGG) model'; and people—the fourth component must be fully engaged with them. The emerging social practices and with best fit with the rural society is likely to empower them more and more by improving their quality of life.

Future Scenario Envisioned

Scenario planning is preparing responses to imagined changes in conditions; it is not about predicting the future. It is a tool for learning. Earlier planning during the downturn allows them to move quickly when the time for action comes. Scenario planning can be used to plot potential responses to business upturn.

We envision scenario planning for India's rural economy. Rural economy is confronting ongoing array of challenges as discussed; to come to at par with the mainstream urban economy and to participate fully in national economy development. It has to develop unique economic strength by following the Paradigm shift 1: focusing on people's efforts; Paradigm shift 2: focusing on PPP and P4 models; and Paradigm shift 3: focusing on government's efforts to meet the challenges of boosting rural economy.

Envision a future communication scenario in 2000 decades where rural telecoms are being set up. Cyber-schools are set up for computer literacy, training and e-commerce in the villages and for low-income group people. Women are being trained in Internet working technology. They are using satellite technology to disseminate critical knowledge. Many websites are put up for e-commerce of arts and crafts; for information, knowledge and entertainment for youths and teenagers.

People are making tremendous efforts for e-readiness. In fact, they are leap-froging in ICTs applications for development and self-reliance for socially and economically deprived segments of the society with the economic aid from many international organizations. On the other hand, educated groups, though comparatively much ahead in communication consumption also leap-frog by using the update communication applications, products and services, and supporting and facilitating the efforts of the unexposed segment. This scenario was different a decade back, when people were exposed to mostly traditional interpersonal communication channels and a smaller percentage of the population was exposed to other conventional media such as radio and television. The current rural scenario whether banking, markets, business product growth, agro growth, and technology use are all pointers to leapfrog growth in many fields especially technology, cell phone and TV.

People around the world are making demands and efforts to leap frog in communication technologies and its applications in rural India. Such efforts are resulting in changed communication scenarios, innovations and innovative applications of the old and new technologies for changing people's aspirations and demands with new ways to deal with communication issues that are arising overtime; through different communication plans, strategies, models and channels. How ruralites deal with it makes significant differences to their lives. Self-initiative makes difference in how communication channels are utilized.

Envision a changing work ethic and life style scenario in 2000 decades. It will be equally challenging for people to envision what their future world could be and to change their mindset to work towards achieving that vision. It will be the unique perspective about what their world could be that can change the stagnant systems and stagnating or low rural economy.

Envision about rural integrated transformation. We are aware of the fact that peri-urban people are migrants from rural areas. Do we envision bringing them back to rural roots with a promise and future of better quality of life? Or we let them be at peri-urban where they have assumed a significant role in development of urban economy by contributing through tertiary services? If second is the option then we must focus on social sector programs to give them quality of life. Better education, employability, skill development, sanitation and hygiene, healthcare, housing, and social security schemes should benefit them also.

Discussions throughout the book on the dynamics of rural economy—the factors, the plans, programs, attitude and behavior of village community and various other stakeholders highlight the low level of rural economy, high resource spending by government for uplifting the economy, the discontent and dissatisfaction of various stakeholders in the past decades.

These discussion-analyses are also pointer to the fact that lack of experienced development administrators, lackadaisical attitude in handling the implementation of such schemes and negligible involvement of local community and impediments of caste and creed at the local level hindered the expected development and success of those plans and programs till 2000.

Further, these discussions-analyses point that government, industries and other stakeholders have redressed this problematic issue by total community participation by: (i) sensitizing them to demand driven development programs; (ii) active and timely implementation of those programs; (iii) checks and balances on corrupt practices on delivery of these programs intended for them; whether it is the doctor not attending the rural clinic, or the school teacher being absent, or medicines disappearing from the clinics; (iv) or even when political activists craving for their own vested interests nullify the benefits in land compensations and job training offered by the industry/business entrepreneurs who plan to acquire their lands. Thus, monetary benefits and job opportunities may delude them.

We do notice change since 2000 in rural communities' attitude and behavior in handling these issues and participating in P4 model.

The odds are ruralites will be growing now and so will be rural economy. They are no longer complaining though discontented, rather they demand and are taking actions; and are sensitized to a better quality of life. Government is getting aware of the fact that rural economy must grow and integrate with mainstream national economy for better GDP growth. Government's realization that, a large rural work force should be dividend to rural economy and also for India's national economy; both will let India grow as global power. Businesses are fast realizing that bottom of pyramid means more volume and money in business and expanded opportunities for social corporate responsibilities. NGOs can be active in creating more business for themselves, active IEC campaigns in diverse fields and for philanthropy.

If these trends remain consistent overtime; rural economy will grow and so will be rural people. We do expect rural economy to grow fast in the next two decades.

Appendices

Appendix 1. Rural Communication Models

Coding Key for Figure 1.1: Indian Development Decades

Gandhian Metamodel	GMM
Etawah Project	EP
Nilokheri Experiment	NE
Community Development	CD
Panchayat Raj	PR
Cooperatives	COOP
New Paradigm	NP
Dominant Paradigm	DP
Agriculture Extension Model	AEM
Administrative Decentralization	AD
Basic Minimum Need Model	BMN
Extension Model	EM
Diffusion Model	DIM
Integrated Development Model	IDM
Multidisciplinary Approach at Local Level	MAL
Operationally Integrated Strategy	OIS
Block Plans	BP

(Broken lines denote a period in which a subsequently revived model was dormant.)

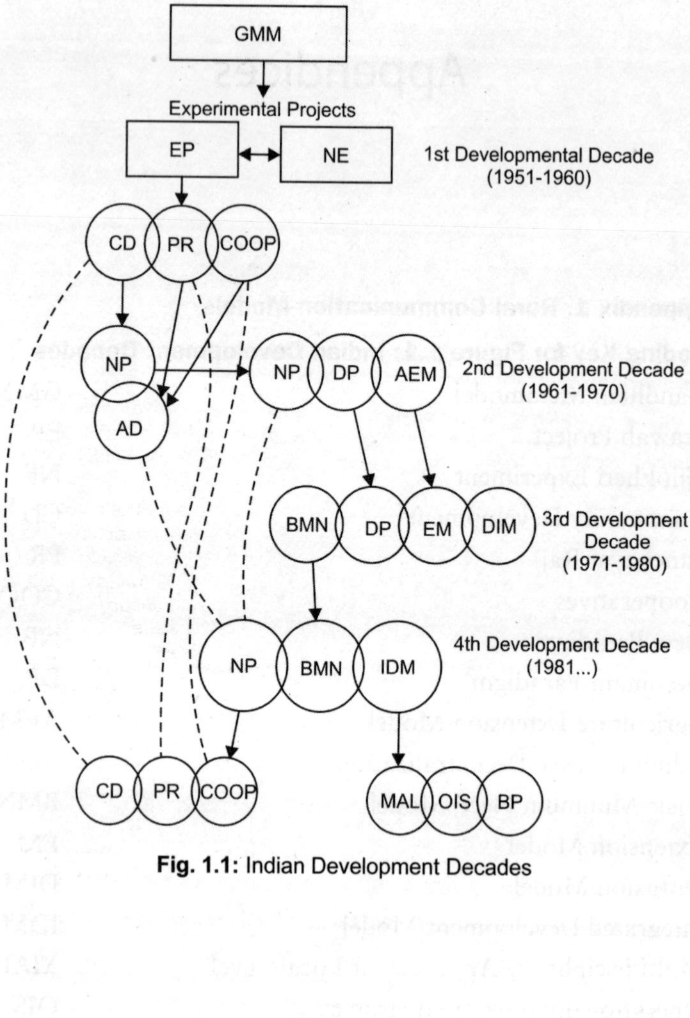

Fig. 1.1: Indian Development Decades

Fatalism	Characteristics Perceived as Problems	Government Intentions	Development Efforts	Actual Effects
Contented	Yes	Improved quality of life	Motivate (*e.g.*, create discontent-ment with things as they are)	Discontent
Dependent	No	–	–	Dependent on the government rather than on fate, land-lords, or social hierarchy
Unaware of innovations	Yes	Inform	Educate	Aware of innovations
Exploited	Yes	Emancipate	Legislate protect policies; inform people of rights	Well informed of personal rights; attitude of having been victimized and now entitled to unearned benefits. Government offered itself as paternalistic; to the extent development communication is successful; people take the role of clients.
Participation limited to the local social hierarchy	Yes	Develop self-awareness as an individual with rights and powers	Intrude into existing hierarchies with radio, TV, and personal linking individuals to the government	Learned dependency; participation consists of accepting things offered as owed, and of complaining: (i.e., "informing the government that it is not doing its job well enough.")

Fig. 1.1 a: Villageism Efforts

Gandhi Meta Model is Gandhian concept of 'sarvodoya'—describes a democratic socialist pattern of economics and institutions suited to the conditions, needs and realities of Indian society. It emphasized rural reconstruction rather than heavy urban industrialization and rather than specific economic indicators it established as its goal a just social and political order devoid of exploitation.

Gandhian plan is based on his concept of 'villageism'. In practice, this was an attempt to produce powerful village communities by initiating participatory communication, developing self-reliant village republics in the form of Panchayats, enforcing of land ownership and encouraging the development of rural industries providing employment.

Model 1.2 based on the researches done in 60s to 70s shows that development communication patterns have changed over the past 20 year due to developmental efforts. This model emphasizes the central role of local leadership who expresses development demands and imposes sanctions. Secondly, masses discontent was focused on communication strategies of the government and perceived government planning as irrelevant for them. The processes of development communication have made the social environment of the villages more complex than they were. They were deeply enmeshed in traditional social patterns and were resistance to change and modernization. The masses have to be made aware of a problematic familiar condition. They have to be informed about a new practice that would solve the problem and they were urged to accept it.

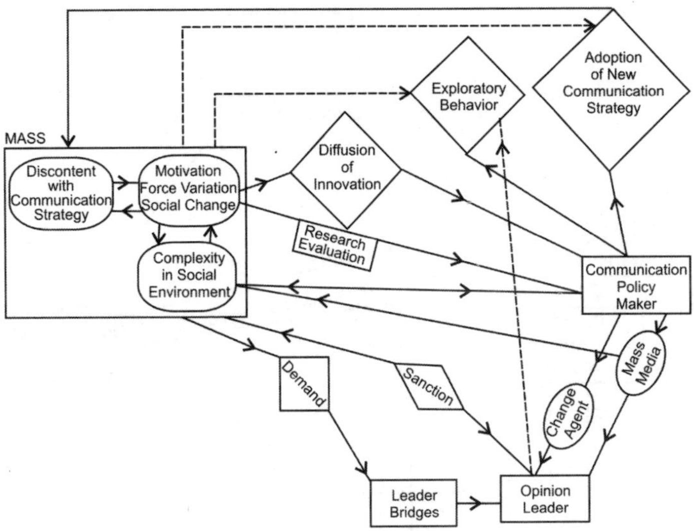

Fig. 1.2: Model of Development

Model 1.3 based on the researches done in 80s highlight the changes in the development attitudes. Researches reveal masses are aware of developmental needs and projects, and are discontented because their demands have not been met. They have moved from earlier belief that government has no concern and interest in their economic and social conditions to a perception of the government as a failed provider of goods and services (this persists). They are more knowledgeable about development bureaucracy and have a much improved notion as which communication channels ought to be useful to them. The resistance to change is less and attitude towards modernization has improved. Now the masses are aware of the existing problematic conditions, and the new practices to solve them. Now the diffusion is needed to make masses adopt the new practices with which they are already familiar.

Both the models highlight that masses do not display high level of active participation from 60s to 80s; and the prevailing passive participation is a major threat to the goal of self-sustaining development.

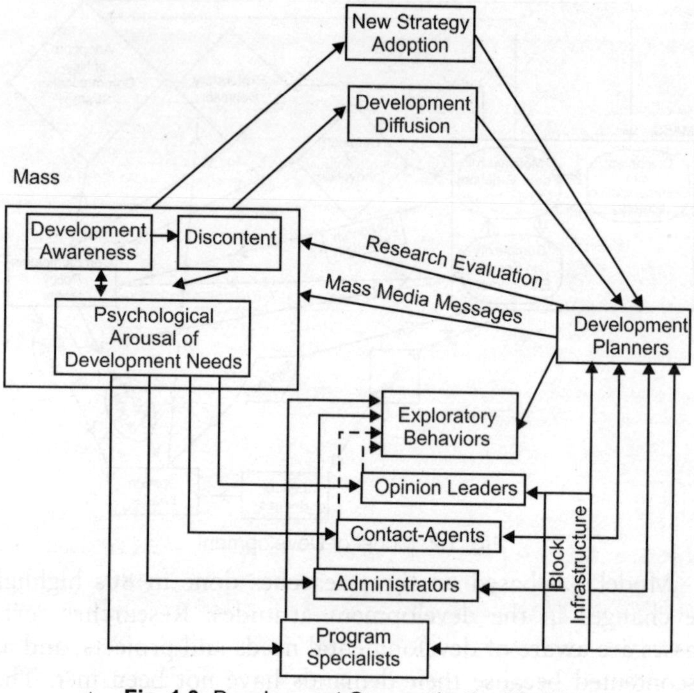

Fig. 1.3: Development Communication Model

Urbanization → Literacy → Economic and Political Participation

↘ ↙

Mass Media Exposure

Fig. 1.4: Lerner's Model of Modernization

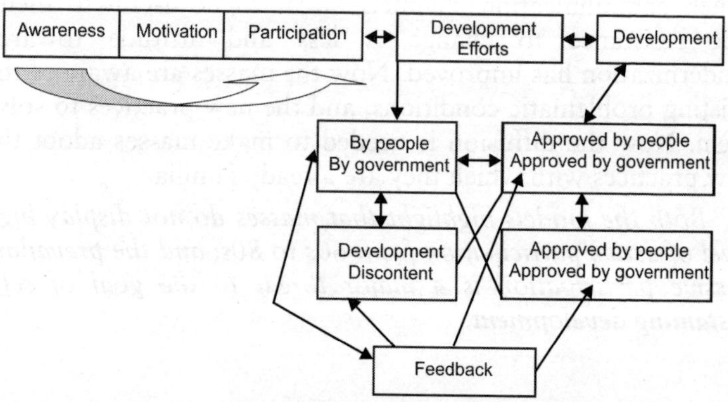

Fig. 1.5: Rogers diffusion of innovations Model

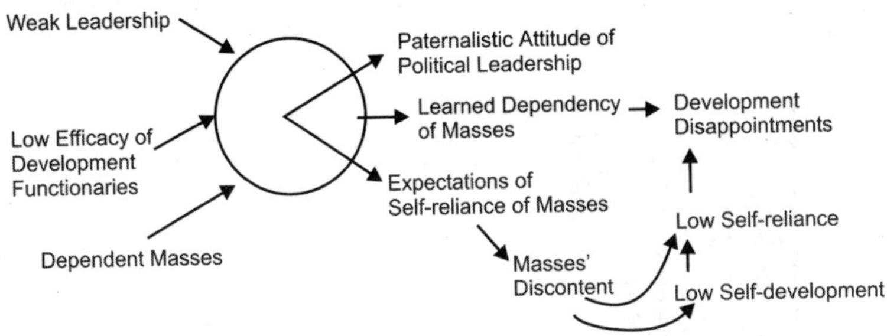

Fig. 1.6: Dysfunctional Factors in Development

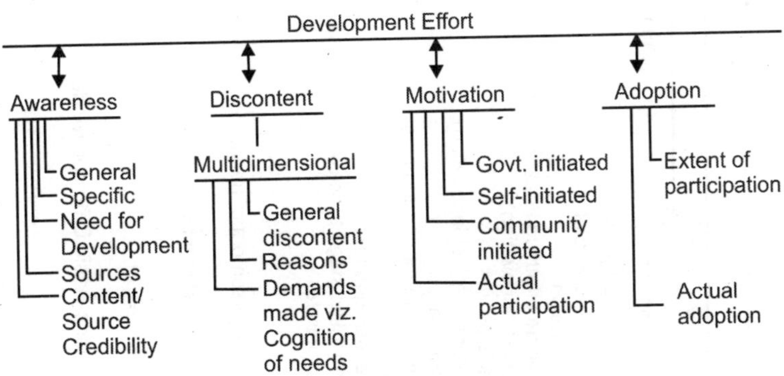

Fig. 1.7: Development Efforts

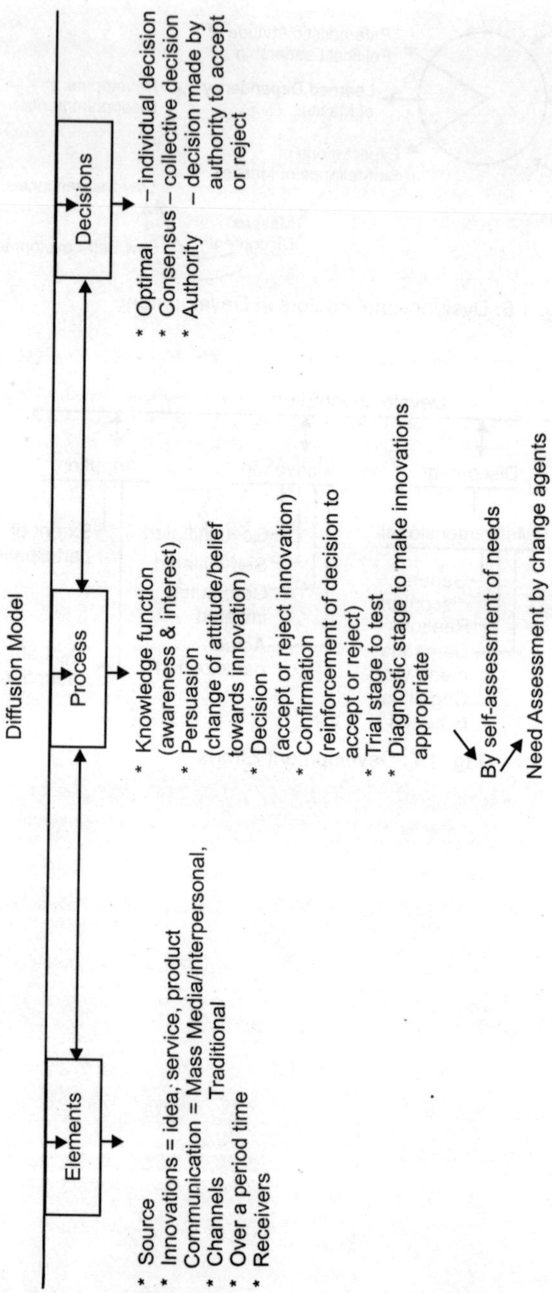

Fig. 1.8: Roger's Basic Diffusion Model

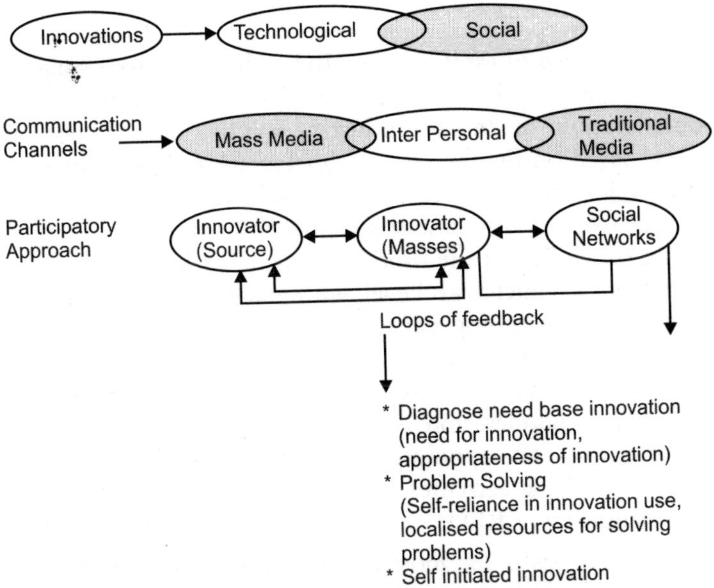

Fig. 1.9: Diffusion—A Communication Strategy for Development

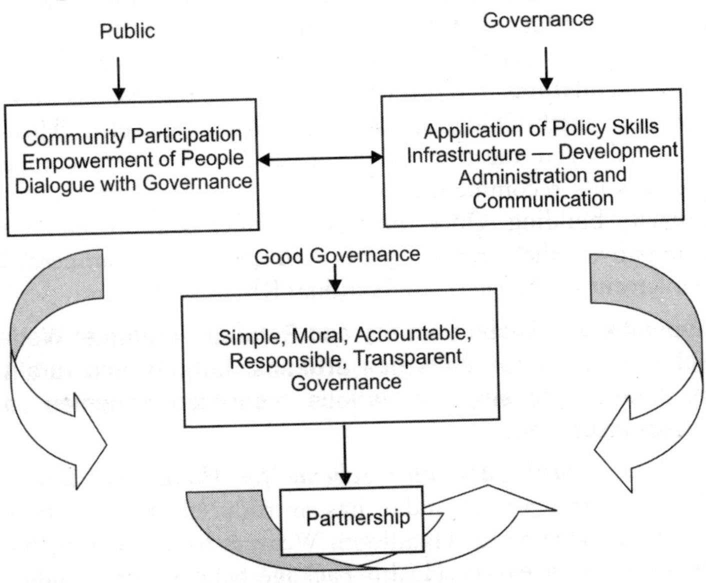

Fig. 1.10: Development Dialogue Strategies

Appendix 2: Process of Establishing Rural Business Hubs—RBH

The process of establishing RBH is divided into 6 stages. In the first stage, the Ministry of Panchayati Raj and the Confederation of Indian Industry, jointly identify potential RBHs, based on the interest of panchayats and companies and the profile of the products. It is followed by a process of dialogue—screening—assessment, which finally culminates into signing of MoUs. At the time of MoU, a Task Force is formed at the Block Panchayat Level with participation of different stakeholders, including various government agencies involved in area developmental activities. The Task Force provides backward linkages, monitors the project and ensures active support and cooperation of local villages. The task force is supported by an appointed Facilitator, whose role is to coordinate all the activities at the local level, to ensure smooth implementation of RBH.

Gap analysis is the most important activity in RBH which is aimed to provide value addition to make products nationally and internationally acceptable. In the next step, the samples of the agro-produce and products are collected by the company, which does detailed analysis and comes out with its recommendations in terms of raw materials usages, technology, process, methodologies, design, packaging, etc. This is followed by a meeting of the Task Force, where company presents it's recommendations and future course of action for capacity building. Once the final product is approved by the Company, the RBH starts functioning commercially. Implementing Agencies are National RBH Councils.

Appendix 3A. Social Security and Related Programs: Welfare Schemes for rural industries artisans, farmers and ruralites in general focusing on various insurance schemes, and health insurance.

New Health Insurance Scheme for Handloom Weavers: The Government of India has introduced a New Health Insurance Scheme for Handloom Weavers from the year 2005-06 in place of earlier Health Package Scheme for Handloom Weavers. Under the Scheme, the total premium payable to the insurance company would be Rs. 1000/- per weaver per annum. Out of this, Rs. 800 will be Government of India's contribution and Rs. 200 will be weavers' contribution. In Tamil Nadu, the weavers' contribution of Rs. 200 is being paid by the State Government. Under this scheme, the weaver's family of four can avail of the medical treatment in any one of the empanelled hospitals and nursing homes in various districts throughout the State without actually having to pay for the medical treatment up to a maximum of Rs. 15,000/- per annum. In the year 2007-08, a sum of Rs. 1.00 crore has been allotted as state share towards premium payable for the existing beneficiaries. In the year 2008-09, an addition of 5000 new members will be enrolled in this scheme at a cost of Rs. 1.60 crore.

The Co-operative Handloom Weavers' Savings & Security Scheme to encourage the saving habit among handloom weavers. This scheme is being implemented by the State Government since 1975. From the year 1985-86, the Government of India is also participating in the scheme and contributing its share as part of the Central Thrift Fund Scheme. Under this scheme, while a weaver-member contributes 8 paise pér rupee of wages earned, the State Government contributes 4 paise per Rupee of wages and Government of India contributes 4 paise as matching contribution under Central Thrift Fund Scheme. Thus, 16 paise per rupee is deposited in the Government account for which the State Government allows 9.5% interest. Out of the 9.5% interest, 6.5% is credited to Weaver-members' account and the remaining 3% is used for implementing the Old Age Pension Scheme and Family Pension Scheme for handloom weavers. A sum of Rs. 4 crore has been allocated for the year 2007-08 and the scheme will be continued in the year 2008-09 at a cost of Rs. 4.25 crore.

The various *welfare schemes* proposed to be implemented in the Palm Board Sector during the Eleventh Five-Year Plan are distribution of tools and equipments for processing of Neera, opening of Sales outlets with infrastructure facilities, training for artisans to improve the quality of the palm products, provision of margin money and interest subsidy for state federation and district federations.

3B. Healthcare Technology: EDPS 2000 Software

The Early Detection & Prevention System (EDPS 2000) is a software system developed by Dr. Abraham George, the founder of The George Foundation, a non-profit trust. It can provide early diagnosis of patient's health status. EDPS 2000 screens patients and identifies those who need prompt attention by qualified physicians, while recommending treatment for others with minor illnesses.

It provides a probable diagnosis of disease conditions based on the complaints narrated by the patient along with the results of a few relevant laboratory tests and the patient's medical history. It must be understood that this software does not aim to give a confirmatory diagnosis in most cases, but only a probable diagnosis. Several conditions are supported by laboratory tests, which in turn, may enable the user to make a confirmatory diagnosis. It should, therefore, be seen only as a first line of intervention whereby the patient, equipped with a probable diagnosis, can then go on to the next level, like referral to a specialist, when required. Several minor or common illnesses will be treated at this level on instructions given by the software.

As of now, the diseases covered by EDPS 2000 are based on the common disease patterns seen in South India. This lists approximately 300 diseases presently covered by the software. A special team from both India and the United States has designed this software over the past two years, and The George Foundation has exclusive license to use in selected areas in rural India. The system is being maintained and enhanced under license by eMedexOnline LLC, a U.S. based company. It has been extensively tested with over 10,000 patients in three leading hospitals in Bangalore for accuracy and acceptance by both the user and the patient. Another aspect of the EDPS software is maintaining a database of doctors and hospitals/clinics to which referrals are made.

The EDPS 2000 software has been designed to be extremely user friendly. Persons involved in primary health care in remote, rural and backward areas will be able to use it easily. The basic qualifications expected of a person who will use this software are knowledge of English, a simple understanding of computers, and a strong motivation and aptitude for primary healthcare. It does not require someone with a medical degree or even formally trained health workers and nurses. Users will undergo specific training to use the software, and will have extensive hands-on training before they are allowed to use it in the field.

There are two main persons involved in the use of this software: the patient and the interviewer (computer user). The software will prompt the interviewer with the questions to ask. The software will keep on evaluating the answers and posing new questions until it has narrowed the list of possibilities down to a probable diagnosis or a future course of action. The interviewer is, therefore, passive in this process. This feature has been incorporated by design to minimize the medical knowledge expected of the interviewer. For cases referred to specialists or hospitals, the interviewer is responsible for following up and making sure that the paperwork, diagnosis, and results of lab tests are entered into the computer to maintain the full and up-to-date medical history.

EDPS 2000 shall assist the technician in maintaining, in a protected and confidential manner, the medical history of all patients, in suggesting tests to perform, and to evaluate possible causes based on the symptoms displayed or the description given by the patient. It will also incorporate the medical history in making the probable diagnosis. In addition, based on this diagnosis, it will also prescribe medicines for minor illnesses, which will be sold at cost by the PHC. In cases of probable major illnesses or when the diagnosis is not clear, the computer output will propose a future course of action—further tests and possibly a visit to a specialist. In the latter case, the computer will print out the patient's relevant and essential history that can be taken to the specialist. We anticipate that the majority of cases will be handled at the level of PHCs, thus drastically cutting down the burden placed on hospitals and doctors.

Each PHC will have a full time staff consisting of a paramedic individual to perform initial screening with the computer, a trained nurse or physicians' assistant, and a laboratory technician. We anticipate that a qualified medical doctor will be shared between 3-5 PHCs in a given area. Training of this staff in the novel technology and in the holistic approach should be extensive and continuous, and their performance should be monitored continuously.

Patients visiting PHCs will also be provided health education by the staff through posters and through audio-visual demonstrations. Providing information and help with family planning, and awareness on communicable diseases, will be a key role of the staff. Community programs for which we shall form collaborations with NGOs and social workers will supplement these activities.

At present, we envisage each PHC to be an isolated unit. All software updates and sharing of information would have to be uploaded/downloaded periodically by a person traveling from center to center. We plan to connect each PHC to its assigned doctor through wireless communications and a palm computer. Over a three-year time frame, we propose to connect the computers at different PHCs through standard telephone and/or cell phone link to a central coordination and support center. Thus, ***enhance the capability of PHC through technology.***

Rural India faces many serious problems. Notable amongst them are potable water, emerging pandemics, population control, good hygiene and sanitation practices, basic education, and simple techniques for improving their crops and lives. One cannot expect to upgrade the people's health without simultaneously making an impact on these issues, and vice versa. The staff at the PHCs should be trained and empowered to spread awareness on some of these issues, build trust within the community, and to take a holistic approach to health care.

Using the telephone link to the central facility, relevant training and educational material and specific health

instructions will be periodically transmitted to the computers at all PHCs and the status of various educational programs need be monitored.

For the PHCs to be effective, people have to believe that the PHCs are there to serve them and to provide value. To facilitate this, the local population in the operation and in the community outreach programs should be involved. We also plan to encourage cultural activities, self-help programs, and health education through the PHCs. The monitoring role of The George Foundation will be to evaluate the performance of PHCs and to provide guidance. Evaluation will be based on one simple criterion—whether the PHCs have significantly improved the health and well-being of the community.

(Suggestions based on The George Foundation, a non-profit trust based in proposed plan for improving rural health care through technology.)

Appendix 4: Telecommunications in India

Table: Growth of telephones over the years

(in million)

March 06, Fixed lines 40.23, CDMA 32.67, GSM 69.19, Wireless (CDMA & GSM) 101.86

March 07, Fixed lines 40.77 CDMA 44.62, GSM 120.47 Wireless (CDMA & GSM) 165.09

March 08, Fixed lines 39.41 CDMA 68.38, GSM 192.70, Wireless (CDMA & GSM) 261.08

Feb 09, Fixed lines 37.73 CDMA 92.14, GSM 283.98, Wireless (CDMA & GSM) 376.12

Gross Total 142.09 205.86 300.49 413.85

Annual growth (%)* 44 45 46 37.72

Facts and figures about telephone in India in 2009

Telephony Subscribers (Wireless and Landline): 452.91 million (May 2009).

Cell phones: 415.25 million (May 2009) Land Lines: 37.75 million (Jan 2009)

Yearly Cell phone Addition: 113.26 million (2007), Monthly Cell phone Addition: 15.41 million (Jan 2009)

Tele-density: 38.88% (May 2009) Projected tele density: 626 million, 46% of population by 2010.

(*Source*: Department of Telecommunications)

Telecom Technologies: After formation of Telecom Commission in 1989 and with the start of economic liberalization in 1991, C-DoT had taken a decision to induct a few more technologies particularly for large Digital Switches with state-of-the-art features available internationally with a proviso that the equipment are produced indigenously and only indigenously manufactured equipment was to be procured by C-DoT.

The period 1991-92 exhibited increase in the volume of traffic and thus the need was felt to induct high capacity telephone exchanges and accordingly, DoT had short-listed six technologies developed by Siemens, Ericsson, AT&T, Fujitsu, NEC and Alcatel. As procurement was to be made from the indigenous companies, except NEC all these companies had set up their manufacturing bases in India either directly or through technology tie up with Indian companies. Transfer of technology did not include the software portion including transfer of source code. But because of intensive trainings and experiences, ITI and HTL as manufacturers and DoT as service provider with in-house training program, managed to acquire adequate skills in operating and maintenance of these systems. Still, the software level maintenance support, remained with the technology providers.

During the period 1995 to 2000, both on account of growth in private sector telecom operations as well as deployment of newer technologies, MTNL and BSNL have also followed the trend and in their tenders, the clause "Indian manufacturers" was amended to "Indian manufacturers/ suppliers". This led to a situation where the procurement was made from Indian suppliers who were just importing and supplying the equipment to these PSUs. On the other hand, the private telecom operators have been importing directly from foreign suppliers. With the change in telecom product requirements from fixed line switch to GSM/CDMA, the Indian manufacturers (mainly C-DoT) could not keep pace with the changing technology resulting into stoppage/closure of manufacturing units whereas, MNCs who had the technologies, preferred to do trading than technology transfer to India.

Additionally, with a view to meeting emerging demand in 90s, large capacities were created for PIJF Cables and Optic Fiber Cables both in public as well as private sector. One of the companies has also setup integrated manufacturing plant for manufacture of Optic Fiber from raw material stage and managed to export fiber even to Europe and USA.

IIT, Chennai developed core-DECT technology for providing access through Wireless in Local Loop. After successful evaluation, the technology has been inducted in BSNL/MTNL networks. For manufacture of equipment, IIT through Midas Communication transferred the technology to 2-3 indigenous manufacturers. Some individual efforts have also resulted in development of indigenous technologies viz. Tejas in Bangalore is stated to have developed DLC and STM transmission technologies. However, the fact is that none of the manufacturing units could migrate to GSM and CDMA equipment being used now extensively in Indian Telecom network.

Telecom Manufacturing

A growing number of telecom companies have set up manufacturing facilities for the production of mobile phones and other telecom equipment to cater to India's growing telecom market and exports to. Nokia's plant, located in a Special Economic Zone (SEZ) at Sriperumbudur near Chennai, manufactures mobile handsets and network infrastructure equipment including base stations. Nokia's plant produces 8 million handsets a month. Other telecom equipment manufacturers already have or are in the process of setting up production facilities in the same zone. These include Aspocomp Group (HDI printed circuit boards), Perlos (handset mechanics/moldings), Salcomp (mobile phone chargers),

Motorola (mobile handsets), Foxconn (mobile phones), Flextronics (mobile handsets, base stations and other electronic items), Sanmina-SCI (network components), Jabil, Laird (antennas, battery packs and EMI shielding products) and Wintek. Elcoteq's telecom plant located near Bangalore manufactures handsets among others. Samsung Electronics' mobile handset plant is located in Gurgaon, near Delhi. Alcatel and Ericsson manufacture base station and mobile switching equipment at plants located in Rae Bareli and Jaipur respectively. BPL Telecom manufactures GSM phones and LG Electronics India produces GSM phones in a plant near Pune. Kolkata based Xenitis Group plans to set up a mobile phone manufacturing facility located near Kolkata.

Until recently, only the PSU's BSNL and MTNL were allowed to provide Basic Phone Service through copper wires in India. MTNL is operating in Delhi and Mumbai only and all other parts are covered by BSNL. However, private operators have now entered the fray, although their focus is largely on the cellular business which is growing rapidly. Mobile handsets account for 26% of the total telecom equipment industry in India. The lion's share was held by the carrier equipment business while the enterprise equipment segment accounted for the remaining 14%. The market size of the telecom equipment industry has grown to Rs. 954 crore (US $22 bn) by 2009.

Appendix 5: The 'Loop Model' and Interconnected Interactions

The 'Loop Model' comprises of people, businesses, governance and political will as primary components and the learned dependency of people, think tank, as support for policies and market forces are the major dimensions of this model. It interconnects its primary components through interactions. The essential nodes in this loop are People, Businesses, Governance, and Political Will. All nodes are important and facilitate each other; therefore, for real empowerment, it is important they should be in tandem with each other and are on good wavelength for understanding. The forces that can pull them apart or bring them close are 'Learned dependency' and market forces.

This is the primary empowerment loop. The government and the politicians draw their implied empowerment from the people and the businesses but for explicit empowerment, they need a 'Think Tank' of civil society for policy making as well policy implementations in various domains. The objective research analysis and observations of the think tank should provide that input to the government and the politicians to act upon. The think tank will be independent of the primary empowerment loop but part of the secondary loop in which governance, politicians, and the civil society are the primary nodes and the policies in various domains are the forces to pull them together. The people and governance are connected by this loop to primary loop.

The other secondary loop that businesses need develop to empower people is to develop special segments consumer markets. They would follow Business Models for Rural Markets, Co-Creation Business Model for Poor and Bottom of the Pyramid Model; and Microfinance Practices. The businesses and the people from special segment consumer markets are the primary nodes. The various business models for these segments will empower each other.

The interconnection of the two secondary loops to the basic primary loop and interactions among the various nodes in the primary and secondary loops will give real empowerment to the people through governance, businesses and politicians. These are the positive approaches to participatory communication.

Appendix 6: Energy

India's energy supply is inadequate to meet the demand arising from dynamic economic growth. Energy consumption is rising by between 9 and 12 per cent per year. Some of the power generating plants are obsolete and the state utilities are operating at a loss, thus imposing a further burden on the national budget. Power stations are fired by low-grade coal and achieve a very poor level of efficiency. India is now the fifth largest carbon dioxide emitter in the world and is playing an increasingly large part in the international oil market. A stable, environmentally sound energy supply is a basic precondition for sustainable economic growth in India and for global climate protection. The important issues include energy efficiency, renewables, emissions trading, and the Clean Development Mechanism (CDM).

Improving efficiency in the generation, transmission and consumption of power is therefore an important objective. The use of renewables (hydropower, wind energy, solar energy, and biomass) is seen as particularly important. Support is also accorded to programs that help reform the structures of the energy sector.

Bibliography

Alagh, Yoginder K. *Panchyati Raj and Planning in India: Participatory Institutions and Rural Roads*. Presentation at Asian Institute of Transport Development, 2007, New Delhi.

Aspen Institute's Roundable on Community Change. *Our Shared Fate: Bridging the Rural-Urban Divide Creates New Opportunities for Prosperity and Equity*. A report October 2008.

Bindé, J. (ed.). *The Future of Values*, Oxford/New York, Berghahn Books, 2006.

Bremer, Ian. *The J. Curve,* Simon and Schuster, New York, 2006.

Christensen, Clayton. Interview with *Economic Times* Mumbai edition (2006, 2008).

Christopher, Marquis et al. *The Geography of Corporate Giving,* 2005.

Conference *Hindustan Times Leadership Summit*, New Delhi, India, Nov., 2006, 2008, 2009.

Conference of Chief Secretaries on *Public-Private Partnership*, New Delhi, Oct. 2007.

Conference on *Digital Learning India 2006, e-Learning in India: Vision 2010,* egov India 2006 and Indian Telecenter Forum, New Delhi, India, 23-25 August, 2006.

Conference on *Infrastructure Development Private Investment*, New Delhi, Oct. 2007.

Deployment in Developing Countries—Role of Markets and Institution, 2008.

Dhanendra Kumar. *Rural Telecommunications Reform in India*, Secretary Telecom Commission, Government of India, 2007.

Diamond, Jared. *Collapse: How Societies Choose to Fail or Succeed.* Viking, New York, 2004.

Douglas F. Barnes. *The Challenge of Rural Electrification: Strategies for Developing Countries*, Resources for future groups, 2008.

Dussani, Rafiq (ed.). *Telecommunication Reforms in India.* Quorum Books, Connecticut, 2007.

Easterbrook, Cregg. *The Progress Paradox: How Life Gets Better While People Feel Worse,* Random House, New York, 2003.

Economic Survey 2008-09, Government of India, New Delhi.

Economic Survey 2010, Government of India, New Delhi.

Fluharty, Charles. *The Great Beyond: Developing Stronger and More Equitable Rural Policies*, Presentation Texas Conference of Rural and Community Hospitals, Dallas, TX, April 15, 2009.

Frankel Francine, Zoya Hassan et al. eds. *Transforming India—Social and Political Dynamics of Democracy*, Oxford University Press, New Delhi, 2000.

Gasmi, F. and Virto, L.R. *Telecommunications Technologies Deployment in Developing Countries—Role of Markets and Institution, 2008.*

3G World Focus 2007 by Mobile Communications International.

Hanson, J. and Narula, Uma. *New Communication Technologies in Developing Countries,* Lawrence Erlbaum Associates, New Jersey, 1990.

Indira Purushottaman and Shukla. *NCAER Survey*, Economic Times, Feb. 2008.

Inkles Alex and D.H. Smith. *Becoming Modern: Individual Change in Six Developing Countries,* Cambridge: Mass Harvard University Press, 1974.

International Copper Promotion Council India, *Rural Electrification Program*, India Copper Forum, 2007.

ITP Division, Ministry of External Affairs, GOI, *India in Business,* Indianbusiness.nic.in.

Jennifer Keller. *Rural Broadband: A RUPRI Policy Brief* rupri.org December, 2008.

Kapila, Uma et al. *Changing Contours of Asian Agriculture: Policies, Performances and Challenges,* Academic Foundation, New Delhi, 2009.

Kellogg Foundation. *Entrepreneurship Development Systems in Rural America,* Project 2008.

Lerner Daniel 1958. *The Passing of Traditional Society: Modernizing the Middle East.* New York, Free Press.

Lodge, George. *A Corporate Solution to Global Poverty: How Multinationals can Help the Poor and Invigorate their Own Legitimacy*, Princeton University Press, 2006.

Madaswamy, Moni, Mohan Rao, Durai and Sikdar Jain. *Impact of Economic Reforms on Indian Agricultural Sector: Application of Geomatic Technology to Reduce Marginalization and Vulnerability of Small Farmers in India,* Agricultural Informatics Division, National Informatics Center, Ministry of Information Technology, New Delhi, 2009.

Ministry of Rural Development *Bringing Sustainability to Drinking Water Systems in Rural India*, New Delhi, 2007.

Ministry of Rural Development. *Rural Housing in India—Problems and Prospects*, New Delhi, 2000.

Mulay Sumati and Uma Narula. *Satiation in Family Planning Message Receptivity,* Indian Institute of Mass Communication, New Delhi, 1972.

Narayan, Deepa and Patti Petesch (eds.). *Voices of the Poor: From Many Lands,* World Bank, Oxford University Press, January, 2001.

Narayan, Deepa, Patel, Schafft, et al. *Voices of the Poor: Can Anyone Hear Us?* World Bank, Oxford University Press, 2000.

Narula, Uma and Pearce, W. (eds.). *Culture, Politics and Research Programs*. Lawrence Erlbaum, New Jersey, 1990.

Narula, Uma and Pearce, W. *Development as Communication: A perspective on India*, Southern Illinois University Press, Carbondale, 1986.

Narula, Uma. *Development Communications,* Haranand Publishers, New Delhi, 1999.

——. *Let Us Do It Ourselves*, Mimeo. World Bank, 2000.

——. *Technology Revisited: India Case Study*, Mimeo, 2003.

——. *Indian Economy: Visions and Reality,* Atlantic Publishers, New Delhi, 2006a.

——. *Business Practices: Modern Trends,* Atlantic Publishers, New Delhi, 2006b.

——. *Handbook of Communication Models, Perspectives, Strategies.* Atlantic Publishers, New Delhi, 2006c.

——. *Global Empowerment: Emerging Practices.* Atlantic Publishers, New Delhi, 2008a.

——. *Globalization: People Empowerment Practices.* Atlantic Publishers, New Delhi, 2008b.

——. Dynamics of Development Communication: Awareness, Motivation and Participation Ph.D. Dissertation, University of Massachusetts Amherst, 1984.

Nilkeni, Nandan. *Imagining India*. Penguin, New Delhi, 2009.

Nye, Joseph. *Soft Power: The Means to Success in World Politics*. Public Affairs, New York, 2004.

Pardeshi, Geeta. *Primary Health Care in India—An Ideal Approach*, Asian Health Management, 2008.

Patel, Neesha. *Evaluating the Role of Primary Health Centers in India*, Express Health Care Management, 16-31 August, 2005.

Prahlad, C.K. (2004b). *The Fortune at the Bottom of the Pyramid: Eradicating Poverty through Profit.* Wharton School Publishing, Upper Saddle River, New Jersey.

Prahlad, C.K. (2005a). *Bringing Down the Digital Divide: How Mobile Communications will Underpin the Economic Uplift of the World's Aspiring Poor.*

Ramana Murthy, M.V. *Mobile based Primary Health Care System for Rural India,* Mobile Computing and Wireless Networks, CDAC, Bangalore.

Rao, Manmohan. *Digital Asia Pacific Review Reports.*

Report. *Empowering the Next Generation: Youth in the Developing World Development Gateway,* 2006.

Rogers, Everett M. and F.F. Shoemaker. *Communication of Innovations: A Cross Cultural Approach,* Beverley Hill, Sage, 1971.

Rogers, Everett M. *Communication and Development: Critical Perspectives*, Beverley Hill, Sage, 1976.

——. *Diffusion of Innovations* 3rd ed., New York, Free Press, 1983.

RUPRI.org *RUPRI Center for Rural Entrepreneurship.*

Rural Health Care System in India—The Structure and Current Scenario, Ministry of Health *mohfw.nic.in/*Rural, New Delhi, 2007.

Sachs, Jeffrey. *The End of Poverty*: *How We can Make It Happen in Our Lifetime,* 2006.

Scherer, F.M. *New Perspectives on Economic Growth and Technological Innovations,* 1999.

Schoolnet Research. *Enhancing Human Capital Index: New Approaches for the Knowledge Economy.* Education background paper presented at the GIIC Conference, New Delhi, 14-15, March 2002.

Sciadas, G. *Monitoring the Digital Divide and Beyond.* Paper presented at the "Digital Bridges" Conference (International Telecommunication Union, Busan, Republic of Korea), 10–11 September, 2004.

Seminar on *Sustaining Growth: In A Downturn Through Technology*, Mumbai, May 2009.

Seminar *on Transformation: From NGOs to Formal Institutions*, at the Indian School of Business, Hyderabad, December 12–14, 2002.

Sharma, Rita. *Integration of Agricultural Research and Extension*, APO 2003.

Singh, G.B. *Green Revolution in India—Gains and Pains*, 21st Indian Geography Congress, Nagpur (India), January 2-4, 2000.

Singhal, Arvind and Everest M. Rogers. *Indian Communication Revolution, From Bullock-carts to Cyber Marts*, Sage Publications, New Delhi, London.

State Bank Institute of Rural Development, *Shelter for all by 2010: Prospects for Rural Housing*, Hyderabad, State Bank of India Monthly Review.

Surjit Singh and V. Ratna Reddy. *Changing Contours of Asian Agriculture: Policies, Performances and Challenges*. Academic Foundation, New Delhi, 2009.

Swaminathan, M.S. *Reaching the Unreached: Technology as on Ally in Skill and Knowledge Empowerment of the Poor*. Presentation at the Conference of the World's Scientific Academies, Tokyo International Forum, 15–18 May 2000.

Telecom Regulatory Authority of India. *The Indian Telecom Services: Performance Indicators*. July-September 2005. Retrieved, February 1, 2006 from http://www.trai.gov.in/

Tharoor, Shashi. *The Elephant, The Tiger and The Cell Phone*. Arcade Publishing, New York, 2007.

UNDP. Human Development Report 2003: *Millennium Development Goals: A Compact among Nations to End Human Poverty*, Oxford University Press, New York/ Oxford. (http://hdr.undp.org/reports/global/2003).

UNDP. Human Development Report 2004: *Cultural Liberty in Today's Diverse World*, New York, UNDP (http://hdr. undp.org/reports/ global/2004/english/), 2004.

Waverman, L., Meschi, M. and Fuss, M. *The Impact of Telecoms on Economic Growth in Developing Countries*. Report World Bank, 2006.

Wireless Networking in the Developing World. Online e-Book, June 2006.

WirelessFederation.com/news.

World Bank Report. *India and the Knowledge Economy: Leveraging Strengths and Opportunities*, 2005.

World Bank. *Sharing Knowledge: Innovations and Remaining Challenges,* Washington DC.

World Bank. *Constructing Knowledge Societies: New Challenges for Tertiary Education*, Washington DC, 2004.

World Bank. *Engendering IC: Incorporating Gender into Information Technology Projects*, Washington DC, 2002-2003.

World Bank. *Human Development Report 2007-08: Fighting Climate Change: Human Solidarity in a Divided World,* Washington, 2009.

World Bank Human Development Report 2009. Overcoming barriers to human mobility and Development 2009, Washington 2009.

Xie M., Kuffner U. and Le Moigne G. (1993). *Using Water Efficiently*, World Bank Technical Paper 205, Washington DC. 1993.

Yoffee. *Competing in the Age of Digital Convergence, Competing on Internet Time, and Judo Strategy.* Harvard Business School Press, 2004.

Yoon, S. Symposium on The Impact of Environmental Degradation and Poverty on Women and Children, *Water for Life* 27-30 May, 1991, Geneva.

Subject Index

A

Aravind Eye Health Care Technology Use, 166

B

Bharat Nirman Programs, 174, 185, 357

Biogas, 29, 67-68, 190, 195-96

Bio-Center, 199

Bio-fuel, 222

    biofuel for rural wireless, 269

Business Correspondents, 338

C

Citizen Service Centers, 281

Clean Development Mechanism, 217, 221, 446

Community Participation Framework, 238

Community Safe Water Systems (CSWS) model, 187

Core Network Plan, 229, 232-33

core-DECT technology, 443

Country Operations Business, Plan, 237

Country Partnership Strategy, 237

D

DDG projects, 220

Digital divide, 241, 251, 268, 273, 288-89, 295

Digital Economy, 275, 288-89

Digital opportunities, 242

    Center for Digital Inclusion, 275

District Rural Road Plan, 232-33

DRUM Project, 225-26

E

e-Choupal, 55, 274, 308-09

e-commerce hub, 308

EDPS 2000 software, 438-39

Electrification of Remote Villages, 221

Environment policies, 201

Environmental Health Surveillance, 196, 407

Environmental pollution, 189, 201, 240

F

Fluoride contamination, 187

Fuel Pellets, 293

G

Gasifier technology, 293

George Foundation

    Technology use, 165

Golden Quadrilateral, 237

Gram Vikas model, 202
Grey Water management, 199
Grey Water Use, 199

H

Housing schemes, 203, 412
HUDCO, 207-08, 210
Human Settlement Management Institute, 208
    National Mission for Rural Housing and Habitat, 209
Hygiene Education, 146, 196, 239

I

India Infrastructure Finance Corp Ltd., 236
Indian Energy Exchange, 220
Indira Awaas Yojana, 204-06, 373, 375, 385
    Innovative Streams, 207-08
    Rural Building Centers, 207-08
    Samagra Awaas Yojana, 207-08
Infrastructure Policy, 236
Integrated Watershed Development Program, 36, 188
Irrigation, 51, 187-88
    Accelerated Irrigation Benefit Program, 187
    Micro irrigation, 188
    Rain harvesting, 187
    Rainfed Area Development Program, 187-88

L

LED solar lanterns, 222

M

MARR technology, 263
Mobile Grameen Sanchar Sewak scheme, 255
Mobile Phone Health Monitoring System, 162
Mobile-based PHC Management System, 164

N

National Food Security Act, 374, 386
National Mission for Female Literacy, 376
National Rural Livelihood Mission, 374-75, 385, 392
NGO SCOPE, 196
Nirmal Gram Puraskar, 193

O

Optic fiber, 443

P

Pradhan Mantri Adarsh Gram Yojana, 206, 374-75
    Credit-cum-Subsidy Scheme, 206
Pradhan Mantri Gram Sadak Yojana, 274
Public-Private Partnership Appraisal, 235

R

Rajiv Awas Yojana, 205-06
Rajiv Gandhi Gramin LPG Vitrak scheme, 294
Rashtriya Mahila Kosh, 375
Researchers
    TIER project, 168, 170

UC Berkley, Intel, 166, 168, 170, 172
UC San Diego and IIT Khargpur, 172
Reliable media, 253, 260, 264
Rural community phones, 255, 258
Rural electrification programs, 218
Copper Wiring—Rural Electrification, 222
NARI study, 223
Solar Electrification, 222
Rural Electricity Supply Technology mission, 224
Road information system, 232, 234
Rural Broadband connectivity, 284
Rural BPOs, 277
Infosys BPO, 279-80
Wipro BPO, 280
Rural e-Governance, 275
Rural Housing Policies, 355
Holcim Initiative for Rural Housing, 212
Hydropower, wind energy, solar energy, biomass Projects, 217, 221, 446
National Rural Road Development Agency, 229, 234
Prime Minister Rural Roads Program, 228
SDC Initiatives and Rural Housing, 213
Rural ICT initiatives, 289
'jagruti' initiative, 272
kiosk models, 290
Rural Housing, 174, 203-10, 212-13, 215, 354
Rural ICT centers, 106
Rural Micro-utility Initiative, 223
Rural Mobile Market in India—report, 261-62
Rural mobile telephony programs, 266
Google rural mobile, 268
NOKIA, 269
Reliance Communications, 257, 267
SIDA – SPIDER, 269
SMS Servers, 268
TCS, Qualcomm, 268
Transclick USA, 266
Unified Communications, 268
Vihaan Networks—rural mobile telephones, 266
Rural Power cooperative, 224
Rural shelters, 206, 209
Rural telecommunications, 251
New telephone policies—NTP 94 and NTP 99, 260
Rural mobile telephony, 257, 264
Rural telephony, 174, 251
Telecom infrastructure, 265
Telecom Mission Plans, 259
Tele-density, 251-57, 270, 275
Telephone kiosks rural, 259
Rural Transport system, 238

Rural vision centers, 167-68, 171

S

Sanchar Dhabas, 263
Self-help groups, 65-66, 113, 117, 154, 277, 295
Sewage system, 200
Social change, 3-5, 266, 311
Student Loans to Weaker Sections, 376
Sustainable Sanitation Initiative, 200
  Central Rural Sanitation program, 191
  Community-led Total Sanitation, 191
  Ecosanitation, 190, 197
  Sanitation technology, 189
  Sehat Saathi, 163
  SIDA, 200, 269
  Village Health and Sanitation Committees, 128, 130, 197
Sulabh International, 195-197
Sustainable sanitation, 184, 190, 194-95, 198-99, 406-07
SWANs, 257

T

Telecommunication infrastructure policies–rural, 243
Telecom Technologies, 263, 442
  C-DOT-PMP technologies, 263
  GSM technologies, 263
  INMARSAT, 263
  wireless in local loop (WLL), 263
Tele-density—rural, 251-57, 270, 275, 288, 396
Television, 216, 241, 243-49, 296, 299, 424
  Cable Television Networks rules, 249
  Cable TV, 245
  Satellite INSAT 1B, 246
  Satellite transmission, 245
  Satellite TV, 266
Transformative technologies, 242
Training Facilitators, 324
TRAI, 255-56, 264, 266

U

USOF, 255, 265, 283-85

V

Village Medicine Depots, 372

W

Waste Management, 189-90
Wi-Fi Long-distance (LD), 167, 169, 242
WiMAX broadband, 272, 283, 285
Wire line rural broadband, 284-85
Wireless technologies, 167, 256, 258, 295
Women Self Help Groups, 377